WORDS OF FIRE, DEEDS OF BLOOD

: : : : : : : : : : : :

The Mob, the Monarchy, and the French Revolution

OLIVIER BERNIER

ANCHOR BOOKS

DOUBLEDAY

NEW YORK LONDON TORONTO SYDNEY AUCKLAND

An Anchor Book
PUBLISHED BY DOUBLEDAY
a division of Bantam Doubleday Dell Publishing Group, Inc.
666 Fifth Avenue, New York, New York 10103

ANCHOR BOOKS, DOUBLEDAY, and the portrayal of an anchor
are trademarks of Doubleday, a division of Bantam Doubleday
Dell Publishing Group, Inc.

Words of Fire, Deeds of Blood was originally published
in hardcover in 1989 by Little, Brown and Company.
The Anchor Books edition is published by arrangement
with Little, Brown and Company.

DESIGNED BY JOYCE C. WESTON

Library of Congress Cataloging-in-Publication Data
Bernier, Olivier.
    Words of fire, deeds of blood: the mob, the monarchy,
    and the French Revolution / Olivier Bernier.
    —1st Anchor Books ed.
        p.   cm.
    Reprint. Originally published: Boston: Little, Brown, c1989.
    Includes bibliographical references.
        1. France—History—Revolution, 1789–1799—Causes.
    2. Monarchy—France—History—18th century. I. Title.
    [DC138.B42   1990]   90-30686
    944.04—dc20   CIP
    ISBN 0-385-41333-5

CONTENTS

Words of Fire, Deeds of Blood

. . . .

LIST OF ILLUSTRATIONS

(Illustrations follow pages 150 and 278)

PREFACE

THE French Revolution, in less than four years, changed the world. From the moment Louis XVI walked up the steps of the guillotine, no other European monarch felt safe again; by the time France had given itself a constitution and a legislature, it became obvious to the peoples from Sicily to Siberia that this was indeed the way a government should rule. The liberties the French claimed for themselves — of religion, of the press, of assembly, of thought; their right to be taxed only if their representatives had first consented; equality before the law and the end of privileges — all these startling innovations soon appeared to be the normal requirements without which no state could claim legitimacy.

That these liberties had already been won by the American people hardly seemed to matter; it was well understood that a new country like the United States was in no way comparable to the old European monarchies. It *did* matter that the results of the *French* Revolution were all a very far cry from the previous practices of the French and the other European governments. There, inequality was determined by law: certain taxes were paid only by commoners, certain punitive laws applied only to them; and conversely, many important or lucrative positions — in the army, at court — were reserved for the nobility, while, in the Catholic countries, the Church was altogether free from the jurisdiction, financial and legal, of the state. The story of the Revolution, therefore, is to a great extent that of the fall of the monarchy and the replacement of a privileged society by one in which the ringing claim of "liberty, equality, fraternity" was at least partially implemented.

Of course, it did not happen all at once; but one of the fascinating aspects of the Revolution is the speed with which, after timid beginnings, the National Assembly claimed, for the very first time, what we have since come to think of as inalienable human rights. How the supposedly all-powerful King reacted to all this, how his government crumbled or tried to resist, how his very conscience helped the process along is a story worth telling impartially, without the sentimentality that so often affects those historians who regret the monarchy, without the selective optimism displayed by those whose Marxist training colors their judgments.

Of course, the French Revolution had societal and economic causes; but it was also a moment when people mattered, when cleverness or stupidity, eloquence or insensitivity could make an enormous difference. With a different cast of characters, the ancien régime might not have collapsed so fast or so completely. After the elimination of the King and Queen, the Revolution continued on an increasingly wild and bloody course. Dissent became a crime, repression the order of the day. The very goals of the Revolution — liberty, equality, fraternity — were forgotten as the Republic struggled against domestic and foreign enemies, until, in yet another convulsion, Robespierre and his tyranny were overthrown.

Ever since that day, the Terror has fascinated many; and yet, spectacular though it was, it matters less than what came before. In May 1789 Louis XVI was an immensely popular monarch, and the French felt confident that they were entering a new Golden Age. Less than four years later, this revered monarch was beheaded. The real story here, the one that terrified all other European monarchs, is that of the rapid and irremediable collapse of the ancien régime. The structure of the state and the methods of government that had endured since the Middle Ages were suddenly seen to belong to another, dead, era. As for the trials and executions of the King and Queen, these were vivid symbols of the new order: if the people, through their elected representatives, could sit in judgment on those who had been considered the chosen of God, then a new era had begun. When the consent of the governed replaced the obedience of the subject, a new legitimacy was defined, and the modern world was born.

Words of Fire, Deeds of Blood

PROLOGUE

IT was hot and muggy early on the morning of June 20, 1792, in Paris, just the kind of day on which, after three years of revolution, more violence could be expected. For weeks, King Louis XVI had kept a history of Charles I of England at his side; now it looked as if history was about to be repeated.

The evening before, Parisians had heard some of the rumblings that usually announced a revolutionary outburst. Jérôme Pétion, the Mayor of the city, and his political friends were seen talking to the leaders of the Faubourgs Saint-Marceau and Saint-Antoine, men who could, with a little preparation, produce screaming mobs of unemployed and hungry workers. Conveniently, the date itself offered a perfect pretext. Three years earlier, the National Assembly, meeting in defiance of the King's express orders, had sworn a dramatic oath. "We are here by the will of the people," the comte de Mirabeau had told a royal envoy, "and will leave only by the force of the bayonets"; on that day, for the first time in French history, the King found himself the servant of his subjects.

What was required, Pétion said, was the kind of mass demonstration that would celebrate the day while terrifying the remaining monarchists. This demonstration was especially important since there was another, even more inflammatory anniversary that everyone remembered. Exactly one year earlier, Louis XVI and his family had made their escape from Paris, only to be caught at Varennes, near the Austrian border. Rumors, carefully circulated by the Mayor's friends, had it that the King was ready to try again. He must be shown who was the master now.

These were fighting words in the two faubourgs, where most of the city's working class lived. Not everyone there was literate, but even those who weren't knew about the plots hatched at the Palace, the King and Queen's hatred of the Revolution, their hope that France would lose the war declared on Austria just two months earlier, and their reliance on the Austrian emperor's army to restore the ancien régime.

The people of the faubourgs also knew that they were the vanguard of the Revolution. Time after time they had marched into central Paris, down the narrow, winding streets which they filled with their numbers. They were prompt to respond when they were told that plots were afoot to defeat the Revolution, all the more ready, in fact, since most of them were unemployed and had nothing to lose except their newfound importance; and they knew that the bourgeoisie was not about to resist the will expressed by bands of armed and angry men.

Then, too, they had been abundantly forewarned. On June 1, in *L'Ami du peuple* (The Friend of the People), Jean-Paul Marat had denounced the Palace's maneuvers. On June 3 he had gone on: "Never has the danger . . . been more imminent. . . . The King, hiding his dastardly plans behind a mask of hypocrisy, is getting ready to flee again." After denouncing the war as the road to despotism, he concluded: "A few more days, and the Parisians who refuse to kneel before the despot will be slain by the tyrant's sword."[1] Then on June 9 Marat raised his tone yet another octave. "All is lost, dear friends of the Fatherland," he wrote. "Without a general insurrection, we are lost forever. . . . The court intends to slaughter all freedom-loving citizens by fire or famine under the pretext of defending the state against its foreign enemies."[2] So when Pétion arrived on the evening of June 19, the population of the faubourgs needed no encouragement.

At dawn the next day, a screaming, sweating mob armed with pikes, cudgels, axes, truncheons, and rifles marched toward the center of the city. By the end of the morning, some eight thousand strong, they reached the *Assemblée législative*, France's Parliament, and demanded admission. They had come, they said, to lay petitions before the Deputies (as the members of the Assembly were called).

There was no keeping them out: the National Guard, a body composed of the increasingly frightened bourgeoisie, had, ever since 1789, been charged with maintaining order. In the last two years the Guard had been unwilling to put down the ever more violent revolutionary riots. Now, as usual, they did nothing, so for some three hours the Deputies and their president watched as the *sections** filed past, thousands of men, hundreds of women, smelling of sweat and wine, waving their weapons, and shouting that the people were ready to take their revenge and that if Capet** did not improve his behavior he would come off the throne.

That the Palace of the Tuileries, less than a quarter of a mile away, was next no one doubted, not even the King. Only the day before, he had found posters glued on the doors of his apartments. "No more king," they read. "A king is an obstacle to the happiness of the people."

Indeed, a little before three o'clock, on that hot, sultry afternoon, the mob moved on to the Palace; and there was no one to defend it. On May 30, by order of the Assembly, the King's bodyguard had been disbanded. Now he was under the sole protection of the National Guard, and everyone knew that faced with violence, the Guard would flee or, at best, remain wholly passive.

The quickest way to the Palace was through the gardens, so the mob asked that their gates be opened. Louis XVI forbade it, and with good reason: the Tuileries had originally been a country palace, and all along the ground floor French windows opened right out to the park. From that side, the Palace was indefensible. But to no one's surprise, the National Guard ignored the order.

Inside the Tuileries, the royal family and their few remaining courtiers knew that the mob was coming. Soon they could hear a great swelling noise as the gardens filled up and the narrow streets leading to the other facade were taken over; within less than an hour, that side, too, was besieged. Whenever they looked out of a window, they saw the men, some holding up signs denouncing the King and Queen, all fully armed; they could also see a cannon, pulled by ropes, being trundled to the main gate. It was hotter than ever, inside the Palace and out.

For some time Louis XVI and Marie Antoinette had been expecting an

---

* The equivalent of a constituency, a section consisted of the voting members of a given, usually not very large, area.

** The first King of France (or of the Francs), in 987, was Hugues Capet; Louis XVI was, very indirectly, descended from him. Calling him Louis Capet, therefore, denied his royalty by suppressing his title.

attempt against their lives; now the day had evidently come. Massacres by an enraged mob were a revolutionary tradition: it seemed quite likely that before evening most of the occupants of the Palace would be torn limb from limb. Indeed, the royal family, huddled together in the King's apartment, could hear the screams just outside: "Down with the veto! Long live the nation and the *sans-culottes!*"* At the main gate two of Pétion's men, Panis and Sergent, demanded admission; at that, the National Guard gave up. The gates were opened; the soldiers massed in the Palace's courtyard threw away their arms and joined the mob. "Men and women, soldiers and brigands, rage on their faces, steel in their hands, rushed to the Palace's great staircase," Mme de Tourzel, governess of the royal children, an eyewitness, reported. "In one moment they were up. A cannon . . . was set up before the King's apartment. The first door was smashed open with axes."[3]

Inside, "the King, realizing that the door to his room would soon be forced open, decided to try . . . to quiet the mob . . . by appearing before them," Mme de Tourzel continued. "He ordered the Queen and his children removed so that they would not be exposed to danger; that princess, as she left the King with tears streaming from her eyes, exhorted [the few Guardsmen who remained gathered around him]: 'Frenchmen, my friends, save the King!' "[4]

By then, the smashing of the door in the next room could be heard clearly; so, ordering the bolt withdrawn, Louis came forth to meet the mob. " 'What do you want?' he asked them. His calm, the serenity of his appearance, some remaining respect for the royal majesty halted the enraged crowd. For a moment, they seemed ready to put down their arms and fall to their King's feet."[5] The moment did not last: soon a man with a pike, and another with a sword, lunged at the King; they were stopped by the little group around him, who then surrounded him as he retreated into a deep-set window, while his sister, Madame Elisabeth, who had refused to abandon him, took refuge in the next window, followed by the ministers. "It was then she was taken for the Queen. Seeing the rabble advancing toward her, shouting: 'The Austrian, where is she? We want her head,' she said: 'Don't tell them who I am; if they could take me for

---

* The King had recently vetoed several acts passed by the Assembly. The sans-culottes were the revolutionaries, who wore trousers, not breeches.

the Queen, there would be time to save her.' One enraged man put a pike to her breast: 'Take it away,' she told him softly; 'you do not want to hurt me.'

"Shouts of all kinds were now heard everywhere. Banners covered with threats were held up to the King: 'Tremble, tyrant, the people are in arms,' one of these read; and the men spoke to him only to insult him."[6]

All through this, Louis XVI, a stout man with a big, aquiline nose, stood firm and apparently unmoved. "Sire, do not be afraid," a National Guard grenadier told him. The King took his hand and, pressing it to his heart, "Grenadier," he answered, "put your hand there. Is that the heartbeat of a fearful man?"[7] Soon afterward, when his entourage drew their swords to try to fight a way out, he stopped them.

Still the violence grew. Louis was forced to put on a red Phrygian cap, the emblem of the most violent revolutionaries, while a young man paraded before him with a bleeding veal heart stuck on the end of a pike with a banner reading "Heart of the tyrant and the aristocrats." By this time, late afternoon, the sultry heat in the old Palace was almost unbearable, and it maddened the crowd still more: the shouting got louder, the threats more menacing.

Throughout all this, the Queen and her children had been in the next room. " 'My duty,' she said, 'is to die with the King. If you stop me from joining him, I will be dishonored.' 'No,' M. d'Aubier [one of her attendants] answered, 'if the King sees the Queen surrounded by the mob, he will rush to save her and be killed.' "[8] At that, as the din in the next room apparently came closer to the doors, Marie Antoinette ran forward, shouting to Hue, the King's valet, "Save my son." She herself went off down a different passage, and for a while, closely followed by the mob, she ran from room to room, finally finding refuge behind a door so flush with the paneling as to be unnoticeable.

It was nearly five o'clock before one of the King's valets convinced some additional grenadiers of the National Guard to come to the rescue. Clearing one of the rooms, they set a table against the door. Louis XVI stood behind it; he was joined by Marie Antoinette and their children, whose presence the mob had been demanding. At that point, a delegation from the Assembly finally arrived, looked around, and tried to talk the crowd into leaving the Palace. Failing even to make themselves heard, they went back across the gardens to the Assembly. Meanwhile, the crowd forced Marie Antoinette and the little Dauphin in turn to don red caps.

By then, there seemed to be no reason why the siege should ever end. At six, the Mayor, Pétion himself, appeared and, making his way to the table, told the King: "The people have come here with dignity, they will leave in the same manner, Your Majesty can rely on it,"[9] but he carefully refrained from giving the necessary orders and went off to the Assembly to report. At last, the Deputies decided to act: carefully choosing a group of violent antimonarchists, they dispatched them to the Palace, where they proceeded to surround both King and Queen. Their presence and, no doubt, the length and heat of the day finally seemed to quiet the mob. Instead of milling about, it began to pass before the royal family in an almost orderly manner, thrusting forth models of the guillotine and banners reading: "Tremble, Tyrant, your hour has come!" "Sign the [vetoed] decrees or die!" "Down with Veto and his wife!"

It was now a little after eight; the siege had lasted more than five hours. "Night was falling. It was time to end this long agony. The King, racked with heat and fatigue, was escorted back into the Council Hall by the Deputies and the Guard; from there, he went on to his bedroom where his family joined him. There . . . he held the Queen, his children, and Madame Elisabeth in a tight embrace. The Deputies, moved by this, tried to console him. 'I have done my duty,' he said."[10] Even then, it was quite a while longer before the royal family was at last left to itself in its devastated apartments.

"I am still alive," Marie Antoinette wrote her friend Count Fersen the next day, "but it is a miracle. The twentieth was a frightful day. They are not after me the most anymore; they are after the very life of my husband. Danger can surge up again at any moment."[11] She was right, of course, in every way. The hatred that, at first, had been directed against her now paled before the revolutionaries' loathing of the King. It is true that on June 20 they had stopped just short of murder, but as everyone soon realized, the day had simply been a rehearsal. Having found its way into the Tuileries, the mob was bound to return, and when it did, it was not likely to stop at threats.

PART ONE

CHAPTER ONE

The People Aroused

.   .   .

THE French, as everyone knew, were the easiest people to govern. Unlike the English, those perpetual rebels who had beheaded one king and sent another one off into permanent exile, the French loved their monarch; even when, on occasion, they no longer did, they still obeyed his orders. The King of France, in fact, was much envied by his European brethren: he ruled over a large, polished, disciplined nation; with the smallest of efforts he could make himself extremely popular; the resources available to him were immense.

That it should be so was no surprise. The French, it was agreed, were the most cultivated, the most reasonable people on earth. They set the fashion for buildings, paintings, books, and clothes, and, by the 1780s, they had reached a new, unparalleled degree of civilization. Their court was the most brilliant in Europe, their aristocracy the most sophisticated; as for their politeness, it was legendary.

Still, something was changing. France, whose wealth had always come from agriculture, was beginning, slowly and tentatively, to develop industries as well. There had always been workshops in which artisans made furniture or cloth or tableware of extraordinary quality; but in the last two decades, a number of larger manufacturing concerns had been set up in the eastern suburbs of Paris, the Faubourgs Saint-Antoine and Saint-Marcel, thus concentrating an easily dissatisfied proletariat in one spot. The employers ranged from the Réveillon wallpaper factory, with its 350 workers, to the Santerre brewery, with a hundred workers, to family businesses employing four or five men, and it was among these varied manufacturers that unemployment was spreading. There was, of course, no planned assistance for the families of jobless men, and their wages were, at the best of times, so small that they could not conceivably save against a rainy day. A man of all work, in 1789, made 30 sous* a day, a mason 40, a carpenter 50. Against this must be set their expenses: a four-pound loaf of bread usually cost 8 to 9 sous, but in bad times could go as high as 20. Bread alone normally took up half a man's wages; vegetables, fats, and wine another 16 percent; clothes 15 percent, with the balance, 19 percent, spent on rent and incidentals. Obviously, it was a hard life: observing normal religious holidays, laborers could expect to work no more than 250 days a year. Thus a carpenter might make about 625 livres to keep himself and his family in a world where, at the other extreme, the King and the royal family were spending 30 million a year.

Because the winter of 1788–89 had been unusually severe, unemployment was high in the two faubourgs that spring; at the same time the price of bread kept rising. It might not have been so bad, perhaps, if all had suffered equally, but the workers had only to walk into the center of Paris to see the most lavish luxury displayed everywhere. The streets were filled with gilded carriages, the fashionable parks with elegantly dressed men and women; as for the court, it was as formal and as splendid as ever. Clearly, while the workers froze and starved, the upper classes were enjoying themselves.

Then, on April 28, 1789, with the price of bread still rising and unemployment painfully high, Réveillon, the great wallpaper manufacturer, announced that wages were quite high enough as they were. The result came swiftly: a crowd of angry unemployed workers attacked and sacked his factory and his house. As it happened, that day horse races were being run at Charenton. This immensely fashionable amusement had been recently imported from England by the duc d'Orléans, the King's cousin and a well-known liberal; on April 28, therefore, most of Society was at Charenton. The way back into Paris, however, led through the Faubourg Saint-Antoine; and there something surprising and alarming happened. Réveillon's house had just been sacked; now, as the carriages began to drive through, "a troop of men stopped the people returning

---

* There were 20 sous in a livre; a very approximate 1989 equivalence would be about 25 cents to the sou and $5 to the livre.

from the races at the Porte Saint-Antoine,'' an eyewitness reported, ''asking them whether they were for the Nobility or the Third Estate . . . , insulting those it thought noble. They forced the women from their carriages and made them shout: 'Long live the Third Estate!' Only the duc and the duchesse d'Orléans were free from this humiliating obligation; the populace cheered them to the echo.''[1]

Still, the very people who had endured that unpleasant moment found little reason to be alarmed: the rising was promptly repressed, and, in any event, seemed to belong with the various affrays taking place all over France, caused by the scarcity and high price of grain; it had happened often before, it would soon be ended by the reforms the King had promised. Of course, there was one novelty, the act of forcing women to shout ''Long live the Third Estate''; but that was seen as a meaningless excess, not the affirmation of a new political force. Nor was anyone surprised at the duc d'Orléans's popularity: he had, after all, visibly backed the liberals. Having a prince of the blood at the head of the opposition was an old tradition in France; he was a conveniently visible, legitimate leader. As an observer noted, ''Among those who wanted changes in the government, many Deputies [to the Estates General, which were to meet in May] . . . who were not yet aware of his incapacity were delighted to see a prince of the blood royal at the head of the people's party.''[2]

Orléans, a feckless, spendthrift debauché, was hardly an inspiring leader, but as a member of the royal family, he lent credibility to any cause he joined. Simply by proclaiming himself a liberal, a believer in the rights of the people, he had put himself at the head of those who wanted a change. If, as the result of some as yet unforeseen crisis, Louis XVI were to lose his throne, Orléans was a ready-made replacement; if the King needed a prime minister who would personify a commitment to reform, the duc again seemed like a possible choice. As noted, that, in itself, was nothing new. Although Orléans appeared to be taking a modern, left-wing stance, he was in fact playing a very old game; it was far from the first time that one of the King's relatives had tried to govern in his place.

Still, there was nothing to worry about; that was the consensus. With the opening of the Estates General, the old abuses would be corrected, and France would slide peacefully into a golden era of enlightened peace and plenty. Of course, that consensus was expressed by those who were in a position to do so; what the mostly illiterate workers thought was not even a consideration. After all, they wrote no pamphlets, attended no salons, were not Deputies at the Estates. The only danger, clearly, came from the King, who, despite his generally recognized good intentions, might be reluctant to share his power with an elected Assembly. That danger increased when the Estates, having transformed themselves into the National Assembly, began to write a constitution. Indeed, Louis XVI's dislike of this body was well known.

Originally, the Estates General had consisted of three separate Orders, the Clergy, the Nobility, and the Third Estate — all according to tradition. The very arrangements in the building that housed the Estates reflected the inequality of the Orders: while smaller halls had been furnished specifically for the meetings of the Clergy and the Nobility, the *Tiers,* or Third Estate, was given no space of its own. It was to hold its sessions in the great hall used also for the ceremonial occasions on which the King addressed the three Orders together. Given the additional fact that, at the mass celebrated the day before the opening of the Estates, the Clergy and the Nobility had found reserved seats, but the Third Estate had not, this smacked of deliberate insult.

As it turned out, the arrangement worked to the advantage of the Tiers: because it sat in the ceremonial hall, it looked as if it were the only Order that really counted; and the extra room proved very convenient when, faced with the dithering of the government and the arrogance of the Nobility, the Third Estate called to itself all Deputies of goodwill who belonged to the other Orders, and rechristened itself the National Assembly. Henceforth it claimed, with every appearance of reason, that it, and it alone, could represent the people. And it proceeded to work on a constitution that would severely restrict the King's powers.

Nothing like this had ever happened in French history: the Estates General, which, in any event, had not met for a hundred and seventy-five years, had, on certain occasions, suggested reforms, but they had never had the means to force anything on the King. Now, as the representatives of the nation, they claimed the constituent power. They passed a motion — the famous Oath of the Tennis Court — resolving not to separate until they had given France a constitution, and there could be no doubt they knew what they were about. Although some liberal noblemen and even some members of the Clergy had joined the Assembly, the Deputies for the most part were lawyers and businessmen, and they were used to writing contracts. They also had every intention of reforming the iniquitous fiscal system, not only planning on ending the largely tax-exempt status of the Nobility and Clergy, but even going so far as to take action to prevent the King from lavishing money on his courtiers. If Louis XVI was going to stop it all, there was no time to waste; and the only way he could do it was by using the army.

By the beginning of July 1789, troops were encamped in the plain just outside Paris; they had been given a commander, the old maréchal de Broglie. It was all very clear: the King was preparing himself to put down resistance and resume his full, his absolute power. At the National Assembly, which sat at Versailles, some quarter of a mile from the Palace, they understood it all too well: if the reforms were to be implemented, the soldiers must be sent away, and Louis XVI must be convinced he did not need them. On July 8 Mirabeau, one of the liberal leaders in the Assembly and a man of extraordinary eloquence, proposed that a message be taken to the King. It asked:

> How can people make you doubt, Sire, of your subjects' love? Have you heedlessly spilled their blood? Are you cruel, implacable? Have you stopped the course of justice? Does the people make you responsible for its unhappiness? Does it accuse you of its calamities? . . . Always ready to obey you, Sire, because you command in the name of the law, our fidelity to you is boundless. . . .
>
> Send back the soldiers to the garrisons from whence your advisers have called them. . . . Your Majesty does not need them. . . . Sire, in the middle of your children, you will find your safety in their loves.[3]

There was a warning here, as well as an exhortation: the French, Mirabeau said, were ready to obey *because,* which meant *as long as,* the King obeyed the new laws restricting his power. Even so, the picture painted in the message was not all for show: for most of the nearly twelve hundred Deputies in the Assembly, Louis XVI was still a father figure.

Versailles is only some twelve miles from Paris; perhaps the Deputies should have traveled to the city that day. The minister of Saxony did, and there was nothing reassuring about the report which he wrote on July 9:

Although Paris no longer seems as rebellious on the outside, the fermentation is the greater for it, and the more to be feared. The arrival of the troops, instead of causing fear, has created a feeling of vengeance and hatred which has progressed amazingly in the last two or three days. If the King gives in to the Assembly's request, he will discourage, and thus lose all control over, his army, which unfortunately already shows the most decided ill will. . . .

Any attempt at a coup supported by the troops will set Paris aflame, bring about a tax strike throughout the kingdom, a bankruptcy of the state, and generalized civil war.[4]

In fact, a new protagonist had just appeared in the unfolding drama: the King, the court, and the Assembly all thought that, as usual, only the middle and upper classes mattered, but the mob had felt its first taste of power on that day in April when it sacked the Réveillon house and stopped the carriages returning from the races.

It was still an ill-defined, unsure, inchoate mass, without real leaders, without real goals; but it knew well enough that it had been oppressed for centuries. It was no longer ready to starve obediently; it heard the liberals who claimed that all men were equal, but it was also discovering its own raw strength, its ability to impose its wants and to suppress, physically, by the use of violence, any opposition. Suddenly, in early July, Paris was no longer the safe place it had always been.

The mob was easily recognizable, and not just by its ever-fluctuating numbers. It looked different: the men wore trousers, not breeches, plain, straight hair instead of powder and curls. They were dirty, they smelled, and so did the women who appeared in growing numbers. They shouted, they pushed, often they attacked; and now their numbers were often swelled by supporters who were not largely unemployed factory workers like themselves, but artisans who made only a bare living, jobless servants, soldiers who were deserting their regiments, street vendors whose trade was disrupted by the growing unrest.

They knew they wanted cheap bread and jobs, of course, but more than anything they yearned for revenge. The collective memories of centuries of humiliation, of aristocratic arrogance were vivid. They did not like the King much, and they loathed Marie Antoinette, but the aristocrats were their real enemies. And now they no longer stayed in their slums on the outskirts of Paris. Already they were in control at the Palais Royal, whose palace and gardens belonged to the duc d'Orléans and were consequently free from police control.

The Palais Royal had always drawn all kinds of people. A long rectangle right in the heart of Paris, three of its sides consisted of shops on the ground floor where you could find everything from a good meal to some of the wildest brothels in the city. In the garden at the center, elegantly dressed people strolled and would-be politicians orated. So far, the atmosphere had been animated but civilized. By late June that had all changed.

On the twenty-sixth, the Spanish ambassador described the scene there:

All these last days, there have been such crowds in the Palais Royal that one could hardly get through: everywhere one saw groups of people who were listening to a discussion or to the news read by others standing on a chair or a table. The partisans of the Tiers and the National Assembly were so numerous that one could not safely offer an opinion which seemed opposed to their ideas. Thus, they threw two men out of the garden, after punching and kicking them, and an abbé who tried to defend, in the most moderate way, the Archbishop of Paris against [verbal] attacks was properly whipped on a table; he was forced to beg forgiveness, to retract on bended knee and to kiss the feet of a waiter in one of the cafés. . . .

Yesterday . . . around six in the evening, more than fifty soldiers from the regiment of the *gardes françaises,* without rifles, but their sabers held high, appeared in the Palais Royal, shouting: "Long live the Third Estate! We belong to it and will never fight, except in its defense and against the enemies of the nation."[5]

The gardes françaises were part of the Royal Guard, and it was normally on them that the King relied to keep order in Paris. That they would not obey an order to march against the crowds in Paris was becoming exceedingly clear.

Indeed, it soon became clearer still. Eleven of these soldiers had been imprisoned when they were caught helping an angry mob and had refused orders to stop them. On June 30 another mob broke into their prison and freed them. Since there was obviously no question of rearresting them, M. Necker, the principal minister, came up with a stratagem: the

Assembly would ask the King to pardon them, Louis XVI would do so, and all would look well. This, in fact, is what happened; but there was no ignoring the fact that the government no longer ruled in the capital. Worse, from the King's viewpoint, was the probability that most of the troops encamped outside the city would also refuse to fight the mob.

Old habits die hard, especially when it suits people to hold on to them. Obedience to the King had long been a fact of life. Necker, who was in touch with reality, knew that the world had changed; Louis XVI, Marie Antoinette, and the comte d'Artois* refused to believe it could. Normally, therefore, the King should have looked for a minister whose ideas he shared; but in June, when Necker had tried to resign, there had been something very like an uprising in the streets of Versailles. Then, he had stayed in office and the people had quieted down. Now, prompted by the Queen and Artois, Louis XVI decided things had gone far enough. Necker was a liberal; Necker was in favor of the reforms and advised his master to accept them; Necker must go.

It was Jacques Necker's singular fortune that he was worshiped by two immensely talented women, his wife and his daughter, who were also propagandists of genius: together, they convinced enlightened opinion that Necker was the only man who could save France. Necker himself, of course, did his best to help them, partly through the publication of a number of pamphlets, partly through his ability to say very little. In an age when quick and eloquent conversation was the rule, his silences were taken as a sign of profundity; it occurred to no one that, perhaps, he had nothing to say.

To be sure, Necker had certain specific talents. A native of Geneva, he had come to Paris, worked in a bank, and done so well as eventually to become one of its owners; upon which he went on to make a very large fortune. He understood the handling of money, therefore, and was completely familiar with the Paris financial market; he was also thoroughly acquainted with the nature of credit. All this was bound to be of the greatest help in his new office of principal minister, as was the fact that he was financially honest — there would be no secret speculations on the side of the kind the former finance minister, Charles-Alexandre de

---

* The King's youngest brother, a fervent reactionary, and a man of considerable charm but very limited intelligence.

Calonne, had indulged in. Because he was already so rich, Necker was also not eager, indeed not willing, to receive any favors from the King; nor, as an austere Swiss Calvinist, did he covet a title.

Unfortunately, set against these great advantages was a central drawback: Necker had no political sense at all; and because he was convinced of his own superior knowledge, he exhibited a righteousness that not only alienated his opponents, and, indeed, some of his friends, but also prevented him, not infrequently, from becoming aware of the most urgent problems. Thus, within the months of June and early July 1789, he had managed to alienate completely the King's always reluctant support by forcing him to make sacrifices that, apparently, had all been in vain, since they had not appeased the Assembly.

Early on the afternoon of July 11 a letter was carried by one of the King's footmen to the principal minister. It said:

> Ever since I asked you, Monsieur, to remain in office, you have asked me to adopt a consistent attitude to the Estates General and you have shown me several times that complete acceptance was the one you preferred, that you did not think yourself of any use if another plan were followed, and that you asked my permission to withdraw if I should do so. I accept your suggestion that you leave the kingdom during this crisis and I expect that, as you promised, your retreat will be quick and secret.[6]

Necker did as he had promised. Leaving Versailles secretly that afternoon, he arrived in Brussels the next day and went on to Basle, which he reached on July 20. On that same July 11 a new ministry was announced by the King; it was led by the baron de Breteuil, whose positions made him the very symbol of the extreme reactionary party. Marie Antoinette and Artois triumphed: they had known all along that ending the decay of the monarchy simply required energy.

In Paris, attitudes were a little different. The minister of Saxony wrote:

> It is in the midst of fire, blood, and carnage that I write this dispatch. . . . Ten thousand men gathered at the Palais Royal after looting all the armorers' shops; two companies of grenadiers and one of fusilliers . . . ran right over their officers to join their [deserting] comrades [from another regiment]. . . . M. du Chatelet [the colonel

commanding the gardes françaises] could not see any solution other than to send word that the cavalry, which was still drawn up in battle order on the Place Louis XV,* must withdraw immediately to their quarters so as to prevent a massacre.[7]

What the minister of Saxony did not see was that the Royal-Allemand, a regiment of mounted foreign recruits led by the prince de Lambesc, a cousin of Marie Antoinette's, had charged the crowd in the Tuileries gardens at five that afternoon, July 12, killing an old man and wounding several of those present. Otherwise, he was right; by ten o'clock, even the Swiss regiments, which had not done any of the fighting, were sent back to their barracks. From that moment on, Paris, to all intents and purposes, had become an independent city.

The mob had triumphed, and this time on a large scale. In April it had merely sacked a harsh employer's house; on that warm and cloudy Sunday it took over the capital. This was obviously bad news for the King and the new ministry. As Necker had predicted, the troops, by and large, deserted so as not to fight the people. Without troops, without the support of the National Assembly, Louis XVI was powerless.

In his *History of the Revolution,* Necker commented that the coup Louis XVI planned might have succeeded if the court had moved to Compiègne, one of the royal palaces some sixty miles north of Paris, and gathered the troops there, thus preventing an early contact with the crowds; in retrospect, it seems probable that the attempt would have failed. What in any event was all too clear, on the evening of July 12, was that the King had lost all authority. The Parisians, many of whom were men (and women) of property, were now at the mercy of the mob. It was not a position they relished.

Worse, they found themselves menaced by opposing forces: outside the walls, there were the King's soldiers who, for all anyone knew, would start besieging the city so as to make it submit to royal authority; inside Paris, anarchy seemed about to prevail. At 1:00 A.M. on July 13 the mob burned down forty of the fifty-four excise offices at the gates. At six, it broke into the convent of Saint Lazare, where, rumor had it, there were huge stocks of grain; but the most thorough pillaging had shown them to

---

* Today the Place de la Concorde.

be a myth. No one knew where the enraged mob would turn next; clearly something had to be done.

At eight that morning, therefore, a group of 400 men met at the Hôtel de Ville, the Paris City Hall: they were the electors of the Parisian Deputies to the Estates General and had themselves been selected by a much larger electorate; together, they represented the bourgeoisie of Paris. Immediately, they chose a "permanent committee," which, despite its modest name, was, in fact, a city government, and set about creating a militia composed of 48,000 men, 800 per district. Many of the deserters from the gardes françaises joined this new troop. That very evening the first patrols began their rounds.

It was not a moment too soon. Even as the new committee came into being, the mob had broken into the Garde Meuble, the repository of crown furniture, on the Place Louis XV, and seized some old armor that had been stored there. All through that Monday, in spite of the cool, windy, rainy weather, the great open space in front of the Hôtel de Ville was filled with crowds demanding more arms. "The whole city," the British ambassador reported, "offered a picture of consternation. . . . The streets were almost empty of people."[8] It was one of those moments when fate seemed to hesitate. Stunned by Necker's dismissal — "We felt," wrote an eminent Parisian, "like a family who have just lost their father"[9] — terrified by the possible excesses of the mob, anxious about the troops outside the walls, the new committee hesitated. It might still have appealed to the King; instead, it chose to deal with the situation by itself: it was the birth of self-government. At five that afternoon, a delegation of Parisian electors arrived at the Hôtel des Invalides, where 32,000 rifles were stored, and requested that the arms be turned over to the new militia; the governor, the marquis de Sombreuil, refused.

Nothing more happened that evening; the cold winds, the heavy rains took care of that. But on Tuesday, July 14, although the weather was cool and cloudy, a mass of people was seen moving toward the Invalides soon after daybreak. "Some of my windows look out onto one of the streets leading to the Invalides," the Spanish ambassador reported;

We have seen all day the most singular spectacle. . . . Several groups of civilians, well dressed and of all ages, often numbering 900 to 1,000 or more, marched past to the beating of drums; with them went soldiers from many different regiments. Some were armed with rifles, others with swords, others with different arms. . . . I also saw some artillery with its ammunition passing by, it was escorted by the militia in arms. . . . It looked like a complete, well-disciplined army led by a few officers on horseback.[10]

Another diplomat, the minister of Saxony, was present at the Invalides itself. "Seven or eight thousand unarmed bourgeois," he noted, "rushed into a moat twelve feet wide and eight deep and, by passing on one another's shoulders, they crossed it in no time. They began to fill the Esplanade and seized twelve cannons of 24 bore, ten of 18, and a mortar."[11]

There and then, it became clear that no part of Paris could be defended any longer: the cannons were fully loaded, but the Esplanade was defended by troops who simply refused to fire on the Parisians. Clearly, the King no longer had a single soldier on whom he could rely. When Ethis de Corny, assistant attorney general in the Parlement of Paris, the chief law court, and the official envoy of the committee, arrived, therefore, and handed the governor a requisition for the arms stored at the Invalides, the latter was in no position to refuse. The gates of the building were opened to let the envoy in; the crowd immediately followed him; and 28,000 rifles were seized. Still, rifles are of no use without ammunition, and most of the cartridges that were used with them were stored at the Bastille. Obviously, that must be the next objective. Already, at ten-thirty, a deputation from the committee had arrived at the old fortress and demanded that it be turned over to them.

What they found was more a symbol than a fortress. To be sure, the Bastille, in 1789, still looked impressive enough. Built in the fourteenth century by King Charles V, it had once been a mighty defense. But, although its eight stout, crenellated towers still looked formidable, and the guns that crowned them were quite able to sweep away a crowd, the governor and the garrison were anything but warlike; and the moat had long since become a garden.

The Bastille, in fact, had last been used as a fortress during a civil war in 1651. It was, of course, still a prison; but on July 14 it held only seven men: four crooks, who had falsified bills of exchange; two madmen, one of whom thought he was God; and an accomplice of Damiens, who had tried to murder Louis XV in 1759. It was so uneconomical to keep the Bastille open, in fact, that, over the years since 1780, the government had seriously considered tearing it down. Unquestionably, the old fortress was no longer much use. Yet it remained a potent symbol, the visible manifestation of the King's power to imprison anyone at will.

Like all such symbols under Louis XVI, it was allowed to deteriorate: on the morning of July 14 its garrison consisted of eighty-two partly crippled veterans and thirty-two Swiss soldiers. None of the men was really expected to fight; as for the governor, the marquis de Launay, he was stupid, weak, and indecisive. Given that a fortress is only as strong as the men who defend it, it was clear that the Bastille was bound to fall if ever it was attacked.

What followed upon the arrival of the deputation from the committee reads more like a drawing-room comedy than the beginnings of a revolution. Courteously received by the governor, the envoys sat down with him to discuss the situation and merely asked, at first, that the guns aimed at the Faubourg Saint-Antoine be withdrawn. De Launay, who obviously felt he was dealing with reasonable, civilized people, immediately agreed to do so, and, while he was at it, invited the deputation to lunch; that is where the second deputation, which included Ethis de Corny, fresh from the taking of the Invalides, found them.

What had caused the sending of this second delegation was the misreading, on the part of the crowd outside, of de Launay's order. There, some six hundred men, mostly artisans from the neighboring Faubourg Saint-Antoine, watched and assumed that the guns had been withdrawn only so that they could be loaded. In great alarm, they sent a warning to the district headquarters, and it was from there that the second delegation had come.

Upon their arrival, the drawing-room comedy resumed. De Launay promptly reassured them about his intentions and promised he would not fire on the people unless he was attacked. Then, taking both luncheon party and new arrivals to the top of the towers, he showed them the unloaded guns; taking them downstairs again, he had the garrison swear not to shoot except in self-defense. Faced with such an obvious desire to avoid trouble, the second delegation asked de Launay to surrender the fortress; most politely, almost regretfully, de Launay declined to do so.

There seemed to be no reason why this polite dialogue could not go on forever; but the crowd outside, which was growing larger and angrier, began to shout, not "Take away the guns," but "We want the Bastille." At that, the second delegation went off to report — the Hôtel de Ville was not very far from the fortress — and was sent right back in order to tell the crowd, which was rapidly turning into a revolutionary mob, that the Bastille would fire only if attacked. That, of course, made no difference to them: what they wanted was the surrender of the fortress, not an assurance that they were safe. So they began pushing against the outside gate; men soon scaled the walls connecting it to the towers and broke the outer gate down from the inside. A little after one, the mob rushed into the main courtyard of the Bastille. So far, not a single shot had been fired.

The drawing-room comedy was now drawing to its close; against all the rules, in fact, it transformed itself into something very like a tragedy. Panicking before the onrushing mob, some of the veterans fired their rifles, while high above, the boom of a single cannon was heard. That was enough. The mob, most of whom had assumed the gates had been opened voluntarily, thought it was being let in only to be massacred and in reaction turned violent. It was their turn to shoot at the garrison, which then defended itself. Just then, at about three o'clock, a fourth deputation arrived from the Hôtel de Ville to demand the fortress's surrender. It was unable to do anything except watch the battle: by now, above the roar of the crowd, shots echoed and the smell of gunpowder grew stronger. Appalled, the delegation returned to the Hôtel de Ville. On its way it passed a troop of a hundred gardes françaises bringing a cannon with them to besiege the Bastille; within a few minutes, sixty-one more soldiers and some five thousand armed citizens joined the crowd. The cannon was aimed first at the walls and proved useless; then it was aimed at the inner gate; that was the end. De Launay, who told the garrison he wanted to set off the fortress's gunpowder magazine, was easily dissuaded by the veterans. At five o'clock, he surrendered: the Bastille, that most visible symbol of oppression, had fallen.

"Thus, my Lord, the greatest revolution in history has taken place. . . . From this moment we may regard France as a free country," wrote the English ambassador.[12] It was, to say the least, an exaggeration: free countries do not allow massacres, but that, in fact, is what followed the surrender of the Bastille. More than a hundred men had been killed in the attack; now the survivors in their thousands were determined to avenge what they thought of as the betrayal of their friends. At least four of the garrison were slaughtered on the spot; de Launay was taken to the Hôtel de Ville, but he was literally torn apart before he entered the building; and Jacques de Flesselles, the *prêvot des marchands,** who had had nothing whatever to do with the Bastille or its garrison, was massacred as well, simply because he was unpopular. The two men's heads, carefully cut off by an unemployed cook, were stuck on the ends of two pikes and taken to the Palais Royal, where they were paraded until a heavy downpour convinced the mob to go home.

Those were the excesses, and they were significant. The mob had progressed from the sacking of a house to murder. But what most observers noticed was that virtually all elements of the population had come together. "The troops of the city attacked the Bastille and took it by force after it had resisted for three hours," the Austrian ambassador wrote his minister,[13] and he was right. Paris now had an army, and it had no intention of obeying the King.

It normally only took two hours to go from Paris to Versailles, but on July 14 nothing was as it used to be. The news that the Bastille had fallen did not reach Versailles until nine o'clock. Even then, Louis XVI, who did know about the break-in at the Invalides, had ordered that all royal troops were to leave Paris. When the news that the Bastille had fallen reached him, however, he failed to understand it — partly because he could hardly believe it was happening, partly because his reactions were always slow. It was left to a liberal aristocrat to explain it all to him.

The duc de La Rochefoucauld-Liancourt, who belonged to one of the great French families, had fought in America. There he had discovered the benefits of freedom. Since then, while engaged in a busy career as a public benefactor in which he spent his own money abundantly, he had also become a leader of the reformist party, both before the meeting of the Estates General, and within their new incarnation as the National Assembly. At the same time his high rank gave him access to the King. So it was that as Louis XVI was proceeding with the ceremony of the *coucher,***

---

* The prêvot des marchands was both a representative of all Paris merchants and the conduit for the application of the government's economic policy.

** The elaborate ceremony in which the King undressed and went to bed.

he decided to speak clearly to His Majesty. . . . He went into the alcove and said: "Sire, I bring my head to Your Majesty to save your own." He spoke to the King lovingly and frankly, without concealing anything from him, then he said that the situation was such that the kingdom was at the edge of the precipice, and that the bloodiest of civil wars would break out if His Majesty did not entrust himself completely to the National Assembly. He added that, while everyone loved the person of the sovereign and praised his virtues, people were publicly offering 300 livres for the head of the Queen, 100 livres for that of the comte d'Artois, and so on for all those who were thought to advise distrust of the people. . . . He concluded by saying that there was not a moment to be lost.[14]

These were bold words in a court where the King was treated as a living divinity. They may have been bolder still; according to the duc's son (whose life of his father was not, however, written until the 1820s), Louis XVI, upon hearing them, said: "But then, it is a revolt?"

"No, Sire, it is a revolution," La Rochefoucauld supposedly answered.[15] In any event, whether the words were said or not, the fact was clear: what we now call the ancien régime had ended at five that afternoon.

Whatever doubts Louis XVI may have still felt were dispelled by the arrival of the baron de Besenval at Versailles early on the fifteenth. Besenval, a Swiss, was the commander of the Swiss troops in the French service. He was also an assiduous courtier, part of Marie Antoinette's coterie, and a man not likely to err on the side of liberalism. Thus, when he reported that even his troops, which were, after all, foreign, refused to fight against the people, his words carried conviction: from that moment on, even Louis XVI knew that he no longer had an army.

Earlier that morning, at two, Dupont de Nemours, one of the more forward-looking members of the National Assembly, had been sent to the Hôtel de Ville with the King's order to remove his troops from Paris. At eleven, realizing the consequences of the previous day's events, Louis XVI went to the Assembly without any of the pomp required by the normally unbreakable etiquette; and that was the first visible proof that all had indeed changed.

"I have assembled you to consult you on the most important affairs of state," the King told the Deputies. "There is none more urgent, or that affects my heart more tenderly, than the dreadful disorders prevalent in the capital. . . . Help me now to ensure the salvation of the state. . . . Counting above all on the love and fidelity of my subjects, I have ordered my troops away from Paris and Versailles."[16] It was a full capitulation.

Oddly enough, the King, against whose absolute power Paris had just risen, was popular at the very same time that he was not trusted. This apparent paradox was due to what everyone recognized as his utter inability to make up his own mind. Louis XVI, in July 1789, had been on the throne for just fifteen years and two months. Immensely popular when, at the age of twenty, he succeeded his grandfather, it soon became obvious that, despite the best of intentions, he was too slow and too indecisive ever to become an effective ruler. As a result, the people who really mattered were those who were in a position to influence him.

Even his physical appearance confirmed his political inadequacy. He was, in fact, immensely strong, but he merely looked fat. He was terribly nearsighted and thus seemed perpetually surprised, at a loss, but he refused to wear glasses on the grounds they did not look dignified. He walked with an awkward waddle. After a strenuous day's hunt, he was given to falling into a deep sleep, sometimes in public, from which he awoke in a state of stupor. Almost worse than all that, until an operation in 1777, he had suffered from phimosis, a condition that led to functional impotence, and about which everybody knew. It seemed all too emblematic: Louis XVI was as impotent physically as he was inadequate politically.

The consequence of all this was that whoever had the King's ear also controlled the government. By the middle eighties, it seemed clear that Marie Antoinette was the person in question. In fact, her influence was not nearly as great as people supposed; like all weak people, Louis XVI could occasionally turn obstinate; but she had unquestionably chosen the last three principal ministers, Calonne, Loménie de Brienne, and, most recently, Necker.

That might not have mattered so much if the Queen had not been so unpopular; but by 1789 she was almost universally loathed, and not without reason. Although she was kind in private life, Marie Antoinette's blend of self-centeredness, frivolity, and financial irresponsibility had contributed heavily to the fiscal catastrophe that had brought the state to the edge of bankruptcy and forced Louis XVI to call the Estates General. As if that were not enough, the Queen was widely — and on the whole, accurately — seen to be arrogant, lazy, and interested in little besides her own pleasures. She had largely given up the charitable duties carried out by her predecessors, was thought, with some reason, to have spent vast sums on gambling, jewelry, and the redesign of the Trianon gardens, and was deemed to care nothing for the people's welfare.

Unfortunately, during her fifteen years on the throne, Marie Antoinette had remembered she was Queen only when she wanted something; she was incapable of sustained application or long-term interest in a policy. "The Queen," the comte de Mercy, the Austrian ambassador, noted, "has retained an inclination for her fatherland, some attachment for her family, and feeling for her brother [Emperor Joseph II], but she is incapable of acting in consequence. In her ignorance and distaste for serious business, she understands neither its value nor its consequence; she considers it tedious, often adopts contradictory positions and chance sometimes determines her stance as a result of the most bizarre reasoning."[17]

The minister of Saxony, reporting to Dresden on March 15, 1787, unknowingly agreed with Mercy. "It must not be imagined that the Queen is as thirsty for power as people think. Content with preventing whatever might harm her [Austrian] family as explained by M. de Mercy . . . who has a great deal of influence on her, she spends her time in pleasures and being good to the people who are close to her. That is why she tries to get places for her favorites, but she never intervenes in the general European developments about which Your Excellency may rest assured she cares not at all."[18]

At the same time, Marie Antoinette's behavior was governed by one basic tenet: nothing, to her, was more important than maintaining the King's absolute power. Far from feeling, as Louis XVI did, that the monarch was on the throne only to ensure his subjects' prosperity and happiness, she saw the kingdom as a possession, a kind of larger private estate whose population's first duty was unquestioning obedience, in return for which it was to be looked after.

Obviously, then, the current situation struck her as dreadful. Further lessening her ability to adapt to the events of July 1789 was the fact that personally she was deeply unhappy owing to the collapse of the relationships on which, earlier, she had been wholly dependent. From the beginning of the reign, she had found an escape from the dullness of her husband in a circle of close friends, first centered on the princesse de Lamballe, but then, for the last thirteen years, on Mme de Polignac. This attractive, charming, and rather lazy young woman, who sang prettily and knew just how to run a salon, was also extraordinarily selfish and greedy. Prompted by her husband and her official lover, the comte de Vaudreuil, she extracted favor after favor from Marie Antoinette: titles (her husband was made a duke), court sinecures, estates, and pensions. She herself was given the highest possible position, that of governess of the royal children,* a post that came with a large salary and precedence over all the other duchesses. In return for all this, the Queen enjoyed the privacy of evenings spent in Mme de Polignac's Versailles apartment with a group of lively, frivolous people on whom she came to rely for affection and amusement. By 1786, though, it was becoming clear that Mme de Polignac felt no lasting gratitude at all to her friend: when Marie Antoinette asked her to stop inviting a man she disliked, the duchess answered placidly that she would do as she pleased in her own salon, and that no one was forcing the Queen to come.

This was insolence of a high order, and, for a while, the Queen stopped her visits; but then, boredom and loneliness drove her back. Something had changed, though. Until then, she had thought that Mme de Polignac's incessant demands were due to the pressure from other members of her circle; now she began to see the young woman for what she really was: selfish and uncaring. Then, in 1787–1788, the Polignacs came to be seen by the populace, rightly, as the symbol of everything that was wrong with the system; and the Queen was already so hated that she could no longer afford to spend her days with them. Because she had no inner resources, no taste for literature, or indeed, knowledge of any kind, her consequent isolation left her bored, lonely, and depressed.

Nor was that all. Although often an indifferent mother, Marie Antoinette did care greatly about her children. A baby had died at birth in 1787, but she still had a daughter, Marie-Thérèse, called Madame Royale, who was born in 1778; an elder son, the Dauphin, born in 1781; and a younger son, Louis-Charles, born in 1785. Madame Royale, a

---

* She emigrated on July 15, 1789, and was replaced by Mme de Tourzel.

graceful, rather melancholy child, gave her mother nothing but satisfaction. The Dauphin, however, always fragile, became gravely ill in late 1787. On February 22, 1788, the Queen wrote her brother: "My eldest son worries me terribly. . . . His back is becoming crooked, because one hip is higher than the other and because the vertebrae are out of place and jutting out. For some time now he has had a daily fever, and is thin and weak."[19]

In fact, the little Dauphin was suffering from that scourge of both the Bourbons and the Habsburgs, tuberculosis; and given the current state of medicine, the disease was not only incurable but, except in its pulmonary form, not understood to exist. As a result, the little boy grew progressively sicker. In February 1789 Mercy reported: "For the last three weeks, M. le Dauphin's condition has grown steadily worse; the articulations of the hands and feet are losing their flexibility, and tumors have been noticed. . . . The physicians do not know what remedy to use and unless nature itself produces some happy change, there will be no saving the young prince. . . . The Queen . . . is deeply affected."[20] There was, of course, no "happy change." All through the politically tempestuous spring of 1789, the lonely, isolated Queen watched her child slowly dying; on June 4 he finally expired.

As for the royal family — the comtes de Provence and d'Artois, and their wives — it also failed to provide any solace to the Queen. "The difference of opinion and behavior between Monsieur* and M. le comte d'Artois . . . has caused a schism; parties are forming. The Queen sees with sorrow that the monarch is not disposed to settle this. . . . Madame . . . is given to drink, the result has been some disgusting scenes. All that together deprives the Queen of the resources she might have found . . . in the royal family. The well-known danger of the favorite set [the Polignacs] keeps her away from it."[21] In April the ambassador of Saxony commented that the Queen now lived in absolute solitude within her private apartments.

Naturally, she disliked the National Assembly: its Deputies struck her as not merely insolent, but also as an illegitimate obstacle standing between King and people. She had been essentially responsible for

---

* Monsieur, without a title, was the appellation given to the King's next brother; his wife was Madame. Here, of course, these titles refer to the Provences.

Necker's dismissal on July 11; the notion that the people had the right to control their government struck her as both ludicrous and sickening. Again, it was not that she enjoyed meddling in politics: given the choice, she would have preferred to go on living a purely frivolous life, with, of course, enough influence to get her friends appointed to important positions. Louis XVI's weakness, however, and the current crisis left her no choice. Because her mother, the Empress Maria Theresa, had been a remarkably effective ruler, Marie Antoinette believed that she herself had the same capacities; as she saw it, it was now her duty to save the monarchy.

Unfortunately, although courageous, she was also, as Mercy had suggested, unintelligent, ill informed, and incompetent. She had thought of Necker's dismissal as an act of energy that would stop the Revolution, when it was clear to most observers that it would have exactly the opposite effect. She had believed the troops would follow orders although she had been warned they would not. Even the fall of the Bastille failed to give her a clearer sense of reality: at the Council of Ministers that followed, she suggested moving to the fortress of Metz in eastern France; there, amid loyal troops, the King would prepare to reconquer the realm.

Whether or not the garrison of Metz was still obedient is in itself a very large question; but even if it was, the whole plan was predicated on talents Louis XVI was very far from possessing: he was, in fact, the very last man who could be expected to reconquer a rebellious France at the head of his troops. In any event, Marie Antoinette was virtually alone in advocating this course. The ministers pointed out that the King had neither the ready money nor the foodstuffs necessary to provision an army cut off from the rest of the country. The maréchal de Broglie, who had been made war minister in the new administration, said gloomily: "Yes, we can go to Metz, but what will we do once we are there?"[22]

It was a hard question to answer; Monsieur (the comte de Provence), himself the liberal member of the immediate royal family, joined the maréchal in opposing the move. Sadly, the King agreed: there was nothing to do but give in. Almost immediately, however, he regretted his decision. In February 1792 he would tell Count Fersen, Marie Antoinette's Swedish friend: "I know that I missed the moment, it was on July 14. I should have left [for Metz] and wanted to, but what could I do when Monsieur himself was asking me to stay and when the maréchal de

Broglie [agreed with him]?''[23] By then, of course, the Revolution had progressed a long way. In July 1789 Louis XVI was extremely averse to any violent course. He really did feel a responsibility for his people and preferred to give in rather than risk a civil war — an admirable stance but one that also happened to comfort his natural passivity. As for the Queen, who did not have her husband's scruples, she angrily told one of her secretaries: ''You can well imagine that if we wanted to, we would soon put an end to all this business; but we would have to spill our subjects' blood. . . .''[24]

Unlike the Queen, Louis XVI could see positive aspects to an otherwise dreadful situation: he was, after all, growing more beloved by the hour. As the press, now to be freed from all censorship by a newly approved decree, described it: ''It is impossible to depict the universal and moving impression [the King's] speech made on the National Assembly [on July 15].'' The *Journal de Paris* continued,

> Gladness and loving tenderness were at their uttermost. The King and the princes, his brothers, returned to the Palace on foot, accompanied by all the Deputies, and cheered by a numerous crowd; it took His Majesty more than an hour [to walk a quarter of a mile]. Once His Majesty was back in the Palace, he soon reappeared on the balcony with the Queen, Monseigneur the Dauphin, and the princes and princesses of the royal family. Indescribable acclamations and applause gave further evidence of the people's love and gratitude.[25]

All very pleasant, no doubt; in Paris, however, the people were behaving very differently. There, the alliance of the bourgeoisie and the mob endured. To all intents and purposes, the capital had become an independent state, unwilling to defer, not just to the King, but to the Assembly as well, a fact which caused that body considerable and justified concern. So the Assembly decided to send a delegation to the Hôtel de Ville, and to put at its head the one person in France who was familiar with revolutions.

Because he had at the age of nineteen sailed away to America in spite of royal orders to the contrary, the marquis de La Fayette had become the very emblem of the fight for freedom and independence then being waged by the fledgling United States. His courage, his hard work, his heavy financial contributions to the cause had soon transformed the awkward and shy young man into the Hero of the Two Worlds. His close relationship with George Washington had taught him the merits of a free government, and he now stood as one of the leaders of the much-fragmented liberal party in the Assembly. He also knew what a people's militia was, and had just proposed that France give itself a Declaration of the Rights of Man to guarantee the liberty of every citizen. If anyone could cope with the new power in Paris, therefore, it was La Fayette.

Unfortunately, La Fayette was not quite all he seemed to be. Although he had indeed become a hero to the Americans and his compatriots alike, although he was certainly brave, he lacked both common sense and decisiveness. His success in the United States had been due, in good part, to George Washington's advice; left to himself, he tended to dither. Worse, he had become fond of popular applause and was likely to behave unwisely in order to be liked. Finally, he all too fully believed himself uniquely able to cope with the situation, whatever it might be. Still, as he set off toward the capital, he was unquestionably not only the best known of the Deputies, but also the one most likely to be heard by the Parisians.

It is impossible to say how the delegation would have been greeted had he not led it; as it was, he was seen as the right man in the right place: the Parisians promptly offered him the command of their new militia. This was everything La Fayette had ever dreamed of: he would be the French Washington, bring liberty to his fellow citizens, and then, just as the General had retired to Mount Vernon at the end of the war, go off to his own country estate. So, suggesting that the militia be renamed the National Guard, he proceeded joyfully to organize it: order would now be kept, not by the troops of an absolute king, but by the people themselves. Of course, La Fayette had a somewhat restricted idea of who the people were; it included neither working men (of whom the mob was almost exclusively composed), nor servants, nor people who were too poor to pay taxes. Rather than the nation in arms, in fact, the National Guard was to be the bourgeoisie triumphant.

As such, it included small and large shopkeepers, and also the members of what we now call the professions and public employees. Landlords were part of it, and so was the fairly numerous *rentier* class, people whose small fortune afforded them a sufficient income so that, although not rich, they did not have to work. In a word, the National Guard was composed of the small middle and upper bourgeoisie, who at the moment were, like La Fayette, very much in favor of a constitution and thoroughly opposed to the Breteuil ministry. As a result, the Guard was neither a professional army nor really reliable: duty was a part-time obligation, enthusiastically accepted, to be sure, but likely to be discharged neither very effectively nor very fearlessly; the very fact that the Guardsmen kept their guns and uniforms at home made the new body even more unwieldy. It was widely thought, in 1789, that just such men would be the best defense against disorder because, as property owners, they had so much to lose; in fact, just because they were afraid of losing so much, they were, on the whole, reluctant to oppose the mob. And it cannot be emphasized too much that the Guard, although allied to the mob for the moment in a joint rejection of royal absolutism, had interests that were very different from those of the workers and the unemployed.

Still, the very fact that it existed implied an immense change, a decisive shift of power away from the King. The Guard was not restricted to Paris. It was to be truly national, with battalions in every city and town. And in Paris itself, a new city government was set up with, as its Mayor, Sylvain Bailly, a committed liberal, a deputy to the National Assembly, and one of the foremost astronomers of his age. Now, all that remained was for the King to endorse these innovations. The Parisians made it clear that he had better do so in person.

Louis XVI, for all his indecisiveness, did not lack courage. When, on July 17, he set off for the capital, it was in the expectation that he would be held prisoner, or perhaps even killed. "Full powers as lieutenant general of the kingdom were [secretly] given to Monsieur," the Austrian ambassador reported.[26] As for Marie Antoinette, she prepared to go to the Assembly. "The Queen . . . wrote a short speech . . . for the Assembly," one of her ladies noted. "It began by these words: 'Messieurs, I come to entrust you with your sovereign's wife and family; do not allow those whom God has united to be put asunder here on earth.' As she rehearsed this speech, her voice was interrupted by tears and by these painful words: 'They won't let him return.' "[27]

She was not alone in her worry. "The Queen . . . sent for several members of her court: their doors were found to be padlocked. Terror had sent them away, the silence of death reigned in the Palace and fear was at its height."[28] Indeed, early that morning, the comte d'Artois, the King's youngest brother, his cousins the prince de Condé, the duc de

Bourbon, the duc d'Enghien, and the prince de Conti, the Polignacs, the Queen's greatest friends, Breteuil, who had headed the three-day ministry (he was dismissed on July 15), and many other members of the nobility were on their way out of France, most of them wearing disguises and moving with all possible speed. "At Versailles," the Austrian ambassador noted, "the Palace was deserted."[29]

In fact, if Louis XVI had tried to resist, these apprehensions would probably have been justified; but it was an outwardly penitent King who came to his capital on July 17. He had withdrawn his troops, he had agreed to the creation of the National Guard, he was ready to acknowledge the existence of the new city government; and, most important of all, he had recalled Necker: his brief attempt at reaction was well and truly over. Still, the Parisians thought he needed a lesson.

It was cloudy, with occasional showers, when the King's carriage arrived at the city gate. There, he was joined by most of the Deputies; but conspicuously absent for the very first time in its history was the Royal Guard. It was an undefended monarch who came to meet his subjects, and he was made to feel their power.

"One hundred and fifty thousand men in arms lined the streets, three deep on both sides, for more than a league,* from the gate [of the city], along the quay, through the Place Louis XV, down the rue Saint-Honoré to the Hôtel de Ville," the Sardinian ambassador reported. He continued:

> Four cannons placed near the Pont Royal were aimed down the quay on which the King was to drive . . . and four others . . . could start a crossfire on the Cours-la-Reine where the King entered Paris. . . . Nothing could be more [imposing] than to see this armed multitude standing in the deepest silence; the very mix of arms and social classes made the sight more awesome. . . .
>
> People had been warned that it was forbidden to shout "Long live the King" at the monarch's arrival and that, upon his return, the order would be given, if need be, to shout "Long live the King! Long live the nation!" . . . In that immense crowd, not a single word was heard.[30]

It was as sharp a lesson as any king had ever received.

On arriving at the Hôtel de Ville, Louis XVI was greeted by Bailly, the

---

* About two miles.

new Mayor, bearing, as was traditional, the keys of the city. "Sire," he said, "I bring Your Majesty the keys of the city of Paris; the very same ones were offered to Henri IV; he reconquered his people; now the people has reconquered its king. Your Majesty has come to enjoy the peace you have restored to the capital, you have come to enjoy the love of your faithful subjects. . . . Today begins an august and eternal alliance between the monarch and the people."[31] At that point, after the crowd had cheered, Louis XVI was supposed to answer; but he appeared so choked with emotion as to be unable to speak. Unlike the press, who attributed this silence to overwhelming joy, we may suppose it was either relief at still being alive, or fury at being told he had just been conquered. In any event, Louis was seen to whisper to Bailly, who then announced that the King had come to end whatever concern the Parisians might still feel and to enjoy the love of his people, that he wished peace to reign once more. Then there were more speeches, to which, choked once again, the King answered only, "My people can always count on my love,"[32] before getting back into his carriage and driving back to Versailles amid the cheers of the hitherto silent multitude.

In many ways, the events and attitudes of July 17 were even more important than the explosion three days earlier: they set a pattern and provided the Revolution with its own, unstoppable dynamics. Because both Bailly and Louis XVI pretended to feelings they did not have, because the Assembly claimed to be pleased when, in fact, it was terrified at the possibility that it would be eclipsed by the ad hoc government in Paris, speeches were made that had virtually no relation to reality. Louis XVI, who expected to be lynched, had not come to enjoy the Parisians' love. There was no alliance between monarch and people — resentment and distrust, on both sides, would be closer to the reality. But everyone then went on to behave as if the pretense was the reality, as if the real power was virtually anywhere except among the armed Parisians.

Had the situation been dealt with realistically, it might perhaps have been stabilized; by behaving as if hypocritical, sentimental, and high-flown speeches actually described the real world, both the King and the Assembly ensured further disorders. Indeed, more disorders began almost immediately. Although La Fayette in Paris and the Assembly in Versailles had happily announced that order was restored and the Revolution, as such, ended, on July 22, the Parisians proved them both wrong: that day, they seized two men, Louis Berthier and Joseph Foulon, his son-in-law, whom they quite wrongly accused of starving the city. Firmly ignoring Bailly's and La Fayette's pleas, they proceeded to hang them from a street lamp, cut off their heads, and parade them through the city at the end of a pike. "The heart of the traitor, stuck on a knife, was carried about the streets," one of the new revolutionary newspapers reported approvingly.[33]

Of course, there was an outcry. La Fayette resigned as commander of the National Guard — it was, after all, supposed to maintain order in the capital — upon which a group of Guardsmen marched to his house and begged him to resume office on the grounds that he alone could preserve liberty. Without further ado, the General (as he was usually referred to) took back his resignation, and the world of illusion, after this brief interruption, resumed its sway.

All through these trying days the Queen consulted the Austrian ambassador, gave him the latest news, and told him just how she felt; it was a reflection of her devotion to her homeland, and of the ambassador's cleverness, that he remained the one person she trusted absolutely. When, in 1770, the fourteen-year-old archduchess had left Vienna, her mother had urged her to depend on the ambassador, and the ambassador alone, for advice; only he, she said, would have her true interest at heart.

Naturally, that was a lie: the comte de Mercy-Argenteau, who had already spent several years representing the Empress at the French court, had as his sole object the triumph of Austria. If, in the process, Marie Antoinette was to be sacrificed, well, that was the price she would have to pay for being a Habsburg; and indeed, one of the major causes of the Queen's unpopularity was the accurate perception that she always favored the interests of Austria.

Mercy himself was a typical Habsburg statesman: a thorough cosmopolite, a free-spending grand seigneur who kept a series of dancing girls, he was Belgian,* not Austrian at all. French was his first, virtually his only, language; and indeed, all his diplomatic correspondence was written in that language. At first glance, he seemed the very model of the

---

* The Austrian Netherlands, as Belgium was then called, was part of the Habsburg empire.

frivolous aristocrat, witty, well mannered, thoroughly at ease in the midst of court intrigues; he dressed in the latest fashion, knew the latest gossip, and was universally acknowledged to be superb company. Behind that glittering facade, however, was a wily and penetrating mind. He maintained a secret correspondence — as distinct from his official reports — first with Empress Maria Theresa, then, after her death in 1780, with Emperor Joseph II, Marie Antoinette's brother, and the letters are as accurate and informative as they are well written.

Early on, he gained Marie Antoinette's trust by using a simple, highly effective stratagem: the one thing she as Dauphine,* later as Queen, dreaded most was a scolding from Vienna, so Mercy pretended to be on her side. In fact, far from defending her, his confidential reports provoked the Empress's wrath; but the secret was well kept and Marie Antoinette never found out. Thus, early on, she came to rely on Mercy for help and advice; then, because she found politics dull and impossibly complex, she trusted him to provide her with ready-made positions. When, as happened frequently, Louis XVI annoyed her, mostly because he refused her something she wanted, money or the appointment of one of her friends, she consulted Mercy about the best method for overcoming her husband's obstinacy.

All that was naturally shrouded in the deepest secrecy; but in 1788 Mercy's influence became more visible. Years of improvidence had finally brought about a partial bankruptcy of the royal treasury; the prime minister was discredited, the government paralyzed. Mercy, who could see the catastrophe approaching, went to the Queen, urging the dismissal of the then ministry and the appointment of the universally respected Necker. To this Marie Antoinette, after some initial resistance, agreed; Mercy then directed her campaign with Louis XVI. The King loathed Necker and had sworn never to employ him, but he could not withstand the combination of the ambassador's intelligence and Marie Antoinette's insistence: as usual, when sufficiently pressed, he sullenly gave in, and the ambassador brought the negotiations between the court and Necker to a successful close.

Even then, Marie Antoinette was not always a reliable tool: it was very much against Mercy's advice that she had talked Louis XVI into

---

* The heir to the throne was called the Dauphin; his wife, the Dauphine.

dismissing Necker on July 11, 1789. Pride and personal dislike had superseded the ambassador's advice. But now, with everything collapsing around her, it was, as usual, Mercy whom she called to the rescue. Indeed, as the tempo of the Revolution increased, the Queen, who was rapidly growing to loathe the French, felt there were only two men she could rely on for disinterested advice: Mercy and her Swedish friend, Count Fersen.

It was the ambassador, therefore, whom she consulted on July 17. Necker had, the day before, been reappointed principal minister, but the letter sent to him by the King had not yet reached him. The Assembly, too, had written him, telling him, among other compliments: "Your talents and your virtues could not receive a more glorious recompense or a more powerful encouragement. . . . Every minute counts. The nation, her King, and her representatives await you."[34] For the first time, a minister would depend for support on the Assembly rather than the King, and there would be no preventing the reforms he wanted to carry out. "The Queen," Mercy reported in one of his secret letters, "agreed with me that because of the violent pressure to which the Assembly is subjecting the King, their decisions can, in principle, be considered illegal. In spite of this, it is best for the King to consent blindly to everything that requires his consent, with, however, the understanding that later, according to the circumstances . . . he would take advantage of various occasions to take back little by little . . . the power and consideration he has lost." And with perfect accuracy, he added: "The city of Paris is now really the king."[35]

Indeed, the vacuum at the center, after July 14, was virtually total: the King had become utterly powerless; the Assembly, busy writing a constitution, reforming France, and listening to itself, kept looking nervously over its shoulder, wondering what the Parisians would do next. These apprehensions were all the sharper now that Louis XVI behaved very much as if he were on strike, and refused to approve — or disapprove — many of the reforms; this was likely to provoke a new uprising. Worse yet, the longed-for prime minister, the savior of France, the great Necker was wholly out of his depth; and the Deputies knew it.

CHAPTER TWO

The Failure of M. Necker

: : :

AS he set off from Basle on July 24 and prepared for the third time to govern France, Jacques Necker wrote his brother: "Thus I return to France, but as a victim of the esteem they bear me. . . . All is in motion there. There has been yet another scene of disorder and open sedition in Strasbourg. I feel as if I am falling into an abyss."[1] It was an apt diagnosis.

The outcry at Necker's dismissal and the demands, both in Paris and at the Assembly, for his recall were themselves typical of the new world of unreality in which so many people moved — for Necker's immense popularity had virtually disappeared before July 11, as the Deputies became aware of his incompetence. Even then, Necker was out of his depth: a gifted bookkeeper and a speculator of some talent, he was completely unable to develop a policy of rapid but limited reform.

A good part of Necker's reputation, in fact, was due to the enduring myth that says successful businessmen are ipso facto suited to run the government. A small man with a beaklike nose, a sharply receding chin, and a protruding stomach, Jacques Necker looked strikingly like a pouter pigeon. He had come as a young man from Geneva, where he was born, to Paris; there he had gone to work for a bank, done well, eventually started his own establishment, and finally retired in his forties with a considerable fortune. From that moment on, it had been his ambition to become principal minister, an ambition ardently supported by his wife. Luckily for him, Mme Necker was a gifted hostess and an effective propagandist: had she been born in the twentieth century, she would no doubt have enjoyed a dazzling career in advertising. As it was, she devoted herself to the selling of a single product, her husband; and, typically, she did not scruple to exaggerate his merits; then, from the late 1770s on, the Neckers' daughter Germaine (the future Mme de Staël) joined the family enterprise. A woman of extraordinary intelligence and courage, a writer of talent, an acute and sensitive critic, Mme de Staël also devoted herself to ensuring her father's elevation.

In fact, Necker had a gift for figures; he was thoroughly honest; and he cared nothing about perks and honors: those were his good qualities. During his first term as finance minister, between 1777 and 1781, he had managed to make some fairly substantial savings in the runaway budget; since returning to office in September 1788, he had continued to pare away at some of the most extravagant expenditure; but even then, he found himself quite unable to reduce the uncontrollable deficit. Thus, the main reason for the calling of the Estates General had been to improve the tax system so as to ensure the solvency of the state. At the same time, Necker held liberal principles. He thought France — and the King himself — would be better off under a constitutional monarchy, and that, further, taxation without representation was wrong.

He also favored a measure of limited reform: he wanted to end the King's right to arrest anyone arbitrarily; he advocated a limited freedom of the press; he thought that all the French, no matter what their social origins, should have access to all offices, ranks, and titles. In a word, he wanted to import something very like the English system of government. What he could not do, on the other hand, was manage a representative assembly or stop the revolutionary measures that were impending.

At the opening meeting of the Estates General, he had gravely disappointed the Deputies by reading — or rather, having read; his voice gave out — an interminable speech full of incomprehensible figures and totally devoid of any suggestion for reforms. Then, as the days passed, it became clear that he was floundering; unable to deal with demands for radical change, whether in the political system or the tax structure, he was also incapable of negotiating solutions with people whose opinions differed from his. Infatuated with himself, he was far too rigid to compromise; willing, indeed eager, to adjust the system, he could not conceive of replacing it altogether. As a result, it had become evident that he was no longer fitted for his post — until, that is, Louis XVI dismissed him; and then he became the very symbol of liberty. It required no great insight, therefore, to see that the returning minister, faced with a vastly more radical set of demands and the transfer of effective power from Versailles to Paris, would be even more out of his depth than before. The very triumph of his supporters ensured their disappointment and his failure.

What the revived ministry faced, in fact, was an impossible situation: it had, most reluctantly, been appointed by the King, but did not have his confidence; it was in place because the Assembly wanted it, but it had no majority there, no control over it, no ability to get its proposals enacted; finally, it had no links whatever with the one group likely to determine the future course of France, the people of Paris.

All through July, August, and September, the government and the Assembly plunged deeper into their world of make-believe. Both were determined to set up a new, constitutional system in which the executive, embodied by a hereditary monarch, and the legislature, in the form of one or two chambers, would cooperate to rule France. From the very outset, however, this proposed solution ignored a significant fact: you cannot have a constitutional monarchy without the King's cooperation; and, unfortunately, Louis XVI considered the Assembly not a legitimate representative of the French people, but a lawless usurper intent on wrenching away powers God had entrusted to him. At best, therefore, he was prepared to give his reluctant consent to measures he hoped to annul as soon as possible; at worst, he either procrastinated or refused his approval. Under those circumstances, the new regime was doomed from the start.

At the same time, the Assembly, although faced with an impossibly difficult task, shamelessly played to the public. This was partly because power was so new an experience for most of the Deputies that they behaved as if they were still in a salon where eloquence and a finely tuned argument counted far more than the real consequences of what they advocated. Even more important, though, was the fact that the speakers were often playing not to their colleagues but to the public in the tribunes.

"The crowd of spectators who were allowed into the galleries so excited the orators that each wanted for himself that applause whose newly discovered enjoyment so flattered his pride," Mme de Staël wrote. "The democratic declamations which ensured the speaker's success were transformed into terrorism in the provinces: the [Nobility's] castles were burned down as an application of the epigrams spoken by the Assembly's orators, and the kingdom was disorganized by their rhetoric."[2] This is an accurate perception: the public in the tribunes usually consisted of the most revolutionary elements; thus, the quest for their applause radicalized the atmosphere, and the decisions, of the Assembly. At the same time, like all her contemporaries, the usually perceptive Mme de Staël remained blind to one key factor: the real power was in Paris, and its people were far more radical than the average Deputy; so while the speakers unquestionably courted applause, they were also attempting to stay in touch with the reality in the capital. That, of course, made the more conservative Necker and the government almost completely irrelevant. As they functioned in a vacuum, their requests, and even their acts, belonged to another, nonexistent world.

The result of all this should have been prompt and total catastrophe; and yet, Mme de Staël was right again when she noted: "It is to the reforms carried out by [the National Assembly] that the nation owes . . . the treasures of reason and liberty which it wants to, and must, keep at any cost."[3] In fact, the Assembly found itself attempting to deal with such a multitude of problems that it seems amazing it succeeded in its attempts at creating a more just society: there was still the gaping deficit to provide for; order to reestablish; a constitution to be written; a brand-new judicial system to be created; a position for the Church to be defined; and reforms to be made so as to end the old abuses as soon as possible. As it turned out, however, a majority of the Deputies were well-educated, practical men who could easily agree on a minimum program: personal liberty, a separation of powers, an end to autocratic government. These seemed reasonable, indeed necessary goals. Between its first meeting, on May 5, and July 14, the Assembly had essentially fought for its own rights as the representative of the nation; after July 17, the issue was largely settled to the detriment of the King. The Assembly was then free to begin on its great work of reform.

The first major question it tackled was that of the rights inherent to any French citizen; there it followed the example set in the United States. Not only was the new Declaration of the Rights of Man to be inspired by the Declaration of Independence and the brand-new Constitution of the United States, it was proposed by La Fayette, the individual whose inspiration was most wholly American — so much so, in fact, that the group of liberal noblemen that followed him came to be called the Americans.*

The Declaration, as the Assembly finally passed it in late July, is still incorporated today in the French Constitution; indeed, two centuries later, it still has a very modern sound. "The representatives of the French people . . . consider that the ignorance, the contempt, and the oblivion of the rights of man are the sole causes of public unhappiness and of the corruption of governments, [and] have resolved upon setting forth, in a solemn Declaration, man's natural, sacred, and inalienable rights. . . . I. Men are born and remain free and equal" — thus begins the Declaration.[4] It then goes on to say that among these inviolable rights are liberty, security, and resistance to oppression; that sovereignty belongs to the nation, and not to one particular individual; that laws must be the same for all; that no one can be arrested arbitrarily; that punishment may result only from the breaking of a preexisting law. It establishes freedom of speech and of the press; ends all privileges, whether noble or ecclesiastical; guarantees freedom of worship; and finally asserts that the right to own property is inviolable and sacred.

At one stroke, the old system, based on the supremacy of two privileged Orders, the Clergy and the Nobility, was ended. So was the King's absolute power: God-given right was replaced by the consent of the governed.

Unfortunately, that summer the governed were not in a very good mood. On July 29 Necker, arriving at Versailles, had been received by the King and the Assembly; on the thirtieth he went to Paris, where he was greeted by the Mayor and city government amid scenes of the wildest enthusiasm. That, the minister thought, would enable him to rectify some of the errors committed by the people. There was no resurrecting the dead, of course, but the baron de Besenval, the former commander of the Swiss Guard, who had been wrongfully imprisoned, could at least be released; accordingly, at Necker's request, a motion granting him amnesty was passed both by the city government, sitting at the Hôtel de Ville, and by the representatives of the districts. Bailly, however, refused to sign it; the next day, both motions were repealed, and the National

---

* Many of them had also fought in the War of Independence.

Assembly decreed that Besenval would stay in jail until his trial.* The limits of Necker's power had just been clearly drawn.

At least, he was still thought to be financially competent. The treasury being empty, the Assembly, at his urging, agreed on August 9 that 30 million livres' worth of government bonds would be offered to the public; on August 28, with the treasury still bare, the Assembly raised the sum to 80 million; but even that did not help much. Government bonds hardly looked like a safe investment; the old tax system was moribund, and no one knew what its replacement would be. Necker's mere presence at the head of the government had been enough in the fall of 1788 to induce oversubscription; one year later, it had almost no effect at all.

That, and the need somehow to keep the government afloat, were enough to occupy Necker and the other ministers: every day, yet another section of the old order collapsed, with no replacements in sight. Taxes were hardly paid anymore. Soldiers were deserting right and left. The countryside was racked by local uprisings in the course of which, most often, the repositories of feudal titles were destroyed; but, occasionally, muniment rooms, and indeed entire castles, went up in flames along with the parchment. More rarely still, but frequently enough to induce general terror, the noble owners of the castles were massacred as well. Suddenly, anarchy was everywhere and the government could do nothing to stop it. "The King's authority is paralyzed," the Spanish ambassador reported. ". . . [He] will not even use his executive power."[5] He was both right and wrong: the deeply disapproving Louis XVI remained wholly passive; but the problem was also that no one was any longer willing to carry out his orders.

Indeed, no one knew just what orders he was entitled to give, what role, precisely, he was supposed to play. The old order was dead, everyone agreed about that, but the new constitution had yet to be written, and the position of the Assembly was deeply ambiguous. Those who looked to the United States for a model — La Fayette among others — saw clearly that France had combined Congress and Constitutional Convention, the very thing the Americans had carefully avoided; thus, the Assembly lurched uncertainly between discussions of constitu-

---

* He was eventually acquitted and released.

tional principles and ad hoc measures prompted by the day-to-day emergencies. The result, not surprisingly, was total confusion.

Even that most fundamental notion, what is a law? had to be clarified. Could the Assembly, alone, make the law, and was the King's only task to carry out what the Assembly had decided? Or was his agreement required before a decree of the Assembly became the law of the land? Was the King to be given a veto? And was it to be absolute or, as in the United States, conditional? Then the composition of the legislature remained to be decided. Would it be bicameral, the way it was in England, with its hereditary House of Lords and elected House of Commons? Or bicameral the way it was in the United States, with a lower House elected by almost universal male suffrage and a Senate whose members were chosen by the legislatures of the several states? Or was there to be just one, all-powerful chamber? All this had to be decided, as quickly as possible, if the current paralysis was to be overcome; and since it concerned the King quite as much as the Assembly, it would have been logical for him, or at least for Necker, to stake out a position that could be defended in the Assembly.

Unfortunately, neither Louis XVI nor Necker ever attempted to do this, in part because neither really understood what was happening, in part because both were completely unable to work with potential supporters in the Assembly. That, in turn, was due to the novelty of the situation, and also to the fact that the potential "King's party" was badly fragmented by personal rivalries.

The most destructive of these was the conflict between Necker and Mirabeau, the greatest, most influential orator in the Assembly. Of all the extraordinary figures thrown up by the Revolution, Mirabeau was among the most striking. Born into a noble family, and proud of his lineage, he had spent his entire life fighting for freedom. Partly because his parents loathed each other and used him as a weapon, partly because he refused to bow to his father's tyranny, Mirabeau was, early on, the object of incessant persecution. The irony was that the father in question, a philosopher and Physiocrat, spent his life publishing books meant to improve the condition of the people, so much that he was often called *l'Ami des hommes*, the Friend of man; but like so many reformers who love humanity in the mass, he had a tendency to despise individuals. To make it all worse, Mirabeau, who was brilliantly intelligent and gifted with the most compelling natural eloquence, was also extraordinarily ugly and heavily marked with smallpox, and his father claimed that looking at him made him sick.

Because Mirabeau had sided with his mother, less because he liked her than because he wished to annoy his father, the latter simply treated him as an out-and-out enemy. It was possible, in eighteenth-century France, for the head of a noble family to ask for, and be given by the King, a lettre de cachet authorizing the imprisonment of one of his children. This Mirabeau's father did repeatedly, using his son's mistakes to punish him further; thus, a scandalous love affair with Sophie de Monnier, the young wife of an old husband, led to yet another period of imprisonment. As of the young man's late teens, his father's hatred kept him confined in a series of fortresses — on the island of Ré, in eastern France, at Vincennes — altogether for some seven years. This did not normally involve acute discomfort: Mirabeau had a decently furnished room and was given books, pens, paper; and although not allowed visitors, he usually made friends with the commander of the fortress. Still, it was more than enough to teach him that liberty was a good thing.

In between, in a rare moment of such liberty, Mirabeau, besides having a fiery, frantic, and altogether public affair with Mme de Monnier, tried, unsuccessfully, to earn a living by writing a series of pamphlets. These were about state prisons, about the situation in France — devised, at least in part, to provoke the government into paying him not to publish them. In this, he failed utterly. He also gambled, incurred debts, seemed obviously for sale, and in general appeared to be an unprincipled, thoroughly corrupt debauché. These appearances were misleading, though: in the midst of all this foolishness, Mirabeau showed what he could do by publishing an excellent analysis of the Caisse d'Escompte, the main, government-controlled, credit institution. He was, in fact, a man with enormous talents but without an opportunity to use them; his father had seen to that by traducing him constantly. In the existing scheme of things, there was no room for Mirabeau. Without the Revolution, his name today would be utterly forgotten; but he loved liberty, could see far more clearly than most, and was the most compelling orator of his time.

Because he had suffered so badly from the combination of his father's and the King's absolutism, he always defended the cause of liberty. So it was that while the Nobility in Provence, where he had an estate, refused to elect him as one of its Deputies, the Third Estate did so eagerly. His membership in the Assembly gave him his chance: he was heard, he was influential, and he knew himself capable of governing, not least because he was not afraid of facing reality. Indeed, in late May 1789 he realized that a major crisis was impending; and while he wanted freedom and a constitutional monarchy, he also feared the complete collapse of the system. Improbably enough, he was on friendly terms with the staid Pierre-Victor Malouet, a center right lawyer and Deputy, who advocated only minor changes in the status quo. "It is now a question," he told Malouet, "whether the monarchy and the monarch will survive the coming storm or whether past mistakes, and the mistakes which will undoubtedly still be made, will drown us all."[6] At that point Malouet, who had become part of Necker's circle, arranged a meeting; but Necker, who still thought he needed no help, felt nothing but contempt for so corrupt a man as Mirabeau. "When Mirabeau came into the minister's room," Malouet recounted, "they bowed to each other silently and spent a moment observing each other.

" 'Monsieur,' M. de Mirabeau said, 'M. Malouet has assured me that you had understood and approved the reasons for the conversation I wish to have with you.'

" 'Monsieur,' M. Necker answered, 'M. Malouet told me you had something to propose to me. What is it?' Mirabeau, wounded by the coldness of the minister's manner, and by the meaning he gave the word *propose* [that is, that he was asking for a bribe], got up in a rage and answered, 'I propose to wish you a good day.' "[7] One can see that, to so very honest — and prissy — a man as Necker, Mirabeau's whole history and personality must have appeared revolting; but that day the minister threw away one of his few opportunities to control the uncontrollable.

Mirabeau, in fact, could have led the monarchy down the road of least damage; he believed deeply that certain reforms were necessary — enough to give France an English-type government — but he could see clearly that if the King were made powerless, anarchy was likely to replace liberty. Unfortunately, even the reasonable concessions Mirabeau demanded went far beyond what Louis XVI was prepared to grant of his own free will; and to Marie Antoinette, the great orator seemed to be an especially dangerous rabble-rouser.

This might not have mattered so much if the court had enjoyed the support of a solid party in the Assembly; but, of course, that was hardly the case. The extreme right, composed mostly of reactionary nobles, was against any change whatever. Totally devoid of political experience or instinct, it rallied to the *politique du pire,* favoring the most ardent left-wing extremists in the hope of bringing about, first, a disaster, then a violent reaction that would restore the old order.

The center right, which favored a limited measure of reform, was led by Malouet and his friend Jean-Joseph Mounier, a lawyer from Grenoble. It was largely ineffective because it tried to preserve more of the King's power than the center left wanted, without, however, enjoying Louis XVI's confidence. In combination with the extreme right and sections of the moderate center, it would have had the numbers to prevail. That combination, however, was not a possibility: rather than agree to limited reforms, the extreme right, as noted, preferred to bring about a total catastrophe, and its members were far too arrogant ever to listen to a mere lawyer like Mounier. As for the moderate center, although it was worried by the speed and extent of the changes, it had an uneasy feeling that it would not be right to stop them — indeed, that an attempt to do so might result in yet another explosion in Paris, something only the extreme right and the extreme left could contemplate with any equanimity. The vast, ill-defined center might itself have supported Necker, but that could not happen because of his — and the Queen's — personal dislike of men such as Mirabeau.

On the other side, the left, from moderates to extremists, was not only united in wanting a constitution that guaranteed many freedoms; it also felt that it held the right ideas, that it *truly* represented the people. Because of this assurance, the left held much greater power than that of its mere numbers.

The two great constitutional questions that the Assembly discussed in August gave the moderates their last chance to become a majority: if the new legislature had a hereditary upper house, if the King had an absolute veto, then the compromise for which they yearned could be achieved, and a "mixed monarchy" with a parliament would come into being. The veto would enable the King to resist revolutionary measures; the upper house would give him a measure of protection from the lower. Typically, Mirabeau, who thought liberty most likely to prevail through a system of checks and balances, and who hoped one day to become principal minister, came out for the absolute veto.

Here was Necker's, and the monarch's, great chance: working together with the moderates, they probably had the votes to prevail; separately, they were bound to fail. Unfortunately, at the Palace, no one could see this. Marie Antoinette agreed that concessions must be made, since they could not be resisted, but she felt only disgust for the Assembly and thought of Mirabeau as a dangerous firebrand. For her, it was simply a question of waiting until the King had, once again, an army capable of imposing his will. The notion that present compromise might save the future did not occur to her: she felt nothing but dislike for the rebellious French, knew that such episodes in the past had always ended in the monarch's triumph, and could therefore see no reason why it might be necessary to work with the Assembly. As for Louis XVI, indecisive but obstinate, he felt much the same way, although he was prepared to accept periodic Assemblies with the power to vote the budget and taxes; so he tried to resist by being wholly passive, and continued simply to postpone signing the measures he especially disliked.

Thus there was no leadership from the top. Necker, who might have supplied it, remained largely absorbed in financial details; besides which, he never seems to have understood the notion of a parliamentary government party. As a result, the upper house was turned down on September 10 by a vote of 849 to 89 and 100 abstentions — perhaps unavoidably, given the Nobility's extreme unpopularity.

The veto, however, had a much greater chance. There was Mirabeau's always powerful oratory in its support. Necker might have brought pressure to bear on many centrist Deputies; he was, at least, prepared to make his position known. And a great many moderates were worried that the Revolution might become uncontrollable. So, all through August, negotiations took place. La Fayette saw clearly that this was a key issue; he favored a suspensive veto because he thought that an absolute veto would place the King in the impossible position of directly opposing the will of the people, instead of the more moderate stance of merely giving it a chance to reconsider.

As it happened, there was someone in Paris La Fayette could consult about all this, someone who loved liberty and understood constitutions, Thomas Jefferson, the minister of the United States, and a friend from the days of the campaign in Virginia. Jefferson's house was also neutral ground, so La Fayette organized a meeting there that brought eight of the leading men in the Assembly together. There, a compromise was reached: no second chamber, but a suspensive veto. There was a very good chance that the Assembly would agree to this; by September, it was quite ready to trade the veto for the King's signature on a whole series of revolutionary decrees it had passed in August.

These measures were, uniquely, not the result of a popular uprising. Rather, a liberal young noble, the vicomte de Noailles, had stood up, late in the night of August 4, and renounced all the privileges his class had enjoyed for so many centuries. "The troubles that afflict France," he told the Assembly, "can be calmed only by relief [from onerous burdens] and by our generosity."[8]

As the *Journal de Paris* reported,

> This motion caused an outburst of generosity. . . . One motion was immediately followed by another; all were adopted as soon as offered. . . . It was decided to abolish feudal courts, hunting laws, feudal tithes, *main-morte,* all the pensions not due to proved service to the nation. The taxes were to be equally supported by all . . . , justice would be free, and the venality of all judicial offices ended. . . . All provinces would give up their privileges. . . . All men would be admitted to every office or military rank.
>
> M. de Lally-Tollendal asked that Louis XVI be given . . . the name of Restorer of the Liberty of France. . . . This was decreed by cheers so loud they shook the walls.[9]

Main-morte was a rare, but still existent, form of feudal slavery, so shocking that, in fact, Louis XVI had urged the nobles to end it. Ending venality meant that it would no longer be possible to buy an office in any of the Parlements, the courts of the ancien régime where would-be judges bought their seats. The privileges being given up by various provinces entailed exemption from certain taxes. At one stroke, the system under which the French had lived for some seven centuries was to end, and the movement was led by noblemen drunk with love for their fellow men. As for the new title given the King, it was in the nature of a sop. No one thought he would really approve of what they were doing that night, but they hoped he might give in to the Assembly's wishes. It was almost dawn before the Deputies went home, and it took them nearly a week to give legal and reasonable form to what had been done that night. Many nobles, after all, depended on the income provided by their feudal rights, which, indeed, were considered to be a form of property, so arrangements had to be made for buying them back. But, finally, on August 11, the decrees were passed. "The Assembly destroys the feudal regime altogether. . . . All feudal rights and duties . . . are ended," they began;[10] and, indeed, they ushered in a new era in which no man would have privileges, none obligations that would not be shared by all.

On August 13 the decrees were brought to the King for his signature. He had already expressed approval of some parts of them at least so there was therefore good reason to hope that he would promulgate them without delay. Indeed, the Deputies, the King, and the court immediately proceeded to hear a Te Deum in the chapel of the Palace, after which Louis XVI was solemnly offered, and accepted, his new title.

Unfortunately, as much as a sop, it was the product of wishful thinking. While the King was, in fact, pleased with the abolition of the main-morte, while he could accept the exchange of feudal pecuniary rights for compensation, the revision of all pensions and the opening of all ranks and offices horrified him. Worst in his eyes was the abolition of the tithes, an important source of income for the Church; this directly attacked the established religion. Unlike other feudal rights, there was to be no buy-back for them. In their great burst of selflessness, Noailles and the other young nobles had wanted to make all men equal before the law — in this way, perhaps, preempting the agitators who were again getting busy in Paris. It was an attempt to go the revolutionaries one better, to offer so much that nothing would remain to be taken by force. But, in order to succeed, it had to be implemented immediately; and that required promulgation by the King. Louis XVI, however, had no intention of approving what he saw, accurately, as the end of the traditional monarchy.

The very next day, in fact, he showed just what it was he really cared about. In a proclamation that executed an Assembly decree he had requested, he ordered that "all the city administrations of the kingdom preserve the public peace. . . . All persons arrested are to be turned over to the courts."[11] As for the decrees brought to him on the thirteenth, he simply took them under advisement. He announced that he approved of the spirit of the decrees, but left it at that.

His unfavorable attitude was only reinforced by what happened next. The Assembly had already discussed the Declaration of the Rights of Man; on August 19 it proceeded to pass it as a further decree that also required the royal signature. From the King's point of view, this merely added to the horror. He could not, he felt rightly, refuse his consent outright without provoking an explosion; the fall of the Bastille had taught him that much. So he delayed in the hopes of better days to come. And this attitude, in turn, singularly complicated the fight for the veto, since the King showed himself, once more, unwilling to work with the Assembly.

Today, with the benefit of hindsight, we can see that Louis XVI was simply deluded; but in the summer of 1789, the reality of royal power was still so close, the tradition of obedience so strong, that many thought it possible there would soon be a reaction. If, therefore, the King simply held on long enough, equivocating all the way, he might prevail in the end. It was a stance Marie Antoinette fully supported; and so the deadlock lasted.

Naturally, as it did, the tension became more acute; and that was when Mounier, Malouet, and their group, now known as the *Monarchiens* because they supported the monarch's power, came up with that eternal standby, the suggestion of a retreat of the King and court to some place more distant from Paris than Versailles — Compiègne or Soissons, in this case. The Assembly was to follow; and away from the capital's agitators, it would become more docile. Unfortunately, the implementation of that plan would have been possible only if Louis XVI was convinced the Monarchiens were on his side; but because they had supported the transformation of the feudally divided Estates General into a National Assembly, he thought that they were no better than the rest. Then, too, a move away from Versailles would have required just the kind of decisiveness he lacked. Finally, of course, the rationale behind the plan was that the provinces could be relied on to support the ancien régime, that they were less revolutionary than Paris. In the summer of 1789, this was a largely unjustified assumption.

So the deadlock continued and the mood in Paris grew uglier, in part because the King was represented, once more, as influenced by his reactionary entourage, in part also because the duc d'Orléans was subsidizing whole groups of agitators. Like his cousin, he still thought of the situation in traditional terms; with luck and effort, he felt the French might produce a replay of the English revolution of 1688, and he, Orléans, hoped, and indeed expected, to play William III to Louis XVI's James II. Once more a younger branch of the ruling family would accept constitutional restraints in order to seize the throne.

The duc was well placed to create disorder. He was immensely rich and could thus afford to pay crowds to appear at the right place and at the right time. Also, the gardens of the Palais Royal, right in the center of Paris, belonged to him; because they were his private property, the police had no access to them, and they provided revolutionary orators with a perfect forum. Finally, he was careful to cultivate his image as a liberal, a backer of the people's rights. With all that, he should have been irresistible.

Unfortunately for him, however, he was also lazy, frivolous, not very bright, and far too fond of pleasure to give much energy to anything else. One of the most spectacular debauchés in Paris at a time when riotous living was the norm, he was incapable of the seriousness needed to gain his ends; nor was his reputation improved by the fact that, instead of choosing a serious and cultivated nobleman as the governor of his children, he had given the job to his mistress, Mme de Genlis. She turned out to be a highly competent educator, but the impression remained that the duc was controlled by his sensuality. This was all the more readily accepted because he was also a coward, unwilling to assume responsibility and quick to take cover. Thus, in spite of the flood of pamphlets he financed, in spite of the shouting crowds, he failed to progress as he should have.

Still, he did protect the revolutionaries. It was, typically, in the garden of the Palais Royal that one of the most fiery revolutionary orators, the young Camille Desmoulins, spoke nearly every day, and he was listened to by increasingly large crowds. "The [Austrian] Empire has just made peace with the Turks so that it can send its armies against us," he said, for instance, on August 30. "The Queen, most likely, will want to join them, and the King, who loves his wife, will not want to be separated from her. If you allow him to leave the kingdom, we must at least take the Dauphin as a hostage; but I think we would do much better, so as not to lose this good king, to send him a deputation that will urge him to confine the Queen at Saint Cyr and bring him to Paris where we can secure his person."[12]

This was a simple, but highly effective, theme. By opposing a good, yet easily influenced, Louis XVI to the evil Marie Antoinette, it was possible to attack his acts while still pretending to respect him, thus creating the widest possible consensus. In most ways, in fact, the Queen was a godsend for the revolutionaries. "The people's anger is turned mostly against the Queen," the Sardinian ambassador noted,[13] and Mercy agreed with him: "It is impossible to explain the causes of the frenzy . . . against the Queen," he wrote Joseph II in late July. "She is said to have sent several hundred millions [to Austria], to have asked for an imperial army to crush the nation, and these, and similar, absurd notions have made a deep impression."[14]

That impression soon became even more prevalent because of a new development: on August 23, the National Assembly guaranteed the freedom of opinion; on the twenty-fourth, the freedom of the press. Although the King did not sign these decrees immediately, the government's loss of control in Paris meant, in fact, that these laws had been anticipated by the newly emergent press. Now, anything could be printed; and because, earlier, the censors (now unseated) had been responsible for banning most libels, there was no existing law to contain the excesses of the new publications. As a result, while some papers like the *Journal de Paris* were content to report the news accurately and promptly, others, exhibiting all the signs of the most violent prejudice, did not hesitate to distort or invent whenever convenient, and that added greatly to the general unrest.

Naturally, speeches like those made by Camille Desmoulins could now be widely published, often in the form of pamphlets selling for a few pennies. On September 12, Marat started his first paper, *Le Publiciste parisien,* in which he promptly attacked the veto, writing: "To create the veto before having completed the constitution is the same as building a house and starting with the roof. . . . To begin with, the promulgation of the laws would mean giving the monarch the power to oppose the constitution."[15]

It was a convincing argument, especially since many people thought that the nation should first give itself a constitution before allowing the King to enjoy his powers as the executive. They felt that the King could not veto constitutional decrees because the ability to write the constitution belonged to the nation alone.

The newfound freedom of the press did not protect political writings only: suddenly a flood of pamphlets appeared in which calumny triumphed. Marie Antoinette, for instance, was commonly accused of being as cruel as she was depraved. A leaflet entitled *Antoinette of Austria, or a Dialogue between Catherine de Médicis and Frédégonde, Queens of France* was typical of this. Both Catherine and Frédégonde were stock figures of evil queens, and in the leaflet they exclaimed: "So long an object of horror to God, the universe, and Hell itself, our crimes will at long last be forgotten. . . . [Our] misdeeds are mere games, bagatelles compared to those of Antoinette of Austria. . . . Incest, adultery, the most infamous and shameful lust are just pastimes for this Messalina. . . . Paris will be burned down, blood will flood its streets, and all those atrocities are the work of this cruel and vindictive woman."[16] This last accusation had a long and successful career. In 1792, the revolutionary mob would sing: "Madame Veto had promised she would burn Paris down to the ground," and that in itself is a measure of the success of this pamphlet and dozens of others like it. Because the monarchy had so long been revered, the attacks, when they came, were all the more violent and all the more believable: maddened crowds will always be quite sure that their enemies are plotting their extermination.

In a sense, however, these attacks were not wholly without a wider truth: Marie Antoinette had not yet called on the Austrian army, she certainly had not sent her brother hundreds of millions of livres, but, as noted, she was wholly pro-Austrian, even to the detriment of French interests. She did not think of destroying Paris, but she loathed the Revolution and its mobs and, unlike her husband, would have seen a little bloodletting without any displeasure, providing only that it restored the ancien régime. But what of the "unnatural lusts" with which she was widely credited?

Although she may well, in fact, have fallen in love with Count Fersen, a handsome Swede who spent several years in France, there can be very little doubt that the affair, such as it was, was never consummated. The circumstances of her life at Versailles, her lack of privacy, the Count's infrequent visits, all make it virtually certain that nothing sexual actually happened. Other than that, Marie Antoinette, who does not appear to have had a very strong sex drive, seems to have been wholly faithful to the King. It had, however, become a habit, in France, since the 1750s, to accuse one's enemies of all sorts of excessive or perverted sex acts as a way to destroy their reputation; this habit came not from the people, but from the court itself, where nobles would commission pamphlets attacking their rivals for the King's favor. That method had been used against the Queen in the late 1770s and 1780s by people who resented being left out of her little coterie. Now it was enthusiastically picked up, so that, although the accusations were absolutely false, they were widely believed among the people and helped ensure that she was considered a monster, the evil power constantly perverting a well-meaning King.

Marie Antoinette's extreme unpopularity, the duc d'Orléans's intrigues, the King's failure to sign the decrees passed by the Assembly in August, and, just as important, the high price of bread, all combined to make the situation in Paris highly explosive. Necker knew it, and so did the moderates among the Deputies. It was obviously time for a serious negotiation leading to a settlement, and that, in early September, is just what happened. The liberals in the Assembly were ready to trade a veto for the King's promulgation of the decrees. Necker agreed to the bargain; all was settled. On September 11, 679 Deputies voted in favor of a conditional veto, with 329 opposing it. On September 21, the veto was defined as valid for two consecutive legislatures; the third legislature, if it concurred with its two predecessors, could override it. Each legislature was to have a two-year term.

Now the Assembly expected the King, finally, to promulgate the decrees ending feudalism and setting forth the Declaration of the Rights of Man. But that supposed a feeling of obligation on Louis XVI's part, the acknowledgment that the Assembly was indeed a valid partner. In fact, the King considered himself faced with a group of usurpers to whom he owed nothing, while, on the other hand, he was accountable to God for the powers he had inherited along with the throne. The misunderstanding could not have been more complete.

Because Louis XVI had given in to pressure so often and so visibly, because he was slow and passive, almost bovine, he seemed most often a hapless tool, of his wife or a minister, a man capable of resenting the loss of his power, but not of doing anything about it. That, however, is a misperception: below all those layers of inadequacy was the bedrock of his conscience, and there, for him, all was clear. He had inescapable duties to God, the Catholic Church, and the throne. No explanation could ever convince him that he was wrong about this: like many rather dim people, he could be very obstinate — a trait with which Marie Antoinette was quite familiar. Faced with an unacceptable situation — the demand for his signature to the August decrees — he was not capable of counterattacking; but he could resist passively and, if necessary, he was ready to equivocate, renege on an agreement, and betray the people who had relied on him. That is just what he proceeded to do throughout September.

The Assembly had created the veto on September 11. On the fourteenth the King ordered the Flanders regiment to Versailles in the mistaken belief that it would provide him with the force he needed to resist the Assembly, whose president that day brought the decrees to him with the request that he have them promulgated. On the eighteenth, finally, he gave the Deputies, who had trusted him, his answer in a long letter. He declared that he was willing to allow the buy-back of the feudal dues, the free admission to all offices, and the suppression of all privileges. He noted that he had some reservations about the end of the hunting laws, the suppression of the venality of the offices in the Parlement because it would be so expensive to compensate the current owners, the revision of the pensions because he could not allow the Assembly to conduct an inquisition into them, and the end of the annates, a Church tax, because it was part of the concordat with the Pope. Finally, he said that he would not allow the suppression without compensation of any of the feudal rights, the end of feudal courts, or that of the tithes.

Naturally, the Assembly, having kept its end of the bargain, was horrified. On the nineteenth, it cheered Mirabeau when he said: "Let us dare to tell the King: you are mistaken about the nature of our request. We have not asked you for advice, we simply want your signature; justice and the current circumstances make it necessary."[17] Indeed, the "current circumstances" Mirabeau mentioned were pressing; in his newly renamed paper, *L'Ami du peuple,* Marat commented: "There is only one way to save the state, and that is to purge and reform the National Assembly by throwing out ignominiously its most corrupt members [i.e., the conservatives]."[18] Two days later, Marat went a good deal further: "It is certain that the aristocratic faction has always dominated in the National

Assembly and that the Deputies of the people have always blindly followed it. . . . Let the nation finally invoke its rights. Let it dismiss the Assembly and annul its decrees."[19]

Of course, Marat only spoke for the extremist fringe, but tempers were rising in Paris, and the Assembly could see clearly where the King's resistance was likely to end: reform was one thing, continued popular violence quite another, and this was just what Louis XVI was provoking. Necker saw it, too, and he pressed the King to carry out his end of the bargain. Typically, Louis XVI said neither yes nor no; he simply gave orders in late September for the decrees to be published without having been promulgated, in the apparent belief that they could not be carried out until laws had been passed to spell out their mode of execution. Thus he hoped to fool the Assembly and the people: publication without promulgation and the regulating laws would seem to imply approval on his part, and would disarm the liberals, without actually allowing the August decrees to be applied.

It was the worst possible attitude. Once again, as when he had dismissed Necker, the King set up a confrontation with the Assembly and the people that he could not possibly win. It required a complete lack of realism to think that the regiment of Flanders, alone, could protect him against a repetition of the July 14 uprising. At the same time, partly because of the monarchy's lingering prestige, partly because France was living in a constitutional vacuum, Louis XVI was just strong enough to be a serious obstacle, and one that must be overcome. There might have been a case for his leaving Versailles, going off to one of the fortresses on the eastern border, and trying to reconquer the country; there was an excellent case for accepting the August decrees and reigning as a popular constitutional king; there was none at all for taking half measures.

Mirabeau saw it clearly. As always, he wanted to blend liberty and order: he had demanded that the King sign the August decrees and was ready to support him if he would. By the end of September, however, he realized that the situation was virtually hopeless. "What are those people thinking of?" he asked his friend La Marck, speaking of the King and Queen. "Can't they see the abysses gaping before them?" And, La Marck adds, "Once, when he was in a state of exasperation even more violent than usual, he exclaimed: 'All is lost; the King and Queen will perish, and you will witness it: the people will stamp on their corpses.' "[20]

CHAPTER THREE

Paris Takes Over

: : :

VERSAILLES, the great golden Palace set in its majestic park, remained unchanged in the summer of 1789. The ormolu on its furniture gleamed as brightly as ever, the costumes worn by its occupants lost nothing of their splendor, and the inflexible etiquette ruled as firmly as ever. The court could, if it chose, think that, after all, the monarchy was intact. In Paris, though, they knew better: while the Assembly waited for the King to promulgate its decrees, the Revolution went right on — more quietly, and even more effectively. A new city government was set up with a central body, the Commune, elected on September 18. Far more important, each of the sixty *districts,* originally a mere constituency, became a little self-contained republic with its own assembly and its own executive.

All the legal voters of the district could attend its assembly, but they, in fact, did not amount to very many: women, servants, soldiers, and workers were ineligible. Those eligible to attend were much the same kind of people who served in the National Guard, and their political views differed from area to area: the district of the Filles Saint-Thomas, near the Tuileries on the Right Bank, for instance, was fervently royalist, while the districts of parts of the Left Bank counted among the more revolutionary.

The district assemblies, in turn, were modified by actual circumstances: the well-to-do seldom attended, but then again, in 1789 at least, the very small shopkeepers rarely found the time to leave their business. The result was that the district assemblies consisted mostly of the small to middle bourgeoisie, the very people who were most in favor of the reforms and who, knowing how to read, were devouring the papers and pamphlets being poured out by the Parisian presses. As a consequence, and with two or three exceptions, the district assemblies were very much more radical than the National Assembly; in addition, because their meetings were attended by the local nonvoters, who came as eager spectators but did not make the trip to Versailles, they felt the pressure of the mob far more strongly than the Deputies away at Versailles, and, being less in the public eye, they were even more inclined to give in.

All the great questions were debated in the district assemblies, along with issues of local interest only; and it was there, not in the National Assembly, that new policies were forged. Even more important, these districts could fill the streets with angry crowds at a moment's notice, and the Assembly knew it. It also knew that the government's writ no longer ran in Paris. Each district had a police committee on whose orders searches and arrests were carried out and which also functioned as a court; a military committee that effectively controlled the local battalion of the National Guard, itself the only remaining force left in the city; a subsistence committee that controlled the markets, the bread supplies, the movement of foodstuffs, all exceptionally important and sensitive matters throughout the summer when shortages were constant; and all this was done in public sessions usually very well attended by the people. Thus, virtually every Parisian could watch a new, democratic government at work and learn that many of the most important functions of the royal administration needed neither king nor minister to be accomplished. It was a triumph of grass-roots power; it also greatly weakened whatever prestige the monarchy had retained until then.

Even so, there were still street disturbances. Although the excellent 1789 crop promised a winter of abundance, the first grain did not reach the markets until middle to late October. All through the summer, the price of bread, that essential staple, remained at a historic high. At the same time unemployment spread rapidly: on top of the ravages caused by the unusually long and cold winter of 1788–89, many employers emigrated in the second half of July. Even the nobles who still remained in France cut down severely on their expenditures. Because Paris was the center of France's luxury manufactures — everything from jewelry to clothes to furniture — many artisans were thrown out of work, as were many domestic servants. On August 18 tailors and barbers took to the streets demanding work and higher salaries; on September 22 the butchers followed them.

Today, we are accustomed to being told that recessions are caused by economic laws that government can only palliate at best. In 1789 abundance was taken to be the norm; distress, when it happened, was invariably thought to be the result of a plot, either on the part of grain dealers intent on making huge profits, or, in this case, on the part of the Queen and her friends, who were deliberately starving Paris to punish it for the Revolution. When, day after day, people are hungry, when they blame a ruler (or his wife) who has already been humiliated once for trying to resist the people's will, then, obviously, a new revolutionary outburst is near. And, once again, conditions were right for an alliance of the mob and the middle class.

For the mob, in late September, two issues really mattered: the price and scarcity of grain, and the arrival at Versailles, on the twenty-third, of the thousand-man Flanders regiment. This looked very much like a repeat of the military concentration of early July; it seemed to demand very much the same response. As for the middle class, although food prices did not affect it nearly as much, it, too, was worried about the King's intentions. Whether the Flanders regiment was supposed to march against the city or, as seemed more probable, protect the royal family in a flight to Metz, a possibly fatal blow would be dealt to the Revolution. Then, too, the bourgeoisie very much wanted to see the August decrees promulgated because they were the charter of a new kind of government in which it would hold power. By the end of the month, therefore, it was clear that the city was preparing for another *journée,* a Day, as the revolutionary outbursts were called.

Lafayette,* as commander of the National Guard, and Bailly, as Mayor, were in a position to know this; both, unquestionably, felt the rise of the people's anger. Neither did anything about it, Bailly because he approved of it, Lafayette because he was anxious to retain his extraordinary, but fragile, popularity. Indeed, they had only to read the papers: on October 2, for instance, the *Révolutions de Paris* announced: "We need a new bout of revolution, and everything is ready for it."[1] This paper

---

* At this time, he changed the spelling of his name from La Fayette to Lafayette.

continued the next day: "The plan of the aristocrats is to kidnap the King and take him to the fortress of Metz so as to make war on the people in his name."[2] As for Camille Desmoulins, that fiery young man whose speeches so roused his rapidly swelling public, he published, anonymously, a pamphlet whose very title was a provocation: *The Speech of the Lantern to the Parisians.* Purporting to be spoken by the streetlight from which Berthier and Foulon had been hanged in July, it described the pleasure it took in being admired by vast crowds. "It thrills me so," Desmoulins has it say, "that I am surprised they don't hear me exclaiming: 'Yes, I am the queen of lanterns!' "[3] After praising the August decrees, the lantern goes on to attack all nobles and demand their expulsion, as well as that of all ecclesiastics, from the National Assembly; only the Deputies of the communes, the former Third Estate, should remain.

It was a clear, if especially picturesque, expression of an increasingly widespread feeling: a more revolutionary Assembly was needed, and it alone should rule. To think, therefore, that the Flanders regiment's presence at Versailles could change the situation bespoke a very remarkable degree of blindness; and yet, because they did not want to see, that is just what afflicted both Louis XVI and Marie Antoinette. As for Necker, the darling of the people in July, the savior of France whose recall the Assembly had demanded, he was so busy with schemes for loans, new taxes, balancing the budget, and finding ready cash to keep the government going that, to all intents and purposes, he was already irrelevant.

The Queen herself, like so many limited people, saw history only in terms of dazzling and heroic deeds, especially those of her family. No doubt she remembered the famous episode in which her mother, the Empress Maria Theresa, having inherited her many crowns only to discover that the empire was falling apart, had gone to the Hungarian Diet and made such a rousing speech that its members had shouted enthusiastically: *"Moriamur pro rege nostro Maria Theresia"* (We will die for our King Maria Theresa). What Marie Antoinette did not know was that this great moment had been preceded by lengthy negotiations, in the course of which her mother had given way to many of the Diet's demands. So, in the full confidence that what the Empress had done, she could repeat, Marie Antoinette helped to provide Paris with just the provocation it was awaiting.

On the evening of October 1 the officers of the King's bodyguard, noblemen all, invited their colleagues from the Flanders regiment to a banquet in the Versailles Opera hall. After this banquet had proceeded for some time, with wine flowing freely, the King, the Queen, and the Dauphin made their appearance, and were greeted with rapturous applause and shouts, upon which the officers took the tricolor cockades off their hats, threw them to the ground, and stamped on them. The tricolor flag, or cockade, which juxtaposed the blue and red colors of Paris with the white of the monarchy, was a symbol of the new order; the white or black cockade, of the old. Then, as if that were not enough, shouting a variety of ultra-royalist slogans, and with black or white cockades now adorning their hats, the officers accompanied the royal family back to its apartments.

Marie Antoinette, as she acknowledged and encouraged all this, must have thought it was a replay of Maria Theresa's success with the Hungarian Diet. That, obviously, was pure fantasy: the bodyguard and the Flanders regiment combined could no more have stopped the Revolution than they could have conquered the rest of Europe. Indeed, the foreign envoys treated the whole episode dismissively; the Spanish ambassador, for instance, after describing this silly episode, added: "This gesture has received much unwarranted publicity."[4]

And so it had. Within forty-eight hours, the Parisian press was describing an innocent Louis XVI unknowingly taken in by a group of reactionaries: "The King, coming in from the hunt, is taken to [the banquet], which he is told is very cheerful. The Queen, holding monseigneur the Dauphin by the hand, comes forth to the edge of the floor. A voice rises above the shouts of joy and these sacrilegious words are heard very distinctly: 'Down with the colored cockades, long live the black cockade, it is the only good one.' Immediately the sacred symbol of liberty is trod upon."[5] With that, the exuberance of a few half-drunk officers became a concerted attack on the Revolution and all it stood for, the visible manifestation of the plot whose existence the Parisians had suspected all along.

Now it was the Assembly's turn to feel alarmed. On October 2 a deputation asked the King to sign the decrees incorporating the Declaration of the Rights of Man and presented him with the first nineteen articles of the constitution. These essentially defined the framework of the new regime: the nation, not the King, was sovereign; the King would be bound by the existing laws; he would be given the executive power, the legislative being entrusted to a unicameral legislature which alone would be able to propose and enact the laws and vote taxes and loans; the King would have a conditional veto and the right to ask the Assembly to consider any particular subject.

Immediately, the King resorted to his habitual tactic: he expressed himself willing to accept the nineteen articles, but only with grave misgivings, while asking for a strengthening of the executive. As for the Declaration of Rights, in a letter dated October 4, he replied: "It contains very good maxims which can guide your labors, but these principles, being capable of different applications, and even different interpretations, can only be properly appreciated . . . when their true meaning is fixed by the laws to which they must serve as a base."[6] Once again, Louis XVI had said neither yes nor no. Together with the banquet, it was more than enough to make the Parisians feel it was time to show him who was actually in charge.

"The alarm is universal. . . . There is not a moment to be lost: all good citizens must come together in arms," Marat urged on the evening of the fourth.[7] By then, at the end of a day during which the orators of the Palais Royal had explained it all, the crowd knew just what to do. There were no more fortresses to be taken in Paris; but, away in Versailles, the King was constantly subjected to the influence of a reactionary court clique that at the same time was starving the capital. The solution to both these problems was as simple as it was obvious: if only the King were in Paris, surrounded by his loving people, he would accept the Revolution wholeheartedly and see to it that the city was fed properly; if he would not come of his own free will, then he would have to be brought back by force.

Of course, on an obvious level, that appeared to make sense. Yet, in the people's attitude toward Louis XVI, at this moment, there remained a powerful nonrational element: although the God-given monarchy was dead, the King himself was still something very much like the totem of the tribe, the magic intermediary whose physical presence would heal all wounds. This was not incompatible with the view that Louis XVI was weak and easily fooled: just as some primitive tribes whip the statues of their gods when the crops fail, so the person of the King seemed an essential component of the public welfare. Needless to say, this was wholly unrelated to the belief widely held among the educated elite that, except in very small cities, republics inevitably degenerated into anarchy followed by a military dictatorship, and that France must, therefore, always have a (constitutional) monarch. What the people felt was simply a superstitious belief whose roots went back to the Middle Ages.

It thus seemed to make perfect sense when, on October 5, a troop of several hundred women, after coming together at the Hôtel de Ville, started to march on Versailles. By the time they reached the city limits, they numbered some five to six thousand. Then, as the bells tolled, 15,000 men of the National Guard decided to follow them in spite of Lafayette's exhortations to the contrary, leaving the General nothing to do but accompany them.

At that point, of course, Lafayette could have resigned: a general whose troops pay not the slightest attention to him can hardly be very effective. In fact, he did not consider resigning for a moment: he cared far too much for his popularity to endanger it in this way. When, after the murder of Berthier and Foulon, he had resigned, it was done safe in the knowledge that he would be begged to change his mind; but, on October 5, that would not have happened.

Of course, Lafayette's behavior broke two of his cherished principles: the first was that the Assembly, and the Assembly only, should be in charge, and that the laws must be obeyed; the second was that an oath, once taken freely, was unbreakable — and he had sworn to obey the constitutional King. Against that, however, two far more weighty motives determined him: the first was indeed a fear of becoming unpopular, but the second was exasperation at Louis XVI's endless delays. A scare would do the King good; and if he were to be brought back to Paris, then the easily influenced monarch would no doubt prove far easier to handle. Still, a scare would be enough: the General had no intention of allowing the royal family to be massacred, and his presence at the head of the Guard would ensure the King and Queen's safety. Thus it was that he left the capital prepared to play a thoroughly ambiguous role.

The presence of the Guard was all the more necessary since behind them came a great mass of armed Parisians. Once again the mob and the bourgeoisie had come together to impose their will; and this was made particularly clear by the presence of a two-man deputation from the Commune, charged with demanding that the King move to Paris.

In fact, this great eruption toward Versailles was not nearly as spontaneous as it seems. Much remains murky about the organization of this new journée, but there can be no doubt that the women were carefully brought together and the National Guard forewarned and urged to accompany them. The movement took place much too fast, much too smoothly for it to have occurred of itself. Even the placing of the women — some of whom were in fact men wearing dresses — in the vanguard was carefully thought out: if royal troops tried to stop the Parisians at the Sèvres bridge, they might be willing to shoot at armed men, but certainly not at hungry women come to ask for bread.

It is, however, much more difficult to determine whose hidden hand was responsible for all this. Obviously, there were many groups in whose interest it was to give the King at least a good scare: all those, in fact, who stood to benefit from the new order of things, all those who wanted the King to accept the August decrees and the Declaration of the Rights of Man; and then, there was the duc d'Orléans. Although nothing can be proved, it seems extremely likely that his money and his agents were strong contributory factors. If the King became a prisoner of the Parisians, then he, the duc, might well be appointed lieutenant general or regent, the first step toward a change of dynasty. Many papers were burned in the weeks following October 5; many people were afraid of telling what they knew; but it remains a fact that Orléans was made to leave France in early November, under the pretext of a mission to England, and he would certainly not have gone had he not feared embarrassing disclosures.

October 5, as it turned out, was not a good day for a walk. By the time the Parisians reached Versailles, they were soaked and muddy, and still the rain continued. In Versailles itself, all was disorganized. The Queen was at the Trianon; she came back hurriedly to the Palace in mid-afternoon. The King, as usual, had gone hunting — nothing, not the gravest political tension, was allowed to take him from his favorite sport — and though he was hurriedly brought back from Rambouillet, some eight miles away, to Versailles, he did not reach it much before seven. As for the local National Guard, which was supposed to maintain order in the town, it simply refused to serve. Thus, when around four-thirty the women arrived in the big open square in front of the Palace gates, the Place d'Armes, they found only a thin line of bodyguards blocking the entrance. Naturally, they asked to see the King. On being told that he was still away hunting, they moved back down the Avenue de Paris, up which they had just marched, and into the National Assembly, shouting all the time that they wanted bread.

"All through the afternoon, the tumult increased," the *Journal de Paris* reported. "Gunshots resounded in the streets. . . . When the Deputies reached the Assembly's hall, they found it filled with women. . . . Some were shouting, others singing, all were talking. . . . Several of them had hunting knives or half-sabers hanging over their skirts."[8] Under the circumstances, clearly, all deliberation was impossible — indeed, many of the Deputies found themselves unable to enter the building. Mounier, who was president of the Assembly that week, and a deputation went off to the Palace; and there they waited for the King's return.

Finally at seven, Louis XVI, muddy, disheveled, and exhausted, came in through a gate at the back of the park.

> The president of the National Assembly was immediately taken to him, and, with him, a deputation of fifteen women who complained about the poor administration and the lack of foodstuffs. The King answered that he loved his good city of Paris too much ever to want it to lack for anything; that as long as he had been in charge of its provisioning, he thought he had done well; but that since these gentlemen, pointing at the members of the National Assembly [who had accompanied their president], had tied his hands, it was not his fault . . . but that he would give orders and consult with the Assembly so that, the very next day, as much would be done for them as possible.
>
> As soon as they came out to tell the others about this satisfactory answer, there were shouts that it was not true; that they had surely been bought off; they were about to be hanged when some of the Deputies asked that they be given permission to get a written confirmation of what they had said. They were taken once again to the King, and His Majesty wrote and signed the confirmation.[9]

By then, alarm reigned in the Palace, but for the wrong reasons. No demand had yet been made that the royal family move to Paris; just as the fall of the Bastille had forced Louis XVI to recall Necker, so it was thought that the current crisis would end when he signed the August decrees and the Declaration. At eight, a letter went off to Mounier signifying the King's complete and unconditional acceptance of them. Still, there was the huge crowd outside the Palace gates. Marie Antoinette pointed out that the royal family was hardly safe; some of the courtiers advocated prompt military action. "M. de Narbonne-Fritzlard, who was then with the King, begged his Majesty to give him a few troops and some cannon, assuring him he would soon be rid of these bandits. 'We must put a watch on the bridges at Sèvres and at Saint Cloud,' he said. 'Either the mob will give up, or it will go through Meudon. Placed then on the hill, I will decimate it with my cannons and use cavalry to pursue it in its flight so that not one of them will get back to Paris alive.' " Mme de Tourzel, the governess of the royal children, who was there and reported this, adds: "The King . . . could not accept a plan to spill his subjects' blood."[10]

This last is a constant note, both in contemporary accounts and in later histories: much is always made of Louis XVI's refusal to massacre his subjects. On the political right, of course, this is deplored as an inexcusable weakness; on the left, it serves to make him a more appealing figure. In fact, as no doubt he knew, there was not an army corps left in France who was willing to end the Revolution by force. Typically, the Flanders regiment that evening stayed in its barracks; when it was summoned by the King, it refused to obey. Even with the King's encouragement, therefore, M. de Narbonne-Fritzlard would have found himself quite unable to carry out his project.

This was, in fact, soon evident. "It had poured all day; at nine, since nothing seemed to be happening, the King ordered the bodyguards back inside, they started forming into a column; the people, thinking they were about to charge, prepared to defend itself; the Versailles National Guard [which had now joined the Parisians] . . . started shooting at them, wounding fifteen or sixteen men; the bodyguards fled and could only be rallied well inside the park."[11] By then, it was nearly eleven, and news came that the Paris National Guard would soon reach Versailles. For a while still, the King was reluctant to leave, in part because he was afraid the Assembly would offer the throne to the duc d'Orléans; but then, summoning his energy, he ordered that six hunting carriages be readied —

they were lighter and faster than the court's usual traveling coaches — and he prepared to flee to Rambouillet with his family. "The carriages had to cross the Place d'Armes [where the Parisians were camped]; they were stopped by the people, who were shouting: 'The King is leaving!' "[12] There was now no exit.

At eleven, the Paris National Guard having arrived, Lafayette came in with four of his officers. "He crossed the room where we were on his way to see the King," Mme de Staël remembered. "He was eagerly surrounded, as if he had been in control of the situation when already the people's party was stronger than its head. . . . He seemed very calm."[13] In fact, this eternal optimist thought the situation highly positive: he had, it is true, been forced to follow his troops, but now at last, the King could be made to accept the new order. Still, tact was required.

"Sire," the General said to Louis XVI, "appearing before you in these circumstances and in this fashion makes me the most unhappy of men. If I had thought I would serve Your Majesty better by sacrificing my life for you, you would not see me here." The King answered: "You can have no doubt, Monsieur de Lafayette, of the pleasure with which I always see you and my good Parisians; go and report these feelings to them." The General went out immediately to meet his troops . . . and M. Mounier came in soon after. The King told him: "I wanted you to come so as to be surrounded with the representatives of the Nation, but I have already seen M. de Lafayette." As soon as the General had taken the necessary measures outside, he came back to the King with whom he stayed until one-thirty. As he came out, he said to the courtiers waiting in the Œil de Boeuf [an antechamber just outside of the King's bedroom]: "Messieurs, I have just convinced the King to accept some painful sacrifices: His Majesty will have no guards other than those of the nation [i.e., the National Guard]. He has allowed me to garrison two thousand men in the Palace. Let all retire; I will see to everyone's safety and send the rest of the troops back to Paris." Immediately, the Palace was occupied, with the bodyguard remaining only at the doors of the royal family's apartments. All seemed quiet.[14]

By then, it was two in the morning. The King had given in completely to all demands — except the one, made by the two representatives of the Commune, that he move to Paris. Lafayette, having seen to the posting of the National Guards, and sure that the worst was over, left the Palace to spend the night at the Hôtel de Noailles, a mansion belonging to his father-in-law. The Palace settled down for what remained of the night.

Still, the people of Paris were encamped, not just on the Place d'Armes, but in the courtyards of the Palace as well; and at daybreak, they began to move. "The guard placed at the bottom of the King's staircase was insulted by the mob and . . . called his sergeant. The latter . . . shot a man dead, and so then did the guard. Immediately they were seized by the mob who broke into the Palace."[15] It was barely six o'clock.

On the way from Paris, the women had shouted they would kill the Queen and use her guts to make cockades: now they went to find her. "One of the Queen's bedchamber women heard [the beginnings of] the assault. . . . Rushing into the Queen's bedroom, she shouted: 'Quick, Madame, get up, don't get dressed, run to the King.' The Queen sprang terrified from her bed, threw on a petticoat without even tying it on, and her two ladies took her to the Œil de Boeuf. A door of the Queen's bathroom opened into it and was usually locked only from the inside. At this dreadful moment, it turned out to be locked on the other side. The ladies knocked frantically; the servant of one of the King's valets came to open it; the Queen went into Louis XVI's bedroom but found it empty: fearing for the Queen's life, he had gone downstairs to the corridor under the Œil de Boeuf, which allowed him to go to the Queen's without crossing that room."[16] Almost immediately, though, Mme de Tourzel, who was just as alarmed as the Queen, burst in with the children, and, a minute later, the King himself was back. A few of the bodyguards still held the doors to his apartment; but the royal family was besieged; and if the mob prevailed, anything might happen.

At that moment, Lafayette appeared: rushing over from the Hôtel de Noailles, he now set himself to protecting the royal family. He was able to count on a battalion of grenadiers belonging to the Paris National Guard. Here, in fact, was the first confrontation between the mob and the bourgeoisie: the former cold, wet, and enraged, the latter still anxious to avoid a massacre. "The grenadiers arrived, pushed back the crowd, which was about to break down the doors of the [outer room of the King's apartment]. . . . They made themselves known to the bodyguard, who, from the inside shouted: 'Swear that you will defend the King's life.'

" 'We swear . . . we will die before any harm comes to His Majesty,' they answered. The doors were opened, the grenadiers came in, followed by the rest of the Paris National Guard; they surrounded the bodyguards and filled the Hall of Mirrors and the apartment all the way into the King's bedroom."[17] By then, several of the bodyguards had been killed; Lafayette managed to save ten of them who were about to be massacred by the mob. Still, the crowd outside was becoming louder and angrier. At first, the King went out alone on the gilded balcony overlooking the great courtyard of the Palace and tried speaking, but his voice was drowned by shouts of "The Queen! The Queen!" So Marie Antoinette, dressed now, and holding her children — ten-year-old Marie Thérèse-Charlotte and the four-year-old Dauphin — by the hand, joined him, but the mob yelled: "No King! No children!" For a minute everyone went back in; but the crowd kept demanding the Queen with increasingly hostile gestures. In an act of great bravery, since she expected to be lynched, Marie Antoinette went out on the balcony. For a while the hostile yells persisted. The Queen curtsied, and the mob quieted a little; then Lafayette came out on the balcony and, with a bow, bent and kissed her hand. Suddenly a dead silence fell, soon broken by cries of "Long live the Queen! Long live General Lafayette!" The Hero of Two Worlds had just saved his sovereign.

Still the crowds kept yelling, but now it was "To Paris!" So Louis XVI came out again and shouted: "My children, you want me to follow you back to Paris: all right, I will, but on condition that I will not be separated from my wife and my children."[18] Mme de Tourzel then describes what happened:

The King got into his carriage at one-thirty. . . . He sat next to the Queen and Madame, his daughter. I faced him with Monseigneur the Dauphin on my lap and Madame [the comtesse de Provence] next to me. Monsieur [Louis XVI's brother, the comte de Provence]* and Madame Elisabeth [the King's twenty-five-year-old sister] were on the door-seats; M. de Lafayette, commander of the Paris National Guard, and M. d'Estaing, commander of that of Versailles, rode on either side of the carriage. . . .

We saw around us, first the bulk of the Parisian troops, each soldier

---

* The King's other brother, the comte d'Artois, had emigrated on July 17.

having a loaf of bread impaled on his bayonet; then came a wild mob carrying the heads of the massacred bodyguards on pikes. There followed carts laden with bags of flour.[19]

At intervals, the women surrounded the carriage, shouting: "We won't lack for bread anymore, we've got the baker, the baker's wife, and the little apprentice!"[20]

That day, October 6, the weather had changed; it was dry, sunny, quite warm. Going at the crowd's pace, the royal carriage took more than six hours to reach Paris. After a while, the little Dauphin complained of being hungry and thirsty; but there was nothing to give him. Finally, at seven, the carriage reached the gates of Paris. There, Bailly waited with the keys to the city, just as if this had been an ordinary visit, but when Louis XVI said he wanted to go straight to the Tuileries Palace, the Mayor refused and said he must come to the Hôtel de Ville first; so the dusty carriage trundled on, finally getting there at eight-thirty. "Once at the Hôtel de Ville, M. Bailly told the crowd that the King had said it was always with pleasure he found himself amid the inhabitants of his good city of Paris. The Queen then added: 'You forget he said also: and with confidence.' There were shouts of 'Long live the Queen.' . . . Then Their Majesties came to the Tuileries, where, incidentally, the King had never slept before."[21]

Indeed, the Tuileries was anything but ready for the arrival of the royal family: it had not served as a royal residence since Louis XIV had moved to Versailles in the 1670s. Most of the apartments had been given to courtiers as grace and favor lodgings; now they had to be cleared in a few hours; and there was a shortage of everything from bed linen to furniture. Still, the King and his family were alive and unharmed.

"Don't worry, my health is good," Marie Antoinette wrote Mercy the next morning. "If one forgets where we are and how we came here, we must be pleased with the feelings of the people, especially this morning. I hope that much can be regained, if only bread is no longer lacking. I speak to the people; militiamen, fishwives, all offer me their hand; I take it. Inside the Hôtel de Ville I was personally very well received. This morning, the people were asking us to stay. I told them, on the King's behalf — he was next to me — that whether we stayed depended on them; that we asked for nothing better; that all hatred must cease; that the first drop of blood that was shed would make us leave with horror."[22]

A new revolution seemed, in fact, to have taken place: the angry, menacing mobs of October 5 and 6 had, within twenty-four hours, become loving subjects. Milling around the Tuileries, the people kept calling for the members of the royal family and cheering them. One group of women asked Marie Antoinette for the flowers and ribbons in her hair as souvenirs; graciously she gave them. Still, there remained a menacing undertone. "A woman told . . . the Queen that she must now send away the courtiers . . . and love the people of her good city. The Queen answered that she had loved them at Versailles and would love them equally in Paris. 'Yes, yes,' another woman said, 'but on July 14 you wanted to besiege the city . . . and on October 6 you were about to flee to the border.' The Queen answered pleasantly that that was what they had been told, and that they had believed it; that these [calumnies] were the cause of the unhappiness of the people and of the best of kings."[23]

This was all very well; but the royal family had no illusion about their true situation. It was not just that the Tuileries needed rearranging: when the Palace was built in the sixteenth century, it was in the middle of the country and the facade on the garden side opened wide through windows and French doors on to the outside. Both the Queen and Mme Elisabeth, the King's sister, had apartments on the ground floor, where the crowd could literally press against their windows: there was neither privacy nor safety. The interior also reflected the drastic change that had just occurred. Until October 6, the life of the royal family had been conducted according to the inflexible rules of the complex etiquette codified by Louis XIV. Access to the royal presence was carefully controlled; only people with three hundred years' proven nobility were admitted at court; the most careful gradations were observed when it came to who had access to which room of the royal apartments. Now, in one day, all that was gone.

On his first visit, the minister of Saxony described it all:

[I saw] a courtyard, a vestibule, a staircase filled with people, a rather small antechamber where the grenadiers are together with the body-guards, who spent two nights there as if in prison, without clothes or anything because all they had was pillaged, footmen, pages, ladies of the court, bishops, ambassadors, officers, in mud-covered boots and spurs, in a word all those who could not fit in the so-called audience room, and amid all that, the Queen.

Imagine a M. Jauge, banker, one of M. de Lafayette's aides-de-camp, walking into the King's study as a duke could not have done before and saying to the comte de Montmorin, the foreign minister: "I saw they would not allow your carriage into the courtyard, that was because I ordered the gates kept shut due to the circumstances. You must learn to suffer. Another time, if I know when you are coming, I will give them orders to let you in."[24]

Immediately, though, efforts were made to recreate a court. On October 9, it was announced that the King and the royal family would receive the ambassadors on Sundays and Thursdays, that, on those days, there would be card playing, as well as on Tuesday evenings, and that on Sundays the King and Queen would, as ever, dine in public. Several of the faithful courtiers kept their positions near the King; the etiquette was observed once more; but even so the Tuileries was nothing like Versailles.

The events of October 6, in fact, marked the first great acceleration of the Revolution. In a city whose people had demanded, and won, their liberty, the King himself had lost his. He was now a hostage, prisoner in an easily attacked palace, unable to do anything except consent endlessly to whatever might be forced on him. Much as he disliked what had happened before, he had felt able to delay, to palliate, and, of course, he was personally free. Now, he had to give up not just his principles, but also his daily habits. In spite of his passion for the hunt, for instance, he had to stay in the city; in spite of his need for exercise and fresh air, he was forced to use either the always crowded Tuileries gardens or the equally popular Bois de Boulogne; as for the Queen, she was never to see her beloved Trianon again. From this moment on, therefore, Louis XVI, that virtuous man, felt perfectly justified in lying and deceiving: he was under duress, and nothing he did counted anymore.

He felt this so strongly, in fact, that as early as October 9 he sent Charles IV of Spain, his distant cousin,* a secret letter in which he set the record straight. "I owe myself," Louis XVI wrote, "I owe my children,

---

* Louis XVI and Charles IV were, respectively, the great-great-great-grandson and the great-great-grandson of Louis XIV.

I owe my family and my entire House not to allow the royal power, which many centuries have maintained in my dynasty, to be made worthless now. . . . I have chosen Your Majesty, as head of the second branch [of our family] to hold the solemn protest I make against the acts which are contrary to the royal authority and into which I have been forced since July 15 of this year."[25]

Louis XVI was not alone in considering himself a prisoner. While Lafayette felt triumphant, Mirabeau, who was more practical and better able to look into the future, was appalled. On October 7 his friend La Marck noted: "He said to me as he came in: 'If you have any means of being heard by the King or the Queen, convince them that they are lost, and France as well, if the royal family does not leave Paris. I am working on a plan to get them out of the city.' "[26] Indeed, a week later, Mirabeau handed his plan to the comte de Provence, the King's liberal brother. He first underlined the fact that the King was no longer free, that the Assembly (which moved to the capital on the nineteenth) was also controlled by its fear of the mob, and that the ministers were powerless. Adding that the King was not even safe, he suggested that Louis XVI announce solemnly that he was visiting Rouen,* and that once there he publish a proclamation saying that he was entrusting himself to his people, that he had been a prisoner in Paris, that he now adopted without any reservation all the measures voted by the National Assembly, and that, finally, he intended to live simply and without pomp on one million livres a year.** Then he would ask the Assembly to join him and, if it was prevented, call for new elections.

In itself, it was not a bad plan; but it ignored a few salient facts. The first was that the comte de Provence, in whom Mirabeau confided, was both ambitious and jealous of his elder brother; in October he still hoped to replace him on the throne; he had, therefore, every reason to oppose any plan likely to save Louis XVI. Further, Mirabeau's suggestions required both guile and decisiveness, qualities the King wholly lacked. Then, Louis XVI, far from accepting the Assembly's reforms, found them wholly vile. Finally, the great orator underestimated the dislike felt for him at court, where he was still seen as a corrupt debauché and a

---

* The capital of Normandy, some seventy miles west of Paris.

** In 1788, 30 million livres had been spent on the King and the royal family.

dangerous revolutionary, the dregs of the new regime. Just two weeks earlier, in fact, Marie Antoinette had told his friend La Marck: "We will never be so wretched, I hope, as to be forced into the painful extremity of seeking help from Mirabeau."[27] The painful extremity had come closer since then, but it was still not close enough.

Oddly enough, despite his solemn protest, Louis XVI, and Marie Antoinette with him, felt distinctly more hopeful after October 7. Partly because the people really thought that having the King among them would improve their lives, partly because their triumph on October 6 had been so great, the royal couple as noted suddenly seemed to be immensely popular. They were greeted with cheers whenever they showed themselves, Louis XVI was endlessly praised as the liberator of his people, and even Marie Antoinette, so hated until now, found herself, apparently, as well loved as when she had arrived in France nineteen years earlier. "This change in the public's opinion . . . is striking," Mercy commented on the twelfth.[28] To some, once again the Revolution seemed to be over. Friedrich Grimm, that acute observer of the intellectual and political scene, in his newsletter noted that the Salon, the yearly exhibition of new paintings, which opened in mid-October, was particularly brilliant, and he praised the works shown by David, Vien, Hubert Robert, and Mme Vigée-Lebrun.[29] That the last-named had already emigrated, however, perhaps said something about the real state of affairs.

Mme Vigée-Lebrun had sharper eyes than most. The French reputation for urbanity was so well established that foreign visitors flooded into the capital in vast numbers. The occasional street movements that still took place that autumn were seen as the last subsiding aftershocks of the great July to October earthquake. The English, the Duchess of Devonshire at their head, came, not just to enjoy the usual pleasures of Paris, but to see France in its new incarnation as a free country. Because the English revolution was the only precedent, it seemed clear that the people, having won that essential reform, a constitutional government, would now consider itself satisfied. The theaters were full; the opera season was particularly successful; the liberal salons, better attended even than before, enjoyed their triumph to the full. Clearly, in this most civilized of centuries, a great revolution could take place with minimal bloodshed.

Indeed, the recent events could easily be seen as the proof that women ruled the world, after all: not so much the women who marched on Versailles as those in whose salons the new constitution was so earnestly discussed; and after July 14 and the first wave of emigration, the great hostesses were all liberal. In their circles, under the influence of Voltaire, the *Encyclopédistes,** and, often, Rousseau, it was understood that everyone had certain basic rights, that privileges of all kinds were wrong, that no taxation should be imposed without the consent of the nation's representatives, that the lack of aristocratic birth should prevent no one from rising to the highest levels, that freedom of speech and religion were everyone's due. To that, they added equality before the law and the end of all class-defined exemptions. Some of them, like the duchesse de La Rochefoucauld d'Anville, Benjamin Franklin's friend, and the comtesse de Tessé, who was born a Noailles, belonged to the greatest families in France; Mme Necker, the minister's wife, also presided over an important salon; but none was quite so admired, or so influential, as that of her daughter, Mme de Staël.

A woman of extraordinary intelligence, Germaine, baronne de Staël, was witty, eloquent, incisive, and a convinced liberal. Although quite plain — a fact she endlessly deplored — she had beautiful arms and breasts, which she showed off with remarkable pertinacity. More important, hers was the kind of compelling personality that made men fall in love with her and everyone listen to her: only those who heard Mme de Staël, the contemporaries noted, knew just what an art conversation could be, for it was not a question of her holding forth to a spellbound audience, but of her encouraging dialogue so that, in her presence, everyone seemed to shine.

She was a devoted daughter, constantly praising her father, but she was, if anything, a little to the left of M. Necker. She wanted the Assembly to have rather more power, and the King less. In fact, like her friends, she favored something approaching the English system: there would be liberty and a court, an Assembly and powerful salons. She was herself wholly free: married to a Swedish diplomat without means of his own or much personality, Mme de Staël ruled her life, her household, and her salon; the fortune her father had given her maintained it all. Naturally,

---

* The Encyclopédistes were those liberal intellectuals who questioned the authority of the King and the Church. They were beginning to advocate a limited, constitutional monarchy.

like almost all her upper-class contemporaries, she had lovers — at the moment, and rather briefly, Maurice de Talleyrand-Périgord occupied the post. More important, it was in her salon especially that the liberal aristocrats and the new men of the Assembly came together; and in the course of the discussions she led, many important decisions were made. This, all present agreed, was the civilized way to do things. As for the return of the royal family to Paris, it was a convenience: there was no need, any longer, to make that boring journey to Versailles.

Because of all this, what the English, and most other foreign observers, saw was a simple transfer of power from the monarch to the middle class and liberal-thinking members of the aristocracy: the idol of the Parisians was the marquis de La Fayette, the scion of an old and illustrious family; the end of the feudal system had been urged by the vicomte de Noailles, all of whose relatives belonged to the very top rank of the court; the duc de La Rochefoucauld-Liancourt counted among the most ardent reformers; even Mirabeau was noble and proud of it. As for the bourgeois leaders of the Revolution, men like Bailly and Mounier, they, too, had always belonged to the Establishment.

It was thus typical that the next great reform was suggested by a young man who seemed the very incarnation of the ancien régime. Maurice de Talleyrand-Périgord belonged to a family whose nobility went back to the year 1000, but, as the eldest son of the head of the younger branch, he was far from rich. Worse, because his nurse had dropped him and broken his foot, he was a cripple; so very much against his inclinations, he was forced into the Church, a fate normally reserved for younger sons. In 1787 he became Bishop of Autun as the result of a court intrigue: Louis XVI, who appointed all members of the hierarchy subject to the Pope's automatic approval, knew that his nominee was not likely to make a good pastor, and he was right.

Blond, blue-eyed, snub-nosed, witty, and impertinent, Talleyrand was one of the most elegant young men in France. He drank; he gambled heavily (but profitably); he had mistresses, Mme de Staël among them. Still, that was not enough to keep him entertained: he was also extraordinarily intelligent, with a sharp, analytical mind and a highly cynical view of people's motives. As a result, he had been a complete success as the Clergy's financial agent, a role that should have tied him closely to the right in 1789; the Clergy's fiscal immunities were, after all, the first to go.

Instead, having taken the measure of the King and Queen, and realized they were, in their different ways, hopelessly inadequate, he joined the winning party. He was among the Deputies of the Clergy who answered the Third Estate's summons and now belonged to the center left. It must also be said, however, that his political position was not the result of mere expediency: he quickly saw the benefits of liberty, and continued to defend them for the rest of his life.

When, on October 10, he got up in the Assembly to speak, he was thus able to draw on his thorough knowledge of the Church's finances. "The state," he said, "has long been faced with great needs; to meet them we need great resources; the treasury is empty and the people overtaxed. Yet there is one immense reserve whose use . . . can be allied with the most thorough respect for the rights of property. I am sure that the Clergy . . . will rush to make it available"; and he added: "The value of the Clergy's property is close to two billion livres."[30]

That, of course, was an immense sum: in comparison, the entire budget of the state ran at around 550 million a year. Nationalizing the Clergy's properties would thus rescue the treasury without requiring the taxpayers to make even the slightest effort. Of course, all those vast estates — about 10 percent of all the land in France — served to support the Church; but, Talleyrand pointed out, the state could start paying salaries to all ecclesiastics instead. It made sense; more, it was a productive way of reforming the shocking disparity between the huge incomes enjoyed by most bishops and the grossly insufficient stipends on which most country priests were expected to survive. And there was yet another boon: while ecclesiastical property was tax-exempt, its sale to lay owners would generate new tax revenues. It was no wonder, therefore, that Mirabeau promptly joined Talleyrand in backing the change, or that most of the Assembly concurred.

As for the Church itself, it was so divided as to be ineffective. A number of bishops who belonged to the great aristocratic families were either frightened or gone; the vast army of impoverished country priests had nothing to lose — indeed, their salaries were likely to be less miserable than their former stipends. A few churchmen were liberal themselves; there was really no one to protest. On November 2, less than a month after the proposal was first made, the estates of the Clergy were duly taken over by the nation, which, in turn, was charged with adequately providing for the upkeep of the Church.

Still, there was one difficulty. The Clergy owned mostly landed estates — a notably illiquid form of property. The treasury needed ready cash, not fields, streams, and forests. In the best of circumstances, it would take several years to make a complete and accurate list of all ecclesiastical properties and the debts attached thereto; and it was obviously impossible to put them all on the market at once without causing land values to collapse. This is where the financial expertise of Talleyrand and of Necker came in. A special department of the treasury was created, the *caisse de l'extraordinaire* (temporary resources fund). To it was immediately assigned 400 million livres in Church property against which it put forth that same sum in paper money, the *assignats,* or assignations against the sale of these properties. There would be no depreciation — the usual fate of fiat money in troubled times — because of the solid guarantee behind the assignats; and the treasury would get 400 million unexpected livres. That, in fact, is what happened on December 21.

Of course, these decrees required the King's signature, especially since they were ordinary acts and not part of the constitution. Equally naturally, the pious Louis XVI was horrified. But he had also adopted a new policy: partly because the memories of October 5 and 6 remained vivid, partly because his conscience was assuaged by the protest he had sent to Spain, and partly also because he hoped that if enough radical reforms were made, there would be a strong conservative reaction, he now made it a policy to sign anything that was brought to him. The Assembly understood this. On October 19, its first day in Paris, it required that the King immediately promulgate the August decrees,* giving him eight days to accept or reject them, and telling him that his choice was between full acceptance or full refusal. To no one's surprise, Louis XVI promptly did what was required of him. The nationalization of the Church lands was promulgated even faster: the Assembly passed its decree on November 2. The King signed it on November 4. The Assembly had finally triumphed.

---

* Louis XVI had accepted them in his letter of October 5, but they had still not been promulgated.

Nor was it just a question of royal compliance. Mme de Staël, Talleyrand's former mistress and now one of his friends, thoroughly approved of this new development, but she was beginning to worry about the government's — and therefore her father's — utter lack of power. She was embarking just then on an affair with another liberal nobleman, the comte de Narbonne, yet she still had time to see clearly what was happening. "All the government's power had fallen into the hands of the National Assembly, although its function was supposed to be merely legislative," she wrote. "The distrust of the King's intentions . . . prevented his being given the means necessary to reestablish order; and the heads [of the parties] in the Assembly nurtured this mistrust so as to have a pretext for controlling the ministers. . . . The action of the executive was hampered by the Assembly's decrees, the ministers could do nothing without its authorization."[31]

It was, in fact, one of the two situations the Americans had specifically striven to avoid in their constitution: all the powers, executive, legislative, and, as it soon became clear, judiciary, were concentrated in one, all-powerful elected body; the government no longer governed; and anarchy spread. For here was the supreme paradox, one of those ironies that history, now and again, records: as the Assembly made itself a king in all but name, it also lived in fear and subjection; the object of its terrors was not the once-mighty monarch, but the people of Paris. When, on October 19, it moved into the former riding academy of the Tuileries, which had been hastily reconverted, it found itself drowning in the seething mass of the mob. Not only was its hall, like the Palace, virtually indefensible against popular attack, its very architecture made it critically vulnerable. At Versailles, there had been large tribunes for the spectators; in Paris, the tribunes were even larger, and here the spectators were the unemployed mobs who were the vanguard of the Revolution.

"You ask me my opinion on the Revolution," a Paris lawyer called Dumont wrote his colleague Sir Samuel Romilly, a British barrister and M.P. "Alas, my friend, what can I tell you? This land is so volcanic, the movements are so sudden, the government is so weak that we have every reason to dread the coming of the National Assembly [to Paris]."[32] He was perfectly right to worry: real power had already moved, not just to the mob, but also to a variety of political clubs.

Originally, these clubs had been started by groups of like-minded men who wanted to discuss the political issues of the day. This had made a great deal of sense before May, when there had been no public forum, no other way of forming one's own opinions. With the advent of the National Assembly, however, the clubs had multiplied, each reflecting a shade of opinion, and as the numbers of their members grew, they turned into replicas of the Assembly itself, complete with public debates, motions, and votes. It was thus possible for all the members of a club to arrive at a single position on the issues, and for those who were Deputies to behave as a bloc, always a fruitful tactic in a divided legislature.

More than that, the issues could be debated freely, and often violently; it was within the clubs that new men, such as Danton and Robespierre, began, slowly, to gain notoriety. And their eloquence mobilized the crowds who had come as spectators. The aroused people had made the Revolution so far, and the clubs knew it. Because they were able to produce large, angry crowds, they could overawe the other Deputies. Thus, the political decisions that were taken in the Assembly often reflected the prior debates and decisions made in the clubs.

Even worse than a growing, quite rational apprehension of another *journée* was a confusion about the source of the government's legitimacy. The nation, not a divinely appointed king, was sovereign — that was well understood; but the key question was, how would the nation express itself? The Deputies — their very appellation is expressive — who sat in the Assembly were the *representatives* of the people to whom they owed their legitimacy; but the members of the political clubs, the men who were active in the districts, *were,* in their own persons, the people, and felt it was their duty to control the representatives, to denounce any gap between the ideals of the Revolution and their application by the Assembly, to relegitimize the Deputies by forcing them to adopt the right measures.*

The great conflict, from October 19, 1789, to the end of the Revolution thus became one of jurisdiction, a conflict between the successive Assemblies, who tried to rule, and the clubs and the districts, who tried to tell them how to do it. The Deputies could claim that, having been duly elected, they represented the popular will; the Paris mob answered that it *was* the popular will, and that the Assembly's only duty, therefore, was

---

* This was first pointed out by François Furet in his *Penser la Révolution française.*

to listen to it. What no one mentioned until quite late in the Revolution, and by then it was too late, was that perhaps the active population of Paris — some fifty thousand men, probably — might well be out of step with the majority of the French.

These should have been circumstances in which the duc d'Orléans could take over. It was all he had originally hoped for: an impotent and discredited King in Paris, the mob in virtual control of the Assembly. But this man whom Louis XVI most dreaded, although capable of ambition, lacked every quality necessary to a popular leader except, perhaps, for wealth.

"His Serene Highness was little spoken of and he is latterly become a subject of as much indifference here as he was formerly an object of popularity," Lord Edward Fitzgerald, the British minister in Paris, reported to the Duke of Leeds, the foreign secretary. "When he is spoken of, it is with the utmost contempt and in thorough detestation of his character by many and with extreme indifference by others. . . . Among the people he is only kept from sinking entirely by the shattered remains of his popularity which has decayed with a fortune that, all agree in saying, was scattered amongst them with a degree of liberality all the more extraordinary as that Prince was never before distinguished for that quality."[33]

What Lord Edward does not make altogether clear is that every time the duc had had a chance to lead, he had funked it. Always afraid of retaliation, constantly hiding behind his confederates, Orléans signally failed to use one opportunity after another. Immensely popular in May because of his liberal stance, he had gained still further approval by sitting as a Deputy of the Third Estate, a position to which he had been duly elected by his tenants at Villers-Cotterêts, rather than with the rest of the princes of the blood royal. From then on, however, it had been all downhill: he was incapable of speaking in the Assembly, unable to make up his mind, unwilling to keep his promises. As it became obvious that he was unreliable, weak, and indecisive, not unlike the King his cousin, in fact, he had lost much of his popularity. The events of October 5 and 6 had finished it off.

As noted, everybody assumed that he was in part responsible for the march on Versailles; certainly he had helped to finance it; but throughout those days, he hid in one of his suburban villas. When he finally joined the royal family, he tried commiserating with the King *and* rejoicing with the mob, and, in the days following, quite failed to indicate whose side he was on. This kind of cowardice, so visible to all, finally did away with whatever popularity he had retained. From then on, he could, almost automatically, take extreme revolutionary positions: no one cared anymore.

He was not alone, however, in his drastic loss of popularity. What was most striking, in fact, was the entire lack of effective political leaders. With the duc d'Orléans discredited, the active part of the Assembly was divided among loosely drawn confederations given to imprecise and shifting memberships. As a result the Deputies were easily swayed, by eloquence, by fear, by envy, by ambition — and, occasionally, by their real desire to establish a fair and stable government.

It was thus possible for various men, whether representing the clubs or acting on their own, to take charge of certain questions: Talleyrand with the nationalization of Church property, for instance, or more obscure Deputies like Armand Gaston Camus, whose great subject was that touchy issue, royal pensions.

There was also Lafayette, of course, the one man whose popularity was immense and solid, the commander of the National Guard, whom many saw as the next prime minister. There can be very little doubt that Lafayette could have taken charge, had he chosen to. But while he was certainly disinterested and a true lover of liberty, while he had done very well indeed as long as he was under the guidance of George Washington, it was also quickly becoming clear that he had no political head at all. That crucial shortcoming was compounded by another weakness: Lafayette was, most often, incapable of coming to a decision if the question to be resolved was at all complex. Thus, the one man who was in a position to lead the Assembly altogether failed to do so. Instead, he dithered, organized parades of the National Guard, and wasted month after month.

That left Mirabeau, who lacked neither ambition nor political instinct. In October as in June, he could sway the Assembly: his eloquence, contemporaries agreed, was irresistible. He saw clearly, argued well, could gauge the changing moods of the Deputies; most important, perhaps, he had a vitality, an energy that swept all away before it. When that deep resonant voice was heard, when the scarred and pitted face was transformed by the fire within, Mirabeau cast a spell.* But, like all spells,

---

* Like many eighteenth- and nineteenth-century speeches, Mirabeau's today seem overlong, overemphatic, and unconvincing: different times, different oratory.

it tended not to last. Worse, Mirabeau was listened to but not trusted. He was well known to be always in search of money to support an extravagant life-style and heavy gambling losses; the very love of life that gave him such power as a speaker also meant that he was a great frequenter of brothels, an insatiable seducer, a man who often drank too much in public.

Of course, Mirabeau wanted power, for the satisfaction of exercising it as well as for the money he needed desperately; but he was shrewd enough to see that, alone, he could never conquer it — if there was anyone who distrusted him even more than the Assembly, it was the King. So he looked around and saw the obvious: if he and Lafayette were to become allies, they would be irresistible. This was a matter of some urgency: all ambition aside, Mirabeau realized that the Revolution was likely to devour the monarchy, the Assembly, and France itself unless it was stabilized. By October all the great reforms had been made; now was the time to stop and consolidate. As it happened, that was a position with which Lafayette could agree.

It was also the right time publicly to advance this sort of consolidating policy. The return of the royal family to Paris had brought a lull; the price of bread was rapidly going down as the result of the summer's excellent harvest; the mob, while still present, was fairly quiet. But none of that was likely to last. The winter, as usual, would bring a measure of hardship; Louis XVI could be counted on to blunder; and the clubs, which just then were busy dividing and reorganizing, would soon regain power and start defending the extreme left's agenda. If the opportunity to stabilize were ever to be seized, this was the moment to do it.

In early October, therefore, Mirabeau approached the General and apparently convinced him — so much so that he promptly borrowed 50,000 livres from Lafayette. Indeed, on the seventeenth, he wrote his friend La Marck: "The business is under way and Lafayette decided inasmuch as he can by himself. He is taking me this morning to Montmorin's [the foreign minister]."[34] The plan was to recast the ministry, with Lafayette in a leading post; Mirabeau, as necessary, was to be a discreet but powerful adviser, with perhaps a place as minister without portfolio.

Two days later, Mirabeau was still busy convincing Lafayette that a radical change was needed. "If you have thought about the perfidious collusion of the ministers with the brutal, or rather insane, pride of the contemptible charlatan [Necker] who has brought France to the edge of the abyss, and who will push it over rather than admit to his own incapacity, you will no longer feel that one can possibly work with them all,'' he wrote the General.[35]

Just as in July the Assembly had forced the King to recall Necker, so now Lafayette could make the King appoint a new ministry: it required only a little determination; but that, of course, was just what Lafayette lacked. He would listen to Mirabeau and be convinced; he would then consult his friends, most of whom distrusted the orator, and decide to do nothing. Thus, all through October, he indulged in a peculiar political dance, one step forward, one step back. Still, there did seem to be progress. On the twenty-sixth Mirabeau wrote La Marck: ''I have been offered the embassy to Holland or to England, with the nomination to be made today, not that I would go to either country, but so as to position myself and make me worthy and capable of the supreme honor of holding in my pocket a letter from the King assuring me that I will become a minister in May. It is M. de Montmorin who has taken Lafayette this pompous proposal. The latter will only speak to the Queen this morning, but, in fact, he seemed less decided than ever . . . as for me, I go back into the fight, and am firmly decided not to give an inch, *which is important even for them if they really think me necessary.*''[36*]

In spite of Mirabeau's doubts, Lafayette evidently spoke to the Queen; on the twenty-ninth he put the following question to his confederate: ''What would you say if M. Necker threatened to resign in the case where [you] came in? Think about it. . . . Mutual trust and friendship: that is what I give and expect.''[37]

That was just the sort of problem which fired Mirabeau's imagination. No one could forget what had happened when Louis XVI had dismissed Necker in July; but the mere fact that the first minister of finances — that was his official title — loathed Mirabeau could not be allowed to stand in the way. Within forty-eight hours, the plan was ready.

Necker was to be bought off by being made prime minister, a title that had been in abeyance since 1661, but without being given real power:

---

* Mirabeau's italics.

"we must make him as impotent as he is incompetent and yet keep his popularity for the King." There followed the plan for an entire ministry of liberal, serious men, including Talleyrand (as finance minister), Lafayette, promoted to be a marshal of France and commander in chief of the army, and, of course, Mirabeau himself as minister without portfolio but with all the power. As for the comte de Montmorin, the current (and thoroughly mediocre) foreign minister and the man closest to the king, he was to be created a duke and made governor to the Dauphin.[38] It was an ingenious combination, but it depended entirely on Lafayette's determination; and by November 5 Mirabeau knew exactly what to think about that. "You saw him as he is," he wrote La Marck, "equally incapable of reneging on a promise and keeping it ad tempus; besides, powerless except after an explosion in which he could, and up to a point might want to, do everything."[39]

Mirabeau saw it clearly. Of course, Lafayette distrusted Mirabeau; he claims in his memoirs that he had been put off by the great orator's gamy reputation, and that he realized too late that he should indeed have backed a joint government. In fact, then as ever, Lafayette was incapable of making up his mind.

The negotiation was at an end; the Lafayette–Mirabeau ministry never came to be, and the government drifted on. Worse, rumors of the plan began to circulate, and Champion de Cicé, the keeper of the seals,* who was slated to lose his place in the change, promptly put an end to any possible scheme by proposing to the Assembly that it forbid any Deputy to accept any employment under the crown. That, to a body always expecting its members to be bought by the court, seemed an admirable idea. Of course, no one doubted that the exclusion was aimed at Mirabeau; but, equally with de Cicé, there were many of his colleagues who had no desire to see him running the ministry. "Mirabeau fell in the Assembly, partly because of his enemies' maneuvers, partly because of the deluge of pamphlets attacking him, but also because of the endless mistakes caused by the violence of his character, that rage to dominate and that impatient ambition which betrayed itself. They could not bear to see him becoming a minister," wrote one observer.[40] The exclusion was voted on November 7.

---

* The official title of the minister of justice.

*   *   *

At the same time, the Assembly was as wary of the King as ever and could see that there was equal danger in the continued popular unrest. Of course, the extremist press fanned it. Already Marat was publishing *L'Ami du peuple* on a fairly regular basis and gaining a wide audience. A former physician — he had been a surgeon in the comte d'Artois's guards — Marat was a failed scientist. His *Traité sur les principes de l'homme* (Treatise on the essence of mankind) received dreadful reviews, from Voltaire among others. From then on, Marat pursued his research in physics with sour fanaticism: the one object of his life was not actually to extend knowledge, but to humiliate the Academy of Sciences by invalidating one of its tenets. In this, he failed utterly. The Revolution, however, gave him the chance he had longed for: now he could humiliate, not just the Academy but the entire ruling class.

Incapable of making a major role for himself as an orator — he suffered from a painful and disfiguring skin disease and had neither the looks nor the voice — he wrote prose that was fiery and convincing. Because he shared them, he appealed to the people's deepest-seated fears and prejudices; because his solutions were direct and bloody, they had all the appeal of simplicity, not to say simple-mindedness. Thus he became one of the main voices of the left, tirelessly warning, threatening, exhorting. And always, he remained a loner, refusing several proposals from political friends that he and they publish a paper together.

Camille Desmoulins, the fiery orator of the Palais Royal, could not have been more different: young (he was twenty-nine), handsome, happily married to a pretty and amiable wife, he had trained to be a lawyer but burned with resentment at the injustices of the ancien régime. He loathed the King, the court, and the upper classes equally because they all exploited the people. When the convening of the Estates General, and the duc d'Orléans's plot, gave him his chance, he made a name for himself as the most popular of the spokesmen of the left; but he soon realized that speeches were not enough: a paper could reach a much wider audience, a fact that other, more obscure writers understood as well. More important, papers were to be the medium of the Revolution whenever the Assembly seemed lacking in zeal.

On October 19 the *Révolutions de Paris* warned about a plot to abduct the King and start a civil war, citing the keeper of the seals as the chief culprit. This was an absolute lie, but, in the absence of libel laws, it could not be stopped or punished; and day after day, the paper, like many others, kept denouncing the aristocratic plot against the new institutions. Camille Desmoulins, having now started his own paper, the *Révolutions de France et de Brabant*,* began by pointing out, complacently: "Today, in France, it is the journalist who is the great censor and passes on the acts of the Senate, the consuls, and the dictator himself."[41] For Senate read Assembly; for consuls, ministers; for dictator, King. And Desmoulins went a step further; far from defending the new institutions, he thought them insufficient: "I have already publicly said I am . . . for the constitution of Pennsylvania. . . . Do not be mistaken. . . . We are rapidly advancing toward a Republic."[42] In the next issue Desmoulins predictably attacked the Queen: "There cannot be a Queen of France, the salic law is clear. Marie Antoinette of Austria is the King's wife, nothing more."[43] The salic law was an ancient one that precluded women from succeeding to the throne, but had nothing to do with the position of the Queen. The Queen, here, was simply a convenient target, a useful symbol of all that was wrong with the ancien régime. Because she was, barring some very fleeting enthusiasms in early October, so very unpopular, any calumny would be believed; and even if, temporarily, it was awkward to attack the King directly because he was, once again, liked, he could still be wounded indirectly through his wife. This was the start of a consistent, two-pronged campaign: first, Marie Antoinette was to be denied all legal status, so as to make her unworthy of the respect that still belonged to the persons of the monarchs; and at the same time pamphlets accusing her of a variety of sexual depravities began to appear.

For Marat, though, it was structure and policy that mattered: in *L'Ami du peuple,* he consistently harped on the notion of a vast, well-organized, and bloodthirsty anti-Revolutionary plot. In the space of a week in December, for instance, he advocated abolishing the mayoralty of Paris because he thought Bailly dangerously moderate; he repeatedly attacked the ministers and complained that a denunciation of the comte de Saint-Priest, the minister of the King's Household, had been suppressed by the aristocratic faction in the Assembly; he described the misbehavior

---

* Brabant, then a part of the Austrian Netherlands, was having its own revolution, which was suppressed by the end of 1790.

of several of the *intendants,* the chief representatives of the administration in the provinces who had frequently clashed with the local Parlements; and related the (imaginary) murder of a sentinel of the National Guard.[44] All these denunciations were heard by those to whom they were addressed: the mob, fresh from its October triumph, was beginning to fear that its conquests might be reversed. Another radical paper, the *Révolutions de Paris,* explained it all convincingly:

> The nation is virtually prostrate as the result of the tremendous effort it has just made . . . and seems to wait for the horrible shocks being prepared by the secret fermentation of the aristocracy. . . .
>
> The enemies of the Revolution want us to yearn for a counterrevolution. . . . All the different aristocrats will coalesce and form a private assembly within the Assembly that will carry decrees outrageous to the people. . . . To this highly dangerous measure, the aristocracy has added another that is not less likely to make the people disgusted with their freedom: the continuation of the anarchy.[45]

As usual with the revolutionary press, this was a blend of truths and untruths, but it was also highly believable: human nature, after all, is such that men do not usually give up great privileges willingly. Thus it stood to reason that, although temporarily vanquished, the aristocrats must be plotting to regain what they had lost, and in the process they could be accused of fomenting the very disorders from which they suffered.

In fact, though, this argument is riddled with fallacies. While, undoubtedly, many great nobles were totally opposed to the Revolution, they were also mostly abroad and hardly in a position to affect events in France; and, in the late fall of 1789, there was still a substantial group of liberal aristocrats who thoroughly approved of the recent changes. As for a right-wing majority in the Assembly, it simply did not exist: rather, a center-left coalition normally prevailed; and, of course, no one wished more than they for the end of the various uprisings. Still, the resentments unleashed by the Revolution were so great, the domination of the aristocracy so recent, that reality hardly mattered. Even the use of the word *aristocrats* reflects this. Originally, the aristocracy and the Nobility were the same: aristocrats were titled people who belonged to the Second Estate. Now, however, an "aristocrat" was anyone who opposed the extreme left wing; thus, for instance, Mounier, that living incarnation of the bourgeoisie, was considered an "aristocrat." This new usage was all the more convenient in that it created the perfect target: it was far easier to attack "the aristocrats" than the King, especially since he had regained much of his popularity, and this even allowed the press to proclaim loyalty to Louis XVI while demanding further revolutionary change.

In one respect, however, the journalists were right: many people around the King yearned for a counterrevolution, without, however, doing anything about it. The Spanish ambassador saw it all clearly:

> The King . . . seeks only to prevent the shedding of blood . . . but around him are people who, either out of loyalty or because they are self-seeking, can see no way out other than a counterrevolution which, for lack of means, cannot succeed. These strains put the crown in an unnatural position which dissipates the credit earned by its compliance [to the Assembly's policies], destroys the people's trust when it is so sorely needed. . . . Hesitation and inconstancy are even more to be feared than mistakes.[46]

Louis XVI, however, had good reason to be resentful. Policies loathsome to him were being implemented; his God-given right to rule had been seized from him; he was forced to live in Paris much against his own wishes. As if all that were not enough, the Assembly passed a decree that he considered to be a direct insult: on December 21, it decided that "the crown lands, except for the forests and the royal houses His Majesty wishes to keep for his own enjoyment, will be sold."[47] Not only was that outright theft, as the King saw it; it also forced him into an undignified scramble to retain at least some of his country palaces and the forests in which he loved to hunt. Amid all these discomforts, however, at least one of the Assembly's reforms must have pleased the monarch: on November 3 that body, having announced its intention to set up a new court system, suspended* the Parlements, whose systematic and sterile opposition to his government had so annoyed him. It was a measure of the discredit earned by the judges that this truly revolutionary measure caused neither comment nor opposition from anyone outside the Parlements themselves.

Meanwhile, the Queen, unlike her husband, had suddenly become much less visible. She held court twice a week, but otherwise spent much

---

* They were formally abolished on March 24, 1790.

of her time supervising her daughter's education or, alone in her study, writing her family and her friends. This new low profile did not, however, prevent her from working as hard as she could against the Revolution, both by corresponding with potential rescuers and by influencing her husband. There was perhaps a small chance that, in spite of his protest to the King of Spain, Louis XVI might have grown to accept many of the reforms; but Marie Antoinette made very sure that would never happen. Thus, although the King and Queen publicly claimed to be in sympathy with the reforms, they surrounded themselves with opponents of the new regime and treated all non-nobles with marked disdain; leaks, usually made by servants, indicated that they detested all that was happening. As a result, their insincerity was clearly felt and caused great apprehension among the people.

On December 23, 1789, Mirabeau wrote his friend La Marck: "The evils of indecision, weakness, envy, and bad faith corrupt, soil and dissolve all things. At the Luxembourg [where the comte de Provence resided] they are afraid to be afraid. . . . M. Necker does not know what he can, wants, or should do."[48] He was right; and to make the atmosphere heavier still, on the twenty-eighth a murky, and still partly mysterious affair broke into the open: the marquis de Favras, who was known to have ties with Monsieur, was arrested for plotting to take the King's life.

Still, amid all his anguish, Louis XVI must have had a moment of pleasure. On December 29, from London where he had been virtually exiled, the duc d'Orléans, now a political cipher, wrote dutifully, and in proper style: "At this time of the new year, when all Your Majesty's subjects hasten to bring you the tribute of love and respect which is due you on so many accounts, I beg you to receive with kindness my respectful homage and my wishes for your happiness and your glory."[49] At least, there was no longer any fear that Orléans would usurp the throne.

It was, indeed, the world turned upside down. The most popular prince in France, the idol of the crowd that sacked the Réveillon house in April, was discredited and forgotten in December. Versailles was just an empty shell; all signs of centuries of royal absolutism had vanished. For Louis XVI, living reluctantly at the Tuileries, it was all too clear: he had somehow lost most of his inheritance, that right to rule entrusted to his ancestors by God and belonging forever to the eldest male of the eldest branch. Just as clearly, it was his duty to pass on to his son the monarchy as he himself had received it; thus, no matter what he might say or do, there could be no compromise with the Revolution. And had he ever doubted, Marie Antoinette was there to give him new conviction. Although they frequently disagreed about tactics, the King and Queen were now utterly united when it came to their common goal, the total reversal of everything that had happened since May.

For the liberals, for the people itself, on the other hand, these events were little short of miraculous: in less than six months, freedom had been won, the old abuses ended. Everyone now was equal before the law. Much still needed to be done, the reorganization of the institutions was far from complete, but the main point had been established: henceforth, government was to be based on liberty and the consent of the governed. The presence of the King at the Tuileries was a shining symbol of this new state of things. Back among his people, where he belonged, he could be the slightly impotent father figure they believed themselves to want.

The Revolution had come a startlingly long way in a startlingly short time. The great question now was whether it was time to consolidate. Mirabeau thought he knew the answer, but he was almost alone. Paris, although quieter, still rumbled; and the optimism displayed by many sometimes looked like a thin disguise for anguish about the future.

CHAPTER FOUR

A Constitutional Monarchy?

:   :   :

A reluctant King, an incapable prime minister, an increasingly restive mob of badly dressed, rude, unwashed men and women, mingling in the Tuileries gardens and the Champs-Elysées with the elegant habitués of the salons, all in a setting where the old ties were broken but new habits had yet to be formed: stability, early in 1790, was hardly the order of the day. The Assembly itself, looking anxiously over its shoulder, was busy creating a brand-new society. Everything was to be reformed, the law, the courts, the Church, the government, the manner in which property could be held; but in the meantime uncertainty prevailed and, as is so often the case in times of uncertainty, the new governing classes relied on the magical power of the spoken word. If they said often enough that France had now entered an era of liberty, peace, and prosperity, it might perhaps become true.

More and more, the upper bourgeoisie and the liberal aristocrats worried because nothing was settled: six months earlier the Assembly had decided to give France a constitution but, except for a few fragments, the charter had yet to come into being; the financial crisis that had forced the King to call the Estates General was unresolved; and at either political extreme, there was a substantial group of people who utterly despised the current state of things.

On the left, of course, the powers that be were blamed for their inordinate conservatism. "Let us punish right now so as to not have to keep punishing. . . . Let us execute all the seditious plotters," the *Révolutions de Paris* demanded in January,[1] adding, a few weeks later,

"All these evils have only one cause, the prodigality of a rotten court . . . where each pleasure was paid by the labor of a million men . . . and racehorses more highly prized than the French nation."[2]

It was a powerful message and the Assembly heard it. On January 5 it decreed that the pensions paid to people who normally resided in France, but who were now absent, would no longer be paid.[3] The people in question, of course, were the *émigrés,* the nobles who had prudently left France, and who included not only the Queen's friends, the Polignacs, but also the King's youngest brother, the comte d'Artois, and his cousins the prince de Condé, the duc de Bourbon, and the duc d'Enghien. In its way, this, too, was a radical break with the past, in that it rejected part of French society and denied the King's power to reward as he chose. Of course, the Assembly was justified: although it did not know it, the comte d'Artois had already written Emperor Joseph II asking him to invade France so as to end the Revolution. Clearly, for much of the French aristocracy, class mattered far more than nation.

Amid all these uncertainties, one man at least was in a position to prevail if he chose: as noted, Lafayette, with the National Guard behind him, was the only obstacle to chaos in Paris. This fact was clearly understood by the King, who listened to him carefully, and by the Assembly, where he could, if he chose, rally a majority. The problem was that most of the time he did not so choose. Although he was devoted to the best possible principles, and wanted nothing more than the welfare of France, although, unlike practically everybody else in Paris, he was utterly oblivious of his own interests, he also lacked the resolution and the clarity of mind needed to govern under difficult circumstances. So, just as he had in his negotiations with Mirabeau, he wavered endlessly while slowly his enormous influence shrank.

Occasionally, his dithering took on highly comic forms; one scene in particular, described by the Spanish ambassador, has all the earthy humor of a Molière farce.

His Majesty had agreed with M. de Lafayette that he would see him . . . at 11:30 with M. de Saint-Priest to decide on a new minister [of the navy, Count de Fernan Nuñez reported on January 4, 1790]. Lafayette meant his friend M. de Bougainville to have the office, and the

King would have appointed him as he did all the others who sit today in the council if chance had not interposed itself.

Lafayette takes a laxative every morning before he goes out. If that medicine fails to take effect, he takes a second one, then a third. M. de Bougainville's bad luck was such that, on this particular day, all these doses were required, so that the time of the appointment was past. Realizing this, the General promptly ordered a review [of the National Guard] so as to have a pretext to give His Majesty in the afternoon. . . . The monarch, who was tired of waiting . . . finally gave the appointment to M. de Fleurieu.

That evening, Lafayette appeared at court and announced that he had been forced . . . for reasons of public safety, to hold a review; but when he brought up the appointment of a minister of the navy, the King administered a fourth and unexpected laxative by telling him that M. de Fleurieu had already been appointed.[4]

Whatever the state of Lafayette's digestion, it was clear to those who could see that the General was quite incapable of running the government. Necker, so popular only six months earlier, was also now largely discredited: the Assembly was still sometimes willing to listen to him, but seldom acted on his recommendations, while, among the mob, he was seen as shortsighted and conservative. On January 18, a new pamphlet appeared, written by Marat; it was entitled *Dénonciation contre Necker* (Denunciation against Necker) and essentially accused him of preparing a return to the ancien régime.

As for the King himself, he was once more under attack. In a rare display of irony, Camille Desmoulins wrote on January 16: "The hatred I feel for all kings does not blind me. . . . So good-tempered a king [Louis XVI, of course] . . . deserved consideration and a Christmas present. So it is that the National Assembly has sent sixty of its members to wish him a happy New Year," and he went on: "Who will dare to assert that the nation's representatives do not have all the powers?"[5]

Clearly, it no longer much mattered whom the King appointed as minister of the navy. Because, throughout the eighteenth century, ministers had been so powerful, people, Mirabeau among them, assumed they still must be; in fact, Desmoulins was right: the Assembly had all the powers. Not only were the various chains of command now utterly ineffective, the ministers no longer dared to take action without the Assembly's approval. To all intents and purposes, one branch of government had swallowed the others.

That was perhaps to be expected given the key role of the Assembly in carrying out the reforms; but it is also obvious that its role was made very much easier by the continued incompetence of the King. "What cowardice!" Mirabeau wrote about the court in late January, "what carelessness! What a grotesque assemblage of old ideas and new projects, little repugnances and childish whims, decisions and nondecisions, aborted love and hates!"[6] He was right, of course. Even when he was still at Versailles, Louis XVI had shown himself hidebound and indecisive; now he proved himself utterly unable to influence events. "The King is in effect a prisoner at Paris and obeys entirely the National Assembly," Gouverneur Morris, the future United States minister, noted accurately,[7] while Count Fersen, on his side, echoed Morris. "The King is still a prisoner," he wrote. "His position, and especially that of the Queen, who feels much more acutely, is dreadful."[8]

Fersen knew what he was talking about. Long a close friend of Marie Antoinette's, and almost certainly in love with her, he now devoted himself to helping the royal family in a variety of ways — by forwarding messages from or to the Queen, by conferring with Mercy about what should be done, and so advising the Palace, by corresponding with possibly helpful foreign governments. All through this period, he had the entire confidence of both Louis XVI and Marie Antoinette and is thus a completely reliable witness when it comes to their reactions.

By the end of January, it was clear to both the Palace and all intelligent royalists that, in a deteriorating situation, it was crucial that the King do something. No doubt, leading a counterrevolution would have been his first choice; but the events of July and October 1789 had taught him that it was not a possibility. So he decided to be clever instead.

Dishonesty has long been a tool of state. Machiavelli, who knew how men are governed, assumed its use by the Prince, and many democratically elected leaders since that day have not scrupled to use it. Still, if lying is going to be effective, it must also be convincing: a lie perceived as such does no good at all. Louis XVI was not a good liar. Thus, when he decided to endorse the Revolution, he set up yet another situation in which people felt constrained to say one thing while believing, and acting on, another.

The occasion, on February 4, 1790, was the taking of the civic oath by the members of the National Assembly: instead of swearing obedience to the monarch, as formerly, they, and the rest of France, would now offer their allegiance to "the nation, the law, the King." It was following on this ceremony that Louis XVI addressed the Assembly; and what he said had been carefully thought out, not just by the ministers but by his wife as well.

At first, the King complained about the general state of the country: "The progressive loosening of all the ties of order and subordination, the suspension or the inactivity of the courts, the resentments born of personal deprivations, the oppositions, the wretched hatreds consequent on long dissensions, the critical situation of the finances . . . and finally the general turmoil all seem to come together to worry the true friends of the prosperity and happiness of the kingdom," he said sternly.[9] That, of course, was just yet another reiteration of his favorite theme, the fact that reforms brought disorder with them, a disorder which was proving extremely harmful to the country; but then, he went on to add some very surprising things.

"The time has come, I think," he continued, "when the welfare of the state requires me to associate myself in an even more express and manifest way with the execution and the success of the measures you have adopted for the advantage of France. . . . I will favor by all the means in my power the success of this vast organization."[10] This, obviously, was new: until very recently, the reforms decreed by the Assembly had been accepted by the king only with the most visible and extreme reluctance. Now, suddenly, he praised and professed to like what until now he had seen as violence and usurpation.

Speaking to a hushed but elated Assembly, he promptly went even further: "All enterprise," he added, "which would endanger the principles of the constitution itself, all efforts which would tend to upset them or weaken its happy influence would only introduce among us the terrifying ills of discord. . . . The result would be to deprive us of all the happiness we can expect to find in the new order of things. Let everyone know that the monarch and the representatives of the nation are united in the same interest and the same wish!"[11] Here was a clear, plainly stated commitment: Louis XVI, that afternoon, was endorsing the Revolution.

Having done so, he addressed yet another plaintive appeal to the Nobility, and most particularly to those members of the order who were attacking him for failing to contain the revolutionary flood. "Those who have given up great pecuniary privileges . . . will have to make sacrifices of whose great extent I am fully aware," he said, "but I feel sure they will be generous enough to find a compensation in all the public good we may expect from the existence of National Assemblies."[12] Except, of course, for the liberal nobles, many of whom, being Deputies, were among his audience, that plea had virtually no chance of being heard, but it no doubt soothed the King's conscience by helping him to convince himself that he had acted out of concern for the good of France, and that he had no reason to feel guilty for the losses suffered by the nobles.

Having thus comforted himself, he went on to give a most impressive pledge. "I will defend, I will maintain that constitutional liberty whose principles arise from the people's wish and my own," he said firmly. "I will do more: together with the Queen, who shares my feelings, I will, early on, prepare my son's heart and mind to accept the new order. . . . I will teach him, from his earliest childhood, to find his happiness in that of the French, to recognize always . . . that a wise constitution will preserve him from the dangers of inexperience, and that a just freedom gives greater value of the feelings of love and fidelity of which the nation has, for so many centuries, given its kings so much evidence."[13]

It was quite an undertaking; it might even have borne fruit if the King had stopped there and gone on to prove, in the next few months, that he actually meant what he said. Instead, having, as he saw it, made a great sacrifice, he went on to demand compensation: "As you end your work," he added, "you will surely take care . . . to strengthen the executive . . . [since, otherwise] there could be no lasting order. . . . You can no longer harbor any distrust; thus it is your duty to ensure . . . that stability which can flow only from an active and paternal authority."[14] Making it quite clear that, in his view, enough was enough, he went on to say: "You cannot undertake everything at once; and so I urge you to put off to a later time some of the improvements of which your enlightenment offers you the perspective."[15]

It could not have been clearer: the King was offering the Assembly a bargain, his acceptance of the new constitutional order against a reinforcement of his powers and the postponement of further reform. For people accustomed to seeing politics as the art of the possible, that might have seemed quite reasonable; but the majority of the Deputies were new to politics. For some of them, especially for the men who sat on the left, the world was sharply divided between Good — total liberty — and Evil — a strong executive. They had been raised in the atmosphere of the Enlightenment modified by that peculiarly French taste for logic: the new trend must therefore be carried to its furthest possible conclusion.

Of the Deputies who sat in the center and center left, many were Fayettists, who were in favor of very wide liberties; and many were lawyers and businessmen who believed that a contract must be as clear, as unequivocal as possible and must also serve to avoid future conflict. For them, the sort of tug-of-war set up by the American Constitution between the President and Congress was simply inefficient, and unnecessary: if the Assembly represented the French people, then it must keep virtually all the power.

Finally, in spite of the applause with which it met the King's speech, the Assembly simply did not trust Louis XVI. Even if he sincerely meant what he said that day, chances were that Marie Antoinette would change his mind the next. Besides that all-important feeling was the fact that virtually all the Deputies had been conditioned by centuries of monarchical power. It seemed obvious to them that, given an opening, the executive would soon become tyrannical. And finally, because they had long personal experience of the abuses under the old system, they knew both that the reforms could not wait, and that if they left their implementation to the King, their work would be undone. As a result, the concessions requested by the King, to whom, having given up so much, they seemed highly reasonable, were unacceptable to the Assembly.

That was bad enough; almost worse, many of Louis XVI's statements were simply not believable. No one really thought that either he or Marie Antoinette approved of the new order; it was apparent that he regretted the powers wrested from him by the Assembly, and that he first and foremost wanted his authority reinforced. Still, there was much to be gained by taking the King's words as the expression of the literal truth, and that is just what most everyone did: here, after all, was a way of catching him at his own game, of committing him to the new order whether or not the Assembly granted him his wishes. Thus his speech marked a new step in the divorce between the current political discourse and reality: if everyone pretended to believe that Louis XVI really meant what he said, perhaps it would become true. At the same time, however, the Deputies, and almost everyone else, went on acting as if, in fact, the whole scene had never happened.

Even the extreme revolutionaries could see that there was much to be gained by taking Louis XVI at his word: he had just helped to bury the old system of rule by divine right, after all. More promising still, he could in the future be judged in reference to what he had just said; so Camille Desmoulins wrote, after praising the speech: "The Commune of Paris has just sent the King a deputation to congratulate him on having announced that he was the head and the bulwark of the new constitution."[16] As for the more moderate reformers, the men who wanted a constitutional monarchy, they, too, had much to gain by pretending to believe every word: you cannot very well have a monarchy without a King, after all. There was only one problem: more than the Assembly, it was the mob who set the course of politics, and it was not given to pretending. It was bound to see, quite rapidly, that this was all so much make-believe; and its reaction then was not likely to be gentle.

In the midst of this vast chorus of mutual praise, though, there was one man who insisted, even before the mob did, on seeing the pretense for what it was: Mirabeau. "You will have heard about . . . the King's peculiar speech," he wrote La Marck on February 6, "about the oath, the pantomime, and the true effect of all these movements. . . . Monsieur surpassed himself in cowardice, the King in empty words. . . . All the parties have played out the farce each more zealously than the other and Lafayette himself is among the dupes. . . . What is most lacking in all this is good faith."[17]

It was, indeed; and a precedent was set. By pretending to accept the constitution, Louis XVI hoped either to regain such popularity as would allow him to start a counterrevolution, or to speed the process of disorganization, thereby provoking a reaction. Meanwhile the Assembly counted on consolidating its gains. But when neither party to a contract means what it says, trouble is likely to follow — especially since the constitution everyone talked about did not yet exist.

So far, the Assembly had yet to define the way in which the future government was to function, the precise role of the executive, the prerogatives of the legislature, the relation of Church and state, even the form, nature, and powers of the judiciary. It had given the King a suspensive veto and decided in favor of a single chamber; it had voted the Declaration of the Rights of Man and abolished the feudal system; finally, it had appropriated the estates of the Church and announced its intention of creating a new court system, without actually doing so. Much, therefore, remained vague, and the very act of swearing to observe the constitution was tainted with hypocrisy. That, however, need not bother Louis XVI, who had salvaged his conscience in his protest to the King of Spain. As for Marie Antoinette, she considered the French as rebels to whom she owed nothing, complaining bitterly that "the King and his family are the prisoners of a people in revolt."[18] Later in the spring, as she walked in the park of Saint-Cloud, to which the royal family had been permitted to go, upon seeing that she was surrounded by men of the National Guard (as opposed to the former bodyguard), she told Mme de Tourzel, with tears in her eyes: "How surprised my mother would be if she could see her daughter, the daughter, wife, and mother of kings, or at least of a child destined to become one, surrounded by such a guard!"[19]

Unfortunately, whatever Louis XVI might say in public, he went on behaving as if nothing had changed and thus undermined his own credibility. After the first few days of its residence at the Tuileries, when the emergency had forced a temporary suspension of the etiquette, the court was back to normal. Once again, only persons who had been properly presented* were admitted to the King's lever and to his coucher, only duchesses were allowed to sit (on stools) in front of the Queen, only officers of the Household were allowed to surround the sovereigns; and those were naturally the very people who most resented the Revolution. Worse, they did not scruple to show it, or to snub newcomers in the indescribably offensive manner they had learned at Versailles. Anyone, therefore, who came to the Tuileries — and many of the Deputies, many well-to-do Parisians who belonged to the National Guard did so — was able to watch a display of pomp and pride that was the living denial of the new order. That, alone, was enough to show up the King's new promises.

---

* Only people who could prove that their families had been noble for three hundred years were presented at court.

That all this could remain, visible and unchanged, in 1790 seems, retrospectively, amazing, but even in the new revolutionary Paris, life continued as before — and that, no doubt, helped both the King and the Assembly play their mutual game of deception. It was understood that any attempt at a counterrevolution would cause a renewal of the uprisings of July and October; but short of that, the reputation of the French for civilization was so well established that recurrent violence still seemed unthinkable.

For the liberals, in fact, 1790 turned out to be a golden year. "All the vigor of a free people and all the graces of the old politeness were blended in the same persons," Mme de Staël wrote. "The men of the Third Estate, who were distinguished by their brilliance and their talents, came together with noblemen who cared more for their achievements than for the privileges of their order. . . . Women . . . led almost all the conversations. . . . They softened the political discussions and often lightened them with lively and amiable witticisms."[20] Never had the salons — Mme de Staël's especially — been so brilliant; and that very fact confirmed the liberal nobles — Lafayette, Noailles, La Rochefoucauld, and many others — in their belief that the world was theirs. Rather like their Whig counterparts in England, they felt nothing but disdain for the King and Queen; they had, after all, seen the royal incapacity at first hand; and they thought themselves clever enough, and popular enough, to establish just the sort of government they wanted.

Even so, now and again, they worried a little; the disturbances in the provinces continued through the early winter of 1789–90. In response, on February 9 the Assembly passed a law specifying heavy jail terms for those caught invading private property; on the twenty-third it passed a similar law to ensure tranquillity in the cities, one that forbade street disorders and allowed the government to prosecute publications and people who incited to riot. At the same time, it continued to dismantle the remnants of the ancien régime; on the thirteenth it decreed the end of all monastic vows in France. Henceforth, no one could be kept in a monastery or convent against his or her will. To us, in the late twentieth century, this seems perfectly normal; but to a pious person in 1790 it was extremely shocking because it interfered, not just with ecclesiastical property as had been the case before but with religious life itself — and no one was more pious than the King.

Just as shocking to the ''aristocrats'' was the gradual transformation of manners: at court, etiquette was paramount and defined the order of precedence with the most rigorous exactitude, while an almost endless array of polite formulas prevailed in everyday life and maintained a certain formality even among friends, especially when women were present. No matter how well a man might know a woman, for instance, he always called her Madame in public, and added her title if she had one: she was Madame la duchesse even to her lover. Now the revolutionaries began to single out these observances as a remnant of the bad old days. In January, for instance, the *Chronique de Paris,* a moderate newspaper, ran the following text: ''The first man who, writing to another, signed himself his servant, was probably a wretch in need of assistance; but the man who, having risen above the most basic needs, assured another, his fellow man, that he was his very humble and obedient servant* . . . was a servile coward. . . . All [these formulas] . . . the shameful remainder of our fathers' slavery, must be stricken from the language.''[21]

Living as we do in an informal society, it is hard for us to imagine how important all these rules of politeness seemed at the end of the eighteenth century: in fact, they were the very stuff of life. They expressed not only the structure of the society — if you were a duchesse, you could not be reminded often enough — but also an agreement that made life easy and pleasant by maintaining a certain distance between people. Now a clamorous mob was demanding an end to all these observances. For much of the upper classes, the King and Queen among them, the new rudeness seemed almost more bewildering, more distressing than the actual shift of power: it is, after all, often our daily habits that matter most to us.

Another aspect of this degradation of manners was a rapidly escalating degree of violence in political discourse. In the late spring, for instance, when the royal family had gone to Saint-Cloud, one of the revolutionary papers gave a solemn warning: it was only a first step. ''The most insolent joy is displayed by the aristocrats. Unhappy Parisians, they have you trapped, you will allow your King to leave. The trip has long been planned: does he not already say he intends sometimes to hunt at Rambouillet? Soon, we'll be hearing about Fontainebleau and Com-

---

* This was a standard formula used at the end of a letter and did not mean much more than ''very truly yours.''

piègne; from there, they'll take him to Metz, perhaps even to Vienna. War will burst out here and the aristocrats, rending their prey, will drink your blood and devour your entrails.''[22]

Of course, the remedy to this was not only to make sure the King could not escape — soon, he would complain that everyone was free in France except himself — but also to kill before you were killed. This was the remedy advocated by Marat in *C'en est fait de nous* (We're done for), a pamphlet published in late July. The killing of six hundred ''aristocrats,'' he explained, would suffice to stop the counterrevolution; and those few lives would save tens of thousands who would otherwise be massacred by the reactionaries.

Here, too, it is almost impossible for us to realize how very shocking this was. We live in a century where massacres on an unimaginable scale have become almost commonplace: what are six hundred aristocrats compared with 6 million Jews or 5 million Cambodians? But in 1790 the notion that it might be possible to advocate such bloody reprisals seemed to many literally monstrous: civilization, after all, entailed the respect of human life. The Assembly, whose members consciously felt part of the Enlightenment, promptly passed a law forbidding the sale of this pamphlet — but, as usual, without much effect.

For Louis XVI, who was at any rate well informed, and for his supporters, it was thus becoming clear that a dreadful transformation had taken place. Of course, there had been uprisings before; the people in their anger had killed men they particularly resented; that was the explanation for the murder of Berthier and Foulon in July. But the deliberate incitement to mass murder was new. In speech after speech, therefore, Louis kept reminding his listeners that the French had demonstrated their love for their rulers from the very beginnings of the monarchy. He realized, of course, that there was now a group of revolutionaries who harbored new and highly disturbing feelings, but he remained convinced that they were a tiny minority, and that the mass of the people was sound.

In a number of ways, he was right: Marat shocked even the moderate left and, in 1790, the monarch still retained a good deal of prestige. But there was one key change Louis XVI utterly failed to grasp: whatever the popularity of the King, most of the French loathed the ancien régime and greeted its dismantling with joy. This was manifest as the Assembly took two major new steps. On March 15 it decided that "all honorific distinctions . . . resulting from the feudal regime are ended. . . . The rights of entail and masculine succession are ended."[23] On the twenty-eighth Louis XVI signed the decree. In itself, this outlawed the chief method through which the great noble families had preserved their fortunes: by leaving everything to the eldest son — a practice also current in enlightened England — the patrimony was preserved from endless division. Now, because the law made it compulsory to leave roughly equivalent shares to the several children, within a very few generations, the great estates would be gone.

Three months later, on June 19, the Assembly went even further. Despite numerous pleas from Necker, it decided that "all hereditary nobility is forever abolished; in consequence, the titles of prince, duke, count, marquis . . . will not be used anymore. . . . No citizen will bear any name other than his patronymic; there will be neither liveries nor coats of arms. . . . The titles of Excellence, Highness, Eminence . . . et cetera will no longer be used."[24] This was immensely disturbing to the former aristocrats. Not only did it strip from them the very differences on which their pride rested, it also created immense confusion. The duc d'Aiguillon, for instance, descended from a family whose patronymic was Vignerod, but the dukedom had existed since the 1630s; no one knew therefore who M. de Vignerod was. Since everything the nobles owned was recognizable by their coats of arms, that, too, added to their confusion and distress. But, for the middle and lower classes, who had long smarted under the whip of aristocratic arrogance, this was a gift of the gods. No one in France was superior anymore merely because he had taken the trouble to be born.

Still, it was an extraordinary and shocking measure. Until now, the Assembly had removed various instruments of oppression; here, for the first time, it was beginning to forbid a defined class of people from doing a specific thing, and oppressing the former oppressors. The fact that Necker, that titleless Swiss citizen, fought against it side by side with Mirabeau, his sworn enemy, says a good deal: the abolition of all titles of nobility was something close to an act of tyranny. What, then, was the King to do? He could, after all, veto the decree, and the nobles counted on him to do so. Personally, he found this new law horrifying; and the fact that the members of the royal family would no longer be Royal

Highnesses (even though the King and Queen went on being called Your Majesty) struck him as unthinkable. Yet, within four days, he had signed the decree.

This unbelievable compliance — some of the Deputies who voted for the law did so only because they expected the King to veto it — was, in fact, the manifestation of a determined, and extraordinarily stupid, policy.

Convinced as he was that the Revolution was the work of the Assembly and the Paris mob, and that it was resented by most of the country, the King had decided systematically to allow the Assembly its head, in the quasi-certainty that its excesses would create a reaction through which the monarchy would regain all its power. He would then be able to say that while he had been willing to make any sacrifice for the welfare of his people, it was now clear that chaos prevailed, and that he was resuming his former powers only out of concern for his subjects. On these grounds, therefore, it would have been highly counterproductive to veto the Assembly's more extreme measures, since they were the very ones that would eventually rouse the French against the Revolution. It was wise, Louis XVI thought, to put up with temporary discomforts so as eventually to come out the winner. Unfortunately for him, however, he was completely wrong: he could have vetoed the decree abolishing all titles of nobility, for instance, without provoking a violent reaction; but an immense majority was glad he had not.

One very important person, however, much resented the King's *politique du pire:* for Marie Antoinette, this kind of supine hypocrisy was unbearably humiliating. While Louis XVI hated what was happening, but felt quite able to put up with it in the hope of ending it one day, the Queen suffered a daily torture. Immensely proud (her husband was genuinely humble), she took every act of the Assembly as a personal insult. She knew that royal families were of a different and superior essence; that they were owed respect and obedience; that they were to be surrounded by the well-born; and that the rest of the population could only acquire merit by a prompt and willing compliance. To her, therefore, the apparition of the Deputies and of the National Guard officers at court was a slap in the face; she missed her émigré friends; she missed the Trianon (although that did not prevent her from ordering new and splendid furniture for the Tuileries). Worse, she had to dissemble, to pretend she accepted the new regime when she yearned to have all its denizens thrown into a deep, dark jail: it was all virtually unbearable. And adding to her anger and humiliation was the fact that Louis XVI now often failed to take her advice.

All through the first half of 1790, in fact, the Assembly was busy dismantling the remnants of the ancien régime. On February 23 it made it compulsory for all priests to read all its decrees to the faithful as part of the weekly religious services. On February 26 it decided that the provinces, which had existed from time immemorial, were now only a hindrance to good government and that France would instead be divided into eighty-three *départements*. This strongly centralizing measure went very much further than the monarchy had ever dared: people felt they were Bretons or Normans almost before they were French; now that was all over. On February 28 the aristocracy's monopoly of all officers' positions in the armed services was ended. On March 8 assemblies were created in the colonies — but slavery there was maintained: the Deputies, after all, were men of property. On March 15, reversing itself, the Assembly decided not to reimburse certain feudal rights. On the sixteenth it outlawed the lettres de cachet.* On the twenty-first it ended the much-hated salt tax.

With amazing speed, therefore, all the structures of daily life were transformed. For some, including most of the officer corps, this was literally unbearable, and the wave of emigration began to swell noticeably. For others, it was proof that there were now no lengths to which they could not go. Not many people paid attention, therefore, when, on March 31, a little-known lawyer from Arras, one Maximilien Robespierre, was elected president of the Jacobin Club, but it was as significant an event as all of the Assembly's reforms.

By 1790 the Club des Jacobins had already been through several incarnations. It began in late April 1789 as the Club Breton, a meeting place for the Deputies from that province. Because Brittany had been in a state of virtual rebellion for months, it was the most reformist of all, and such men as Lafayette (who had estates in the province), La Roche-

---

* Letters bearing the King's seal (hence their name), in which he ordered someone jailed or exiled from his usual residence.

foucauld, and Mirabeau belonged to it. With the move to Paris in October, the club settled in the former Jacobin monastery, from which it took its usual name (it was, in fact, officially the Club of Friends of the Constitution) and promptly veered to the left. It was then that Lafayette and most of the liberal nobles left it to found the 1789 Club. By July 1790 the Jacobins had 152 branches in the provinces, which followed the impulse given them from Paris, and some twelve hundred members in Paris; and because the questions coming up in the National Assembly were discussed first at the Jacobins, the club was able to exert significant power through its bloc of Deputies.

The club, however, was under considerable pressure. It has long been understood that competition from the left cannot be resisted by an organization which, itself, claims to be the left; and that was just the Jacobin's problem. In April 1790 a new club opened. It called itself Club of the Friends of the Rights of Man and the Citizen, but was universally known as the Club des Cordeliers, a name taken from the monastery where it had installed itself. Its stars were the two most violent revolutionaries in France, Marat and a thirty-one-year-old lawyer, Georges-Jacques Danton, who distinguished himself by his fiery eloquence and the violence of his views. With the Cordeliers pushing from the left, the Jacobins were obviously in an awkward position; and they made up for it by moving leftward rather faster than might have been expected — hence Robespierre's election as president.

Like Danton, Maximilien Robespierre was a lawyer. Before 1789 he had lived and worked in Arras, in northern France, then had come to the capital as a Deputy to the Estates General. He was, at first sight, an unimpressive figure. Small, slight, ugly, he dressed with the most finicky care but a complete lack of flair. His red-rimmed eyes (his eyesight was very poor), his bilious complexion, his stiff, uneasy manners hardly made him attractive; and unlike most of the great men of the new era, he was a poor speaker, with a weak voice and a preference for involved, endless sentences.

At the same time, however, his austere life-style gave him a great advantage: politics were his only interest, his only occupation, and he nourished absolute certainties about what needed to be done. For him, because the monarchy meant simply corruption and tyranny, the Revolution was to be the triumph of virtue, as free men returned to that state of nature extolled by Rousseau. As a result, and despite all his shortcomings, Robespierre made himself heard: in the last six months of 1789 he spoke more than thirty times within the Assembly alone, and more than eighty times in 1790; and because he so absolutely believed what he said, he carried conviction.

Already, in early March 1790, he had protested what he saw as the Assembly's repressive decrees. "Must we dishonor patriotism by calling it a seditious and turbulent spirit, and honor slavery with the name of love of order and peace?" he asked the Jacobins. "Let us continue our work and close our ears to the importunities of the executive. . . . The people will soon come back to obeying the laws without being forced to do so. . . . We must not allow armed soldiers to oppress good citizens."[25] This was the equivalent of preaching continuous rebellion; and, indeed, Robespierre thought it necessary as long as the new system failed to conform to its ideals.

Just as Robespierre's preeminence at the Jacobins set the stage for an acceleration of the Revolution, so, at the other end of Europe, another event favored the very same course. On February 20, 1790, the Emperor Joseph II died in Vienna. He was succeeded by another of Marie Antoinette's brothers, Leopold, formerly Grand Duke of Tuscany, who now, as Leopold II, inherited the many Habsburg possessions. The change made all the difference in the world from the Queen's point of view, and was deplored by all her friends. Joseph II had been close to his sister and was likely to help her; he was also bold and given to action. Leopold hardly knew Marie Antoinette, did not like her much, and was wholly passive. Thus any hopes that the Emperor would intervene to stop the Revolution and restore his sister and brother-in-law to their former power faded with Joseph's death. Much as they feared foreign intervention, the revolutionaries were, in fact, perfectly safe.

Marie Antoinette, who had begun to long for an invasion, knew it all too well. On May 1 she plaintively wrote the Emperor: "I do not even speak of our present position; it is too dreadful, it must afflict any sovereign in the world, and most especially an affectionate relative like you. Only time and patience can change the people's mood. It is a war of opinion that is far from over yet. In truth, only the justice of our cause and the intimate feeling of our consciences can sustain us."[26] Unfortunately,

Leopold II, who was singularly devoid of family feeling, remained unmoved; but the letter was also a symptom of the Queen's renewed activity. Stunned for a while in the late autumn of 1789, unable in January and February 1790 to overcome her husband's obstinacy, she was able to convince him in the late spring that on most points she had been right all along, and that she understood the new men and the new situation better than he did. As a result, she now, once and for all, took on the role of secret prime minister to Louis XVI.

The people close to the Tuileries realized this; Lafayette never tried to convince the King without first speaking with the Queen. Now, when Marie Antoinette decided on a new policy, it was promptly implemented. Her decisions were based purely on expediency: being, as she saw it, morally right, she need not scruple about the means, or the men, she used. In this instance she looked around and decided to approach the very man whom she had so fiercely, and so publicly, despised. Typically, she used Mercy, still the Austrian ambassador, as her go-between; more than ever, he, and Fersen, were the only men she trusted completely.

"The King and Queen have decided to avail themselves of the comte de Mirabeau's services," Mercy wrote to Mirabeau's friend La Marck* on March 18, "provided he is willing to be of use to them. They trust you to go about it the right way . . . and wish to be in relations with the comte only through you. . . . The deepest secrecy is expected of you. . . . It is essential that M. Necker, with whom they are very displeased, should know nothing about this negotiation."[27] This was followed by a meeting early in April of Mirabeau, La Marck, and Mercy, after which La Marck came secretly to see the King and Queen, who reiterated that they wished to be given only secret advice. To this, La Marck retorted that Mirabeau would hardly do the royalist cause much good if, all the time, the King openly followed Necker's advice; and there, for a short while, things rested.

In fact, this negotiation clearly showed that the Queen understood nothing. Behaving as if she was facing a revolt of the aristocracy, such as had occurred, the last time, during the Fronde in the 1640s, she thought it was enough to bribe the leaders — or, at least, those who were

---

* La Marck was Mirabeau's closest friend, but he belonged to one of the great families from the Austrian Netherlands, that of the princes of Arenberg, and was well known to Marie Antoinette.

amenable to bribes — so as to get them to reverse their policy and bring the people back into obedience. That is just what Anne of Austria had done during the Fronde, with not much success even then. Now it was completely anachronistic.

The Revolution, it is true, had leaders; but their purpose was not to get a large bribe from the crown, it was to create a new, more democratic system. Most of them were thoroughly committed to the new order and simply could not be seduced. As for Mirabeau, who was eager to work for the court, what neither he nor Marie Antoinette realized was that his popularity was due, not to his personality, but to his political stance. The moment he was seen to switch sides, he would also lose his audience.

Still, the alternatives were growing fewer, as the pressures on the court increased, and attacks came from every side. It remained difficult to attack Louis XVI in person after the speech of February 4, so Marie Antoinette became, yet again, the main target. "There meets," Camille Desmoulins wrote, "at the Tuileries, in the presence of the King's wife, a committee composed of the keeper of the seals, MM. de Saint-Priest, de Mercy, and de Reuss, who is well known to be one of the court of Vienna's secret agents. It is said that the ambassadors of Spain, Naples, and Sardinia are sometimes present." The kings of Spain and of Naples belonged to younger branches of the House of Bourbon; the King of Sardinia, who also ruled over Savoy and Piedmont, was married to Madame Clotilde, Louis XVI's sister; all thus were natural accomplices.

Desmoulins continued: "This committee is called the Austrian Committee because it was there that the decision was made, it is said, to renew the alliance with Austria although this is against the interests of France."[28] As it happens, this was pure invention, and therefore pure calumny; but it helped to establish the image of a sanguinary and reactionary Queen anxious for the invasion of France by vengeful foreigners and, by implication, it showed Louis XVI as too weak to stop it all. It was excellent propaganda, in other words, and all the more convincing in that the description of the Queen's feelings, as opposed to her actions, was perfectly correct. Indeed, the continued splendor of the court confirmed its ultimate rejection of the new order; amazingly, Marie Antoinette's always considerable dress budget was just as high in 1790 as it had been in past years at Versailles.

Then, too, there was the pressure embodied in the royal couple's continuing fear of the duc d'Orléans: although still exiled to England, the duc was capable, they felt, of financing the revolutionaries. On the surface, all was well; on March 12, for instance, Orléans wrote the King: "Your Majesty's glory and happiness will always be, as they have always been, the object of my wishes and the reason for all my acts."[29] The very effusiveness of the letter, though, made it less than believable. It was known that the duc kept up his Parisian contacts and that he longed to return — as, in fact, he did, despite the King's orders, in late June. The possibility of his return made Mirabeau even more important to the monarchs: it required little imagination to foresee what would happen if Orléans decided to finance the always needy orator.

As if all that were not bad enough, the Queen was driven nearly frantic by a menace from a wholly unexpected quarter. The Spanish ambassador, as well informed as usual, reported to his minister on it:

> The comte d'Artois has just sent Madame Elisabeth the model of a protest against all the decrees of the National Assembly he would like the King to publish. . . . This gesture would set off a campaign to impose by force . . . the true will of the sovereign. Troops would enter . . . the Dauphiné, where a party would be organized. . . . A civil war would then indubitably follow in which, according to the comte d'Artois, the ancien régime would be restored. . . . This news has greatly upset the Queen, as her unhappy experiences have only too thoroughly convinced her it was essential to eschew new attempts based on frivolous plans and devoid of the necessary means of execution. She has therefore thought it right to let her brother-in-law know that these plans could only worsen [the royal family's] situation and endanger their lives.[30]

Marie Antoinette was right, of course: any invasion of a French province would have immediately provoked a new explosion in Paris, all the more so since Artois could be relied on to botch anything he attempted.

Unfortunately, Artois's interests were no longer identical to those of his relatives in France. His first concern was the restoration of the ancien régime; if the price for that was a massacre at the Tuileries — which would bring him appreciably closer to the throne — it might be worth paying. From that moment, therefore, the Queen dreaded his embarking on some half-baked enterprise that would cost her and the King their lives.

Almost as bad was the effect of Artois's letter on Madame Elisabeth, the King's sister. A highly pious, retiring young woman, Madame Elisabeth had hardly played any role at Versailles; now, as the royal family's horizons shrank, she became the King and Queen's constant companion, sharing their meals and most of their evenings. Like them, of course, she loathed the Revolution; but she also felt that her brother was too weak, that he ought to fight the new order, not give in to it. And so she became, in essence, the representative of the émigrés within the royal family, thus causing great friction, especially since Marie Antoinette suspected her of reporting secretly to Artois. Obviously, this was extremely dangerous: the émigrés were notoriously indiscreet, and revelations of the true position of the King could harm him gravely. Besides which, it made life at the Tuileries even more uncomfortable than it already was.

Thus, day by day, Mirabeau seemed more necessary to the beleaguered Queen — especially since, on April 1, another smart blow had been struck against the monarchy. Pensions, those incomes given by the King to whomever he pleased, and in whatever amount he pleased, had been one of the most resented practices of the ancien régime. The Assembly had ended all that early on; but that did not satisfy those who wanted an exact account of what had been secretly spent. Armand Gaston Camus, the leader of that group, a former judge of the Parlement of Paris, and now a Deputy, finally convinced his colleagues to decree the publication of the so-called Red Book, the list of all the pensions given by the King.

This showed that the King's brothers, in the course of his reign, had received 28 million livres, and the King and Queen themselves some 11.5 million above and beyond their normal budgeted income; and also that various favored courtiers had secretly benefited from the royal bounty. Although it actually revealed nothing that had not already been fairly certain, the publication helped diminish the monarchy's moral standing; it also resurrected, for good, the suspicion that in 1790 the King was still supporting the very people who were busiest fighting the Revolution.

On its side, the Assembly continued in general to remake France. On April 16 it finally made the Jews regular French citizens, with the same rights and duties as everyone else. On the next day, it put government finance on a modern footing. First, it nationalized the Clergy's debts, so that its former estates, which guaranteed the 400 million livres' worth of assignats, became free and clear, and ready to be sold; then it decided that the assignats in question, which would take the form of notes in the amounts of 1,000, 300, and 200 livres, would become legal tender, but that they would also pay 3 percent interest so as to avoid depreciation. Given the presumed value of the Church's former estates, it was clear that the 400 million was only a first step: whenever the state needed more money, it would simply print more assignats to be redeemed at the actual date of the property sales. The deficit seemed to have just stopped being a problem; and therefore the increasingly unpopular Necker suddenly lost whatever authority he still had.

The first violent attacks against the minister, in fact, appeared almost simultaneously with the passing of this measure. On April 19 Camille Desmoulins set the tone:

> Necker has gone so far as to tell the pensions committee that the King was annoyed that the Assembly had the Red Book printed. Was annoyed! Oh, we are much more annoyed that a man from Geneva should speak to the Assembly in those terms; that he should speak thus to the sovereign in the name of him who is now no more than the nation's first subject. . . . We are much more annoyed that you and your like should have wasted, under the reign of Louis the Economical, 135 million in hidden expenses.[31]

Marat's paper, *L'Ami du peuple,* soon joined in. First, in May, Marat accused Necker of fomenting a coup d'état: "It is to the [officer corps] . . . , these men devoted to the prince because of their prejudices, their principles, their interests, and their hopes, that the minister has turned to corrupt the army . . . and bring about a counterrevolution."[32] A month later, under the headline "Discovery of an Abominable Plot," Marat added: "We are informed that Necker is spending great sums of money among the spies of the ancien régime and the destitute people of the capital to buy their votes in the next elections."[33] Of course, both Desmoulins and Marat belonged to the extreme left; but only a few months earlier, they had been among those who supported Necker. The change, however, is easily understood. While the King was at Versailles,

Necker was the guarantee that he would not work against the Revolution; after October 6, with Louis XVI safely held in Paris, these fears were largely over; and, more important, while Necker's position remained unchanged, the two journalists had progressed very considerably, so that their goals of October 1789, which Necker shared, had by May 1790 come to seem almost reactionary.

The climate, in fact, grew more alarming daily. "All is working toward a dissolution of this monarchy," Mercy reported on May 29. "New insurrections are beginning in the southern provinces . . . massacres [of aristocrats] are announced everywhere; alarms, hatreds are spreading faster; in Paris, the people's anger is excited by tales of counterrevolutions. . . . The nation holds the court responsible for events that it can neither provoke nor suppress."[34] Both Louis XVI and Marie Antoinette were well aware of all this; both remembered how close they had come to being massacred in October; obviously something had to be done. Until now, Necker, much though they disliked him, had at least served as a lightning rod against the people's anger; but, these days, he had become a liability himself. Under these new circumstances, only a combination of Mirabeau, who was clever, and Lafayette, who was still popular, was likely to prevail. That the royal couple trusted neither was beside the point: they never meant to do more than use them and eventually discard them.

There was nothing new about this desired alliance: Mirabeau had wooed Lafayette in October 1789. On April 28 he had tried again, writing the General about his "imperious desire to get closer to you and never be separated from you. . . . I will hold nothing back from this union."[35] Unfortunately, Lafayette was still not ready for the alliance. Then, however, the situation changed dramatically: at long last, the King decided to heed Mirabeau's advice — and, naturally, pay for it. As Mirabeau saw it, this was not corruption: while he would work hard on behalf of the monarchy, it would be only to reach results compatible with his principles. There could be no question of restoring the ancien régime: instead, a constitutional system with a strong king was to be set up while the basic liberties guaranteed by the Declaration of the Rights of Man would remain sacred.

That, however, was not what Louis XVI had in mind, so the collaboration was flawed from the beginning. And as Mirabeau was heard to defend the King, his influence declined. Still, he was capable of judging the situation clearly, and that alone was more than any of the King's other advisers could do. As for what he was willing to try, he made that absolutely clear in the first of his secret memos to Louis XVI. On May 10 he wrote:

> Deeply touched by the anguish of the King, who has least deserved his unhappiness, confident as I am that if . . . there is a prince in whose word one can trust, that prince is Louis XVI . . . I would still refuse to play a role in this moment of partialities and confusions if I were not convinced that the reestablishment of the King's legitimate authority is the first need of the country and the only way of saving it.
>
> I see clearly that we are in the midst of an anarchy which worsens every day. . . . I undertake to use all my influence to serve the King's true interest; and so that this commitment will not appear too vague, I declare that I think a counterrevolution as dangerous and criminal as I think unrealistic a government whose leader lacks the power of enforcing the law.
>
> According to these principles, I will give my written opinion on current events, the way to control them or prevent them if they are to be feared; and my main business will be to put in its place within the constitution the executive power whose plenitude must, without restriction, belong to the King.[36]

It was a beginning. For the first time since the meeting of the Estates General in May 1789, Louis XVI had as his adviser a man who understood the times and possibly could exert some influence on them. At the same time, the fact remained that Mirabeau alone was not strong enough to modify a swiftly deteriorating situation. Consequently, at the King's request, he approached Lafayette yet again. He wrote on June 1:

> Monsieur le marquis, our times, our revolution, our circumstances are unlike anything that has happened in the past; neither wit, nor memory, nor social qualities suffice any longer: a blend of meditation, of the inspiration of a genius, and of the power of character are needed today. . . . I may see with one eye only, but in this realm of the blind,

I am more necessary to you than all the committees in the world. . . .
Your great qualities need my impulse, my impulse needs your great
qualities.[37]

Mirabeau was right: neither man alone could hope to stabilize the
situation. Even together, they might well fail, but at least they had a
chance. Lafayette, however, was too blind to see this. He distrusted the
King, and especially the Queen, and was not sorry to see them
humiliated; he basked in the warm glow of his popularity; and when it
came right down to it, he simply did not like Mirabeau. "Lafayette was
wrong about Mirabeau," the General later acknowledged in his
memoirs.* "His immorality shocked him, however much he enjoyed his
conversation, and despite much admiration for such sublime talents, he
could not help showing [Mirabeau] a lack of esteem, which wounded
him. . . . When Mirabeau was consulted by the court, he grew even more
distant from Lafayette. The King and the Queen asked Lafayette to work
together with Mirabeau. . . . He rejected this first request and heard no
more about it."[38]

That the royal couple asked him at all showed how deeply they were
influenced by Mirabeau: by June 1790 they disliked and mistrusted the
idol of the Parisians. These feelings were further reinforced by the way he
rebuffed their suggestion, so they turned to their new adviser, who, once
again, set down a clear and convincing analysis of the situation. First,
however, there was a little flattery for Marie Antoinette: Mirabeau knew
very well that it was she, not the King, who was in charge.

"I defended the monarchy when all I saw of the court was its
weakness, and when, knowing neither the soul nor the thoughts of [the
Queen], I was unable to rely on this august helper," he wrote on June 1.
After stigmatizing "the power which the court's weakness, rather than
the law, allows M. de Lafayette to enjoy," he went on to dismiss the
General:

M. de Lafayette's strength is due to his popularity with [the National
Guard], and that results from the fact that he seems to share the

---

* Like other, later, famous Frenchmen, Lafayette often wrote of himself in the third
person.

opinions of the multitude. But since it is not he who dictates these opinions . . . it follows that, M. de Lafayette having acquired his influence only by adopting the tone of Paris, he will always be forced to follow the torrent of the multitude if he wants to retain it. . . . Upholding the most numerous party whether it be right or wrong, frightening the court by uprisings he will have arranged or which he will predict to make himself needed . . . , there is his destiny. . . . Appointing the ministers he wants will bring the whole kingdom to the same pitch as Paris whereas our salvation lies in letting the kingdom contain Paris.[39]

Once again, Mirabeau saw the situation accurately: Lafayette was indeed the prisoner of his popularity in Paris.

Meanwhile, outside the capital, the mood was very different: the great wave of risings and castle burnings, which had peaked in the late summer of 1789, had ended, and while most of the reforms were popular, there was a feeling, especially in some of the larger cities — Rouen, Lyons, Bordeaux — that things had gone far enough. Virtually no one wanted a return to the ancien régime; equally, however, there was a vast majority against further significant change. Louis XVI was still liked and respected; given the opportunity, that majority was probably ready to support him against the Parisian extremists. That, indeed, was what Mirabeau counted on. And since the King was now willing to follow his advice, it was, he thought, possible to divide and conquer. None of this had been true even three months earlier; but in May, the Assembly, who until then had wrought so many much-needed and widely desired reforms, began on a new course that shocked and angered much of the French population.

CHAPTER FIVE

Liberty vs. the Church

:   :   :

FRANCE in 1790 was a Catholic country. There was, it is true, a very small Protestant minority — probably about 5 percent of the population — and a statistically negligible Jewish group, centered mostly in Alsace. Until 1787, while the Jews were tolerated, under certain disabilities, it was against the law to be a Protestant. All that was over now: the Assembly had decreed freedom of religion, and its decision had met with widespread approval. Still, the French remained much attached to the Church. Most of them, especially outside Paris, took its teachings very seriously indeed, though it was not so much that they were attached to the Pope as that they believed that worshiping according to the familiar ritual would save their souls.

Many of the Deputies, however, whether liberal aristocrats or lawyers, were men of the Enlightenment, raised on the works of Voltaire, Rousseau, and the Encyclopédistes. All their lives they had watched the Catholic Church behave in the greedy and intolerant manner that has so often characterized it throughout its long history. Alone, for instance, the bishops had resisted the restitution of civil rights to the Protestants, so unreasonably, in fact, that even the pious Louis XVI had finally ignored their preaching. What the Assembly failed to see, however, is that the Church is one thing, and religion another; and when it decided to reform what was unquestionably a corrupt clergy, it also, unwittingly, began to suppress freedom of religion.

That people should worship as they please was, as it is still today, one of the basic freedoms: in the United States, for instance (but not in

England), this was guaranteed by the Constitution. Unfortunately, France had an old and solid tradition of interference by the state in religious matters. This tradition was essentially threefold.

First, the concordat with the Vatican provided that the King appointed all the bishops, abbots, and mothers superior in France, subject only to the (automatic) canonical institution by the Pope. What this meant in practice was that the younger sons of the great noble families tended to get all the juicy plums: Talleyrand was a case in point, and so was the cardinal de Rohan, the main actor in the notorious Affair of the Queen's Necklace. Second, the King had assumed the power of rejecting certain doctrines and of favoring others: the Pope could thus usually be pressured, eventually, into agreement. Finally, the Gallican Church benefited from certain "liberties" that, in matters of organization and doctrine, gave it considerable de facto independence from Rome; all through the seventeenth and eighteenth centuries, these liberties had been zealously defended by the Parlements. Thus it seemed perfectly normal to have the state interfere to a considerable extent in the life of the Church; the great difference now was that the King was a devout Catholic, whereas there was a majority of deists to be found in the Assembly.

At the same time, the great properties held by the Church, the splendor in which many of the bishops lived, the manifest lack of sobriety of some of them, all that called for reform. The first step, obviously, had been the nationalization of the Church's estates, a step that had, on the whole, been highly popular. Next, in March 1790 came the closing of the monasteries. That was going a good deal further; but, even so, there was a tradition to justify this sort of interference: monastic orders had, on occasion, been suppressed, and as recently as the 1750s the Jesuits had been expelled from France prior to the dissolution of that order. Thus, while the closing of the monasteries undoubtedly upset some people, it still created no widespread opposition.

In May and June, however, the Assembly took a radical new step: it now decided to reform the very structure of the Church without consulting the Pope. This was naturally a violation of the concordat, that is, of a proper, reciprocal treaty; it was also a grave interference with the way the faithful preferred to worship. By the time the reform was complete, on July 12, the Civil Constitution of the Clergy, as it was henceforth called, had utterly transformed the nature of the Church in France.

First, all the old sees were abolished in spite of their having existed since time immemorial; henceforth, each département was to be a diocese in itself. All ecclesiastical titles, offices, and benefices were abolished. The bishops, instead of being nominated by the King and confirmed by the Pope, were to be elected by the population at large; there would be no papal confirmation although the Pontiff would be notified of the election. The priests, too, were to be elected. All ecclesiastics were to receive a government salary, 50,000 livres (about $250,000) for the Bishop of Paris, either 20,000 or 12,000 livres for the other bishops, depending on the population of the département. All bishops and all priests were to be resident — in the past, many of the former had spent a good deal of their time at Versailles. Finally, all religious life, all current and former ecclesiastical personnel (that is, monks and nuns), was to be strictly regulated.

This massive reform obviously contained some relatively harmless sections — government salaries, the obligation of residence — but others deeply affronted the faithful, among them, Louis XVI himself. This was especially true of the election clause, the end of papal confirmation, and the remaking of the sees. It also opened up a number of disquieting possibilities: would the French Church now split between those who approved of the Civil Constitution and those who thought it a pernicious heresy? Would the government punish the priests and bishops who refused to submit themselves to an election? Obviously, much depended on the attitude of the Pope.

As it happened, Pius VI was a cautious man, eager to avoid a fight whenever possible and far more interested in the museum he was building* than in the welfare of the Church. Further, he had just been through a very bruising fight with Emperor Joseph II, who had made the German and Austrian churches virtually independent of Rome. Thus, the Civil Constitution of the Clergy must have seemed to him unpleasantly familiar, even if it went a good deal further than the Emperor had done. So, for a while, he did absolutely nothing, and it seemed possible that he

---

* The admirable Museo Pio-Clementino, now part of the Vatican museums.

might swallow hard and give his agreement after all. One person, however, soon learned of the Pontiff's real intention, and that was Louis XVI.

Much against his own conscience, but faithful to his policy of systematically agreeing to every reform, the more extreme the better, the King signed the new law on July 22. The very next day — twenty-four hours too late — he received a secret letter from Pius, hinting strongly that he was preparing to denounce the Civil Constitution. Prudently, Louis kept the letter to himself; but now he began to feel that he could not go on pretending much longer, as many of his subjects, horrified by the reform, began looking for priests who would have nothing to do with it.

With the passing, and promulgating, of the Civil Constitution, the Revolution, which until then had relied on a very broad consensus, became divisive — although, at first, this was not clearly seen. Until then, opposition to the new regime had come from largely marginal elements: part of the aristocracy, a small number of bishops, a small section of the upper middle class, and, of course, the King and Queen. Now whole sections of the population were affronted: it is indicative that the very first *anti*revolutionary riots took place in Lyons on July 25. This was important, not just because it was the first step toward civil war, but also because it decisively broke the unanimity that was felt to be essential. Although there had been opinion groups in the Assembly, parties as such did not exist because it was believed that the welfare of the country was at stake, and that the means to attain it existed independently of political nuances: all men of goodwill were "patriots," they put their love of France first, and they could therefore agree on what needed to be done. Now, for the first time, that unanimity was broken.

This opposition, ironically, resulted in a speedup of the Revolution even as the Civil Constitution made its way through the Assembly, because, once again, the mob had a powerful enemy to react against; once again, it felt threatened and therefore prepared to attack before it was attacked. The left-wing press, always a good indicator, became more violent, making the King a target once more. On June 7, for instance, Marat had written: "The surest proof that a new law is good is the consternation it causes at the Tuileries and the sad expressions on the ministers' faces. . . .

"The King has been more often out in the fresh air. He goes hunting and follows religious processions. He gives his thanks to the Paris National Guard. He reviews it on the Champ de Mars and it is with pain I have seen him galloping among endless shouts of 'Long live the King.' ''[1] And the very next day, stressing the loss of unanimity among the electorate (there had just been a disputed election) Marat added: "What! Will the Fatherland be torn apart by its own children? . . . Hidden plots announce a dreadful cataclysm; we are threatened with the direst events, here and at the border; if discord rends us, we are lost forever.''[2]

Admittedly, this sort of ranting struck most people, even in Paris, as repulsive; but it was directed less at the Assembly than at the mob and the members of the two revolutionary clubs, the Jacobins and the Cordeliers, and there its impact was enormous. Marat and Desmoulins, in fact, had just invented a most important motive in the revolutionary process: after fear of repression, which had worked so well in 1789, came the fear of plots by dissatisfied elements; and because plots are by their nature secret and hard to prove, the only antidote was immediate and widespread repression. So, instead of advocating liberty for all, the extremists were beginning to favor the dictatorship of the left.

None of this surprised the King and the Queen, who watched events in the late spring and early summer of 1790 with rapidly mounting fear and disgust. In May, though, they had at least been able to leave the Tuileries for Saint-Cloud, a country palace built on a hill overlooking the Seine and Paris in the distance. It was a great improvement over the Tuileries: not only did they have a vast park and the kind of privacy that the Tuileries so conspicuously lacked, they also found the type of setting they missed in Paris. Saint-Cloud, purchased by the Queen from the duc d'Orléans in 1785, was a seventeenth-century palace designed by Mansart, and had been recently refurnished with all the luxury and elegance typical of Marie Antoinette's residences, so that it was really just as pleasant as Versailles. Even so, the royal couple still felt they were living on a volcano.

It was there, for instance, in a gallery overlooking Paris that the Queen had a typical conversation with Mme de Tourzel, the governess of the royal children. "She told me with a sigh," the latter reported, " 'The life in Paris used to make me so happy; I longed to spend time there. Who would have thought then that this would come about only in so bitter a fashion!' ''³ Whatever the many remaining monarchists might think, whatever the Assembly pretended to believe, the reality was simple: the royal couple knew they were hostages and resented it bitterly.

They could also see that, far from improving, things were rapidly getting worse for them: the Civil Constitution of the Clergy, which was being put together in May and June, was proof enough of that, as was the restiveness of the mob; and the reaction on which the King's policy was predicated was obviously not coming. Under the circumstances, there-fore, three policies were possible: one was to rely on Mirabeau and hope that he would be able to carry out his promises; another was to hope for a quick, effective foreign intervention that would restore the absolute monarchy; and the third was to escape, and return only at the head of an army.

Mirabeau was well aware of this. "In no case and under no pretext must one be the accomplice . . . of an escape. When a King means to be King, he leaves only in the full light of the day," he wrote La Marck.⁴ But so controlling the situation as to be enabled to leave Paris openly was quite beyond Louis XVI's powers, and Mirabeau also knew this. Still, he could see elements of hope in the situation. The destruction of all the former intermediary bodies was, he pointed out, a great possible advantage to the King. No more Parlement, no more Orders, whether Clergy or Nobility, no more provinces with their special privileges: Louis XVI, if he regained some power, would be able to rule far more effectively than before. On the other hand, the complex new administrative structures being set up by the Assembly were a serious impediment, inasmuch as they were not controlled by the central government; but if pressure could be brought to bear on the Assembly by the provinces, that could still be changed. As suggested before, Mirabeau wanted to use the rest of France to control Paris. Now that he was working for the court, however, he had a new problem: Marie Antoinette, who was not as patient as her husband, was already thirsting for revenge. She was also capable of energy.

"The King has only one man, his wife. She can find safety only in the restoration of royal authority. . . . The moment will come, and soon, when she will have to see how much a woman . . . on a horse can do," he wrote the royal couple on June 20.⁵ This was, in fact, only an extension of his earlier plan. The King and Queen were to leave Paris, ostensibly to visit one of the provincial cities, and from there reconquer their kingdom. Unfortunately, it was not as easy to arrange this as Mirabeau liked to suppose, and Marie Antoinette had a very different sort of scenario in mind. If she is to be believed, it was she who influenced Mirabeau.

> The negotiation with M. continues [she had written Mercy earlier, on June 12], and if he is sincere, I have reason to be pleased with him. . . . I think that one of the most reasonable parts of M.'s plan is . . . to convince [Prussia and Austria], under the pretext of the dangers to which they will be exposed if all this consolidates itself, to appear, not in order to carry out a counterrevolution or invade the country, but as guarantors of the treaties . . . and say they do not like the way the King is treated. They could then speak with the tone one has when one is the strongest, both as regards the excellence of the cause and the number of troops. . . . All is going from bad to worse. The ministers and M. de Lafayette lead us daily onto the wrong path, everything is allowed, and far from satisfying those monsters, they become more insolent by the moment while, as regards decent people, one is all the more abased. I am desperate. . . .[6]

The Queen's illusions are all too obvious: a demonstration by an Austro-Prussian army, far from easing her situation, was likely to provoke more and greater disorders. There was also the uncomfortable fact that most of Europe was watching the Revolution with some satisfaction: it was assumed that the French army was rapidly dissolving, and that in another year or two, a victorious war might be highly profitable to the other powers. It was also true, however, that other monarchs were beginning to worry lest the Revolution spread: talks were started on June 26 at Reichenbach in order to develop a common stance, but nothing much came out of them.

In one respect, however, Marie Antoinette could see some progress. On July 3, in the deepest secrecy,* the royal couple met face-to-face with Mirabeau, and the Queen used all her charm on her former enemy. "He returned from Saint-Cloud full of enthusiasm," La Marck noted. "The

---

* This was possible at Saint-Cloud, where the park and the larger palace afforded a greater degree of privacy; it would not have been in Paris.

Queen's dignity, the grace that characterized her, her affability when, with a tenderness blended with remorse, he accused himself of having been one of the main causes of her sorrows, all had charmed him beyond expression. . . . He was no less touched by the King's quiet acceptance and by the moderation of his views."[7] Marie Antoinette could always please when she set out to do so, and Louis XVI was careful to tell Mirabeau only what he wanted to hear. From that moment, the great orator was wholly won over to the royal cause.

Another development came at just the right time. The plan advanced by Mirabeau would require spending 3 million livres. After some debate, on June 9, the Assembly had voted the King a civil list: this was the yearly sum to be paid to the monarch from which he was to cover his expenses, and it was set at 25 million a year. This was much more than Louis XVI needed to pay his bills, and he could thus use the surplus to finance, secretly, whatever people or movements he chose.

Whether the King would have the chance to act, however, seemed to him and the Queen very much open to question: they expected a recrudescence of the Revolution within a month and were not at all sure of surviving it. As the National Guard had taken hold throughout the country, its many local organizations had begun to express a wish to come together, to federate, in a triumphant affirmation of progress and unity. It was decided, therefore, to celebrate the anniversary of the storming of the Bastille by having a grand meeting of all the Guard federations in Paris on July 14, at which all would take the new civic oath to the nation, the law, the King. This *Fête de la Fédération,* as it was called, was enthusiastically endorsed by Lafayette, who expected to see his popularity soar, and, a little more cautiously, was accepted by the Assembly.

Both on the right and the left, however, the greatest anxiety reigned. Louis XVI and Marie Antoinette expected unnamed horrors; Marat and Desmoulins thought Lafayette might well use the presence in Paris of tens of thousands of National Guardsmen, as well as 11,000 regular troops, to do away with their supporters. On July 10 the headline in *L'Ami du peuple* read: "Imminent dangers menace the Fatherland. Dreadful drawbacks of the civic oath," and, on the eleventh: "Enormous errors in the organization of the Paris army [that is, the National Guard]. Imminent dangers with which they threaten our freedom."[8]

Because, with the help of hindsight, we know how things turned out, this constant apprehension on the part of the left seems less than convincing. In fact, in July 1790 there was no guarantee that, in a burst of energy, and perhaps with Austrian help, the monarchy would not reassert itself. Lafayette might feel that things had gone too far; the King might be buoyed up by his popularity among the provincial delegations, who still retained some of the traditional respect for the person of the monarch, in good part because the provincial press was very much more moderate than that of the capital. Marat, on the whole, had good reason to worry, especially since, for the duration of the Fête, the Paris mob would be greatly outnumbered by the well-armed National Guard.

These vast crowds required a setting in which they could be accommodated for the ceremony itself: the King, the Deputies, and the men of the Guard were all to take the civic oath and attend the celebration of a mass. The Assembly had decided to have the Fête only on June 5, less than six weeks before the actual event; so much needed to be done. A vast amphitheater was to be built at the Champ de Mars,* with the King's box at one side and an altar on a tall platform in the middle. It seemed almost impossible it could all be ready on time; but then an amazing phenomenon took place. "We breathed more freely," Mme de Staël remembered. "The imprecise hope of a vast happiness had taken hold of the nation":[9] the Revolution had triumphed, but it had also run its course. The new regime would be consolidated, liberty firmly established, the constitutional monarchy set in place. For one brief moment amidst the turmoil caused by elaboration of the Civil Constitution of the Clergy, a new, moderate age seemed to be in the making. Once again, there was the prospect of a peaceful and golden future.

As a result, great numbers of upper-class Parisians suddenly joined the laborers who were preparing the site. Elegant young men were seen digging, fashionable women pushed mahogany wheelbarrows, fraternity reigned: for those few weeks, the class system vanished in a haze of goodwill. Here again was the unanimity on which the reforms were predicated; all differences were gone, the Civil Constitution was temporarily forgotten, all communed in the love of France and humanity; and on the appointed day, the great amphitheater was ready.

---

* The Champ de Mars, the Field of Mars, was the vast esplanade in front of the Ecole Militaire; it is now occupied in part by the Eiffel Tower.

For most of the people who were present on July 14, 1790, the Fête of the Federation was indeed a great and glorious day, in spite of the rain that fell constantly. There were grand parades throughout Paris, all marching toward the Champ de Mars. There, a great space was bordered on two sides by long, artificial hills on which rows of benches had been placed; the entrance was through an arch of triumph, while opposite was set an elegantly decorated gallery. The royal throne stood in the middle, with seats on either side for the members of the Assembly, those of the capital's municipal bodies, and some of the special Deputies from the provinces, while just above was a space reserved for the Queen, the Dauphin, and the royal family. In the middle of the amphitheater, an altar, placed atop a stepped hill, was surrounded by a group of priests all dressed in white, while Guardsmen stood on the steps.

Early on, the amphitheater filled up with Guardsmen and members of the public, and they waited in the rain for several hours. What happened then can be described quite differently according to the observer's political views. Count Fersen, Marie Antoinette's friend, who loathed the Revolution, wrote his sister:

> That famous federation . . . turned out to be quite ridiculous because of the constant disorder and indecency. . . . There was no order, no one was in their right place, the soldiers who were meant to be on guard obeyed no one, they ran here and there, singing and dancing; before the arrival of the King and the federated troops, they went and got a priest and two monks at the altar, they put grenadier's hats on their heads and rifles on their shoulders and took them all around the amphitheater, singing and dancing just like savages about to eat a Christian.''[10]

Marie Antoinette herself was horrified by the lack of respect shown her in separating her from the King, and the numerous breaches of the traditional etiquette.

For almost everyone else, though, the Fête, in spite of the drenching downpour, left the sunniest of memories, that of a great and joyous communion of a free people with its army, its Church, its King. ''The rain kept falling,'' Joseph Garat, one of the members of the Assembly's left wing, reported, and seemed to want to sadden the festivities, but it quite failed to do so. In the midst of a shower, some of the Guardsmen started a round dance; they soon had imitators, and the dances were seen everywhere. Sometimes the circles tightened, and then there were more, sometimes they widened. . . . Songs and joyous shouts rang through the air. . . . The Queen's arrival provoked . . . many acclamations, which redoubled when, on several occasions, she took the heir to the throne in her arms and raised him to show him to the people. . . .

When the monarch arrived . . . the soldiers and Guardsmen rushed forth from every part of the Champ de Mars. . . . No king has ever been the object of a more sincere or tender love.[11]

Obviously, all depends on the observer's point of view; but what cannot be denied is that only a tiny minority failed to join in the spirit of the festivities.

As soon as the King arrived, the eighty-three banners of the départements were lined up around the altar and, having received a blessing, were then paraded before Louis XVI. At that point, among deafening acclamations, Lafayette rode in and joined the King. It was time for the mass to begin, with as its main celebrant Talleyrand, the bishop of Autun and a man who was famous for qualities quite unrelated to godliness; as Garat commented, it was appropriate to have a priest "who understood that God does not want to be worshipped by slaves." Then came the oath, taken by each of the eighty-three federations. Finally the King himself swore to observe the constitution, after which, in an uncontainable outburst of joy, the ceremony ended.

"M. de Lafayette [swore] . . . to be faithful to the nation, the law, and the King; both the oath and the man who was taking it made everyone trust them. The spectators were beside themselves; the King and liberty seemed to them united forever," Mme de Staël noted, adding sadly, "but those who were capable of independent thinking were far from sharing the universal joy."[12] In fact, the General reached an extraordinary degree of popularity that day; he was surrounded by adoring crowds eager to touch him, or if they could not reach his person, at least his horse; it took him hours to leave the Champ de Mars at the end of the ceremony because the crowd kept cheering him. At that moment, he could have done almost anything he chose; and if, after all, he had surmounted his aversion to Mirabeau, the Revolution might well have been stabilized. Unfortunately, all that applause went to his head instead; he forgot that popularity is often fleeting and failed to use his enormous potential power.

That Lafayette, who had to all intents and purposes created the National Guard, should be greatly loved at the Fête of the Federation was not very surprising; but, far more unexpected, it turned out that the King was also popular. Everywhere he went, he was received with the greatest warmth; shouts of "Long live the King" rang through Paris. Even the Queen was cheered. It looked as if Mirabeau had indeed been right, as if the provinces could be counted on to support the monarchy.

It was, however, highly unlikely that this happy state of things would last. Most of the celebrants believed that the King had genuinely accepted the new order; as soon as it became evident that he had merely been pretending, his popularity would vanish utterly. Potential conflicts between the King and the Assembly were also numerous, starting with the application of the Civil Constitution of the Clergy and culminating in the fact that the constitution Louis XVI had sworn to observe at the Fête of the Federation still did not, in fact, exist. It seems, at first glance, almost impossible to believe: the culmination of that vast ceremony, the guarantee that liberty had come to stay, was in the King's oath; and yet neither he, nor the Assembly, nor, of course, the people knew what it was he had sworn to observe.

As for Louis and Marie Antoinette, they felt great relief: far from being massacred, or even insulted, they had been cheered to the echo. Still, they were well aware that their popularity was wholly artificial — after all, they loathed the very principles which had been so resoundingly endorsed — and that it was not at all likely to last. They should, therefore, have heeded Mirabeau's advice to move to Fontainebleau, some forty miles from Paris, calling troops from Metz, where some supposedly faithful regiments were stationed, to provide for their safety. Most probably, in the happy afterglow of the Fête, they would have been allowed to leave the immediate vicinity of the city. But the King was too passive, and Marie Antoinette did not really trust Mirabeau, so they remained at Saint-Cloud.

They were also, despite their many fears, reassured by a transient phenomenon that they mistook for the beginning of a trend: in the spring and summer of 1790 the monarchist press grew both more eloquent and more numerous, and the royal couple took this as an indication that a powerful royalist party was in the making. Unfortunately, they were completely mistaken: the right might be witty and even occasionally convincing, but it never came close to influencing the course of events. Even today, however, as one reads the pamphlets and papers that so cheered them up, one can almost believe that they were just as influential as *L'Ami du peuple.*

There was, for instance, Rivarol's *National Dictionary,* with its provocative definitions. "The constitution," he wrote, "will be a pact concluded between the father and his children; but we notice that the children have reached their majority, and make demands accordingly";[13] or again, defining the word *insurrection:* "When the insurrection is minor, and when the insurgents, instead of hanging others, are hanged themselves, the word to use is uprising. In the opposite case, and so as to avoid all confusion, the current word is revolution."[14]

This was followed by more vehement, but still amusing productions. In the *New French Dictionary,* an anonymous author, perhaps Champ-cenetz, a right-wing pamphleteer, gave the following definitions: *"Slave:* see King. *Eternity:* Word which until now had no real meaning. It was left to the National Assembly to give us a precise notion of it . . . by the duration of the ills it has brought on the country. *Speaker's podium* [at the Assembly]: fantastic place where the most unreasonable speeches are the ones rewarded with the most applause."[15]

This no doubt made the "aristocrats" feel better, but it could obviously have no real political effect. Other, more earnest publications tried reasoning things out. There was, for instance, *L'Ami du Roi, des Français, de l'ordre et surtout de la vérité* (The Friend of the King, of the French, of order and above all of the truth), a moderate royalist paper. On September 1, it drew a balance sheet of the changes to date, and there was a good deal of truth in what it said.

What did we mean to do? And what have we actually done? . . . We wanted to set limits to the King's authority, and we have done away with it altogether, although it is our only safety against the usurpations of the legislature. We wanted to bring relief to the poor and we have wrenched . . . from them the resources that came from the luxuries and charities of the rich. We wanted to fund the national debt, instead we have made it immensely larger and we have stopped all revenue by destroying commerce and the arts, prematurely ending all indirect taxation. . . . We longed to end the sway of an arbitrary power and we must bow down to the very arbitrary decisions of our envoys [the Deputies] who started out by announcing they were our masters. . . . Instead of that equality we so desired, we have created between the citizens of the same fatherland the most monstrous, the most shocking inequality; the priests, the nobles, the rich, are no longer thought to be citizens, or even men.[16]

Many of these complaints are reasonable, first and foremost that the Assembly itself was rapidly turning into an uncontrollable and despotic body. Although by September 1790 it had existed for only sixteen months, the purpose for which it had been called and the form which it had been expected to retain — that of the Estates General — were utterly remote from its current situation. It had, in all probability, become wildly unrepresentative, and yet there was no appealing its decisions. Then, too, liberty was beginning to be replaced, or at least limited, by selective oppression against the nobles and the priests: on May 28, for instance, wearing a white cockade was forbidden. Finally, most incontestably, the financial situation, which the Estates General had been called to settle, was now nothing short of catastrophic.

The very first effect of the Revolution, in fact, had been almost completely to suspend the payment of taxes. The Assembly, it is true, had said clearly that, until a new revenue system had been established, the old impositions were still valid, but almost everyone ignored that decision. As a result, the deficit, instead of shrinking, had grown enormously, and Necker, who was good at fine-tuning, found himself quite out of his depth. Still, the state could hardly fold up; and while its bills were paid even more slowly than under the ancien régime, money had to be found. The first 400 million livres' worth of assignats had helped for a while; but by August the treasury was empty once more.

There was nothing for it but to print money; and that is just what Necker and the Assembly proceeded to do. On August 8, 40 million livres in promissory notes convertible to assignats were turned over to the treasury, with 10 million more issued on September 6, a further 20 million on the twelfth, and another 25 million on October 4. This was only a beginning; on September 23, the Assembly voted to create a new 800 million in assignats (as opposed to convertible promissory notes), thus reaching a total of 1,200 million livres in assignats, a sum so huge as to be almost inconceivable. Nor was that all; the notes went on being created: on November 12, 48 million were sent to the treasury, and on December 11, 45 million. It required no great financial flair to see what was happening: at a pace of about 45 million livres a month, the government was printing currency supposedly guaranteed by the future sale of the estates of the Church. Unlike the first assignats, these new emissions bore no interest.

As is invariably the case, bad money began chasing out good. People who had gold and silver coins were understandably not eager to exchange them for depreciating paper notes, so that the metallic currency rapidly became almost impossible to find. That, in turn, hastened the contraction of an already ailing economy.

Nowhere was this more true than in Paris. While the peasants grew most of their own food and could barter for the rest of their needs, townspeople lived in a money economy. Paris, especially, was highly dependent on the income brought in by the luxury trades; but in a country where the nobles and the rich were under attack, it stood to reason that no one was doing much ordering of unnecessary goods. By the summer of 1790, therefore, many categories of artisans found themselves out of work: from tailors to coachmakers, from silversmiths to furniture makers, from hairdressers to domestic servants, thousands of men and women suddenly found themselves without resources, at the very same time that prices began to rise rapidly because of the depreciation of the paper money.

This was hardly what the Revolution was supposed to bring about. Instead of a golden era of peace and prosperity, formerly comfortable workers were now unemployed. Because they approved of the political changes, however, the very victims of the Assembly's financial policy felt that the downturn could not be the fault of the new order: obviously, it was all a plot by the rich and the aristocrats to starve the people and punish them for having ended the ancien régime. Thus political radicalization followed on (unplanned) economic distress; and every step taken by the Assembly to remedy the financial crisis worsened the plight of the poor. Nor was it hard to notice that, back again at the Tuileries, the royal family lived in unchanged splendor. Under those circumstances, the goodwill generated by the Fête of the Federation could hardly last very long.

One early and immediate consequence of all this was that Necker, so beloved just a year earlier, was now one of the most hated men in Paris. In part because he disapproved of many of the latest reforms, he had completely lost his hold over the Assembly; worse, he was seen for what he was: an honest but limited, and finally mediocre, banker who lacked the qualities needed in the current emergency. For the minister himself, the situation had become untenable. The King, who had always disliked him, no longer bothered to pretend this was not the case; the Assembly ignored him; and his unpopularity actually put his life in danger. Deeply disillusioned, and the poorer by 2 million livres he had lent the treasury in October 1789, Necker realized he no longer had a choice: on September 3, he resigned his office and left Paris in haste. No announcement had been made, no one tried to stop him: the minister whose dismissal in July 1789 had caused the storming of the Bastille was forgotten as soon as he left Paris. He was not even replaced: the Assembly had in fact already taken control; now the situation was formally recognized. One of its committees took over the management of the treasury, while an obscure administrator, Charles-Guillaume Lambert, was made comptroller of the finances by the King. In yet another usurpation, the legislature had taken over one of the main executive departments.

It was ever more clear that the King ruled in name only: the Assembly decided all important questions, so that the ministers became mere administrators instead of policymakers. Whatever little power Louis XVI might have had in late 1789 was now completely gone. Even the inventive Mirabeau began to despair. "Public opinion is the only tool remaining in the government's hand," he wrote the King and Queen on September 7. "The only minister worthy of his position is he who will know how to influence, and then control that opinion through the choices he still has the power to make, through the use of the cleverest men possible and by all the means of gaining influence."[17] That meant bribes, of course, but also the creation of a newspaper; it should be tightly controlled, Mirabeau explained, but appear to be fully independent. The fact that he was reduced to this sort of expedient tells the whole story: by the fall of 1790 it had become clear to those with political insight that the monarchy was without power or hope.

All through France, in fact, the fabric of order was disintegrating. Riot followed riot, and the Assembly itself became seriously alarmed. The causes were many, and sometimes obscure: here a surge in unemployment, there a rise in prices. Sometimes, the explosion was due to frustration: many of the early backers of the Revolution, among the lower classes, had thought that a constitution meant a safe job and no taxes, instead of which unemployment was spreading and taxes were still due. Elsewhere, street fights followed conflicts between revolutionaries and people fed up with what they saw as excesses, the worst of which was the Civil Constitution of the Clergy. More than anything, perhaps, what the fermentation expressed was the disappointment of all those who were finding out that the Revolution had not brought them an easier life after all.

Then, too, there was a reluctance to obey orders, any orders, coupled with a realization that there was not much to be lost: the government was unable to pay its bills, it owed money everywhere, and the respect it received was inversely proportional to the amount of its debts. In August, the garrison of Nancy, the capital of Lorraine, had mutinied, partly because it had not been paid for several months; and as was invariably the case, the uprising, although provoked by a specific grievance, promptly turned political. It soon became obvious that, if allowed to continue, such uprisings would spread, so that within a few weeks, the entire country would sink into hopeless anarchy.

Of course, Louis XVI thought the revolt at Nancy should be suppressed, but he no longer had the power to give orders to that effect; so Lafayette, with the Assembly's approval, took over. The army in Metz was commanded by one of his cousins, the marquis de Bouillé, and it was still ready to follow its officers. Bouillé was told to put down the rebellion in as spectacular a manner as possible. This he proceeded to do on August 31 after a battle in which he was opposed, not just by the mutineers but also by the city's National Guard, in itself a sinister omen since Paris depended entirely on that same National Guard to preserve order. On

September 3 the Assembly officially congratulated Bouillé on his success; but the day before, the mob in the capital had risen; it was put down with great difficulty; and there was every reason to expect that it would rise again at the first opportunity. Two weeks later, in fact, the sailors on board the French fleet in Brest also mutinied; no attempt was made at suppressing this latest rebellion.

Again, all these risings proceeded from different causes: the National Guard in Nancy had joined the mutineers in part through local patriotism, still a very strong feeling in the newly French (1740) capital of the formerly independent Duchy of Lorraine, in part because its men were reacting against what they saw as the King's attempt through Bouillé to reestablish his former authority. The mob in Paris rose because it was idle, bored, agitated by Marat and Desmoulins's publications, and because it was as good an occasion as any to frighten the Assembly and reduce the King's authority still further. The sailors in Brest mutinied because, like the soldiers in Nancy, their pay was long overdue and because their living conditions were intolerable.

These several risings, although they were not part of an overall antimonarchic plot, served to demonstrate the fragility of the regime and its basic inability to keep order — even if it did better in Nancy than might have been expected. It should be pointed out, however, that the man responsible for the victory over Nancy was himself a conservative monarchist: how long he would go on being obeyed by his troops was thus a very large question.

It was no wonder that, under the circumstances, the Austrian ambassador asked his government to recall him. Austria was hated, and in the next riot its envoy might well find himself murdered. Just before he left on October 4, Mercy sent a last report to Vienna. "I leave all things here in an unimaginable state of confusion and disorder," he wrote. "It seems impossible that the winter will pass without some violent events. . . . I proposed a purely passive policy to the Queen; that may well be the only way to protect her from the personal danger in which she lives."[18] He was right: once again the Queen was vilified and hated. There seemed little doubt that she ran the risk of being murdered in the course of the next insurrection; and no one, except the ever-optimistic Lafayette, doubted that there would be a next insurrection.

Up until August, in fact, the government's situation, though difficult, was not desperate: it seemed just possible that, in a great outburst of patriotism, the situation would stabilize, a free constitution would take hold, in the end France would give itself a system capable of ensuring both stability and liberty. Starting in September, however, that hope rapidly vanished. The atmosphere in Paris grew more dangerous daily. The mob, quelled by the bourgeoisie and its own triumph, began to reappear in the center of the city; and its demands were invariably radical. On September 2 Lafayette was still able to suppress the riots caused by the repression in Nancy, but, as Mirabeau had predicted, he lost much of his popularity in doing so. Soon he found himself under systematic attack by the left. On just two days in October, for instance, the headlines written by Marat for *L'Ami du peuple* read: "Anecdotes about the dictator Motier" (Lafayette's full surname was Motier de Lafayette); and "Horrible project of Motier to disarm the National Guard throughout the Kingdom."[19]

There was no truth whatever to the accusation; but the fact that it was made marks a new step in the development of the Revolution. More than ever, its future depended on the Paris mob. Unlike their brethren in Nancy, the Parisians could not be easily controlled: they were too numerous and there was no marquis de Bouillé ready and able to fight them. One way to incite them to further rioting, to greater demands, was by systematically, and untruthfully, accusing the moderates and the royal family of imaginary crimes. The journalists who had said, on July 11, 1789, that Louis XVI wanted to reinstate the ancien régime were telling the truth, even if they sometimes exaggerated a little. Now Marat, Desmoulins, and Robespierre were prepared to rely on pure calumny. Although the three men hardly agreed on anything else, they all feared a restoration of the ancien régime, they all distrusted Louis XVI, they all wanted to put the people — that is, themselves — in control.

Their campaign of calumny took several forms: there were political accusations, personal attacks, and an always effective weapon — sexual revelation, which was often convincing but always untrue. This had a double effect. First, of course, it undermined the political credibility of the person under attack by making him or her look ridiculous; then, it utterly destroyed that most important element of the old French society, respect, sometimes amounting to awe, for the monarchs, the royal family, and their entourage. In 1790 it was still difficult to attack Louis

XVI politically, since he seemed to be cooperating with the Assembly and had, apparently, accepted the new regime; but if he could be presented as an obese, drunken cuckold, then, when the time came for a more serious attack, he would no longer be protected by what had been a semisacred character.

As usual the way to the King was through the Queen. Already, in the late seventies and in the eighties, a number of obscene pamphlets had been published. Financed by disappointed courtiers who resented the rise of the Polignac clan, they described Marie Antoinette as a nymphomaniac who could never have enough lovers or as a lesbian, even occasionally as both. This was a traditional form of attack that had been used against Louis XV's mistresses; in its updated version, it was supposed to punish the Queen and her friends by making them unpopular; but this had been a limited aim, and a personal one. Now, the new crop of obscene leaflets was meant, not just to discredit Marie Antoinette but to vilify the monarchy through her.

The first of these attacks to be widely circulated was a little book entitled *The Amorous Evenings of General Mottier and the Fair Antoinette, by the Austrian's Little Spaniel*. Supposedly written by a dog whom Marie Antoinette uses for sexual gratification (the real author is not known), it begins with the dog's lament: "I was all, I am nothing anymore and it is to the fair-haired General, to that traitor, that I owe my torments. . . . Alas, we [the Queen] are now completely blind about that man who is false, hypocritical, ambitious, and inept and who, although he betrays daily the party that raised him, is still so stupidly adored."[20] The dog then goes on to lament the fact that he no longer shares his mistress's ecstasies, and to describe her efforts to seduce Lafayette. Her purpose, of course, is to use him in a counterrevolution, and it is made plain in a monologue: "Vile populace, she said, impure gathering of criminals, no, it will not be said that Antoinette, the daughter of the Caesars, will obey your contemptible laws. I feel enough courage to force once again . . . the stupid multitude to submit to me. . . . This people in revolt whom I saw behaving like a bloodthirsty tiger has been dazzled by Lafayette and has put him at the head of its rebellion. . . . [I]t is through him . . . that I will regain my power."[21] The reader is then treated to the description of a series of unsuccessful encounters in which growing sexual passion is interrupted by the entrance of various people, including the King; when, finally, Marie Antoinette takes Lafayette to her bed, he is, greatly to her frustration, unable to perform. These scenes are described in lurid detail and are obviously meant to titillate while serving as a vehicle for propaganda.

There is, however, also another dimension to these pamphlets. That French reputation for extraordinary politeness, for extreme civilization, had as its corollary an increasingly great distance from the realities of life on earth: few things are more artificial than the display of beautiful manners in an elegant salon. In a sense, therefore, this new spate of obscene pamphlets denotes, in an extreme form, the welling up of one long-suppressed aspect of nature. Then, too, the Revolution, because it was an explosion from below, allowed much repressed emotion to emerge into general consciousness, so that the very people who had seemed so exalted as to be almost nonhuman were now depicted as positively swinish.

From the summer of 1790 on, these kinds of pamphlets flourished; but the choice of victims in this relatively early example is interesting. As the left moved on, Lafayette, once its hero, was turned into the greatest of the obstacles in its path: while to the King he seemed to be a dangerous liberal, his belief in the need for a constitutional monarchy and his resolute attachment to the widest possible freedom all put him sharply to the right of the Jacobins and the Cordeliers. As for his power, that was based largely on his popularity: without it, the Guard would not obey him or dare to take on the mob; if therefore he could be discredited, the march of events would be greatly speeded up.

The autumn of 1790 was marked by the end of the virtual unanimity on which Lafayette's power was based. More and more, the streets of Paris grew agitated while its assemblies, in the forty sections, demanded a major political role. The disintegration of the ministry was an event that showed particularly clearly that the Revolution was becoming more and more a local, Parisian phenomenon. On October 10 the sections brought the Assembly a demand: the ministers, they said, were the tools of the "aristocrats" and could no longer be allowed to retain their offices.

This was obviously none of the city's business. First, it was the King's sole and exclusive prerogative, as head of the executive branch, to appoint or dismiss the ministers, just as in the United States the President appoints the Cabinet; only, under the fragmentary French constitution, no confirmation was required. Beyond this, on matters concerning the nation, the Deputies should have been able to deliberate without undue pressure. Instead, the Assembly, its tribunes filled with a vociferating crowd, was fully aware that the mob filled the streets outside, and that it was in a highly exposed situation. Giving in, however, meant that henceforth the demands of the Parisians would be almost impossible to refuse; so there was a delay while the atmosphere of the city worsened. This time Louis XVI, faithful to his policy of nonresistance, gave in first: on October 20 he dismissed most of the ministers. Believing, wrongly, that the situation had all been Lafayette's doing, he turned to the General for advice in choosing his new advisers.

The results were less than brilliant. Montmorin, whom the King trusted, remained as foreign minister and interim minister of the interior until the appointment of Jean-Marie Valdec de Lessart. Lessart was a friend of Necker's but, more important, one of those hardworking, competent men often found under the ancien régime in subordinate positions. Unfortunately, he had neither personal prestige nor political sense, and, in that most exposed of positions, proved unable to protect or properly advise the King.

The war ministry went to Antoine Duportail, a friend of Lafayette's who had served under him in America. He soon found himself attacked both by the émigrés, whom he condemned, and by the Jacobins for being insufficiently warlike; he, too, lacked all political sense, as did the vicomte de Fleurieu, the new minister of the navy. Finally, crowning this assemblage of mediocrities, the key ministry of justice went to François Duport-Dutertre, a lawyer who had played an important role as one of Paris's envoys in the storming of the Bastille but who had no political or government experience. For his second ministry, Lafayette, in a typical display of political incompetence, had brought together just about the least appropriate group imaginable.

From the King and Queen's point of view, the advent of the new ministry proved that France could no longer be governed. None of the new men had any real sense of loyalty to the sovereign; none could do anything except follow whatever leadership came from the Assembly. The degree to which the new ministers felt a lack of responsibility toward the monarchs is in fact quite startling, if the usually well-informed La Marck is to be believed. Soon after Duport-Dutertre's appointment, according to Mirabeau's friend, Montmorin had one day with his colleague the keeper of the seals a conversation about the danger in which the Queen found herself. Factious men, who had not been able to assassinate her on October 6, 1789, did not conceal their intention of trying again. M. de Montmorin having asked whether such a crime would be allowed to take place, Duport-Dutertre answered coolly that he would not be the accomplice of a murder attempt, but that things would be very different if it were a question of putting the Queen on trial.

"What!" said M. de Montmorin, "you, a minister of the King, you would allow such an infamy?"

"But," the other man answered, "what if there is no other way?"[22]

It was hardly a reassuring prospect for Marie Antoinette or the royal family; and any doubts they might have had about the courage or power of the ministers were only confirmed by what they saw.

Daily, in the Tuileries gardens, just outside their windows, the crowds grew more hostile. More and more, they included large groups of sans-culottes: the men in their loose trousers, the women often in rags, they pushed their way through an ever-scarcer general public. Indeed, it was hardly safe for an elegant woman to be there: she was likely to be accosted by a group of fishwives, at the very least reproached for being an aristocrat, more probably insulted, perhaps even beaten. The same, of course, was true for the men, who were likely to be reviled — "fucking aristocrat" was the very least of it — or assaulted. As for the royal family, they found it more and more difficult to go for a walk outside their own Palace: while, occasionally, there were still cheers when Marie Antoinette appeared, holding her children by the hand, more often now she could hear the shouts against "l'Autrichienne."

All this was new. There had been riots before, of course, but this sullen, continuous presence in the heart of Paris, the visible proof that the mob controlled more and more of the once-glamorous city, the tightening of the noose around the Tuileries — all made it very plain to the King and Queen that the Revolution was accelerating, that no one in France would stop it, and that there was no longer any telling how far it might go.

CHAPTER SIX

An End to Hope

:   :   :

A nonexistent constitution, disorder in the streets, ruinous finances, and an incipient religious rebellion: within a year of the King's forced move to Paris, the new regime was facing a situation over which it was rapidly losing control. Because the Assembly was both constituant and legislative, it never had enough time to deal with all the problems of the Revolution. So, on September 23, it appointed a special committee charged with putting together the various constitutional decrees, but that very small step forward was hardly sufficient to fill in the many lacunae left by the fragmentary measures adopted thus far.

Worse still, more of the Deputies and many Parisians had begun to exhibit that taste for rigid, unyielding logic on which the French still pride themselves. As a result, they took increasingly violent and uncompromising political stands, hardly a happy augury; perhaps more than any other form of government a constitutional monarchy requires compromise and, often, actual imprecision. What was happening, in fact, was that the extreme left, now gathered at the Cordeliers, who had just a year earlier yearned for liberty under a monarch with limited power now began to see this as an illogical halfway measure: if the King was no longer God-given — and they knew that he was not — why have a King at all? If the nation was the source of all legitimacy, then a republic was obviously the answer. Thus by the fall of 1790 the first demands for the abolition of the monarchy began to appear.

They were put forward only by small groups of radicals, however, because Montesquieu's views were still generally accepted: republics in large states, he said, invariably degenerated into anarchy or a military dictatorship. Just a century and a half before, in fact, the fall of Charles I of England had been followed by Cromwell's Protectorate, whereas, when it finally established a limited monarchy, England had become the freest state in Europe.

This view naturally supposed the existence of a monarch who was willing to cooperate; and there was the rub. No matter how obediently Louis XVI signed the Assembly's decrees, it was clear to all those who saw him that he was deeply unhappy and thoroughly disapproved of the course of events.

Although he said very little, his depressed look, his manner of speaking, his long silences during meetings of the Council of Ministers all made it plain. More, his opinions were well known: there was no doubt, for instance, about his deep and genuine feeling for Catholicism, or about the fact that he found the Civil Constitution of the Clergy utterly offensive. Then, too, instead of surrounding himself with the men of the new regime, he saw them only when it was absolutely necessary and preferred otherwise to remain among the reactionary noblemen of his Household.

What almost no one knew, of course, was that he had begun to act on his convictions. On October 6 he added to his earlier secret protest in a new letter to Charles IV of Spain, the purpose of which was a denunciation of the Civil Constitution of the Clergy. Later that month, he took a far graver step, in authorizing and considering a plan offered by Count Fersen, Marie Antoinette's friend, for the flight of the royal family. Fersen's purpose was simple enough: once the King and Queen were removed to safety, the momentum inherent to the Revolution would bring about a complete collapse. "Every day the disorder grows," he wrote his father on November 5;

> Misery is everywhere; the [metallic] currency is disappearing; the assignats . . . have little or no acceptance. . . . Merchants are not selling their goods, the manufactures are closing, all the foodstuffs grow more costly, the number of the poor is becoming frightening. . . . The dissatisfaction, which is rapidly spreading, will bring about some great change: once this dissatisfaction grows complete, the new order will collapse as fast as the old.[1]

That was naturally the hope of all the old-line royalists, and their analysis was right, up to a point: the economy was depressed, prices were rising, dissatisfaction was growing. But, as noted, the people who suffered from all this, far from yearning for the good old days, simply blamed it on an aristocratic plot. This was something that neither Fersen nor the court, who had their own reasons for being displeased, could understand; and so they thought that if only the royal family could flee to safety, it would be only a matter of months, perhaps of weeks, before a repentent people called back its good King.

The only problem, as Fersen saw it, with this plan was that during this interval the royal family had to stay somewhere, and that the most obvious choice, Belgium — the foreign country closest to Paris and a Habsburg possession as well — was itself in the throes of a rebellion. That, as it turned out, though, was just a temporary inconvenience: in November the Austrian army entered the country, and by mid-December Leopold II was firmly in control once again.

Unfortunately, Fersen was far from alone in thinking that escaping Paris was the King's best choice: it had early on occurred to the left as well. There was, after all, a tradition of Parisian rebellions and royal escapes followed by repression, starting in the fourteenth century and stretching to the seventeenth. It was also thought that the European powers would be less likely to attack the new French government if the King remained a potential hostage. So, while Fersen plotted, others watched.

Louis XVI, though allowing the plan to be considered, was far from sure that escape was the best solution: it was undignified; it was dangerous. It also required a firm decision and the kind of energy he lacked. Neither accepting nor rejecting the plan, he tried for another solution.

While he had firmly, if secretly, rejected the early changes made by the Revolution, he had still thought they were fairly easily reversible. By the end of 1790, however, he became convinced that he was faced with a fundamental change in the way the French understood the world, and that this new outlook was as great a threat to all the other kings as it was to himself. He felt that, left unchecked, the Revolution would spread, and this feeling was publicly espoused by Catherine II of Russia as well. The Empress was too distant geographically to be of much help; but it seemed obvious to Louis XVI that his neighbors would want to cooperate in reestablishing him as an absolute monarch.

Even so, his conscience forbade him to spill his subjects' blood, so he placed his hopes in a halfway measure: on December 3 he wrote Frederick William II of Prussia suggesting that a European congress, backed by a large, international army, be held; the congress would demand the return of the ancien régime; the Assembly, realizing all Europe was coalesced, would give in; and all would be well. Oddly enough, this phantasmagoric plan was not as silly as it seems: Louis's fellow monarchs were indeed beginning to fear for their own thrones. But Frederick William was unwilling to spend the money required; Leopold II of Austria, having just retaken Belgium, yearned only for inactivity; and, abroad, statesmen had a far more realistic view of what the French reaction was likely to be. Consequently, the letter was largely ignored.

Still, it marked a major step in the King's, and therefore the Revolution's, progress. The letter was naturally secret, and so was the appointment of a pre-1789 minister, the baron de Breteuil, as emissary to the powers; but for the first time Louis XVI considered a foreign intervention as a major hope, a hope in which the émigrés heartily joined. The comte d'Artois, who was as indiscreet as he was light-headed, was traveling around Europe asking that France be invaded, and this was well known. Slowly, therefore, the possibility that the Revolution might be ended by main force became current and, with it, the notion that class and political belief, for the aristocracy at least, came before patriotism.

All these tensions naturally surfaced in the streets and all the other public places, the theater not the least of them. Plays and operas had long been used by spectators to express their political feelings: at the very beginning of the reign, Marie Antoinette was cheered to the tune of an aria whose words were "Let us applaud our Queen!" Now another play, Voltaire's *Brutus*, caused great anxiety among those whose job it was to keep the peace: the subject, after all, was the end of tyrants and fidelity to a republic. For the first night, the guard all around the theater was quadrupled, and Mayor Bailly was present in person. What happened next was chaos.

Each time some of the spectators applauded a line which was not favorable to the Revolution, there arose such horrible shrieks and shouts that the actors could be heard again only after a rather long interval. . . . At the end of the fourth act, Brutus tells his son: "Just like you I will die / Avenging Rome, free still and without a king"; the *without a king* was hissed, and the hiss was booed with rage when a man in the middle of the orchestra, carried away by his indignation, rose and shouted: "What, don't they want a monarchy in France? What does all this mean? Long live the King!" The strength with which these last words were pronounced seemed to electrify the public. . . . All rose . . . and for a few minutes the hall rang to the shout of "Long live the King!"[2]

This should have been no surprise: people who could afford theater seats were likely to be monarchists; as late as May 1791, Marie Antoinette was still cheered when she went to the opera; but unfortunately for her, what she heard was the applause of a tiny minority.

As for the people who really mattered, the Deputies on one side, the Jacobins and the mob on the other, they continued to live in a state of uneasy mutual tolerance. The Assembly was perfectly aware of its exposed position; it was also, to a degree, carried away by its own past achievements; so it went on making reforms that carefully respected the sanctity of properties not belonging to the Clergy or Nobility. In December, for instance, it affronted the King yet again by decreeing the end of the *apanages*. These were properties given to princes of the blood royal for their lifetimes and those of their male heirs; at the extinction of the male line, they reverted to the crown. By 1790 they hardly represented an important mass of property, and ending them was therefore not a matter of urgency; but the very men who urged the King to cooperate seemed determined to annoy him in every possible way.

That same month, it also ended the venality and heredity of all offices. This step followed logically the abolishing of the Parlements, whose judges had bought seats they were then able to leave their children on the payment of a tax; but, aside from the Parlements, there were also a number of other institutions where the same custom prevailed. This was not just unfair and undemocratic; it ensured that justice or efficacy, and often both, would be replaced by collusion and self-regard; thus the new law was an undoubted progress. It was also an affront to the King: the great court offices, from Captain of the Guard and First Gentleman of the

Bedchamber on down, were always venal and frequently hereditary. Once again, this struck a blow at the habits of a lifetime.

What the King saw as hostility to his person, however, was most often a simple desire to improve the condition of the French; but there was also the important fact that all political pressures came from the left. As the Assembly listened to almost daily denunciations of the King, the ministers, and the Church, it was well aware that the Jacobins and the Cordeliers were in ever-closer touch with the mob while Louis's last remnants of popularity were disappearing. But even as it demolished the outmoded structures of the ancien régime, it saw itself less as the voice of the radicals than as the political expression of the Enlightenment. It was quite right: its actions earned the lasting gratitude of all except a few nobles and priests.

There remained the grave problem posed by the Civil Constitution of the Clergy. On October 30 all but two — Talleyrand and Gobel — of the bishops who were also Deputies signed an Exposition of Principles, which requested the government to wait for the Pope's approval before putting the Civil Constitution into effect. This was obviously not an unreasonable request, if liberty of religion was indeed one of the key principles of the new regime; but it could also be considered as an attempt by the Church to oppose the Revolution.

For most of the Deputies, who did not think much of the Clergy, especially the bishops, the Exposition was treated merely as an irritant. On November 27 they voted to require all ecclesiastics to take an oath of fidelity to the nation, the law, the King: since the Civil Constitution was part of the law, that implied swearing obedience to it as well. The penalty for the non-juring priests was to be immediate loss of their position and salary. While they were at it, the Deputies passed a law obliging bishops to give the canonical institution to newly elected priests and bishops.

Here was a great line drawn between progressives and reactionaries, a turning point, in fact, of the Revolution: after property, religion is often what most closely touches people. The Assembly had earlier alienated much of the aristocracy, but that had been balanced by the support of the bourgeoisie; now it was also provoking the opposition of all devout Catholics, and there were still many of them. These devout Catholics now turned their backs on the new Church as established by the Civil Constitution and resorted instead to the ministrations of priests who rejected it. How general a reaction this was may be gauged by the fact that even Mme de Lafayette, otherwise her husband's most devoted follower, refused to attend services celebrated by a conforming priest.

Some, of course, accepted the new dispensation: within the Assembly itself, some fifty priests and two bishops — again, Talleyrand, naturally, and Gobel — took the new oath amid scenes of enthusiasm. But in the country itself, the vast majority of the clergy refused to conform. Worse, those priests who obeyed the law found that the faithful had, by and large, deserted them in favor of their non-juring colleagues. What the Assembly had done, in its attempt at breaking the hold of a selfish, intolerant, and reactionary institution, was in fact to reinforce it. In 1789 most of the priests, as opposed to the bishops, had favored the Revolution because they were poor themselves and lived close to the people. Now most of them turned against the regime.

Still, the new oath-requiring decree could not become law without the King's signature: had he vetoed it, therefore, the Church would have gone on as before. Given the fact that he was the "Eldest Son of the Church," the "Most Christian King," all titles he took very seriously, and a devout Catholic himself, it was clear he could hardly approve of the new dispensation. Moreover, he knew, albeit secretly, that the Pope was certain to condemn the Civil Constitution. Finally, although he was well aware that the upper Clergy left much to be desired, he unquestionably felt sympathy for the thousands of non-juring priests who would be deprived of their stipends. There was, however, no plan to stop these priests from holding such private (that is, nonsubsidized) services as they chose, and the royal family would still be able to have a non-juring confessor.

This last was most important. Hesitant as he was about most things, Louis XVI had no doubts where his conscience was involved. Had he faced the impossibility of confessing to, and taking communion from, a non-juring priest, he would have felt forced to veto the decree. But this was not the case. Except for imposing financial hardships, there was no question of persecuting the non-jurors: freedom of religion was guaranteed by the fragmentary constitution. At the same time, as so often before, the King's approval of the law was seen as the test of his loyalty

Louis XVI wearing royal robes. This was the King's standard image.

MARIE ANTOIN... D' AUTRICHE
REINE   DE FRANCE.

NEÈ À VIENNE AN MDCCLV.

Marie Antoinette, crowned with the plumes that she made the fashion.

The Oath of the Tennis Court, June 21, 1789. The Deputies, locked out of their usual hall, swear not to separate without giving France a constitution.

An orator in the garden of the Palais Royal, June 1789. The property of the duc d'Orleans, it was the center of revolutionary agitation in Paris.

The people of Paris break into the Garde Meuble, July 13, 1789, and seize the arms stored there.

The siege of the Bastille, July 14, 1789. The gate and bridge have already been seized by the rioters; the fortress is about to fall.

La Fayette in 1789 wearing his uniform of commander of the National Guard. His troops are lined up in the background.

Louis XVI arriving at the Hôtel de Ville, July 17, 1789. The troops lining the way are the newly formed Paris militia.

Foulon being hanged from a lantern, July 22, 1789, the first hint that the Revolution had not ended with the fall of the Bastille.

The banquet of the Flanders regiment at Versailles, October 1, 1789. This was the immediate cause of the people's march to the Palace the next day, and of the royal family's forced move to Paris.

The arrival of the royal family in Paris, October 6, 1789. Slightly ahead of the carriage is a cart loaded with bags of flour.

The Fête of the Federation, July 14, 1790. The amphitheater was entered through the triumphal arch; in the background is the hill crowned with an altar.

to the new institutions. If he wanted to avoid a direct conflict with the Assembly, he had no choice; and so, on December 26, he most reluctantly promulgated the new measure.

The law gave the clergy eight days to take the oath. By January 4 ninety-nine of the 250 ecclesiastical Deputies had complied, and an uncertain number of priests throughout the country. What is sure, however, is that only four bishops out of eighty-four submitted and that some twenty thousand priests refused to do so: the Catholic Church, in France, was effectively split. While that seemed to the King like the most dread of catastrophes, the Assembly still thought there was, in fact, a good deal to be said for the situation. The faithful who wanted non-juring priests were free to support them and attend their services; and the centuries-old grip of the Church on the everyday life of the country seemed to be at long last broken. The faith itself was strengthened by the very fact that its ministers were no longer part of the establishment.

One major question remained unanswered, though: as yet, Pius VI had failed to respond to the changes; whether or not he opposed them would, obviously, make a huge difference, since the juring priests and bishops, so far, had not done anything contrary to the teachings of the Church. Of course, Louis XVI, and all those who understood the Pontiff and the cardinals who advised him, were not in much doubt as to what the ultimate ruling would be. Indeed, on March 10, 1791, Pius published the breve *Quod aliquantum,* in which the Civil Constitution was denounced as schismatical, the ordination of new bishops under its terms sacrilegious, and all juring priests and prelates suspended; then, for good measure, the Pope also denounced the Declaration of the Rights of Man, thus firmly putting the Church on the side of the reactionaries. And in April the condemnation was reiterated.

To us in the late twentieth century, who are accustomed to a long series of popes denouncing one modern innovation after another, this hardly seems surprising. For the French of 1791, however, the decision was more unexpected. The papacy had been quiescent throughout much of the century, but occasionally, and admittedly under much pressure, it had taken forward-looking measures like the dissolution of the Jesuit order. In France itself, certain bishops, Talleyrand first and foremost, and many priests had been among the reforming majority at the Assembly: it still seemed possible, therefore, that a compromise could be negotiated with the Pope. Consequently, the reaction, upon the publication of his decree, was all the stronger.

Within the month, the Assembly took a series of countermeasures. On the level of relations between states,* Avignon and its surrounding area, the Comtat-Venaissin, were seized by French forces. That, however, was a fairly standard way of applying pressure: the strictly orthodox Louis XIV had not scrupled to use it. Even the break in diplomatic relations could be seen as a not unusual measure of retortion: it, too, had happened before. Far graver was the dismissal of vast numbers of priests throughout the country, with its attendant stirring of popular emotions. Most of the priests who had taken the oath in January now recanted; and in village after village, they were forced to leave their churches while their newly elected replacements usually found nothing but an empty building. At that, the revolutionaries in the village usually retorted, sometimes by jeering at the people attending non-juring rites, sometimes by seizing a few of the old women who followed their former priests and spanking them in public, sometimes by breaking up the services altogether. Just as the risings of 1789–90 were beginning to subside, a new cause of agitation was thus created; and the situation was not likely to get better soon.

The new law, which stirred up the provinces, also made the King's position more awkward than ever: as of January 1791 he had to choose between juring and non-juring priests, and that choice, which to him was purely religious, was seen by most of the Parisians as political. The higher clergy consisted almost exclusively of non-jurors, and its members came from the great aristocratic families; thus equating non-juring and a generally reactionary stance was easy. Louis XVI always took communion at Easter: the great test would come then.

For Louis XVI personally, the new law had other important consequences as well: it demonstrated to him, once and for all, that there could be no compromise with the Revolution. Until then, he had followed the Queen's advice only reluctantly and partially. Now she had been so fully proved right, in her husband's eyes, that there could no longer be any

---

* The popes, in the eighteenth century, still ruled over a substantial section of the Italian peninsula.

question. To all intents and purposes, therefore, the court's policy was now set by Marie Antoinette, especially since Louis XVI also felt responsible toward her for the unpleasantness of her current position. Just as he was duty bound to transmit the full, unhampered royal powers to his son, so he owed his wife all the privileges that went with being Queen of France. Obviously, he had failed in this respect as well, so he felt all the more obligated to follow her advice.

It was just at this time that an important political group began to find expression. A new paper, *L'Ami des patriotes,* staked out a moderate left position in support of the King and the reforms, that is, of a moderate monarchy. "The King who had long wanted almost all the positive things the National Assembly has done," the paper argued, "and who was prevented from carrying them out by the courtiers, the financiers, the magistrates [of the Parlements], the women [i.e., the Queen's friends] and the priests who devoured everything . . . has endorsed all the measures taken by the Assembly; so that from the earliest time it ceased to be in a state of insurrection and the government became legitimate."[3] And a week later, the paper went on to point out that the King was necessary — an especially interesting stand in view of the fact that, just a year earlier, it had occurred to no one that the monarch was superfluous.

"France needs a King," *L'Ami des patriotes* argued on December 18, 1790, "first, because the constitution established by the National Assembly and adopted by the nation must be carried out as the people's sovereign will and because, today, it is an equal crime to breach the constitutional authority of the King or that of the legislature; second, because this form of government is the only one fit for a country where the administrative tasks are very complicated and the territory immense."[4] Whatever its actual merits, this was an argument believed by the vast majority of the people. It seems exceedingly likely that if a vote had been taken at the end of 1790, a very substantial majority would have endorsed a constitutional monarchy. *L'Ami des patriotes* and its backers — the Fayettists — should, therefore, have been on the right track. Unfortunately, the King himself disagreed violently with their notion of his role, a fact that was becoming increasingly clear, and which gave Robespierre credibility when, almost daily, he attacked what he called Louis XVI's "despotism."

Any doubts the royal couple felt about their position vanished upon listening to the delegation the National Assembly sent the Queen on January 1, 1791: "The Assembly," it informed Marie Antoinette, "offers you the wishes it makes for your happiness. It remembers with the strongest interest that you promised you would teach the heir to the throne that he must respect the people's liberty and maintain the laws. . . . And you, whom Providence has called to wear a crown embellished by liberty . . . [you will not forget that] kings are established only to ensure the people's happiness and that their true power is in their obedience to the law."[5] The Deputies could hardly have been more offensive, or have made it clearer to Marie Antoinette that they did not trust her. That they were right not to do so, however, never struck her as a justification of their behavior.

At the time, the Queen was conducting an extensive secret correspondence, the main purpose of which was to undo everything that had been done since the beginning of the Revolution. The letters, Mme Campan, one of the Queen's Women of the Bedchamber, reports, "were ciphered. The method [the Queen] chose can never be penetrated, but it requires the greatest patience in its use. Each correspondent must have a book in the same edition. . . . Agreed-on numbers are used to indicate the page and the line containing the letters, or sometimes the one-syllable words, one wants."[6] Except for the fact that France was not at war, these are activities that in most countries are considered to be treason.

As it was, however, and most reluctantly, Marie Antoinette had just been working hard to prevent an invasion of France by the émigrés that would, she knew, have put the royal family in great danger. Then, on January 5, she called in the Spanish ambassador, the Count de Fernan Nuñez, and confided in him.

Her Majesty began by asking me to keep everything absolutely secret from all here [the ambassador wrote home], even the comte de Montmorin because, although he is the only minister on whom they rely within the Council, the King and Queen mistrust him, with reason, because they know that he will never approve of a violent, counter-revolutionary policy, or of an action independent from the Assembly.

  She then said that she had called me in to tell me, in the King's name and hers, about the current state of affairs here, about her sad position and her plans to end it if, as seemed likely, all the compliance, half-calculating, half-forced, that they displayed today in order to avoid the worst extremities turned out to be insufficient to prevent them.[7]

First, she explained, she had had to prevent the émigré princes from invading France: this would not only have endangered the royal family, it would have united the revolutionaries in the defense of the country, and, furthermore, it would have failed: the King of Sardinia, who was the brother-in-law of both Artois and Provence, would not march alone. A coalition of Sardinia, Spain, and the Emperor was required, but that had yet to be arranged.

As if that were not bad enough, the Queen went on:

> the aristocrats and the Clergy, who feel the King has abandoned them, are turning their backs on him and denigrating him at home and, therefore, in the rest of Europe; as a result, virtually everyone in France, for different reasons, blames the sovereign and diminishes his prestige. . . . If the King cannot manage to dissolve the legislature, and then have another one elected which, being more moderate, will undo the errors of the first, it will be necessary to take a radical decision and leave here, even if it is dangerous, so as to join those who support the crown in the provinces.[8]

All that, the Queen then added, would be useless, however, unless Spain, Switzerland, Sardinia, and the Emperor brought their armies close to the borders, a move that presumably would frighten the revolutionaries. The Emperor, however, was inactive. The ambassador concluded: "I had before me a desperate woman at the very end of her strength in dealing with the present situation."[9]

It must be stressed here that Marie Antoinette also spoke for the King and that, typically, they both thought of adopting half-measures even in the most desperate case: the plan to rally the monarchists in the provinces is clearly the result of Mirabeau's memos, while the massing of foreign armies on every single one of the French borders shows the influence of the émigrés. This confused, ill-prepared plan, which relied on questionable support in the provinces, and the so far unwilling cooperation of the rest of Europe, was likely to beget a catastrophic failure, and the ambassador so advised his minister.

It remains, however, that as early as the beginning of January, the royal couple had decided to flee, and indeed, in short order, the first exploratory measures were taken. In Paris, Fersen had begun planning; on February 7 he wrote Baron Taube, a close friend who was also First Gentleman of the Bedchamber to King Gustavus III of Sweden: "If the King leaves Paris, which will probably happen . . ."[10] This was not idle gossip: Fersen was determined to save the Queen; Gustavus III, alone among the European monarchs, cared personally about Louis XVI and Marie Antoinette. He alone was determined to do everything he could to help them, and Taube served as a discreet intermediary between Fersen and Gustavus.

La Marck, too, was in on the plot. He was, of course, Mirabeau's friend as well as the Queen's, but that was all right: by February Mirabeau had come up with a modified version of his earlier plan, which was also based on the King's escape from Paris. The idea was that the monarch, once safely out of the capital, would get the provinces to demand the dissolution of the Assembly. New elections would then be held, but not until the electoral districts had been carefully drawn by trustworthy royalists. The new, more amenable, Assembly would then start working on a new constitution that would include, among other features, a bicameral system and the right by the King to adjourn and dissolve it, as well as an absolute royal veto. To make doubly sure of the new legislature, only landowners would be allowed to stand for election, and they would, once elected, receive no salary, thus effectively limiting membership to the well-to-do.[11]

Given the overlap in their plans, there was no reason why La Marck should not work for the King as well as for Mirabeau, and in mid-February he went off to Metz, where he met with the marquis de Bouillé. There was a double point to the trip. First, Metz was the fortress to which certain royalists had advocated a retreat ever since July 1789; it was conveniently close to the border and was thought to be garrisoned by faithful troops. Second, Bouillé was the general who had put down the rebellion in Nancy the year before, and was known to be staunchly for the King. Thus, Metz commanded by Bouillé seemed an obvious destination for the royal family if it decided to flee Paris.

As it turned out, however, the situation had sharply deteriorated within the last few months. "When he spoke to me of the troops placed under his orders," La Marck reported about Bouillé, "he told me that they were all gangrened by the revolutionary spirit, and that there were only a few regiments of cavalry on which he could rely."[12] It was not encouraging. Still, there was the cavalry: if only the King could come within riding range of Metz, those troops would protect him. In another way, however, this was disastrous news: both Mirabeau's plan and the royal couple's preference called for remaining within French territory and reconquering the throne from there; once over the border, there was no telling whether the King would ever be able to return, especially since the duc d'Orléans was now back in Paris. Discredited though he was, might not the Assembly give Orléans the crown if the real monarch had gone abroad?

As if that were not worrying enough, there remained another major obstacle: the powers were vying with each other in evasiveness when it came to a firm military commitment. On February 27 Marie Antoinette wrote Leopold II: "Spain has told us it would help us with its army if you, the King of Sardinia, and the Swiss did the same and came to a direct agreement with us about it."[13] True to his nature, however, the Emperor chose to ignore his sister's plight, answering on March 14: "In spite of my goodwill . . . I cannot help you as effectively as I would like without the agreement of several of the main European courts, especially since an agreement with Switzerland and Sardinia alone would not suffice."[14] And Spain, her ambassador explained, could do nothing without the Emperor.

It was all bitter medicine. The solidarity between sovereigns, on which Marie Antoinette was placing her hopes, simply did not exist. Even she admitted it, adding that Prussia's policy was controlled by England, whose enmity against France caused her to favor the current disorders; that Prussia was likely to attack Austria if the latter came to the help of Louis XVI; and that, therefore, not much was likely to happen. "Her Majesty went so far as to say on two occasions," Fernan Nuñez reported, "that if the other courts did not help extricate the royal family from its present situation, it was to be feared *and even to be hoped that they would find themselves one day in the same situation.*"[15]*

About what was likely to happen if they were not able to flee, however, Marie Antoinette and Louis XVI were completely wrong. Both by now

---

* The ambassador's italics.

hated Lafayette, whom they looked on as a traitor: he had, after all, belonged to the Queen's circle in the 1780s and had proved to be an assiduous courtier; he had been abundantly rewarded by Louis XVI for his American triumphs and had answered by professing loyalty to the monarch. To find him now leading, as they saw it, the revolutionary forces was therefore especially galling. Unfortunately, they failed to understand two important aspects of this situation. The first was that Lafayette was only carrying out his ever-explicit commitment to a free constitution. The second was that he was very far from being in control.

Because the royal couple saw the Revolution only as a personal attack on them (and, of course, in a way it was), because they utterly failed to understand the popularity of the reforms carried out by the Assembly, they saw the events as nothing much more than the latest of the aristocratic rebellions that had erupted so often before in French history; only this time it was Lafayette who was masterminding it all for his own advantage. As the Queen explained it to Fernan Nuñez, Lafayette was hoping that the émigré prince de Condé would cross the border with a body of troops; he, Lafayette, would then march forth as the defender of the Assembly, defeat the prince, and force the King to do exactly as he chose. It was a singularly shortsighted view: not only was Lafayette completely unselfish, he was also, as noted, rapidly losing whatever influence he still had over the revolutionaries.

One thing, at least, was sure: it would not be easy for the royal family to go: the departure of the King's old aunts confirmed that obvious fact. On February 21 the fifty-nine-year-old Madame Adélaide and her slightly younger sister, Madame Victoire, left their residence at Bellevue, just outside Paris, for Rome. They did so quite openly, and with passports provided by the foreign minister; yet two days later, when they reached the little town of Arnay-le-duc, they were stopped by the National Guard, who did not think they should be allowed to emigrate. This was, in fact, absolutely unlawful, as the old ladies did not fail to point out; but the Guards sent to the Assembly all the same; and the princesses were saved only by Mirabeau's disdainful remark that he hardly saw that the Deputies need concern themselves with two old bigots who wanted to live near the Pope. Mirabeau's effort was, no doubt, the result of the King's request: greatly to his relief, his aunts were allowed to continue on their way. But if there had been such an uproar at the departure of two unimportant princesses, it was easy to predict what would happen if the King himself tried to leave Paris.

That, however, did not prevent the Queen from planning a departure; unlike Mirabeau's earlier suggestion that they move openly to Saint-Cloud, then to Rambouillet or Fontainebleau and on to a large provincial city, this departure would have to take place in the deepest secrecy. This would not be a king leaving a factious city to join his faithful provincial subjects, it would be the flight of a prisoner away from his jailers. As a consequence, everything had to be ready: in March, for instance, Marie Antoinette sent her own diamonds — as opposed to the crown jewels — to Brussels, where she ordered complete sets of clothes for herself and her children, and she warned several friends and servants that they must be ready to join her there[16] — not, perhaps, the best way of ensuring secrecy.

Early that month, Fersen wrote Taube: "The Queen's courage is undiminished and one cannot sufficiently admire her. The democrats are outraged. . . . The King feels his position but is unable to express himself," and then he added, in cipher, "Everything I wrote the King [of Sweden] as being my idea in regard to the departure of the King and Queen from France, the way of changing things here and the need for foreign help is a plan which is being worked on. No one else knows about it."[17] More people knew than Fersen realized, but he was basically right: Louis XVI and Marie Antoinette were determined to flee and then depend on foreign armies to recover their throne for them. On March 8 Fersen wrote directly about it all to Gustavus III. After explaining that the court had bought several politicians, including Mirabeau, but that this only ensured the royal family's safety and nothing more, he went on to say: "The King will never be King without foreign help. . . . He must leave Paris, but how, and where will he go? All the members of the King's party are incompetent. . . . The King feels his position deeply but considers it his duty to hide his feelings."[18]

Thus the position in the late winter of 1790–91 was alarming in the extreme: the royal family longed to run away, especially as Louis XVI utterly loathed everything he was ostensibly approving; and, unfortunately, the fact that a flight was being prepared was in the air — in part because there must have been leaks, in part because it was such an obvious possibility. That, in turn, spurred on the revolutionaries, who were willing to go to virtually any length to keep the royal family in Paris as the only means (or so they thought) of preventing a foreign invasion. Amid all these tensions, the Assembly went on legislating as if it were doing so in the midst of peace and plenty.

For the Paris mob, the first months of 1791 were marked by two greatly resented phenomena: a local economic crisis, and a slow movement of the Assembly's majority toward the center and away from a radicalization of the Revolution.

The first was the most generally felt. By March, the assignat had already lost 15 percent of its value. This provoked a corresponding rise in the price of daily necessities — bread, wine — which came just as unemployment was spreading. At the same time, the Assembly ended the old authoritarian structures that bound apprentices and masters in the various trades and dissolved the guilds, which, by controlling supply, had also set the prices of manufactured or handmade articles. The Deputies were acting for the best of reasons: liberty, they thought, ought to apply everywhere and to everyone; the markets must also be free. Unfortunately, that also suddenly deprived many workers of whatever security they had had until then. More and more, the emerging proletariat began to perceive a basic division between itself and the well-to-do members of the Assembly. Far from being better off as a result of the reforms, they were even poorer, and that was not something they were prepared to accept.

Their resentment was shared by the lower middle class, men whose income was too low to qualify them as voters, and who resented this tremendously. What now mattered to them was no longer liberty, which availed them little, but equality, which they were denied: they wanted the same rights as their more prosperous fellow citizens, and began to think a new, violent dose of revolution was needed to bring this about.

To all these causes of unpopularity the Assembly had also added another: just as had been the case at the very end of the ancien régime, the deficit was soaring, and the debts of the state remained unpaid, or were paid very late and partially. Was it for this, people asked, that the Bastille had fallen and Versailles been stormed? If the deficit, before 1789, had been due to the greed of the aristocracy, then the current problem must be due to the greed of the rich. For the first time, in 1791, a split appeared within the middle class; and it promised more agitation.

What France was experiencing was the first instance of what has since become a well-known phenomenon. With the onset of inflation and the sales of the Church's estates, one class of people was markedly helped by the new economics: the farmers who owned their own land. The price of foodstuffs was rising, while the cost of production remained steady, and land was becoming accessible for enlarging existing farms. As the Assembly failed to cope with the deficit, in fact, this became ever truer. The unrealistic budget of 1791 had allowed for some 639 million livres in expenditures, 302 million of which was to pay clerical salaries and pensions; and only 60 million was scheduled to be covered by land sales. Meanwhile, just as had been the case for the last two years, the tax system was thoroughly disorganized, and people repeatedly failed to pay. As a result, between March and September, more than 250 million livres was transferred from the caisse de l'extraordinaire by means, essentially, of assignats; and as the land sales speeded up, the price of land began to drop so that, starting in 1791, a vast restructuring of property took place. More than anything, perhaps, this was a major achievement of the Revolution: not only did it generate prosperity in the long run by eliminating underexploited holdings, it also created a secure and prosperous rural middle class.

None of this helped the unemployed in Paris, though, and Paris was where things happened. That became extremely clear on February 28: as the Assembly was busy debating whether to let Mesdames Adélaïde and Victoire continue their journey, a riot began in the working-class Faubourg Saint-Antoine. In short order the mob, which had been so effective in July and October 1789, was at work again. This time, it was the neighboring castle of Vincennes that they decided to attack.

Although it was also a medieval fortress, with a residential wing that had been added later, Vincennes had not really been used as a proper prison for a very long time.* The Assembly, however, had ordered repair work so as to reconvert it to its earlier use, and that was seen by the mob as a direct provocation, even though the prison was not to be controlled

---

* Napoleon promptly made it a prison again. It is now a museum.

by the King. After taking it over, therefore, the rioters started to demolish the parapets on the towers.

This was clearly an unlawful act, and there was little Lafayette could do except stop it. He called together the National Guard, marched to Vincennes, and retook it from the mob, thus further injuring his popularity and widening the gulf between the Assembly and the people. Luckily for him, however, he was able, the same day, to humiliate the King and the aristocracy by disarming and imprisoning the so-called Knights of the Dagger, a group of noblemen who had come together to defend the royal family.

As the mob began rioting in Vincennes that day, it had become clear that, if it had its way, the Palace might be attacked next. It is only about a mile and a half from the Faubourg Saint-Antoine to the Tuileries; both are on the same side of the river; and the Palace was clearly indefensible. It was not unreasonable, therefore, to suppose the King and Queen were in real danger, and a motley group of about four hundred noblemen, some armed with swords and knives, some carrying rifles, gathered at the Palace in order to protect them.

The very fact that they did showed clearly how little they mattered and how vulnerable the monarch actually was: had the mob really stormed the Palace, the Knights of the Dagger would just have been massacred along with the royal family. Indeed, it would have required disciplined, fully armed troops and several pieces of cannon to make a difference. Still, when Lafayette, returning from Vincennes, reported to the King, he found himself jostled and insulted in the antechambers by the noblemen in question. Nothing could have been sillier: the National Guard was on call; it came, disarmed the group, and removed them to jail, where they spent the next two weeks.

In itself, of course, this was a meaningless incident that simply allowed *L'Ami du peuple* to headline: "Urgent need for the National Guard to take over the posts and lodgings of the Swiss Guard at the Tuileries."[19] Yet it had a number of major consequences. First, it showed conclusively how little the nobles still living in Paris need be feared; then it exposed the King's vulnerability. More important, it positioned him clearly with the former *privilégiés* against the new popular forces. He had, after all, been quite ready to allow the Knights to surround him and had not thought for a moment of calling on the National Guard to defend him.

Thus this unwise gathering played an important role in isolating the monarch and destroying whatever trust the people still had in him. Moreover, for Louis XVI personally, it was the proof that he was essentially Lafayette's prisoner.

The incident also contributed to the weakening of the true constitutional monarchists, who, even as they were becoming more powerful in the Assembly, were losing all popular support. "By what strange fatality do we see the parties endorsing the most dangerous, the falsest opinions?" *L'Ami des patriotes* wondered on March 19. *"L'ami du Roi . . .* claims that the decrees regarding the Clergy are due to the people's pressure, to its menacing attitude, and the author of the *Révolutions de France* [Camille Desmoulins] claims that the Assembly's best decrees result from the people's threats. In every circumstance, this odd coalition of the reactionaries and the [left-wing] factions is clear."[20] In fact, the right's refusal to accept reforms played into the hands of the far left, who could quite accurately claim that no changes were any longer possible without further risings.

It thus seems sadly appropriate that in mid-March Mirabeau fell ill: the solution — constitutional monarchy — for which he stood was no longer viable. By the twenty-ninth he was on his deathbed, writing in a last letter to La Marck: "I take with me the life of the monarchy; after my death, the factions will tear it to pieces."[21] In fact, the great orator's secret association with the King had utterly failed to influence the Assembly; he had ceased making a difference. While his death, on April 2, seemed like a great event at the time, it was simply the passing of an already spent force.

With Mirabeau gone, a new set of leaders gained strength: often called the triumvirs, they were Alexandre de Lameth, Antoine Barnave, and Adrien Duport. All in their early thirties, they had sat on the left of the Assembly in 1789, and had opposed the veto and the second chamber. All were active in passing the Civil Constitution of the Clergy and, eventually, demanding that all priests take the oath to the constitution. Although never antimonarchist per se, they frequently denounced the court and attacked Lafayette for being too moderate. Indeed, Barnave was a theoretical republican: he did not think that France was ready yet for a change of regime, but expected it would eventually take place.

Although the triumvirs were unquestionably liberals, they were also men of property, and they found the trend of events in March 1791 highly alarming; thus, they moved toward the center and even considered restoring to the King some of the powers that had been wrenched from him. The Revolution, they felt, had gone far enough: the time had come to consolidate it and bring it a measure of stability.

They were materially assisted in their efforts by the eloquence of Robespierre — not because he agreed with them but because he frightened the Assembly into supporting them. A lengthy debate on the status of mulattos in the French West Indies helped draw the lines: the triumvirs, backing the men of property, wished the colonies to be governed by their white residents. Robespierre and his friends insisted that the mulattos were entitled to the vote. As for the slaves, no one mentioned them at all. In the end, the mulattos were given the vote, partly because Robespierre's denunciation of racism proved effective. But the ultimate effect of the debate was to frighten the triumvirs and the Assembly's majority into the conservative camp.

Unfortunately, the new support for a stronger monarchy promptly came up against the problem invariably encountered by all the progressives who hoped to work with Louis XVI: absolute noncooperation. As far as the King was concerned, the world was sharply divided between good and evil; the line between them passed well to the right of Lafayette, and the triumvirs had been well to his left. Their recent move to the center, so plain to all intelligent observers, quite escaped the King, for whom it represented merely a different degree of unacceptability. And since a constitutional monarchy cannot function without a willing monarch, the evolution of the majority proved to be wholly ineffective.

Louis XVI, as noted, was getting ready to end the regime altogether by removing himself. Still, Mercy, the Austrian ambassador, in his last communications before leaving his post in April, exuded nothing but gloom regarding the unfulfilled requirements of an escape. "No decisive change favorable to the King can happen in France without a civil war," he wrote home and told the Queen at the end of March. "It remains to be established whether (1) it is possible to escape from Paris without great danger; (2) there is a safe refuge which can be relied on; (3) one can count on a considerable following, some faithful troops, a devoted province, and enough money to last for two or three months."[22] The answer to all these questions, he thought, was in the negative. There was nothing to do, therefore, but wait and hope that the Revolution, by going too far, would provoke a reaction.

That, however, was more than Marie Antoinette was willing to accept: she had waited long enough, she felt, for a counterrevolution to start spontaneously. Now it was time to go. On April 1 Fersen wrote Taube (and therefore Gustavus III) that the decision had finally been made. "The position of the King of France being every day more unbearable," he explained,

> Their Majesties have resolved to use every possible mean to change it: having in vain relied on patience, kindness, and sacrifices of all sorts, they now mean to try force; but since the Assemby . . . has destroyed [the royalist part of the army] . . . they feel they need . . . help from abroad. Their Majesties can rely on a strong party in France and a safe refuge near the northern border. M. de Bouillé is in charge of all that. . . . The King would like to leave Paris in two months at the latest, but the date depends on various answers he is expecting. . . . The departure will be clandestine and take place during the night.[23]

And the next day Fersen wrote Breteuil, Louis XVI's secret envoy abroad, about his master's latest decisions: "The King still intends to leave in the last half of May. . . . He will sacrifice everything in order to carry out his project. . . . He will appear to accept the need to join the Revolution completely in order to fool the factions. . . . He will constantly carry out the wishes of the mob so as to give them no pretext for an insurrection . . . and inspire the trust that he will need so badly when he leaves Paris."[24]

In fact, the King's only regret was that he could not leave sooner. Easter was approaching, he was firmly determined to take communion only at the hands of a non-juring priest. That, strictly speaking, was his right; but the reaction, should he do so in public, was highly predictable: once again, the mob would rise, prompted by what it would consider as an antirevolutionary act. There was no telling how it would all end. Still, the royal family's escape required careful planning; it was impossible to organize everything by mid-March, so the King really had no choice. At least, he thought, he could go to Saint-Cloud, where thc relative privacy he enjoyed would allow him to take communion without provoking the mob.

That decision should not have caused any problem: after all, the royal family had spent most of the previous summer at Saint-Cloud, and virtually no one had opposed their stay there. It was decided that the King and Queen would move there on April 18.

At this point, we can rely, once more, on a very special eyewitness. That it should be Count Fersen, a foreigner, would indeed be extraordinary were it not for the young man's relationship to Marie Antoinette.

Fersen, who was thirty-six in 1791, was tall, slender, and extraordinarily handsome. A great ladies' man, he had broken many hearts and had, at that moment, a mistress to whom he showed very little consideration. It was not so much that he loved Marie Antoinette as a woman; it was more that this passionate and extreme monarchist was fascinated by the Queen. What is certain is that he had always gone to great lengths to protect her good name, even volunteering to fight in America when, in 1780, rumor began linking them. With the coming of the Revolution, he realized, of course, that Marie Antoinette needed all the help she could get; and so, much as the current situation offended his right-wing opinions, he stayed in Paris and began to pay court, daily and often secretly, not just to Marie Antoinette but to Louis XVI as well. Whether, during this period, he also became the Queen's lover is an unanswerable question; but, as noted before, given his and Marie Antoinette's characters, it seems unlikely.

Thus it was that on April 18 Fersen was part of the little group accompanying the sovereigns; he tells us what happened when they tried to go to Saint-Cloud.[25]

At eleven-thirty, the King attended the mass [in the Palace chapel]; before that, M. Bailly had come to warn him that his departure was causing unrest and that the people seemed opposed to it. The King answered that he had given all the French the freedom to go about as they pleased, that it would indeed be extraordinary if he alone could not go two leagues away for a little fresh air and that he intended to leave. He came down with the Queen, Madame Elisabeth, the children, and Mme de Tourzel, and as the carriages had not been able to reach the Court of the Princes,* he tried to go to them in the Carrousel. Upon

* The entrance (and exit) of the Palace of the Tuileries faced the Louvre. First came an

being told that there was a huge crowd, he stopped in the middle of the Court and the Queen suggested that they use the one carriage that had arrived, even though it was only a berlin. They all got into it, and when it reached the gates, the National Guard refused to open them and let the King go. In vain, M. de Lafayette spoke to them, explaining that only enemies of the constitution would behave like this, that by restricting the King's movement, they made him look like a prisoner, and that it would invalidate all the decrees he had promulgated. He was answered only by invective and assurances that the King would not be allowed to leave. The most insulting terms were used to the King: that he was a f[ucking] aristocrat, a b[ugger] of an aristocrat, a fat pig; that he was unfit to reign; that he should be deposed and replaced by the duc d'Orléans; that he was just a civil servant; that he was paid twenty-five millions, that it was too much, and that he must do what he was told . . . that he must send away the aristocrats and the non-juring priests who surrounded him. . . . As the grenadiers [of the National Guard] arrived, they swore . . . they would shoot the King if he tried to leave.

Like many Parisians, the grenadiers feared retaliation by the mob if the King got away. For the next two and a half hours, the scene continued. Inside the courtyard, a crowd of angry National Guardsmen — many of them small tradesmen — surrounded the carriage; outside the gates stood the infuriated mob from which, no matter how angry they were, the Guardsmen protected the King. Bailly, who had been asked by Lafayette to proclaim martial law and thus enable the regular army — still composed of professional soldiers — to intervene, refused to do so; the men of the Guard, who kept arriving, told the General that they refused to use force against the mob; and all the while, the royal family's attendants were at best insulted, at worst severely manhandled. At one point, the carriage was surrounded by National Guard grenadiers who, tears running down their cheeks, according to Fersen, told the King: " 'Sire, your people love you, they adore you, but don't go; you life would be in danger; you are badly advised; we want you to send the priests away, we are afraid of losing you.' " Finally, the King ordered the carriage back to the Palace door. "As he came out of it," Fersen continues, "the soldiers

---

enclosed courtyard, the Court of the Princes; its gates opened on to the Place du Carrousel and the street that crossed it.

crowded around him. Some were saying: 'We will defend you.' The Queen answered, looking at them proudly: 'Yes, we count on it, but now you must admit we are not free.' As they crowded into the vestibule, the Queen lifted the Dauphin in her arms, Madame Elisabeth took Madame [Royale, the King's daughter], and they went as fast as they could; the King then slowed down, and once they had entered the Queen's apartment, the King turned around and said firmly: 'Stop, grenadiers!' They all stopped as suddenly as if they had lost their legs.''

What had happened, in fact, was a combination of something very new with some very old habits. Keeping the King in Paris against his will was no novelty: it had happened first to Charles V in the 1350s. Because the King was not only a ruler but also a kind of totem, keeping him physically present was extremely important. Again, he was, in that respect, rather like the statues of the gods in certain primitive cultures: the people whip them if things go badly, but would panic if they were removed. In 1791 many Parisians still retained the inchoate feeling that as long as the King was there all would work out in the end, but that his departure would be followed by appalling catastrophes. It was, in part, to remove the monarchy from this situation — which he had himself experienced as a youth — that Louis XIV had built Versailles.

By 1791, however, much had changed. Louis XVI was perfectly right to point out that all Frenchmen, himself included, were legally free in their movements; by keeping him at the Tuileries, the people — or rather the mob — were refusing him the very liberty they themselves enjoyed. That this should be the case said something about the transformation of the Revolution. A movement that had begun as a demand for liberty — of the person, of the press, of religion — and fairness was now becoming an instrument of revenge, a means to oppress the former oppressors.

In that sense, a measure of agreement between the mob and the lower bourgeoisie existed: both were intent on preventing the King's departure; both wanted him to send away non-juring priests and aristocrats. But there was also a radical difference between the two groups that Louis XVI and his advisers utterly failed to perceive or exploit, in spite of the fact that it was visible to the naked eye. The shopkeepers and successful artisans not only had premises that might well be sacked in case of widespread rioting, they also were decently if often modestly dressed;

and, when doing their service with the National Guard, they wore the special uniforms designed by Lafayette. Even if their politics were radical, they had something to lose, and they remembered it; they were the people who wanted the King to cooperate so as to establish a stable, but utterly reformed, society in which they could prosper.

The mob, on the other hand, had nothing to lose. It consisted largely of unemployed workers who were rapidly becoming permanent agitators: they filled the tribunes of the Assembly, they crowded the streets, and they looked like what they were. Dirty, badly dressed, wearing trousers instead of breeches, the women often in rags, they were smelly, noisy, pushy, and frequently abusive. Far from wanting stability, they yearned for an upheaval so complete that they would come out on top. To them the King was the enemy.

At the same time, they had something in common with the lower bourgeoisie. Both groups were disenfranchised; thus, while their economic goals were very different, politically they were similar: they hated not just the "aristocrats" but also the well-to-do Deputies who were, at that very moment, turning conservative. It was the National Guard, many of whose members were too poor to have the vote, not the mob, who, as Louis XVI sat in his carriage, insulted him and even threatened to shoot him.

This attitude was something very new indeed. In all the earlier Parisian risings, the King, even if he was a prisoner of the city, was still treated with the greatest reverence. Now, for the first time that respect, that awe, was gone: to this crowd the monarch was just another exploiter who deserved punishment, an overpaid civil servant in a country where civil servants were notoriously disliked. And so it was that the royal family had good reason to fear for its life.

The extent to which the age-old respect for the monarchy had shrunk was made even clearer, on April 18, by the deliberations of the assembly of the Paris département. "An Address will immediately be presented to the King," it resolved, "to ask him to send away from his person the enemies of the Constitution who seek to beguile him by giving him perfidious advice."[26] There was not a word about the riot, not a word about the King's virtual imprisonment at the Tuileries. Indeed, far from commiserating with the monarch, the Address, which was presented to him on the nineteenth, scolded him firmly: "The enemies of freedom, who feared your patriotism, said to themselves: 'We will alarm his conscience.' Hiding their smarting pride under a holy veil, they cry hypocritical tears over the fate of their religion. Those, Sire, are the men who surround you. We see with chagrin that you favor non-juring priests, that you are served only by enemies of the constitution, and we fear that these all-too-obvious preferences may denote your true disposition."[27]

There was the hitch: no matter what he said, or what decrees he promulgated, no matter how often he swore to observe the as yet unfinished constitution, it was perfectly plain from his everyday behavior that Louis XVI loathed the new world in which he found himself. It was bad luck, of course, that he was so pious, and that therefore the presence of non-juring priests struck him as essential to saving his soul; but in any event, he would have been more than human if he had not preferred to have about him the men — great nobles all — to whom he was accustomed and whom he considered his friends.

Because of this, there was no possible compromise. As the Revolution progressed, the King had to be coerced if the people were not to think of him as the fount of all counterrevolutionary attitudes; and the more he was coerced, the more he detested the current state of things. Nor was there any remedy in sight: brought up in a state where legalism was a habit, both the King and the Assembly went on behaving as if the law and legal processes still mattered, when in fact they were despised by the only power that really mattered, that of the National Guard and the mob.

The importance of legalism was clearly evident in the speech Louis XVI made to the Assembly when he visited it on the afternoon of April 18. After complaining about being prevented from going to Saint-Cloud, and referring to "the multitude who thinks it is upholding the law when it is breaking it," he went on:

The nation must prove I am free: nothing matters more to confirm the promulgations and acceptances I have given your decrees. I maintain, therefore, my intention of going to Saint-Cloud, and the National Assembly will understand its necessity. It seems that, in order to provoke uprisings among my faithful people, whose love I have deserved by all I have done for them, an attempt has been made at creating doubts about my feeling for the constitution. I have accepted and sworn to maintain that constitution. . . . I have no wish other than the people's happiness and that can only come about if the laws are observed and all the legitimate, constitutional authorities obeyed.[28]

Here, indeed, was the central dilemma of the Revolution: the reliance on pretense. Louis XVI, when he claimed to be satisfied with the constitution, was lying; we know, after all, that well before April 18 he had decided to flee; and that fact, being widely suspected, meant that all his complaints were, in effect, void. Further, although it is difficult to see how he could have addressed a body other than the Assembly, he was still behaving as if the latter had the power to clear his way to Saint-Cloud; but as long as the National Guard collaborated with the mob, the Assembly was powerless.

Had that body been willing to admit the fact, it is at least conceivable that a reaction against these recent excesses might have taken place. Instead, it went on pretending that all was well, a sure way of causing more trouble. "A worried agitation is inseparable from the progress of freedom," it answered the King. "In the midst of efforts made by good citizens to reassure the people, alarming rumors are started. . . . Sire, the cowardly enemies of liberty and the constitution are yours also. All hearts are yours; as you want the people's happiness, so does it demand yours. When you come in this hall to tighten the links that tie you to the Revolution, you strengthen the friends of peace and the law; they will tell the people your heart has not changed and all concern, all distrust will vanish."[29] It was hardly possible to be more unrealistic: no one really supposed the King had come to tighten his links with the Revolution. As for the prospect of peace, it was, at the very least, elusive; but then, what was the Assembly to do? If it squarely recognized the fact that the King was a prisoner, that he loathed the reforms and was now widely distrusted, then a constitutional monarchy was no longer possible. Given that the majority was not willing to accept this most unpalatable fact, it was bound to ignore reality. Unfortunately, that made both the lower bourgeoisie and the mob, who could see through this unconvincing pretense, all the more determined to reaffirm reality.

As a result, the tumult continued: on the twenty-first, a great crowd assembled before the Palace in response to the rumor that the Dauphin had been spirited away. There was nothing to the rumor, of course, but even so, Bailly wanted to have the gates opened for all to come in, and it was only with the greatest difficulty that Lafayette convinced him this was an invitation to disaster.[30]

As for Lafayette himself, his own position was now crystal-clear: he had ordered the National Guard to clear a path for the King and been disobeyed. Since he could hardly function as commander if his men disobeyed him, he resigned, because once before, after the murder of Berthier and Foulon, this move had been highly effective; but almost two years had passed. Once again, to be sure, he was begged to take back his resignation, but whereas the first time the entreaties were accompanied by promises of good behavior, this time no such reassurances were proffered. In the end he resumed his functions with no guarantees for the future. It could hardly have been clearer: henceforth the Guard would obey his orders whenever it felt like it.

That left Louis XVI and Marie Antoinette virtually unprotected. By the end of the week, most of the remaining courtiers were gone, partly because the King and Queen urged them to seek their own safety, partly because they wanted to have easy access to a non-juring priest, and the royal couple hoped to follow them in short order. On April 19 Marie Antoinette wrote the Spanish ambassador; after explaining that she no longer thought it safe to receive him as before, she went on to ask whether she could count on the Spanish army when the time came, adding that she was demanding similar assurances from her brother and from the King of Sardinia. Naturally, Fernan Nuñez passed the request on to his minister in Madrid, although he cannot have had many doubts about the likely answer. He also provided his minister with a sharply accurate description of the situation: "Even the hard-working artisans are fed up and desperate. They say: 'We took up arms to defend the King, the constitution, and the decrees he has signed, the same decrees we know to be invalid without that signature. And now, after he has signed them and we have undertaken to defend them, the King is trying to find pretexts to annul them, and he lies to us. That we will never allow. When he does not approve of a law, let him not sign it.' "[31] Of course, Louis XVI had signed away in the belief that the very excesses of the laws in question would bring about a reaction; instead, he had created so well set a trap for himself that he could no longer escape it.

He should, however, not be wholly blamed for it: the advice given him by Mercy, for instance, and many others as well, comforted his own inclination. No one could have been more remote from the leaders of the Enlightenment than Louis XVI, but, even so, he shared with them a number of basic (and mistaken) assumptions about human nature. Man, it was thought, was an essentially rational creature, capable of momentary excesses, but bound in the end to see the light; and progress, which was inevitable, was also, by definition, slow and cautious. No one in 1791 still really thought that the people would cheerfully applaud the massacre of an entire class; no one thought that resentment and rage would overwhelm more practical considerations, such as the fact that excessive change was likely to make everyone's life more difficult. As a result, all those who relied on enlightened self-interest to stop the Revolution were utterly wrong at the same time that they were perfectly in tune with contemporary thought. It cannot be sufficiently emphasized that the kind of massive, bloody upheaval with which we have become so familiar still seemed impossible in so advanced a civilization as that of France at the end of the eighteenth century.

After April 18, 1791, however, the possibility that men were not as civilized as all that began to loom. On April 20 Marie Antoinette wrote Mercy, now safely ensconced in Brussels: "The guard which surrounds us is that which endangers us the most. Our very lives are threatened. . . . Our position is dreadful, we must end it by next month, the King wants it even more than I."[32] On the twenty-first, the alarmed La Marck wrote Marie Antoinette: "The peril is great . . . and when my duty is to tell all, the Queen must have the strength to hear all. . . . The King must behave as if he had no other enemy than himself. . . . The salvation of the royal family demands its immediate attendance at the parish mass,"[33] where, of course, a juring priest was officiating. That, however, was advice Louis XVI simply could not accept: he was ready to compromise on everything except the salvation of his soul. Instead, the preparations for flight were speeded up. For the first time, the King was widely menaced; crowds went about promising, at best to humiliate him, at worst to murder him: the respect that, until then, had clung to him was now utterly gone, and that was, in itself, far more important than all the laws passed by the Assembly.

Nor was this a fact deplored only by the royalists. By now, even the moderates were thoroughly alarmed. *L'Ami des patriotes,* on April 23, made it very plain: "There is no denying the fact that the King's departure was forcibly prevented," it wrote. "The authorities were unable to end this violence, this unlawful behavior. . . . There can be no doubt that an army that disobeys its leaders in such an important circumstance will disobey them again in a thousand others. . . . Notice that the National Assembly, long the idol of the multitude, is losing more credibility every day . . . for having too often substituted its own authority to that of the law."[34] This was a point familiar to the Assembly's new majority. Throughout May, it began to pass decrees aimed at restoring order: on the tenth it created a High Court whose jurisdiction was to be crimes against the security of the state; on the twenty-second it carefully defined the right of petition and withdrew it from all organized collectivities; in early June it banned all unions among working men, a measure with obvious economic consequences, but one also meant to prevent the forming of political associations. At the same time, Duport, one of the triumvirs, was elected president of the new Paris Criminal Court; that appeared to ensure that agitators would be treated with due severity.

This was all very well; but the fact remained that no one was in any position to ensure that the new laws would be obeyed. Marat was feeling so confident of the fact that his attacks on Lafayette took on a new tenor: just a few months earlier, he had accused the General of the most dire and bloody plots; now he was content merely to make fun of him. "As soon as Mottié was sure that the gold he had been passing out among the battalions [of the National Guard] had had the right effect . . . he went to the Palace there to start rejoicings and appeared before Antoinette in a grenadier's uniform. When the circle of our gods and goddesses was thoroughly reassured, he went off for a moment, took up a rifle, and stood guard at Antoinette's door. . . . This farce amused everyone, and all competed in making fun of the poor Parisian Guard."[35] It is always galling to think that others are laughing about you, and the General could therefore be expected to resent it; but clearly he was no longer thought to be a dangerous adversary.

Of course, none of this mattered to the King and Queen: they simply tried to ensure that their imminent flight would be successful. On April 30 Bouillé wrote Fersen: "It will be necessary to send us as much money as possible to cover the early expenses. . . . We suppose you must have ready money abroad; it is as indispensable as eight or ten thousand

Austrian auxiliaries.''[36] On May 9 Bouillé added: ''All being considered, the shortest and safest road will be through Meaux, Montmirail, Châlons, Ste Menehould, Varennes, Dun, and Stenay. From Ste Menehould on to Stenay, there will be substantial groups [of cavalry] to serve as the escort. . . . If they leave at night, and travel through the next night, they will arrive on the second day.''[37] Almost all was set, therefore: the itinerary, the escort, the financial provision. There still remained the unsolved problem of help from Austria, though, and Marie Antoinette addressed herself to this on May 22.

She knew, of course, that Leopold II was not about to go to war with France, so this time she scaled down her demands considerably. ''We have always meant to withdraw from this dreadful situation,'' she wrote her brother, ''and to that end, we have dealt with M. de Breteuil* on the one hand and M. de Bouillé on the other. Only the two of them, and a third person here [Fersen] are in the know. . . . We plan to go to Montmédy.** M. de Bouillé is in charge of the troops and the ammunition to be sent there, but he is very anxious to have you order some eight to ten thousand men to Luxembourg, available to come on our request (which will of course be made only once we are safe), so that they may join us, as much to serve as an example to our troops as to keep them within their duty.''[38] From the Emperor's point of view, this was a relatively acceptable request; aware that, after all, his sister's life was in danger, he agreed on June 6 to do what she had asked. It no doubt also occurred to him that having crowned heads massacred by an enraged people would set a deplorable precedent.

Just what Louis XVI and Marie Antoinette were to do once they reached Montmédy, however, remained an unanswered question. Much earlier, Mirabeau had wanted the King to set himself up in a large provincial town, there to gather a new majority around himself; but that was not the plan now. Rather, the royal family was to make for a small fortress right next to the border where they would be protected by Austrian troops. That might well ensure their immediate safety, if indeed

---

* Breteuil, as Louis XVI's secret envoy to the powers, was to arrange for an armed congress aimed at restoring the ancien régime.

** Montmédy was a small fortified town right near the border with the Austrian Netherlands and only some fifteen miles from Luxembourg. It is about 160 miles east-northeast of Paris.

they reached Montmédy; but if the French troops under Bouillé were so unreliable as to need the presence of an Austrian army to guarantee their fidelity, the outlook for a reconquest of France was extremely bleak.

The plan had thus completely changed: instead of the flight serving to change the regime, the most the royal couple now hoped was that it would get them out of Paris. On that basis, planning proceeded apace. On May 29 Fersen gave Bouillé the latest news: "The departure is set for the twelfth of next month. . . . We will be receiving the two million livres of the civil list only on the seventh or the eighth and there is a very democratic chambermaid in attendance on the Dauphin who only goes off duty on the eleventh. The agreed-on route will be followed."[39] As it turned out, however, nothing was ready by that date. On June 13 Fersen updated it all: "The departure is set for the twentieth at midnight, absolutely without delay. A bad chambermaid of the Dauphin, who goes off duty only on the Monday morning, has forced this postponement to the Monday night."[40]

There were other anxieties as well in the interim. On June 13 Fersen noted in his diary that, according to a new rumor, the guard around the Palace was to be doubled and all the carriages searched. That turned out to be untrue. On the sixteenth, Fersen visited the Queen and left with various items that were wanted on the trip; no one suspected anything. On the nineteenth, finally, he saw the King, who gave him the Great Seal and 800 livres in coins with which to pay the postilions: at long last, all was set. The royal family was to travel under false names; the passports, which would be checked in every major town, as was then the custom, were made out to a Swedish national, the Baroness de Korff, who was supposedly traveling with her majordomo, her children, her sister, and her children's governess.

That last day in Paris, Fersen told the King and Queen when secretly to leave the Palace; it was agreed that if they were stopped Fersen himself would go on to Brussels and try to convince the powers to help. Marie Antoinette, weeping abundantly, told her friend that she would never forget what he had done for her, and left him at six. The guard, he noted, was normal: in spite of the rumors according to which the royal family was to flee, no extraordinary precautions had been taken. Lafayette did come to the Palace every night, but he invariably left by ten or ten-thirty: after that, the coast would be clear. In just two years, the Revolution, which so many had wanted and which held such golden expectations, had come to this: Louis XVI's only hope was to escape from his capital; his only friend in Paris was a Swedish count who was in love with his wife. How could things have been allowed to reach such an extremity?

PART TWO

The Revolution was the revolt of one part of the nation against another part, that of the Third Estate against the Nobility. . . . The King was attacked, less as a sovereign than as the head of the feudal system; he was not reproached with breaking the laws, but there was a will for freedom and a new constitution. . . . Louis XVI could have made a key decision . . . , that of transforming himself from the head of the *feudal system* to that of the *nation*.

— Napoleon[1]

CHAPTER SEVEN

Prelude to Disaster

:　　:　　:

JUST twenty-one years before, in 1770, France had celebrated the marriage of the sixteen-year-old heir to the throne and the fifteen-year-old Marie Antoinette, Archduchess of Austria. Although this was a purely political union meant to reaffirm the strength of the alliance between the two monarchies, the young couple soon became a symbol of hope and renewal. The Dauphin and Dauphine, indeed, seemed to embody everything for which the French yearned: they were young, virtuous, a couple in love who provided the strongest contrast to the corruption of the court. They were also the future King and Queen of France, so when they made their official entry into Paris in 1772,* the capital gave them their first taste of popularity. As their carriage crossed the city, it was surrounded by huge, cheering crowds. When, in 1774, the new King and Queen, fleeing the risk of smallpox, from which Louis XV had just died, moved to La Muette, at the edge of the city, they were again able to see and hear for themselves the love their people bore them. Never, observers noted, had monarchs been so popular: here, clearly, was the start of a golden era.

Indeed, the press could not find enough compliments for them. Louis XVI, the papers said, was young but serious, caring, and virtuous; Marie Antoinette was not only beautiful but kind and compassionate; together they would rule, gently and fairly, so as to bring forth an age of peace,

---

* They had been married for two years, but, like the King and court, they lived at Versailles and had not yet officially visited Paris.

prosperity, and progress; and the French agreed wholeheartedly with the press. Every time the new monarchs appeared in public, they received the most rapturous of greetings. No reign, people agreed, had begun better.

When her husband succeeded to the throne in May 1774, Marie Antoinette, Archduchess of Austria and Queen of France, looked like a dream come true. Tall, slender, graceful, she was seductive without being really pretty; but even if her eyes were too small and her Habsburg lip too pronounced, she made up for it with a perfect complexion, a charming smile, and a shapely figure — small waist, generous bosom — shown off to advantage by the current fashions. She walked beautifully, apparently floating over the slippery parquet floors of Versailles. As for her dancing, as critical an observer as Horace Walpole said that when she failed to follow the music's beat, then the music was wrong. She was famous for her grand, sweeping curtsey. Above all, at nineteen, she had the charm of youth.

That so comely a sovereign should also be a model of elegance seemed an added boon. Better yet, the extravagant styles worn at court seemed just right for her: coiffures, by 1774, had become towering monuments of powdered curls, jewels, and feathers, while the richly embroidered dresses that went with them were decorated with more jewels and swathes of fabric looped, overlooped, draped, and tasseled, completed by tight, generously décolleté bodices and skirts held up by panniers so immense that they soon grew to be as much as twenty feet around. In these extravagant costumes the young Queen looked enchanting.

Of course, charm was a great quality in a new sovereign; but there was more to Marie Antoinette than that. She was known to be strictly virtuous, a refreshing quality after the late King's succession of official mistresses. She was obviously in love with her husband, and people sighed with delight as they watched the young couple strolling arm in arm. She was also close to her new family and dined several times a week with her two brothers- and sisters-in-law. She was even fond of the aunts, the sour, old-maid daughters of Louis XV; and she was widely rumored to be kindness itself.

Anecdotes were repeated about her that added still further to her popularity. There was the time, for instance, when in the course of a hunt a peasant had been wounded by a maddened stag. Leaping down from her carriage, she had organized a relief party, ordered the patient into her carriage — an unheard-of breach of the sacrosanct etiquette — and seen to it that he received the best of care. Again, she had taken in one of the children of a destitute family and was having him brought up at her expense while helping the parents. Here, obviously, was a Queen who cared about the people.

Louis XVI, too, seemed the very pattern of a good king. He had simple tastes, disliked luxury, and had no mistresses. In sharp contrast to Louis XV, his grandfather, he was faithful to his wife. He expressed the best of intentions: his first duty, he said, was to his people; and he earned himself immense popularity, right at the start of his reign, by dismissing Louis XV's hated ministers and recalling the Parlement, a judicial body with political ambitions that the late King had abolished. He was, unfortunately, shy and awkward, but already, under his wife's influence, he had improved noticeably. Now, with the assurance of power, he was sure to outgrow these youthful shortcomings. Finally, he was notoriously and strictly pious, and seemed therefore likely to curb the corruption all too prevalent in the Church. All in all, it was no wonder the people loved him.

Unfortunately, these golden appearances were just that: to the few people who knew the young couple well, the future seemed very much less promising. It was true, for instance, that Louis had no mistresses; but then again, he was no husband. When, after much delay and hesitation, he tried to consummate his marriage, he utterly and repeatedly failed to do so. Of course, the court knew it and made fun of him, while all the way across Europe, in Vienna, the Empress Maria Theresa watched with anguish — the marriage was the visible manifestation of the Franco-Austrian alliance — and wrote her daughter letter after letter asking whether there had been any change.

Sadly, the King's impotence seemed all too emblematic of his personality. At twenty, Louis XVI was immensely strong, but already running to fat, and desperately awkward. Naturally shy and uncertain, he seemed even more doltlike because he was so shortsighted as to be almost blind without the glasses he refused to wear. Worse, although not unintelligent, he seemed unable to think for himself; but if he was easily influenced, he was also capable of the most mulish obstinacy, especially when he had at last reached the wrong decision. Comparing him to the world on the first day of creation, his brother-in-law the Emperor Joseph

II wrote of him: "All is still inchoate; the 'Let there be light' has not resounded."[2] It was an accurate and perceptive description.

At first, even this lack of savoir faire seemed like a good quality. The court, thundering across the Palace after Louis XV's death to pay homage to the new sovereigns, had found them, embracing and kneeling, their faces awash with tears; and just as the doors opened, they were heard to say: "Protect us, O God, we are too young to reign."[3] For once, they were right, and they proved it immediately.

Dismissing the late King's ministers — Marie Antoinette insisted on it — was no doubt popular; it was also a serious mistake. Indeed, the seeds of the Revolution were sown on that day. Because, by 1770, the ancien régime had become paralyzed by its beneficiaries' greed, Louis XV had abolished the Parlement, which had blocked reform, and set up a new, fairer, more efficient judicial system to replace it. Far more important, he had begun to modify the tax system so as to shift its burden from the poor to the rich. Unfortunately, the poor had no voice, while the rich were very well able to make themselves heard, so these changes were greeted with a chorus of disapproval; hence the paradox. The very act which earned the new King such popularity also prevented the regime from reforming itself: from that day in May 1774 Louis XVI was hostage to the most reactionary elements in France.

Almost worse, he had acted against his own preference, and given in to his wife, thus setting a dangerous precedent. As for Marie Antoinette, she wanted the ministers dismissed, not because she disliked their policies, but because she thought them friends of Mme du Barry, Louis XV's mistress, against whom she bore a grudge. Thus the most basic of political decisions was made because of one of the Queen's whims, a fact not overlooked by the courtiers. "I can clearly see," Joseph II wrote in 1777, "that all the detail which is connected to personal intrigues is taken care of with the greatest attention and interest, while the essential business of the state is neglected."[4]

In fact, Louis's impotence, as well as the slowness of his mind, made him into his wife's permanent victim. Devoured by guilt at his failure to consummate the marriage, he made up for it by indulging the sexually deprived Queen in other ways; and because, in any event, he was easy to influence, it was obvious that the person closest to him would also be the actual ruler.

Much to her mother's distress, however, Marie Antoinette usually did not choose to exert her power, at least not in the early part of the reign. For a few weeks, Maria Theresa had hoped to run the French government from Vienna, via the Austrian ambassador at Versailles and her daughter; but she quickly realized that the Queen was far too frivolous, far too easily bored and averse to hard work ever to have more than episodic influence.

Unfortunately, Marie Antoinette's thirst for amusement was coupled with a deep reluctance to do her duty. It must, in all fairness, be said that standing for hours, wearing an immensely heavy costume, while unknown ladies pass before you curtseying and kissing your hand, is not particularly entertaining; that receiving ambassadors to whom one has nothing to say is a strain; and that having dinner alone in front of a staring crowd does not make for a pleasant meal; but those were the duties of a Queen of France. Even at Versailles, monarchs had obligations as well as rights. Yet this was a situation Marie Antoinette chose to ignore. To her, being Queen meant having fun; and if that entailed canceling receptions or retreating to her private apartments, then she did just that.

As a result, while still popular with the public at large, she was almost immediately disliked at court. There was the story, for instance, of the way she had laughed at the old ladies who had come to present their condolences on the death of the late King. It was no wonder, people said: had not she dubbed everyone over thirty a "century"? In fact, the teenaged Queen had been responding to the antics of an equally young lady-in-waiting hidden behind her colleagues' vast skirts, and had not meant to offend anyone. Still, in June, a little rhyme began to circulate in Paris and at court: "Little twenty-year-old Queen / You who like to insult people / You will recross the border . . ."[5]

Far worse, it soon became clear that although Louis XVI had given his wife an allowance double that of the last Queen, she was in debt. This was partly because she became obsessed with fashion, spending the equivalent of some two million dollars a year for her clothes by 1777; partly because, although she had the crown jewels at her disposal, she kept buying diamonds; and partly because she gambled frequently and recklessly, often losing the equivalent of hundreds of thousands of dollars at cards in a single night.

All these shortcomings evoked wails from Vienna. Maria Theresa, the greatest as well as the most popular of all the Habsburgs, was a hard-working, intelligent woman who saw all too clearly that her daughter could not afford this kind of self-indulgence. Displaying yet another unappealing side of her character, Marie Antoinette took to denying the truth, to her mother and others, in order not to give up anything that amused or pleased her.

Upsetting the Empress was perhaps not very grave; far more unfortunate, the Queen's own subjects soon got to know her better. It was true, for instance, that she was compassionate when someone suffered visibly; but it was her duty, not just to be kind to her servants but also to be charitable to the poor and sick in general. That, however, bored her; and because she was constantly in debt, she was unable to contribute financially to the various institutions that expected her patronage.

Again, her famous charm seemed to operate best at close quarters. What most people saw, however, was pride and selfishness. That the Habsburgs were superior to everyone else on earth was something Marie Antoinette never doubted. One day, when she was told that a point of etiquette she had just ignored had been most carefully observed by the late Queen, she answered: "It is no wonder a little Polish princess* should have cared about these things, but I am an Archduchess of Austria."[6] Remarks like these, made in the Palace, soon reached the streets; as for the haughtiness of her demeanor, that was visible to all. Once, in answer to a compliment from Mme Vigée-Lebrun, who had just told her that she held her head beautifully, Marie Antoinette said: "Yes, but if I were not Queen, they would say I was arrogant, wouldn't they?"[7] She was Queen, but they said it anyway.

And there were graver matters. One of these, her ownership of the Trianon, may seem trivial to us; to her contemporaries, it was not only shocking, but a clear indication of the way she controlled the King. It had been a tradition in France, since time immemorial, that queens did not own real property; but when, in 1774, Louis XVI gave her the Petit Trianon and its gardens, Marie Antoinette had it enclosed with railings and gates so as to keep the public out (they were allowed throughout the great park of Versailles) and had rules posted in her own name instead of the King's. When, after that, she had a little theater built and had the

---

* Marie Leszczynska, Louis XV's wife, was the daughter of a dethroned Polish king.

gardens completely redesigned in the new English fashion, complete with lake, river, temple of Love, and village, all at great expense, unpopularity turned to outright hatred. So convinced were the people that all the state's money was going to the Queen that, in 1789, many of the Deputies to the Estates General asked to see the well-known — and wholly fictitious — room at the Trianon that had walls covered with emeralds and diamonds.

Then there were Marie Antoinette's friends. It was the fashionable thing, in the 1770s and 1780s — and quite an innovation — for women to have close women friends, and the Queen was certainly fashionable. It must also be said, in all fairness, that she was lonely. Although she eventually grew fond of him, she never thought of her husband as entertaining; the rest of the family was not much better; so she tried to find her company elsewhere. There was, of course, nothing inherently wrong in that; only her two closest friends, Mmes de Lamballe and de Polignac, were nothing if not greedy — for themselves, for their friends, for their families. As a result, the Queen's friendships were soon costing a good deal more than Louis XV's mistresses, a fact with which everyone in France became unhappily familiar because jealous courtiers broadcast it far and wide. Indeed, had the Queen tried to make herself loathed, she could hardly have gone about it more efficiently, especially when her unpopular political influence was added in. This took two equally unfortunate forms.

The first was her clearly visible loyalty to Austria. When, in 1778, the Emperor Joseph II embarked on a foolish and unnecessary war with Prussia, for instance, the Queen repeatedly summoned her husband's ministers, berated them, and ordered them to adjust their policies to that of Austria. As for the King, he too was brought under control. "I was not able to hide from the King the fact that I was upset at his silence," Marie Antoinette wrote her mother in June 1778; "I even told him I would be ashamed to admit to my dear Mama the way in which he was treating me as regards an affair of such interest to me, and one of which I spoke to him so often. I was disarmed by the way he answered me. He told me: 'You see that I am so wrong that I don't have a thing to say.' "[8] And, of course, Louis XVI's obedience to his wife's wishes was no secret.

The second aspect of her political influence was, if anything, even more unfortunate, since it involved the appointment of incompetent ministers and the dismissal of the occasional reformer given office by the King.

Most of the Queen's friends, after all, had characters not unlike her own: they, too, cared most about pleasure, while displaying a remarkable avidity for money, place, and position. Naturally, they urged her to choose members of their coterie as her husband's ministers; when she hesitated, they pointed out that if the appointments were not made, she would look powerless. Such an appearance would be, she felt, deeply humiliating, so she would besiege the wretched Louis, making scenes when necessary, and often end up having her way.

Far worse, the Queen saw to it that reforming ministers were fired as soon as they began to annoy her friends; she was helped in this, until his death in 1781, by the comte de Maurepas. The old man, whom Louis XVI had sent for in 1774 to teach him how to rule, still functioned as the King's mentor. He was present every time a minister was given an audience, thus neatly forestalling any possible criticism of himself; and since a successful reformer might well have become popular and powerful enough to oust him, he saw to it that the minister in question never lasted long enough to be a menace.

So it was that Jacques Turgot, who was both a competent administrator and a man who understood the need for change, was dismissed in 1777, as was Necker in 1781. Calonne, the next powerful finance minister, was Mme de Polignac's friend and behaved in consequence: not only did he provide apparently endless sums for the Queen's coterie, he could also be counted on to prevent all financial reform. It was through this narrow angle almost exclusively that Marie Antoinette saw politics.

Thus, on the highest level, and from the beginning of the reign, the system was blocked. Louis XVI, in his confused but well-intentioned way, realized that the increasingly urgent financial problem kept growing more intractable, but he was not willing to affront either Maurepas or the Queen by acting in ways contrary to their bad advice. Although he unquestionably felt that the people were too heavily taxed,* although he himself disliked luxury, he could not square his impulse toward reform and his overriding desire to avoid complications: in the end, his wife and his minister could, if they chose, make him far more uncomfortable than his conscience.

---

* One of his rare acts of independence was to approve a diminution in one of the taxes as soon as it was suggested by Necker.

At least, in 1777, he was finally able to consummate his marriage. On a visit to Versailles, Joseph II took his brother-in-law aside and asked him just what happened when he tried to have sex. "Just imagine," the Emperor wrote, "he has strong, well-conditioned erections; he introduces the member, stays there without moving for perhaps two minutes, withdraws without ejaculating, and says good night. . . . He says plainly that he does it all purely from a sense of duty but never for pleasure."[9] The phimosis he suffered from was curable by circumcision; and to this operation he now submitted on the Emperor's advice.

"I am in the most essential happiness of my entire life," Marie Antoinette wrote her mother on August 30, 1777. "It has already been more than eight days since my marriage was perfectly consummated; the proof has been repeated and yesterday even more completely than the first time."[10] On December 20, 1778, she gave birth to her first child, a daughter named Marie-Thérèse-Charlotte. That, in itself, made a difference; the King at least ceased being ridiculous, and the Queen settled down a little. It was too late, though, to change the well-established pattern in which the wife ruled the husband.

She was not, however, alone. The ministers, too, could often talk Louis XVI into a policy he neither liked nor, sometimes, understood. Unlike most limited people, though, Louis XVI was at least aware of his shortcomings, and so he repeatedly appointed reforming ministers, promising to back them all the way. The problem was that he would drop them as soon as they upset his wife.

One of these men managed to remain in office, largely because the Queen was not really interested in foreign policy. The comte de Vergennes was responsible for the one undoubted triumph of the reign, the alliance with the fledgling United States. But while England was indeed defeated, the war proved terribly expensive: the fleet had to be kept on a war footing, armies were sent overseas, aid was given to the United States, all as the deficit grew deeper.

It was up to the minister of finance to provide the funds; in this, Jacques Necker, who was in office from 1777 to 1781, was apparently successful. Aside from a very thorough understanding of where the government could find money to borrow, he also had his own ideas about reform; but since he knew he must not annoy the Queen, he cooked the books so as to make the budget appear balanced — mostly by pretending that loans contracted at a very high rate of interest were in fact income. Eventually, however, he, too, tried to restrain the court's spending, upon which he went the way of his predecessor.

After that, a series of incompetents made a bad situation worse. Calonne, one of the Queen's appointees, was a startling example. His policy consisted in spending madly so as to make it look as if the government had all the money in the world, which, in turn, would make it easier for him to float yet more loans. The results, predictably, were catastrophic.

By 1786, in fact, the situation had become desperate. Retrenchment was even tried, although the Queen protected her friends, but it was no longer enough. Clearly, the whole tax system needed changing, since it was not only unfair and inequitable, but also unproductive. Because the poor paid up and the rich did not, the government was destitute, and that at a time when the country was richer than it had ever been.

This situation obviously called for reform, if only to promote greater efficiency; but the problem was so vast that it had become almost impossible to tackle, let alone solve. It was also threefold: first, the actual nature of the taxes, along with the numbers and kinds of taxpayers, was such as to impoverish the state; then, the methods of tax collecting needed examination since they were often both inefficient and unfair; and finally, it was becoming very clear that the government was spending its revenues on the wrong objects.

All this was known only to specialists until, in 1781, Necker, who hoped it would give him added power, and who had asked the King's permission to do so, published his *Compte-rendu au Roi,* in which, for the first time ever, the budget ceased to be a secret. Of course, it created an immense sensation, as its readers discovered that the system, in effect, took from the poor and gave to the rich. That spurred a new attitude toward taxation and spending: government revenue was not, as had been previously understood, the King's private income but the people's money. Once this new notion was accepted, it followed logically that the people had a right to determine what they would pay, and how the sums gathered should be spent; but that, in turn, implied a shift from an absolute monarchy in which the King alone made decisions, to a representative government of some kind in which the King's powers would be sharply limited.

To us, accustomed as we are to constitutional government, it all seems very simple. To the French in the 1780s, however, the situation was so murky as to be virtually incomprehensible. To take a typical example: Louis XVI was firmly determined to preserve his power to rule as he saw fit. Yet, on February 13, 1780, he issued a declaration stating that a specific tax, the *taille,** could no longer be raised by a simple decision of the King's Council, as had always been the case. Henceforth, any upward change would have to be registered by the Parlement, a body known to resist tax increases so as to gain popularity: by appearing to side with the people, it could disguise its own reactionary stance.

This was unquestionably a transfer of power; and yet the King did not see it as such. To him, it was simply a question of protecting the people, whose father he was; essentially an act of kindness and charity, rather than a political decision. The result, in any event, was clear to all: while the rate of the taille had risen steadily throughout the century, it remained constant from 1781 to its abolition in 1789. That, of course, is just what Necker, the author of the reform, had expected; but it was also typical that in his effort to bring about a less oppressive system of taxation, he had reinforced the most reactionary of all institutions, the Parlement of Paris.

A body of judges who had purchased or inherited their offices, the Parlement was in no sense representative: to become a *conseiller* or a *président* required neither real knowledge of the law — though some Parlement men were indeed eminent jurists — nor any kind of election; it did, however, require wealth: a seat as président in the Parlement of Paris sold for around 100,000 livres** in the late eighties.

As a result, that body and its provincial counterparts,*** while gaining popularity by systematically opposing any increase in taxation, in fact were determined to prevent any reform. If the peasantry was to be given relief, then part of the burden would have to be shifted to those better able to pay: the rich and the nobles. In most cases, because their offices

---

* The taille was a flat-rate tax paid only by non-nobles, that is, mostly peasants. Certain "noble lands" exempted their owners from the taille even if they were commoners.

** About $500,000 in 1989.

*** There were thirteen Parlements: Paris, Toulouse, Grenoble, Bordeaux, Dijon, Rouen, Aix, Rennes, Pau, Metz, Besançon, Douai, and Nancy.

carried a patent of nobility, *Messieurs du Parlement* were also legally noble. They made very sure, therefore, that their class would never be taxed, thus freezing the system as it was, and they had a simple way of achieving this goal.

While it was a constitutional maxim that the legislative power belonged solely to the King, his edicts required registration by the Parlement before they could be implemented. Originally, in the fourteenth century, this had merely been a matter of convenience: no one could know what the law was unless there was one central place where a record was kept. That, in turn, brought about a new practice, the remonstrance. If a new law contradicted an older one, the Parlement would bring this to the King's attention; the monarch would then decide to accept or reject the remonstrance.

With the passage of time the Parlement began to behave as if it had the right to remonstrate — that is, not register an edict — not only in the case of a conflict with a preexisting law, but also whenever it disapproved of the new edict. The last word, however, remained the King's. If the Parlement refused to register, in spite of the King's order, then the monarch would hold a *lit de justice,* that is, go to the Parlement and order the registration in person.

Then, in the course of the eighteenth century, the Parlement of Paris began to refuse registration even after a lit de justice. While its resistance to royal authority was often popular among the masses, more intelligent people, Voltaire first and foremost, saw through the pretense. The Parlement, in fact, was an intensely reactionary body, fanatically Catholic and violently opposed to freedom of speech and of publication. It was thus typical that it fought to the last the abolition of judicial torture and the restoration of some civil rights to the Protestants. Last but not least, even in its judicial function, it was not only grotesquely slow and inefficient, but also often corrupt.

Thus it was that the abolition of the Parlements in 1771 met with approval among the very intellectuals whom we would today describe as liberal, while it caused an uproar among the propertied classes. Even then, it was soon noticed that the courts set up as a replacement were both fairer and more effective; but because the abolition was carried out by Louis XV's last ministry, his grandson's first act, on succeeding to the throne in 1774, was to reinstate the Parlement.

Even then, Louis XVI specified that registration must henceforth *precede* any remonstrance; this was, however, a regulation the Parlement began to ignore within the year. As a result, from that moment on, any attempt at reforming the system met with the Parlement's implacable opposition. This had become so clear by 1777 that even Necker, convinced though he was that the taxes were both unfair and unproductive, did no more than tinker with the machinery: some economies were made, some sinecures suppressed with savings of some 2.5 million livres, hardly a significant sum in a budget of some 400 million.

Louis XVI and his ministers did no better when it came to solving the real problems of the state: the court, the increasingly unresponsive administration, the deficit, all were out of control. In one respect, however, Necker did somewhat better than his predecessors. All indirect taxes — and they brought in some 200 million livres a year — were collected by an organization called the *Ferme générale*. This was a group of financiers, the *fermiers généraux,* who signed five-year contracts guaranteeing to pay the King a stated sum yearly, in exchange for which they collected a significantly larger sum and kept the difference. That a small number of already rich men should become very much richer still on the backs of the already overburdened taxpayers obviously made little sense: here was a particularly visible abuse, as a result of which the phrase "rich as a fermier général" had become a standard description.

There could be no question of abolishing the Ferme, partly because the state simply lacked the machinery for collecting the taxes in question, partly because the fermiers généraux were connected to a variety of influential people; but at least, in 1781, Necker forced them to pay the King an extra 5.2 million livres a year.[11] This was obviously a popular move, though, as usual, while taking care of a symptom, it failed to cure the cause of the trouble; even then, the Ferme's yearly profit remained a very high 9 percent of the sums collected — some 18 million livres a year.[12]

Some anomalies in France's system of taxation were less well known but even more costly. A direct 5 percent income tax, the *vingtième*, or twentieth, was in effect, but it was possible for powerful taxpayers to negotiate a fixed yearly amount far lower than the sum they should actually have paid. Thus, once again, the rich managed to evade any significant contribution. Here, at least, Necker thought he saw a full solution. Although the King was, in theory, absolute, the minister knew very well that he did not have the power to change this situation; instead, he suggested setting up elected provincial assemblies that would determine, not the amount of the tax to be paid but its repartition. This would preserve the King's prerogative to tax as he pleased, while making it harder for the rich to evade the tax, since their neighbors, sitting in the Assembly, would then have to make up the deficiency.

On July 12, 1778, the first of these assemblies was set up in Bourges. It consisted of forty-eight landowners, twelve from the Clergy, twelve from the Nobility, and twenty-four from the Third Estate. The first sixteen were appointed by the King, and they then co-opted the thirty-two others. The Archbishop of Bourges was duly made president, and the Assembly settled down to business, with all votes being taken, not by Order (that is, first a vote within each Order, then a second round in which Clergy, Nobility, and Third Estate would have had one vote each), but on a straight one-man-one-vote basis.

Needless to say, this innovation was highly unpopular with the Parlement; that, together with Necker's dismissal in 1781, ensured that this promising development came to very little. In any event, it, too, was merely an attempt at patching up the existing system; it raised no additional revenue, it exerted no significant power; it did not bypass the Parlement's obstruction. That it should have fallen so far short of success says a good deal about the blockage then prevailing.

Taxes were one end of the problematic fiscal situation that plagued Louis XVI; just how the money was spent turned out to be an even more explosive subject. Everybody knew, of course, that the court was splendid and expensive, and that the Queen was more than generous with her friends; but when the *Compte-rendu au Roi* in 1781 listed the sums involved, the outcry was general — except on the part of the beneficiaries, who complained bitterly about Necker's indiscretion.

As it turned out, the Households of the royal family took up around 36 million livres year, an immense sum and very nearly 10 percent of the budget; and that did not include the Household troops. Worse yet were the pensions. Originally conceived as rewards to the meritorious and aids to the needy — the widow of an officer killed in action, say, or an impoverished scientist — they now went mostly to courtiers with already sizable incomes, and they amounted to the shocking total of 28 million livres a year. Among these pensions were two that seemed particularly unearned: 800,000 livres a year (about 4 million dollars) to Mme de Polignac, Marie Antoinette's friend, and 300,000 livres (a million and a half dollars) to the duc de Guines, another member of the Polignac set.

That situation came as no surprise to those who knew the court. Louis XVI, with the best of intentions, was incapable of saying no to any frequently repeated request, especially if it came from the Queen. Still worse, there was no control by the finance minister: during the four years he held office, Necker was never once allowed to be present at those meetings of the Council where expenditures were set. His only task, therefore, was to find the money required by policies over which he had no control. Even so, he occasionally managed to prevent a specific outrage: when Marie Antoinette asked that a million livres (5 million dollars) be given to Mme de Polignac as a dowry for her daughter, Necker talked the King into giving the groom a dukedom and the bride 200,000 livres instead.

For all his efforts, however, Necker also contributed to the financial crisis. The *Compte-rendu*, which was in part self-serving propaganda, asserted that in 1781 the minister had managed to produce a 10-million-livre surplus. In fact, when various misleading accounting practices are corrected, the budget turns out to have had a 50-million-livre deficit: the war with England, although an unquestioned political success, was a financial disaster. Every year, from 1777 to 1783, it cost France an added 150 million livres; since sufficient taxes could not be raised, the balance had to be borrowed.

That essential fact remained largely hidden. Because the debt was neither consolidated nor funded, it consisted of a hodgepodge of loans at various rates and with various maturities; no one but the minister knew what they were. The totals were huge: by 1781 Necker had put out loans amounting to some 530 million livres, and borrowed a further 119 million against the taxes due in the next fiscal year. As a result, the interest rate the state was forced to pay rose drastically, finally reaching a level of 10 percent, and this in a zero-inflation world. It must be said that the capital of some of these loans was not refundable: the holder would be paid his 10 percent for the duration of his life, but the bond became invalid when he died. Still, the public is generally smarter than the officials think: the lenders simply bought the bonds in the name of the youngest member of the family, so that several decades of income could be expected. Worse yet, all this added enormously to the cost of servicing the debt.

Indeed, the figures are eloquent. In 1740 the yearly sum paid out in interest was only 51 million. By 1774 it reached 93 million, an increase of 42 million in thirty-four years. Then came Necker and the American war; in 1782 the cost of servicing the debt was up to 162 million livres, an increase of 69 million in eight years.[9] Finally, since bad habits are hard to break, by 1789 the yearly outlay had risen to 252 million livres,[13] a sum so huge that it alone swallowed over 60 percent of the state's revenue.

It is only fair to add, however, that Calonne, who succeeded Necker after two incompetents came and went in eighteen months, was himself, as noted, an unmitigated disaster. By 1786 the dangers of Calonne's policies were obvious, at least to the comte de Mercy-Argenteau, who had been the Austrian ambassador to the court of Versailles for some twenty years. Not only did Mercy, as noted, enjoy Marie Antoinette's trust and friendship, he also had a network of paid informants throughout the court and the ministries; as a result there was little he did not know. On March 10, 1786, he wrote his master, the Emperor Joseph II: "When waste and profusion empty the treasury, there arises a cry of misery and terror; then the finance minister uses murderous means, like the recent one of recasting the gold coinage according to vicious proportions or the creation of offices. . . . What seems perfectly evident is that the current government passes that of the late King in disorders and thefts and that it is morally impossible that the situation continue much longer without bringing about a catastrophe."[14] The offices Mercy refers to, sinecures mostly, were purchased by people who wanted them. This brought in immediate money to the treasury, but added still more salaries to the yearly expenditure. In the long run, therefore, the measure was self-defeating.

Mercy was right. In the short term also, the growing financial crisis had several effects: the Queen, now dubbed Madame Deficit, became vastly unpopular because it was assumed her spending was largely responsible for the situation; France's international position deteriorated sharply because everyone knew she could not possibly afford another war; and the government found itself more and more influenced by public opinion.

Mme de Staël described it well: "Credit is the true modern discovery which has linked the governments to their peoples," she wrote. "It is the need for credit which forces the governments to bend to public opinion; and just as commerce has civilized the world, so credit, which is its consequence, has made it necessary to have some sort of constitution so as to ensure open finances and the respect of contracts."[15] This led straight to the end of the absolute monarchy.

As the financial crisis worsened, it became all the more clear that the King, although well intentioned, lacked both character and competence. "Louis XVI would have been the most exemplary of private persons but he was a wretched king," Napoleon commented,[16] and, as so often, he was right. Just when clear decisions, firmly supported, were necessary, France was ruled by a man both limited and indecisive. Although he was far from stupid, Louis XVI, after thirteen years on the throne, still understood little about government.

A weakness often disguised as obstinacy was familiar to all who knew the King well. Antoine Bertrand de Molleville, one of his ministers, noted: "M. de Malesherbes [who had been keeper of the seals] said to me one day [about the King] . . . that this extreme sensibility, this tenderness of disposition, so amiable in private life and in times of tranquillity, often becomes, in times of revolution, more fatal to a king than even the worst vices would have been."[17]

Certainly, there was nothing new about a monarch incapable of ruling by himself — but in this case the person closest to him was equally unfitted for the throne. When neither the King nor the Queen was capable of ruling, then tradition required a strong minister. Vergennes had been the closest to taking over, but, after 1785, his health faltered and he died early in 1787. His replacement, the comte de Montmorin, was a well-intentioned mediocrity. "He was a man with good judgment," an observer noted, "but he was shy and able fully to use his abilities . . . only when he was led along, a little like a child learning how to walk."[18] Mercy, as clear-eyed as ever, added: "It has always been clear that the King feels great repugnance against appointing really distinguished men because he supposes that their activity will be too great and that they will too easily be able to dominate him. In that light, the monarch has every reason to congratulate himself on the composition of the current ministry."[19]

All this might perhaps have been well enough if the times had been calm and prosperous; but, in case of crisis, no one at the top was even remotely competent, either to develop a policy, or to maintain it — and the spring of 1787 was anything but quiet.

Averred optimist though he was, Calonne had finally been forced to admit that the regime as it was could no longer survive. Something must be done, and that something, clearly, was a reorganization of the tax system that would give the treasury a significantly larger revenue. It was, however, certain that the Parlement would refuse to register edicts to that effect, so Calonne tried to bypass it by calling an Assembly of Notables.

There had long been, in French traditional usage, two ways in which the King could consult the nation: one was through the Estates General, which had not been held since 1614 and seemed out of the question; the other was through an ad hoc gathering of notables, which had several advantages. First, its members were arbitrarily chosen by the King; second, their advice was nonbinding if unpleasant, and useful if it concurred with the minister's views, since the latter could then say that all France agreed with him; that, in turn, would force the Parlement to accept the new tax system.

The hundred and forty-seven notables who met at Versailles on February 22, 1787, had, therefore, been chosen with care. Although they were supposed to represent the three Orders (Clergy, Nobility, Third Estate), a majority of them belonged to the Nobility, either because most bishops came from aristocratic families or because the men who were supposed to represent the Third Estate were themselves noble. After the opening session, the Assembly divided into seven committees, each headed by a member of the royal family, and the work began. Almost immediately, however, Calonne found that he had miscalculated.

He might have known he was in trouble when a joke had made the rounds: a lady, it ran, had a parrot who knew how to say "Long live the King"; "Hide it," her friends told her, "or Calonne will make it a notable." In his opening speech, in fact, the *contrôleur-général* had managed to affront everyone, the conservatives and the liberals, while owning up to what seemed (and generally was) gross incompetence. Later, when he confessed on March 2 that, after all, the deficit came to 112 million livres, not the 80 he had previously mentioned, he naturally lost whatever credibility he still might have had. Then, as if that were not enough, he managed further to alienate all the liberals present by blaming it all on Necker, and the liberals were the very people who might have been expected to support his proposal for resolving the fiscal crisis.

This proposal, at least, was simple: he advocated repealing the two existing vingtièmes, which added up to a 10 percent income tax but were, as we have seen, evaded by most of the well-to-do, and replacing them with a single, graduated land tax, the *subvention territoriale,* which made sense since in 1787 most of the nation's wealth still was agricultural. This single, and eminently fair, tax, would yield sufficient revenue, he said, to abolish a number of taxes besides the vingtièmes, citing, first and foremost, the highly unpopular salt tax, the *gabelle.* That, of course, is precisely what the upper classes had always rejected: the very last thing they wanted was a graduated income tax that would force them to bear their fair share of the burden.

Having thus unthinkingly alienated both the conservatives and the liberals, Calonne was stunned to discover that he had virtually no support among the notables. Sadly, his proposals were in fact excellent, but after all those years of spending and borrowing, he could hardly expect to be followed when he suddenly shifted positions.

All through March and April, though the work continued in the Assembly, this deadlock persisted between Calonne and the notables; and since it was, after all, the King who had kept Calonne in office and supported his policy, it slowly became clear that the royal authority was also at stake. On April 7 Mercy wrote the Emperor: "It is impossible fully to describe the degree of confusion, disorder, and scandal which this imprudent enterprise [the Assembly] is causing more and more every day. Cabals now lead the opposition to all the contrôleur-général's proposals, and both the form and the publicity of this opposition are compromising in the most unheard-of fashion the dignity of the sovereign, at the same time that it is so striking to public opinion that the state's bankruptcy is thought to be certain."[20]

Mercy, as usual, understood the situation. If the King really wanted the reforms, then he should have forced them through the Parlement; the Assembly's very existence proved Louis XVI's weakness. Then, as long as the notables had been called together, the least the King could do was support his government's policy. Away in Vienna, Joseph II saw it clearly. "If the King weakens and abandons the contrôleur-général," he answered Mercy, "his authority is lost forever, and the Clergy, the Nobility, and the Parlements will come together in a sort of coalition so that he will be opposed in all matters and will in the end be forced to take, as they do in England, the ministers they [the opposition] will choose to give him."[21]

That letter was written on April 26; and while it was still on its way to Paris, Louis XVI did just what the Emperor dreaded. While Marie Antoinette, prompted by her reactionary friends, was demanding Calonne's dismissal, the contrôleur-général came to the King and asked him to dissolve the Assembly and decree the reforms. That would have required just the kind of energy and decisiveness Louis XVI so conspicuously lacked; so, listening instead to the Queen, and helped along by the minister's unpopularity, he dismissed Calonne and appointed a replacement.

Mercy was watching. "During the month of April," he reported on May 19,

> everyone took fright, credit was so low that no paper was being traded in Paris anymore, and the treasury was down to its last coin. Within eight days, people have gone to the contrary extreme; they think that enormous 140 million deficit sufficiently covered, and are all bringing in their money to the new loan . . . and this is all due to their opinion of the dismissed minister and of his replacement. . . .
>
> The King's authority is all the more grievously wounded by his abandonment of the former contrôleur-général because his plans had been so expressly approved by the monarch that he could almost not change his mind. Everybody agrees that the major part of these plans was inefficient, ill-digested, and unadapted to the constitution of the kingdom. . . . The result is a scandalous victory over the government, over the King's dignity, and it is hard to evaluate as yet how far that regrettable circumstance will influence the future. . . .

Mercy adds with an almost audible sigh: "It is to the Queen that the Archbishop of Toulouse owes his appointment."[22]

The ambassador was right on both counts. Louis XVI had just shown anyone who cared to look that, faced with a loud enough opposition, he would back down; and for the first time Marie Antoinette chose a minister, not because be belonged to her coterie but because she felt he was the right man to solve the current crisis. The Archbishop's appointment marked her entrance into full-time politics.

The man she chose, Loménie de Brienne, Archbishop of Toulouse, was known for his ties to the intellectuals and for his eloquence; he had been particularly outspoken in his opposition to Calonne; and to show that, unlike his predecessor, he trusted the notables, he turned over to them, immediately after his appointment on May 1, all the financial records relative to the deficit.

It was a good beginning. Unfortunately, Brienne was the wrong man in the wrong situation. "The Archbishop was neither enlightened enough to be liberal, nor steady enough to be a despot," Mme de Staël noted. "He admired in turn the methods of the Cardinal de Richelieu* and the ideas of the Encyclopédistes. He tried force, but backed down at the first obstacle he met; and in fact he attempted things far too difficult to be accomplished. . . . Under those conditions, the authoritarian stance of the government only showed up its weakness."[23] It is only fair to point out, however, that in this case Mme de Staël had the full benefit of hindsight: she wrote this passage in 1816, and while her analysis is perfectly correct, the consensus, at first, was very different.

"Even the Archbishop of Toulouse's enemies agree that he has a great mind, is thoroughly enlightened, and knows a great deal about the country's administration," the Sardinian ambassador reported. "His skill as a courtier is universally recognized. . . . In this choice, the King seems to have sacrificed to the public good . . . the repugnance he had always shown for having a priest at the head of the government. . . . The public greatly admires the new minister, and feels the greatest confidence in his firmness and honesty. He wants to carry out important reforms. . . . The King shows the Archbishop the greatest confidence."[24]

That was all very well; but even if, with Brienne's appointment, the lenders were reassured, the financial crisis remained. The only way to solve it was by transforming the tax system, so Brienne proposed a plan closely related to Calonne's. Naturally, the Assembly rejected it, but this time there was a difference. On May 21 a new and very shocking suggestion was made within the commission presided over by the comte d'Artois, the King's youngest brother. There, the marquis de La Fayette,

---

* Richelieu was widely credited with having made the King absolute.

fresh from his triumphs in America, asked for a meeting of the Estates General. "What, monsieur," the aghast prince exclaimed, "you are asking for the convocation of the Estates General?" "Yes, monseigneur, and even better than that," replied La Fayette.[25]* It was, indeed, a revolutionary suggestion, one that infringed directly on the King's absolute power, but in fact La Fayette was not alone in thinking this way. Less bluntly, but almost as clearly, the notables said the same thing when they refused to consider Brienne's plan on the grounds that it exceeded their power to do so.

The suggestion that the King call the Estates General into being was, again, nothing less than a direct assault on the power of the monarchy, a fact of which both Louis XVI and Marie Antoinette were fully aware, just as they knew where that assault originated — not in the oppressed and exploited Third Estate, but in the already overprivileged Nobility. No one in May 1787 worried about a popular uprising, but it was rapidly becoming clear that the government was facing the kind of aristocratic revolt which, before the reign of Louis XIV, had caused endless civil wars. The Assembly of Notables' deliberations were tantamount to the beginning of a right-wing revolution.

Naturally, Loménie de Brienne, whose plan had just been rejected, was happy to point this out. The Queen, wounded in her pride, and opposed to the Assembly in the first place, had already begun advocating a dissolution. The King, outraged at what he saw as factious resistance, was easily convinced; on May 25 the Assembly was dissolved. That was not a bad thing, since the notables had merely played their traditional blocking role, thereby stopping any reform of the system; but if the King, the Queen, or Brienne had been cleverer, they might well have seen their chance: had the Estates General been called then, had Louis XVI come before them as a reforming King blocked by the selfish privilégiés, he would very probably have become more popular and more powerful than ever. Unfortunately, much as it might resent the nobles, the royal couple was itself anything but liberal, and the idea of using the Third Estate to overcome the opposition of the two privileged Orders was unthinkable to them.

---

* By "even better," La Fayette wrote some years later, he meant a full representative assembly not divided into Orders.

Instead, they relied on the Archbishop's talents. He was already contrôleur-général; on August 26 he was appointed principal minister, a post that had not existed in decades because the King was supposed to govern by himself and without the help of a prime minister: it was a clear mark of favor. As early as July 14, Mercy had written Joseph II: "The Archbishop of Toulouse, who is considered to be [the Queen]'s creature, is gaining in influence on the King's mind, and he misses no occasion to display the most complete devotion to his august protectress." Mercy added, "[The Archbishop's] greatest difficulty is that the royal authority has been everywhere so badly shaken."[26]

Now that Marie Antoinette had her own man at the head of affairs, she began to take a far more sustained interest in politics, a fact that escaped no one. In some ways, this represented progress. In late July, for instance, she cut down on several sinecures in her Household, thus saving 900,000 livres a year. She also agreed to the suppression of a post especially created for the duc de Polignac, that of director of the post, which paid him a large salary for doing nothing.

What the public saw, however, was not this admittedly rather feeble attempt at economy, but the fact that Madame Deficit was now in charge; henceforth, she was blamed for whatever went wrong. As for the King, who was still relatively popular, pamphlets — illegal but widespread — told everyone that he was incapable of governing. With his usual frankness, Mercy described the situation in mid-August:

The King has so often been told that the Archbishop . . . would try to subjugate him that this monarch, who is enamored of the authority he uses so little, is still hesitating in giving it to him in the degree needed to reestablish order. The result of this repugnance is that there really is no government. The spirit of license and independence is gaining so rapidly that it will be very difficult to contain it, especially under a reign which lacks both energy and consideration. The King's nature offers little resource against so great an evil, and his physical habits diminish him still further; he is getting heavier, and when he comes back from the hunt, he eats so immoderately that he seems to lose his reason. . . . The Queen . . . is feared [and] respected by her husband, who would even obey her if she wanted it firmly enough.[27]

Ruling queens never did well in France. One symptom of this was Marie Antoinette's extraordinary unpopularity. By the summer of 1787, she was undoubtedly the most hated person in France, and she knew it. "Recently," Mercy wrote on September 15,

> the Queen has been much affected by the kind of hysteria which has existed against her in Paris, and unfortunately still exists. The public's injustice, in this respect, and its impertinent delirium, are enough to make one indignant. . . . It is the Queen who is giving an example of economy, and has determined the King to follow suit; . . . she opposed the murderous . . . Calonne administration and was responsible for his dismissal. . . . Her favorite set [the Polignacs] has brought this general ill will down on her. In truth this set, by its rapines, and the abuse of the influence they have on the Queen, have behaved revoltingly.[28]

As a further explanation of Marie Antoinette's unpopularity, this is undoubtedly correct; but even as Mercy wrote, a transformation was taking place: again, because Marie Antoinette was seen, quite accurately, as the power behind the throne, she was now held responsible for everything that had gone wrong. She had once been the delight of the people; her pro-Austrian sympathies, her reckless spending, the favors granted the Polignacs had all turned opinion against her. Now she was seen, moreover, as the enemy of all reform: nothing would improve as long as l'Autrichienne, the Austrian woman, Madame Deficit was in charge.

On July 16 the Parlement, as hungry for popularity as usual, had asked that the Estates General be called, as they alone — it now claimed — could vote new taxes; meanwhile, it refused to register a new stamp tax. On August 6 the King held a lit de justice in which he ordered registration; on the seventh the Parlement declared the previous day's registration illegal. On Brienne's advice, Louis XVI, following precedent, exiled the Parlement to Troyes; but when, on the seventeenth, the comte d'Artois came to the *cour des aides*, a tax court, to have the edict registered, he was hissed by 10,000 angry Parisians.

At that point, having caused the King to announce that he would never compromise, Brienne did exactly that: after a negotiation with the Parlement in the course of which he gave up the new stamp tax, promised to forget all about the subvention territoriale, and announced that the

Estates General would be called for 1792, he allowed the Parlement to go back to Paris on September 4. Once again, Louis XVI had backed down.

That left the treasury just where it had been before, so Brienne decided to float 420 million livres' worth of new loans. In order to avoid seditious speeches, he and Lamoignon, the keeper of the seals, asked the King to hold yet another lit de justice; so, on November 19, Louis XVI came to the Parlement and ordered the loan edicts registered without any previous discussion, adding that he was the sole judge of whether or not the Estates General should be called. To everyone's surprise, as the registration was taking place, the duc d'Orléans, the King's distant cousin,* rose to protest that the registration was illegal. "It is legal because I say so," replied the outraged King, and the duc was exiled to his château of Villers-Cotterêts. In fact, the King was right: all precedents agreed that his was the last word, and that the Parlement, in a lit de justice, was bound to obey; but the duc d'Orléans's speech showed just how low Louis XVI's authority had fallen.

By mid-November the lines were neatly drawn: on one side were the Queen, Brienne, the Polignac set, the comte d'Artois, and assorted reactionaries who wanted to raise taxes but otherwise keep things as they were; on the other were the duc d'Orléans, the Parlement, a number of liberal aristocrats (La Fayette chief among them), and the slowly rising mass of the people; in the middle was the wretched Louis XVI, a marionette controlled, at the moment, by the Queen and Brienne. All in all, it hardly looked promising.

To the rest of Europe, the country appeared to be coming so thoroughly apart that a civil war might ensue. That worried France's ally, Austria, and greatly interested Austria's enemy, Prussia; so, in the fall of 1787, King Frederick William II of Prussia sent Count Alvensleben to Paris. The report he received from the Count confirmed all his hopes:

> The Queen is more hated, but more powerful than ever. She has left her frivolous friends and concerns herself with affairs of state. As she cannot think systematically, she will go from caprice to caprice. . . .
> The principal minister is a poor man who will stay in place only so long as the Queen wants to keep him there and so long as he is weak, for if

---

* The duc sat in the Parlement in his capacity as a peer of France, along with most dukes and several bishops.

he became stronger, he would be pushed out. . . . As for the King's firmness, which is an essential quality when one wants to regenerate a country, he said, before appointing the principal minister: "I don't want to hear either about Necker or about a priest" and three days later the most priestlike of priests was at the head of the kingdom; that does not stop him [the King] from being capricious, short-tempered or even curmudgeonly. . . ."[29]

Having thus accurately described the situation, Alvensleben went on to predict the future. "It is a mistake to believe in the golden era which the partisans of France announce. Yes, the Estates General will revive credit; but . . . waste, disorder, outward magnificence, abuses, pride, all these will prevail and the people will be more heavily burdened than ever."[30] It seemed a logical conclusion in the fall of 1787: since the pressure for change came from the aristocracy, not the people, the Estates General would in all probability simply extend its privileges and give it more power than ever. That, indeed, was just what the Queen dreaded.

Uncertain as the future might be, one thing at least was clear: something was changing in France. No one knew quite what it was yet, but obviously the system as it was could not continue. More and more people of every status spoke of liberty, though that was still a deeply ambiguous word which meant very different things depending on who was speaking it.

Liberty, in its traditional sense, meant, not freedom but the possession of a special privilege: the liberties of a city meant it had the right not to pay certain taxes, for instance; the liberties of a province that it did not have to obey certain laws. Thus, when traditionalists spoke of liberty, they meant a return to a proto-medieval system of government in which the central government would be weak and a myriad of intermediary, nonelected bodies would each be a despot in its sphere. The Parlement was a good example of this: among its liberties, for instance, it claimed the right to exclusive censorship over all printed material, a function that the royal government had long taken over and in which it proved far less repressive than the Parlement wanted to be.

As a result, even the best observers could foresee nothing but a return to a state where the aristocracy would be powerful and the King weak, as was, for instance, the case in England. "The transformation manifest in the national spirit,'' Mercy wrote on November 24, "threatens some great change in the basic principles of the monarchy and if the Estates General, which have in a manner already been granted, do actually meet, the King's authority will sustain attacks against which it will find it hard to defend itself.''[31]

These attacks on the monarchy had, without question, already begun. They were accompanied, in the countryside, by a parallel reassertion by nobles of feudal rights: just as the nobles wanted to reclaim the powers wrested from them by the monarchy over the centuries, so they were now determined to squeeze every penny out of the peasants. Long-forgotten customs were revived, long-disused fees exacted. It was clear, therefore, to the great mass of the peasantry and to all non-nobles that the economic gains they had made in the course of the century were about to be eradicated. Centuries ago, the monarchy had offered the only protection against the predatory feudal lords; now it looked as if an updated version of the Middle Ages was about to become reality. Clearly, the government itself was no longer able to stop this. "Nothing has yet confirmed the idea people had of the Archbishop's talents,'' Mercy reported. "We see nothing but uncertainty and grave errors in his policies.''[32]

Far less visible to observers like Mercy or Alvensleben, because there was no precedent for it, was another kind of opposition: the greed of the nobility was well known and recognizably a difficulty, but the principles expounded in half a dozen liberal salons seemed little more than an intellectual diversion, and in any case unlikely to cause trouble. The liberals, too, like the reactionaries, wanted a weaker king; only, in this case, power was to go to an Assembly of some sort, possibly in the form of yearly meetings of the Estates General. Here, indeed, was a very different sort of liberty.

The reactionaries were hampered by the lack of a single convincing leader; the liberals, on the other hand, had a future prime minister all ready in the person of Necker. Once in power, it was thought, he would bring about the meeting of the Estates General, reform the finances, and usher in a Golden Age of freedom and prosperity. Louis XVI might not like him; but because Necker's supporters were far more articulate than their opponents, he was seen, by the beginning of 1788, as France's last best hope. Nor were his opinions so radical as to frighten the moderates: while he advocated reforms, he also thought, and said, that a country the size of France could be governed only by a mostly absolute monarch.

All this was bad news for Marie Antoinette. She, too, had ideas; unfortunately, they were those of a child rather than those of a thirty-one-year-old woman who had been on the throne for thirteen years. In her simplistic world, kings — and queens — were to be obeyed promptly; as long as they remained sexually virtuous, they were above blame; and they, alone, knew what was best for the people. Of course, they were sometimes let down by ambitious or stupid ministers, and then it was their duty to choose new servants: she never stopped lamenting, for instance, the lack of anyone comparable to Kaunitz, her mother's great chancellor.

Her choice of Brienne was typical: here, she thought, was someone competent enough to manage things and grateful enough to remember he owed it all to her. She knew, of course, that the deficit was a major problem, and that she had been overspending, so she was perfectly willing to retrench — indeed, it gave her the feeling that she was behaving as a great queen should by putting the state's interest before her own. Beyond that, she attributed all the trouble to the Parlement's disobedience.

Thus, when in the spring of 1788 the financial situation became, once again, critical, the solution seemed simple. "We are about to make great changes in the Parlements," she wrote her brother the Emperor Joseph II on April 24. "For the last few months, the King's orders and answers have shown that his principles are firm. The Parlements are surprised and worried, but they still go on making seditious . . . remonstrances. We are thinking of limiting them to their judicial functions and creating another body who will register the taxes and the kingdom's general laws. . . . It is very regrettable to have to make these kinds of changes, but the state of things is such that if we put this off, we would have fewer means to keep and maintain the King's authority."[33]

Mistakenly, she saw a difference between the lower classes, who were innocent but deluded, and the upper classes, who were rebels and ought to be punished. In fact, of course, it was the people who hated her the most. When she described the Parlement as deliberately defying the King's authority, though, she had a point. While cleverly courting — and winning — popularity by asserting it was protecting everyone, that body was actually continuing to behave with its usual selfishness. To start with, on January 4 it declared the lettres de cachet illegal, because (although it naturally did not say so) that was what the King used when he exiled its members. This decision was annulled by the King, who had the power to do so. Then, on April 13, the Parlement voted remonstrances against the "illegal" registration of the loan edicts on November 19, thus provoking the King and causing Marie Antoinette's letter to her brother. As she had announced to her brother, Lamoignon, the keeper of the seals, then defined a new dispensation in a series of edicts: henceforth, all laws would be registered by a plenary court whose members would be appointed for life. To this, the Parlement, who could see that the government was paralyzed, and hoped to win power for itself, replied on May 3 by proclaiming what it called the "fundamental laws" of the kingdom.

First, it claimed, all new taxes must be authorized by the Estates General; then, naturally, the Parlements must retain their right to control the laws; and finally, once again, the lettres de cachet must be abolished. In fact, these were brand-new demands wholly unrelated to any hypothetical fundamental laws: the King had always had the right to tax as he saw fit; registration had been forced by a lit de justice whenever necessary; and no one before then had questioned the King's right to order arbitrary exile or arrest in the lettres de cachet. Far from upholding a (nonexistent) constitution, the Parlement was actually making revolutionary demands; but because precedent was the life blood of the ancien régime, it looked better if novelty was cloaked in spurious antiquity.

These demands were also based on a key assumption, as the Parlement demonstrated abundantly within a few months. Although the Estates General had not been called since 1614, the one thing everyone knew about them was that they were divided into Orders — Clergy, Nobility, Third Estate — each composed of an equal number of deputies, and each receiving one vote. If the Nobility and the Clergy voted together, therefore, they enjoyed a permanent majority over the Third Estate; and they were very likely to do this because virtually every bishop came from an aristocratic family. Thus what the Parlement expected from a meeting of the Estates General was not progress, but violent regression.

Here was clearly an attempt to shift the right to govern from the King to the Parlement — whose only qualification, it must be repeated, was that it was composed of rich men who had bought their offices. Naturally, faced with this direct threat, Louis XVI reacted. First, he annulled the May 3 resolutions; then he put the Parlement on "holiday," an indefinite suspension; then he proceeded with the forced registration of the edicts, a simple process since it meant, literally, having them inscribed in the Parlement's register; and finally, he ordered the arrest of two of the Parlement's most extreme members, Duval d'Esprémesnil and Goilard de Montsabert.

Immediately, all through France, the other twelve Parlements rose against these measures, encouraged, almost everywhere, by the Clergy, which was afraid of losing its tax-exempt status; and at the behest of the local Parlements, the people rioted. In Pau, Dijon, Toulouse, and Rennes, the control of the cities was wrenched away from the administration. In Grenoble, the whole city rose against the royal governor when he tried to close down the Parlement; raining tiles from the roofs, the people overcame the troops and forced the governor to cancel his orders. Within a few days, the Estates of the province, meeting in a rich manufacturer's castle, asked for an immediate convocation of the Estates General according to a new formula in which the Third Estate would have twice as many members as either of the two other Orders, the crucial *doublement du Tiers.*

That, had he only seen it, was the King's great chance. So far both oppositions, liberal and reactionary, had been *united* in fighting his authority; but with the call for the doublement du Tiers, all had changed: while this was the most cherished goal of the liberals, it was anathema to the reactionaries and, of course, to the Parlements. By threatening to grant this, Louis XVI could drive a wedge between right and left, and either consolidate the status quo by frightening the Parlements or join the liberals in order to create a new, strong monarchy based on an alliance with the people against the privilégiés.

It would, however, have taken cleverer advisers than Brienne or the Queen to point this out to him; all he saw, in the late spring of 1788, was generalized upheaval made even more worrying by the financial situation. On April 28, in a praiseworthy but ill-timed attempt at being truthful, Brienne had published a document, the *Compte-rendu au vrai,* which gave a complete and accurate picture of the financial situation; the figures, including a yearly deficit of 161 million livres, were even worse than expected. That, and the conflict with the Parlements, had the usual result: the subscriptions to the state loans suddenly dried up. Everywhere, the people seemed to be on the verge of generalized rebellion.

On July 18 the appalled Mercy wrote the Emperor:

> The French are now prey to such a spirit of excess that it is hard to determine the side on which the hysteria and the lack of reason are the greatest, that of those who must give orders, or those who must obey them.
>
> That is the situation in which, very soon, the Estates General must meet. . . . There is every reason to believe that [this] will not be favorable to the King's authority. . . . The hands holding the reins are neither strong enough nor skilled enough for one reasonably to suppose that the perils of so difficult a moment can be avoided.[34]

Most surprising and most alarming of all, the King himself, who had remained relatively popular, was, as the Queen had been before, blamed for everything. "Such is the people's disposition," the Spanish ambassador reported to his government, "that the day before the King visited the Invalides, he was blamed for never having yet gone there, while the day after, his visit was thought to be a forced gesture to earn the army's goodwill."[35] Now, more than ever, a forceful response was needed; instead, as usual, Louis XVI gave in. First, he announced that the Estates General would meet at an undetermined time; then, on August 8, he set May 1, 1789, as the opening date. That, however, was still not enough to reassure potential lenders. On August 16 the treasury announced that, instead of paying what it owed, it would convert its debts into a forced loan. The long-predicted crisis had finally arrived.

CHAPTER EIGHT

The People's Vote

. : . : . :

NO government can long survive without either money or credit. By August 17, 1788, it was already clear that Brienne had failed disastrously; at the same time civil disorder was beginning to spread. In Paris itself, the "forced loan" was causing riots: crowds, chanting anti-Brienne slogans, demanded his dismissal. But the King, placid as ever, gave no sign of wanting to do anything. Still, at least two people understood that the monarchy was in danger: the Queen and Mercy. Together they set about doing what had to be done.

There was only one man in France who was so widely trusted, so popular, that his accession to power would save the credit of the state while enabling the King to meet the Estates General in the best possible position; one man whose competence was universally recognized and who would not be co-opted by the court; one man who would make sure that Louis XVI was on the people's side. That man was Jacques Necker; and since his dismissal in 1781, he had yearned for a call from Versailles.

On August 19 Marie Antoinette sent for Mercy.

The Queen saw that the problem was becoming more severe every day, and the accurate opinion of her preponderating influence caused people to blame her for the failure of all the ministry's policies.

The Archbishop of Sens,* having announced he would be firm, had shown nothing but weakness and revolted the Parlements and the nation

---

* Brienne had been promoted from Toulouse to Sens, a much richer archbishopric.

for whom he had become an object of loathing. . . . The treasury was about to declare bankruptcy. . . .

I found the Queen greatly worried. She deigned to tell me that, since I had all her confidence, she wanted me to serve her. . . . She told me that, seeing the inadequacy of the principal minister, she had convinced him he must turn the finances over to M. Necker, but that the latter must now agree to shoulder this heavy burden. . . .

After the King's lever, I went to see the Archbishop . . . whose idea was that M. Necker, though he would take over the finances, would still remain subordinate to the principal minister.[1]

At that point Mercy took over. In the intricate negotiations which followed, he was everywhere, constantly traveling between Versailles and Paris and making sure of the right outcome. The Queen had written to him on the evening of the nineteenth, the same day of their meeting, to forewarn him of complications:

The Archbishop came to see me this morning, Monsieur, to tell me about your conversation with him. He is now seeing the King to try to get his agreement [to Necker's appointment]; but I am afraid that M. Necker will not accept office if the Archbishop stays. The public's animosity has gone so far that he will fear being compromised and, indeed, it might well harm his popularity. But at the same time, what can we do? In truth and conscience, we cannot sacrifice a man who has lost his reputation for us. . . .

I greatly fear the Archbishop may have to go altogether, and then whom can we find to put at the head of affairs? We must have someone, especially with M. Necker, he needs someone to slow him down. The person above me [the King] is not capable of doing so and as for me, whatever may happen, whatever people say, I am only in the second rank and, in spite of the confidence the first has in me, he often makes me aware of it. . . . [And a little later, she added:]

The Archbishop has just come from the King; the King is very unwilling, we could only get his agreement by promising we would put feelers out to the person [Necker] without committing ourselves.[2]

At midnight, after receiving word from the Archbishop that he was to proceed, Mercy announced that he would visit Necker the next day.

Indeed, on the twentieth, the two men met for three hours; but, for all the time it took to express it suitably — Necker was nothing if not slow — the answer was simple: the former minister would not come back to office unless Brienne resigned.

All was now clear: the King, very reluctantly, was considering taking Necker back. Mercy and the Queen saw him as the only possible savior, but the latter was not willing to abandon Brienne altogether; and Necker, although eager to be in charge, sensibly refused to accept office if the Archbishop remained as principal minister. A deadlock had thus been reached, but a resolution was urgently necessary. Obviously, someone would have to back down.

All through the next two days, August 22 and 23, the deadlock continued, while letters between Mercy and Marie Antoinette went back and forth at a frantic pace. Necker would not serve under Brienne; Brienne refused to go. By the twenty-fourth matters had become desperately urgent; and since Louis XVI's refusal to commit himself had been part of the problem, Marie Antoinette took care of at least that aspect. Early that morning a note in the Queen's hand went off to Mercy: "I think more than ever that time presses and that it is essential he [Necker] accept. The King agrees with me fully and has just brought me a paper in his own hand which I herewith copy." The paper in question shows how far the King had come: not only was he willing to ask Necker, whom he loathed, to take office, he was even willing to give him that seat in the Council which the minister had never obtained before and from which he was in principle barred by being a Protestant. The note went on: "The King is firmly resolved to hold the Estates at the time appointed and to confer with them about the means of ending the deficit and preventing its recurrence. . . . If M. Necker thinks further retrenchments possible, he may be sure that nothing which concerns the King personally will upset him."[3]

The ambassador, convinced that he was saving the monarchy, was doing his best. On the twenty-fifth he finally tackled the one remaining obstacle. "The Queen had then thought often about the untoward position of the Archbishop and the ill effects it was likely to produce," Mercy reported to Joseph II. "I presume she had allowed the minister to guess that much, but he was still unwilling to take the necessary decision. The Queen gave me the heavy task of deciding him."[4] Mercy succeeded;

Brienne resigned. On the twenty-sixth, after first seeing the Queen, Necker became effective head of the government. When he returned from Versailles that day, his wife wrote Mercy yet another letter that displayed, not only the politeness then so universal in France but also the degree to which the Austrian ambassador was involved in the government of France. "M. Necker has just come back," Mme Necker wrote. "He would like to tell you about his trip and put at your feet the details of a fate whose arbiter you have been. . . . He has much to tell you; be his guide, Monsieur l'Ambassadeur, let your virtues strengthen him; let your esteem remain his even if his reputation, risked so as to remedy the country's ills, is lost elsewhere. . . ."[5] As for the King, on the twenty-seventh he told one of his courtiers: "They made me recall Necker, I did not want to do it, but they will soon be sorry. I will do everything he wants and we will see what will happen."[6]

Thus had the great operation succeeded: on the day Louis XVI made his bitter remark, Necker was appointed director general of the finances and minister of state with a seat in the Council. Clearly, this was to be his administration; even though the other ministers remained, since some — Montmorin especially — were friends and others nonentities, his preponderance was absolute.

Short of the King's actually taking over himself — a complete impossibility — Necker was probably the best choice at that difficult moment, simply because he was so very popular. Still, several questions remain, not least the one about the propriety of a foreign ambassador's involvement in a matter so crucial to the government of France; it says a great deal about Marie Antoinette's attitude that in this crisis the only man she trusted was an Austrian. As for who was actually governing France, the answer is all too clear: no one. Louis XVI was incapable of doing so, and knew it, but his hope that Necker would fail is shocking, both because of the dereliction of responsibility it implies, and because it proves that the King had no idea that his situation was well-nigh desperate. Almost as bad is the fact that Marie Antoinette was now obviously in control of her husband, since she was fully as incompetent as he. All would depend, therefore, on Necker and, public opinion notwithstanding, he lacked most of the qualities necessary to be an effective prime minister.

What is certain, however, is that he had been given office under the most appalling circumstances. "When M. Necker became a minister," his daughter wrote, "only 250,000 francs remained in the treasury. The next day, he was given considerable help by the owners of capital. Government paper rose by 30 percent in one morning."[7] In fact, immediately upon entering office, Necker borrowed 6 million livres from the notaries and 3 million in unpaid wages from the higher-level civil servants in his ministry. Then, on September 4, he floated a first, 15-million-livre loan, followed by another in October. On September 14 he was able to cancel the forced loan edict left over from his predecessor. After this, using 12 million in notes that were accepted at par because he was trusted, he borrowed from the discount bank when necessary, floated further loans, and thus rescued the government from what had seemed an inevitable collapse. This was a laudable achievement, but a very limited one: he had relieved the most acute symptoms, but the cause of the disease remained untreated.

The minister's popularity remained unquestionable. Friedrich Grimm mentions "the frantic rejoicing among the people of Paris to celebrate the dismissal of the two ministers,* the recall of M. Necker and the return of the Parlement. . . . The Archbishop was burned in effigy on the Place Dauphine."[8] But at the same time there was evidence of unruliness on the part of the Parisians that pointed to the deepest dissatisfaction. "The administration of the Archbishop of Sens had become extremely unpopular and there were some trifling commotions in the streets," Samuel Romilly reported. "Crowds assembled on the Pont Neuf and obliged all passersby to take off their hats in token of respect before the equestrian statue of Henri IV. In the coffee shops of the Palais Royal, the freest conversations were indulged."[9] Henri IV was famous for his love of the people: forcing passersby to show his statue respect was a clear criticism of Louis XVI; and it is the first instance in which the Parisians were forced to do something by a mob.

While much depended on Necker's popularity, it was also important to show that the King was capable of steady resolution. This the new administration promptly disproved when, in September, it was announced that the plenary court was dissolved and the Parlements recalled. This

---

* Lamoignon, the author of the anti-Parlements edicts, was very unpopular. He was replaced as keeper of the seals by Charles de Barentin on September 19.

was a mistake for two reasons: first, it precluded any immediate attempt at reform — indeed, Necker announced that the reforms would have to await the Estates General; and, just as important, it showed yet again that Louis XVI would always give in to resolute opposition. There was every reason, therefore, for the Estates to feel, when they met, that they could safely disregard anything the King said: a push, and he would cave in again.

The lack of an announced program for the Estates General was also a key mistake. Everyone agreed that major changes had become urgent; a strong liberal trend throughout the country was becoming evident. If, therefore, the King and the government wanted to retain a measure of control over the scope and nature of the reforms, they badly needed a specific program that could be presented to the Estates. That, however, supposed a measure of agreement among Necker, the King, and the Queen as to what needed to be done, and there was no such thing. Both Louis XVI and Marie Antoinette thought that the Estates' only purpose was to reform the tax system. Necker counted on that assembly to abolish all privileges, legal and fiscal, thus simplifying the various tasks of government and consolidating the state; he also expected it to supply France with a constitution that would stabilize government and preclude the kind of incoherence that had marked the current reign. Because the King would have been horrified and insulted had he been told a constitution was needed, however, Necker kept his ideas to himself and simply hoped that these complex and controversial questions would somehow take care of themselves.

It was, in fact, barely two weeks before the opening of the Estates General that Necker finally tackled the problem in a conversation with the King. "Sire," he said, according to Mme de Staël, "the time has come to grant the reasonable wishes of the French. Deign to resign yourself to [the equivalent of] the British constitution. . . . and as you anticipate the nation's desires, you will be freely granting today what it may demand tomorrow."[10] Of course, Louis XVI rebuffed him, and the often pusillanimous minister dropped the subject, while keeping in mind that the events themselves might prove more compelling than his words.

Perhaps Necker's reticence was wise; although certainly it was sheer folly not to have a policy ready for the meeting of the Estates General, the turmoil in September 1788 was such that no matter what Necker had suggested, he would have met with violent opposition. "The universal spirit was that of independence," Malouet, a provincial lawyer who was soon to be a Deputy, wrote.

> Clergy, Nobility, Third Estate, each wanted an extension of preroga-tives for itself, and the suppression or reduction of all those belonging to the others. The provincial Nobility no longer wanted to be led by the courtiers; the lower Clergy wanted to share in the offices of the hierarchy; the officers and non-coms in the army, espousing the same principle, had similar demands and the grands seigneurs thought it very right for the King to be absolute master of all except themselves for they wanted to be the companions rather than the servants of the sovereign. . . . The result was a misleading unanimity in favor of innovations tending to a free government, something which everyone understood differently.[11]

That disparity of expectations, in fact, became immediately visible. On September 23 the declaration that reinstated the Parlements in their accustomed functions also called the Estates General into being for January 1, 1789. Immediately, a major controversy opened: in what form were the Estates to meet? On the twenty-fifth, in their decision registering the declaration, the judges made their position crystal-clear: they asked that "the Estates General which are to meet next January be regularly called and composed according to the formula used in 1614."[12] In other words, the three Orders were each to have the same number of Deputies; and the voting was to proceed in two stages: first within each Order, then each Order would cast a single vote.

Here was no obscure question of constitutional law. What the Parlement wanted was an assembly where the Clergy and Nobility would have a built-in majority over the Third Estate, and where, accordingly, real reform would be impossible: with the Estates General so constituted, all that could be expected was a strengthening of privileges for the upper classes; and, of course, that fact was perfectly obvious to everyone.

With that decision, the Parlement lost all the popularity it had so carefully cultivated throughout the century: now that it could at last be seen for what it was, grasping and reactionary, it was immediately abandoned by all the liberals who had formerly supported it because it had opposed both taxes and the King's arbitrary authority. What the reformers wanted, of course, was an assembly in which reform would have a majority. To that effect, they demanded the doublement du Tiers: the Third Estate, which, after all, included nine-tenths of the French population, was to have twice as many Deputies as each of the two other Orders; moreover, the vote was to be, not by Order, but on a one-man-one-vote basis, thus assuring that the privilégiés would be in the minority.

New and clearer lines had just been drawn, and they cut right across class distinctions: a significant group of the younger Nobility wanted genuine reform out of a sense of justice and fairness. This group was composed of such men as La Fayette, the vicomte de Noailles, the duc de La Rochefoucauld, the vicomte de Montmorency, and others, the so-called Americans because they had fought in the War of Independence, and returned with liberal ideas. Most of these men were also members of immensely rich families; they belonged to the highest court aristocracy and had very little doubt that, when France had a constitution, they would be its natural leaders. Some of the younger bishops, too, felt that the injustices of the current dispensation should be corrected. In reverse, some of the more conservative members of the middle class felt it was best to keep things as they were: these were men who were willing to acquiesce in a cutting down of privilege, but wanted the King to retain his full, absolute power.

Thus, all of a sudden, the composition of the Estates General became both the key political question, and the way political positions were defined. "Every day, every hour, almost, sees the publication of a new brochure, a new volume on the Estates General," Grimm reported in November, adding that when reading "*Of the Convocation and forthcoming Session of the Estates General in France* by M. Lacretelle . . . we have been struck by the author's frankness: 'Let us tell the truth: we want to be assembled in a body representing the nation, but we do not know how to do it.' "[13] Grimm goes on: "Another brochure, *The Estates General called by Louis XVI,* is by M. Target. . . . The author begins by listing all the happy auguries of the great changes that are about to take place. The Clergy and the Nobility have recognized in the Assembly of Notables in 1787, that proportional taxation was fair. . . . The Parlements . . . have returned to the nation its ancient and unbreakable right of granting all necessary subsidies. . . . All the principles of a national constitution have been admitted, recognized, endorsed by the King himself.''[14] Target, in fact, was an optimist: Louis XVI had done no such thing.

In one respect, though, Target was right: by calling the Estates General for the first time in a hundred and seventy-five years, Louis XVI seemed to be asking for help and advice from the people, and that alone was a major step. As a result, the King, who had been growing unpopular, suddenly became once again the best-loved man in France, a monarch who cared enough about his people to abandon some of his power and under whose reign, no one doubted it, France would be reborn, richer, happier, and more powerful than ever.

That might be all very well in the long run; but, in the fall of 1788 there remained acute and urgent problems. Whatever shape the Estates General might take, it became rapidly evident that they could not possibly meet in January 1789 after all: not only must elections be held according to a variety of local customs, but considerable research was required in order to find out what the precedents actually were. In the end, therefore, the opening date was pushed forward to May; but that did not settle the far more explosive question of the doublement.

The King could, if he chose, endorse the Parlement's stand; but that would deliver him into the hands of an assembly resolved to carry through an aristocratic revolution; while it had, as yet, occurred to virtually no one that the people might one day embark on their own revolution, the intentions of the upper classes were all too clear. Both Louis XVI and Marie Antoinette felt betrayed and insulted by the Nobility's attempt at transferring power to themselves; they knew, therefore, that it must be stopped; but they were far from sure that they wanted the Third Estate representation doubled. As for Necker, he had no doubts: the doublement was the way to the adoption of the constitution for which he yearned.

On the narrow grounds of opposing the Parlement's request, at least, the King and the minister were in agreement; so Necker suggested a possible way out that would spare Louis XVI from actually having to make a decision. On October 5 the notables were recalled for the sole purpose of advising on the manner in which the Estates General were to be composed. When they met on November 6, Necker, in his opening speech, told them: "It is . . . likely that while duly respecting what will seem to be constitutional [precedent], you will nonetheless decide to be guided also by thoughtful meditations and an impartial examination."[15]

In fact, of course, the notables were wholly unrepentant; they proceeded to behave again and as usual in the most reactionary manner. When, on December 12, they brought their conclusions to the King, an imposing majority had decided against the doublement and against the one-man-one-vote rule unless the Orders had all previously consented to it, something they knew would never happen. That Necker ever thought they were likely to say anything else merely shows how naive he remained. Within the overall result, however, there was one interesting new development. Until then the immediate royal family had for the most part stayed out of politics; now two parties were formed within it: the comte d'Artois, the King's youngest brother, and his very distant cousins of the Condé family gave the King a memorandum endorsing the notables' advice. That was hardly surprising: Artois was a frivolous womanizer who was famous for owning several hundred pairs of shoes and being frequently in debt in spite of his huge income. Like the Queen's friends, he simply wanted things to remain as they were; but, being even more stupid than most members of that little circle, he was unlikely ever to be influential. Far more surprising was the comte de Provence's attitude. Provence was the King's next brother, and by far the most intelligent member of the royal family. Although personally unprepossessing — he was very fat, awkward, and often nasty — he had the political sense so signally lacking in Louis XVI. He was also extremely ambitious, utterly without moral scruples, and bitterly resentful of the error of nature that had denied him the throne. Alone of the royal family, he voted for the doublement.

This liberal stance was not, however, due to conviction of any sort; rather, Provence joined what seemed to be the most popular party, in the hope, no doubt, that if things should go really wrong, he might be called either to replace his brother as king, or at least be appointed regent during the Dauphin's minority. And, in fact, there could be no doubt about it: except for the Parlement and the notables, all France was in favor of the doublement.

On November 28 the Spanish ambassador had noted that "the public is speaking out more every day in favor of the Third Estate and that trend is growing ever stronger in the provinces."[16] It was not only a matter of conversations: a flood of pamphlets now appeared to defend the rights of the French people. One of the most typical, written by an obscure commentator named Joseph Cerutti, made it all especially clear. It asked:

> What is the interest of the Third Estate? The welfare of the nation. The people are the sole body which does not live from abuses and which is even sometimes killed by them. . . . What does it request? What the Nobility, the Clergy, and the magistrates have requested, before and apparently for the people, public freedom and national reform. . . .
>
> What did the notables do in 1787? They defended their privileges against the throne. What did the notables do in 1788? They defended their privileges against the nation. The throne has, therefore, no other friend than the nation, and the nation no other friend than the throne.[17]

Here, at last, was clarity: the enemy of the people was not the King, but the privilégiés. It was not Louis XVI who resisted progress, blocked tax reform, and kept the people down, but the first two Orders, aided by the Parlements.

Although this view of the situation was fairly accurate, it also embodied one of the oldest reflexes in French history. All through the Middle Ages, an informal alliance between King and people against the barons had allowed the initially weak sovereign to grow in strength. As late as the seventeenth century, Louis XIV had won a great deal of his enormous popularity by visibly restricting the aristocracy's power. That, of course, was the trend the privilégiés had been fighting for the last fifteen years; it was also Louis XVI's chance. A new understanding between King and people, a call for help against the selfishness of the nobility and the clergy, would have meant immediate support for the monarchy from a very significant part of the population; but it was not a policy Louis XVI could even imagine.

In 1788, however, there was also a new group of people who had yet to cohere, but whose individual views were very much more radical than Cerutti's. For them, what was needed was a drastic reform that would sweep away the privilégiés, weaken the monarchy, and transfer power to an elected body able to guarantee the liberty of every Frenchman. Basing their positions on Rousseau's views, they thought that man was virtuous in the state of nature, but corrupted by society; that the fullest civil rights were inherent in nature and had been unfairly curtailed or abrogated by illegitimate governments; and that the elected body representing the people, which must be the new ruler, should merely express the general will.

These were obviously seductive views in a society where so much was forbidden and where certain people enjoyed immense and unfair advantages simply because of their position at birth. Now that this whole oppressive structure had become vulnerable, it was obviously time to attack it; and no one did so to greater effect than a hitherto unknown clergyman, the abbé Emmanuel Sieyès.

In the fall of 1788, a slim brochure signed by Sieyès and entitled *Essai sur les privilèges* (Essay on privilege) was published; and within days it was read and discussed, not just in the salons but also in the streets of Paris and Versailles. The author started simply: "What constitutes privilege," he wrote, "is that it is outside the common law."[18] Then, on page two, he moved on to a convincing restatement of Rousseau's ideas:

> The long enslavement of the [people's] minds has begotten the most deplorable prejudices. The people thinks, almost in good faith, that it is entitled only to what specific laws allow. It seems unaware that freedom exists before any society, before any legislator; that men have only gathered to protect their rights from evil enterprises, and, protected by this security, to develop more extensively, more energetically and more fruitfully their moral and physical faculties. The legislator exists, not to grant, but to protect our rights.[19]

Here, suddenly, was a truly revolutionary position: at one blow, Sieyès denied the existing government all legitimacy; and while the brunt of the attack was directed at the privilégiés, by extension that line of reasoning leads to the conclusion that the monarch's power is usurped as well. For Louis XVI, and all Europe except England, legitimacy was derived from the will of God and could, therefore, not be questioned by the people. The King might grant his subjects certain liberties, but he owed them nothing except to be as good a monarch as he knew how. Sieyès, however, now claimed that legitimacy flowed from the people; that all power not expressly granted by the people was usurped; and further, that the people could not grant any power that would infringe on its rights. Cerutti asked for improvements resulting from an alliance between King and people; Sieyès said, essentially, that the King was illegitimate and irrelevant.

As if that were not shocking enough, Sieyès then went on to describe what he saw as the only desirable society, one in which there would be no social superiors, no titles, and, of course, no privileges: "The only necessary hierarchy is that between agents of the sovereign.* . . . [B]esides that, there are only citizens equal before the law. . . . All the relationships between citizens are free relationships."[20] In fact, however, the society in which he lived rested on privilege and hierarchy: socially, legally, economically, life was divided into multiple, well-defined layers. A duke came before a count, a noble before a commoner, a bishop before a priest. Innumerable rules defined what each category was entitled to, immunity from taxes or the exclusive right to sell dried fish in Paris. Industry was carefully regulated; publication was a privilege: the entire society, at every level, was held up and restrained by the most rigid of structures. It was this state of being that Sieyès wanted to abolish at one blow.

That, of course, was hardly likely to happen, but the *Essai sur les privilèges* did help to swell the now almost overpowering demand for change; and one by one the old fortresses began to crumble. On December 5 the younger conseillers of the Parlement, made desperate by their sudden unpopularity, convinced that body to reverse itself. By a vote of 45 to 39 — a close call — the members made the following decision: "The respective number of Deputies is defined neither by law nor by precedent for any of the Orders, and it was neither within the power nor the intention of this court to determine it; the said court can only rely on the wisdom of the King for the measures to be taken bringing about such modifications as reason, liberty, justice, and the general wish may demand."[21] This obviously smacked of convenient compromise and did nothing to restore the Parlement's popularity; but it did increase the pressure on the King. The letters patent — the equivalent of the English election writs — calling the Estates into being could not be indefinitely put off.

---

* By *sovereign*, Sieyès meant, not the King but the government representing the people.

Finally, on December 27, the great question was resolved. That day, the King in his Council determined that "the number of Deputies to the Third Estate will be equal to that of the two other Orders together and that proportion will be reflected in the letters of convocation."[22] The doublement had become law. Certain other details were settled as well: the Deputies were to be apportioned according to the population; nobles and ecclesiastics could be elected as Deputies of the Third Estate; traditional methods of voting, where documented, would prevail (this applied mostly to the big cities). One key question, though, was left unmentioned, that of the method of voting within the Estates General, where, on a one-man-one-vote basis, the Third Estate would unquestionably prevail. Certain reforms were promised as well. "M. Necker, in his report published with the result of the Council of December 27, made it clear, in the name of the King, that the monarch would grant the suppression of the lettres de cachet, the freedom of the press, and periodic sessions of the Estates General to deal with financial problems."[23]

This increased Louis XVI's popularity even further. In truth, he had not much to lose by giving up the lettres de cachet: except to exile the Parlements, who would clearly (with the existence of the Estates General) cease to be a problem, they had in the last ten years hardly been used at all. As for the freedom of the press, he cannot have imagined what the results would be. Finally, the periodicity of the Estates must have struck him as a convenient way never again to be dependent on the Parlement.

What the delighted public did not know is that several members of the Council had strongly opposed these decisions. Leading the fight against, Barentin, for instance, argued that "the Third Estate, thus strengthened, would become a fearsome giant whose power would soon be tyrannical."[24]

Necker, in his answer to these opposing elements, had used the one argument most likely to sway Louis XVI: "The King's authority," he said, "has everything to fear from two powerful Orders, everything to gain by binding the people to itself; the smallest improvement made in their life will be enough to tie them to the interests of the crown."[25] It was now for Louis XVI to decide, and he was seen to look at the Queen, who, for the first time ever, had attended the Council. All through the discussion she had remained silent; she still did not speak, "but it was easy to see that she did not disapprove of the doublement of the Third Estate," Barentin noted;[26] and so, the King spoke up in its favor. Having thus backed the liberal position, however, he went on to say that he intended to preserve the division of the Estates into three separate Orders, each voting as a unit — thus, presumably, preventing the natural consequences of the doublement. One more important matter was then raised. Barentin suggested that the Estates meet in Soissons, with the King residing some fifteen miles away in Compiègne, so as to avoid the liberal pressures likely to multiply in Paris; Necker argued for Paris, as the capital of the kingdom; and the King gave his last decision of the day: the Estates would meet at Versailles.

All in all, therefore, a compromise had been reached, or so it seemed to all present; in fact, the future had been heavily mortgaged while several essential precedents were set. Although the King granted the doublement only because he expected to retain control through the vote by Order, he had in fact created a situation where the more numerous Third Estate was bound to insist on a one-man-one-vote rule, thus putting the government in an impossible position: resistance to a majority of the Deputies would obviously be seen as ignoring the wishes of the nation. As for holding the Estates in Versailles, it was almost the same as holding them in Paris: if Louis XVI really wanted to isolate them from the excitement in the capital, then Soissons was the only answer; but it was typical of him that, in a frenzy of indecision, he finally reached a halfway position that had nothing but disadvantages.

Then, too, Marie Antoinette's presence at the Council underlined her importance; henceforth, no major decision would be made without her approval. This was a double mistake, first because she was so unpopular, second because it confirmed Louis XVI's indecisiveness. If either the ministers or the future Estates General thought that he took a stand they disliked at the Queen's urging, then it became virtually a patriotic duty to defeat l'Autrichienne by forcing the King to change his mind.

Finally, the royal couple and Necker, looking firmly backward, completely misjudged the political situation: the doublement was granted so as to protect the crown from the first two Orders, but by December 1788 the world had already changed. It was the Third Estate that held all the cards, and the riots in Grenoble, the main city in the Dauphiné, should have made that clear.

All through the eighties, that province had been in the forefront of resistance to any new tax; its own Estates, after more than a century of suspension, had begun to meet again; more, in that meeting at Vizille following the closing of the Parlements in July 1788, the Dauphiné had actually given itself a constitution that made it virtually independent from the central government. Upon coming to office, Necker, realizing the danger of this innovation, had tried amending the text, but to no avail: his popularity apparently stopped at the borders of the province. On November 8, the reconstituted Estates had written the King a letter: "The Commons include the most numerous part of your subject," they said, "that which pays the most taxes, which owns the most property; it is the Commons who bear the burden of all the abuses. . . . If the Orders, if the provinces were to vote separately, they would become single bodies and it would no longer be the nation itself that would speak through the voice of its Deputies."[27]

Here was a warning indeed: the most economically active part of the province, the middle and upper bourgeoisie, who could to a degree control the workers and artisans, was claiming a share of political power that would reflect its numbers and its wealth. The demand for a one-man-one-vote rule was presented in the name of the nation, which would make it virtually impossible to gainsay; and the logical consequence of this identification of the Estates General — and, in fact, of the Third Estate — with France itself was that the King would become subordinate to the Assembly. It was, however, a warning the Council chose to ignore.

Why it did so may perhaps be explained by the fact that relying on precedent was an ingrained habit; and Necker in particular had a number of other urgent preoccupations: not only must he keep the treasury solvent until the meeting of the Estates General, he also had to prevent a looming famine. In the late eighteenth century the French, and especially the Parisians, still relied on bread as their staple food; it was therefore crucial to ensure a steady and abundant supply of flour. That, under free-trade conditions, would have been no problem, but most provinces either forbade the export of wheat to the rest of France or else put such high tariffs on it as to make it hopelessly expensive. The not infrequent result was glut in one province, and virtual famine in another.

Some progress had been made, notably by Turgot in 1776; but because the population of Paris was so large — some 520,000 inhabitants in 1789 — it was notoriously hard to supply it with enough grain in bad years; and, as it happened, the crops of 1787 and 1788 had been unusually poor.

This was a problem that tormented Necker from the moment he assumed office. He had two very good reasons to keep Paris supplied: humanity, of course, was one; the other was a history of popular disorders, sometimes reaching dangerous levels, when bread became scarce or too expensive. The outlook, in the fall of 1788, was exceedingly poor on both counts. Wheat in 1784 had been selling at 22.75 constant francs for a standard measure; in 1785, after a good crop, it dropped to 18 francs, then, in 1786, to 16 francs. In 1787, however, it rose again to a still bearable 22 francs; after a bad crop that summer, it went up further, reaching a high 25 francs in 1788; and from that summer on, the rise was constant until, in July 1789, it reached a high for the century: an appalling 46 francs.

This was just what Necker had worked hard to prevent. On September 7, 1788, after a bout of hail had severely damaged that summer's crop, he forbade the export of grain. On November 23, he decreed that grain could no longer be bought outside the markets, thus preventing speculators from buying directly in the provinces and hoarding. On April 22, 1789, with the situation rapidly worsening, he gave justices of the peace the power to bring grain to the markets by force if necessary.

None of that was enough, though. On November 23, January 11, and April 20, various measures were taken to facilitate the import of grain into France, but without much effect; so, at immense cost, Necker proceeded to buy abroad a huge quantity of wheat, some million and a half standard measures altogether. Even that failed to make up for the hail of 1788 and what proved to be an exceptionally severe and lengthy winter in 1788–89.

"The cold and the snow continue with such intensity that the Seine has become a place to stroll; my children and I crossed it on foot five days ago," the Spanish ambassador reported. "There is great misery in spite of the numerous and well-ordered measures taken by public and private charity to alleviate it. . . . It is to be feared that it will get worse and that the coming year be a calamitous one."[28]

The severe winter was a disaster on several counts: not only was the next crop in danger, not only was there a great deal of suffering, but also, in preindustrial societies, extreme cold, by cutting resources and interrupting transports, invariably produced the equivalent of a very severe recession: business slowed down, marginal enterprises defaulted, and unemployment spread. That, together with the steady rise in the price of bread, would have been bad enough at any time; combined with political unrest and the forthcoming meeting of the Estates General, it created a catastrophic situation for the government.

The famine, amazingly, was a problem of which Louis XVI was aware; as the cold deepened, he set in motion a variety of rescue schemes. On January 11 the *Journal de Paris* commented, fulsomely but accurately: "While on the one hand our monarch is busy with regenerating the nation and linking with an unbreakable bond the people's happiness and the leader's authority, on the other hand his fatherly generosity is also extended to the most unhappy class of his subjects. . . . His Majesty has everywhere given his help to resourceless indigents."[29] Actually leaving Versailles, the King was seen walking in the countryside outside Paris, visiting the poor, while both he and the Queen contributed substantially to various charitable enterprises.

Perhaps because it was so very cold, there was no serious unrest; had there been, the government altogether lacked the means to quell it. Paris in 1789 had a police force composed of only 1,500 men; worse, they were divided between various organizations and were mostly untrained and incompetent; another 140 men could be called on, but they had to come in from outside the city; and the King's Guard, which was at least stationed at Versailles, close enough to intervene, was largely ceremonial. Paris, therefore, was defenseless.

A wise minister faced with this situation would have tried to set up a more effective police force. Necker, always the optimist, was convinced that there was nothing to fear, so he did nothing — and this at a time when more observant men could see that the situation was highly volatile. "France is threatened with a revolution, a national effervescence such as to be almost unprecedented," Mercy wrote the Emperor early in January. "The government has made error upon error. . . . By recalling so very late the only man [Necker] on whom now rests the safety of the state, he has been left with so difficult a task that he is himself frightened. . . . In so critical a situation, the Queen has taken it upon herself to remain silent about her opinions, avoiding all signs of preference for either party."[30]

She had good reason to do so: her unpopularity was so extreme that anyone or anything she was seen to support would instantly become a target for the bitterest attacks. Indeed, just as her real power was greater than ever, and while Louis XVI turned to her more and more often in the accelerating crisis, she found, not the satisfaction she expected from being able to determine policy but endless bitterness. Her private life was a shambles (the Polignac set had just deserted her), her public life not much better; and still her responsibilities grew.

First and foremost was the political situation. She could see that it was menacing; and she now began to understand that the greatest danger to the King's authority might not come from the privileged Orders, after all. Unfortunately, though, the conclusions she drew from this awareness were diametrically opposed to the policy pursued by Necker, the minister she had virtually forced Louis XVI to appoint; given this, she could no longer rely on Mercy, her usual confidant, who still thought that Necker was indispensable. At that point, she turned to the royal family for support in trying to convince the King that the Estates General must be shorn of power before their opening. Her plan, simply enough, was to have the King issue a declaration stating that the Assembly would have as its sole task the compilation of the *cahiers de doléances*.

These were, traditionally, the list of complaints that the Deputies brought with them from their provinces to the King. They were supposed to show the monarch what was wrong, what needed correcting: after that, it was up to him to act on them or ignore them, as he chose. Limiting the Estates General to the job of adding together and editing these myriad documents would, obviously, deny them any power to modify the status quo.

In great secrecy, Monsieur, who, despite his liberal stand, was growing alarmed, joined the Queen's cabal. It was, however, too late: Necker was necessary, and the King chose to follow his minister rather than his wife. Unfortunately, Artois was incapable of keeping a secret; word of the cabal leaked out. On April 23 the minister of Saxony reported: "A terrible league has been formed against [Necker] headed by monseigneur the comte d'Artois. . . . Monsieur . . . is beginning to vacillate. . . . On Sunday at Versailles, it was taken as certain that the baron de Breteuil . . . would be called to the council that very evening. . . . This would have been the necessary step preceding the dismissal of the [minister, Necker]."[31] This was just the sort of tactic that was likely to create immense resentment outside the court: once again, the King was seen as being maneuvered by a selfish, privileged little clique who were the enemy of the people.

In fact, Necker remained in power; but the fragility of his position was underlined: if the Queen, who was responsible for his appointment, turned against him, precedent showed he would not last long. Nothing more was needed to make the atmosphere even more tense, the Queen even more hated. As Marie Antoinette saw it, however, she had good reason to turn against her former protégé. She had agreed to the doublement to protect the King's authority from the privilégiés; now she realized that the real menace to the monarchy came from a very different quarter. That trend toward the empowerment of the Third Estate, which the foreign ambassadors had noticed in the early winter, became an almost irresistible flood in the early months of 1789. The first sign of this new state of affairs was the tremendous sensation that greeted the publication, in January, of a new pamphlet by the abbé Sieyès.

Entitled *Qu'est-ce que le Tiers-Etat?* (What is the Third Estate), it opened with three questions and three answers which changed French history:

> What is the Third Estate?
> Everything.
> What has it been until now in the political order?
> Nothing.
> What does it ask?
> To become something.[32]

After those six terse lines, the absurdity of a government in which the mass of the population had nothing to say became so plain, and seemed so unacceptable, that great changes were bound to follow; and they were not likely to enhance the King's power. Nor was this all: in its attack against the privilégiés, and, by implication, the monarchy, *Qu'est-ce que le Tiers-Etat?* went a good deal further than the *Essai sur les privilèges*.

> If the privilégiés have managed to usurp all lucrative and honorific functions [Sieyès wrote], it is at the same time an odious iniquity for the mass of the citizens and treachery for the state.

Who would dare to say that the Third Estate does not have within itself all it needs to make a complete nation? It is a strong and robust man still chained by the arm. If the privileged Orders disappeared, the nation would be, not something less, but something more. . . . The Third Estate includes all that belongs to the nation; whatever is not part of the Third Estate cannot regard itself as part of the nation.[33]

Here was not only strong language, but revolutionary politics: in the space of a moment, the time it took to read a thin pamphlet, the world was turned upside down, the classes that had always ruled were rejected from the nation; and, most extraordinary of all, the argument was utterly convincing.

From there, Sieyès went on to demand the doublement — clearly that part was written before December 27 — and a one-man-one-vote rule. Further, he said, only people belonging to the Tiers should be allowed as its Deputies; and he went on: "It is a strange country where the citizens who profited the most from the state gave it the least; where there were taxes it was shameful to pay* . . . where it is honorable to consume and humiliating to produce."[34] A word here is particularly important: *citizens*. The Greeks had been citizens of their cities, the Romans citizens of the Empire, but the French were *subjects* of the King. The very use of the word *citizen,* therefore, embodied a claim and a rejection: the claim was to equality before the law, the rejection that of a God-given authority. And as if it were not yet plain enough, Sieyès added: "The nation alone can will for itself; alone it can create the law."[35] In that one sentence, the old order was abolished.

In fact, Sieyès was expressing vividly what many politically conscious people in Paris and the provinces already thought. It is one of the most extraordinary aspects of the Revolution that in a country where 65 percent of the population was illiterate, certain new ideas were not only widely known but completely accepted: convinced that they were living in a time of high civilization, the mass of the people expected political progress and, indeed, thought it unavoidable.

This can best be seen by looking at some of the cahiers, the registers of complaints, which between January and April 1789 were being

---

* The taille, the tax paid by the peasants and from which nobles and Clergy were exempt, was considered "shameful" because it applied only to commoners.

compiled all over the country; their boldness will become clearer still when contrasted to the letters that were sent out by the government in the King's name. "We need," the official text said,

> the help of our faithful subjects to overcome the difficulties we are experiencing relative to the state of our finances and to establish, according to our wishes, a constant and invariable order in all the parts of the government that concern the happiness of our subjects and the prosperity of our realm.
>
> These great reasons have moved us to call the assembly of the Estates . . . in order to advise and help us in all matters that will be referred to it and to allow us to know the wishes and complaints of our people so that, through mutual confidence and love between the sovereign and his subjects, an effective remedy can be found as soon as possible to the ills of the state, abuses of all kinds ended and prevented from recurring by good and substantial means which will give us particularly the calm and tranquillity of which we have so long been deprived.[36]

The phrasing is interesting in that the King is presented as yet another victim of the abuses — to which, in fact, he had consented throughout his reign. Necker, whose words these largely are, had been careful to leave the door open to wholesale reform. Still, there was no question of transferring power away from the King: what was apparently at stake was pure efficacy.

The letters went out on January 24, and immediately, in every *baillage* (the basic administrative unit that defined the constituencies), the electors began to meet, not just to choose their Deputies, but also, in some cases mainly, to put together the cahiers. Altogether, not counting the Nobility or the Clergy, this involved some 4.3 million men in a population of just under 20 million, an astonishingly high number at a time when the English electorate, for instance, consisted of barely 100,000 voters. In order to vote or to be elected, a man had to be at least twenty-five years of age and pay at least 6 livres a year in capitation, or head tax. This excluded all factory workers (concentrated mostly in and around Paris) and artisans; but it included much of the peasantry. As for women, influential though they were, it occurred to no one that they should have the right to vote.

Voting regulations for the Third Estate were determined by the government; the two privileged Orders set their own rules. The Clergy, many of whose members held liberal views, met in separate assembly and decided that two-thirds of its Deputies must be priests, as opposed to bishops. The Nobility decided that simple hereditary nobility was sufficient to vote or be elected; the possession of a fief was not required, but plural voting was made possible, since the nobles were entitled to one vote wherever they had a fief. That meant, essentially, that the Parlement nobles would count as part of the second Order, but that the grands seigneurs, who owned many fiefs, could make their weight felt accordingly.

Like the Tiers, the privileged Orders gathered their cahiers, and in some cases they asked for reform; but it was the people whose voice came through clearly and forcefully. As Sieyès had pointed out, the Third Estate had become the nation, and the nation, in a surprising show of virtual unanimity, knew just what it wanted.

Throughout France, the same list of demands recurs everywhere, sometimes written in polished words by lawyers, sometimes spun out in pompous phrases by small-town intellectuals, sometimes composed of rough, almost ungrammatical sentences by a group of peasants. To read the cahiers is to feel the breadth and diversity of the country, especially since local issues always follow the great, national questions; but the latter are always clear and simple. They are six in number:

1. All taxes are to be voted by the Estates General, which must be presented with a clear and complete yearly budget. The debt must be nationalized* and consolidated.
2. The taxes are to be applicable to all: there will be no more tax-exempt orders or persons.
3. The Estates General are to meet on a regular (usually triennial) basis.
4. The press is to be free; censorship of all kinds is to be abolished.
5. There will be no more arbitrary arrests; a court order will be required in every case.
6. The ministers are to be responsible to the Estates General.

In those six simple principles a constitution can be found: what France demanded, in the spring of 1789, was the transformation of the absolute

---

* Until then, it was the King's personal debt.

monarchy into a constitutional regime complete with periodic assemblies and a bill of rights. Some of the cahiers, of course, went further: there were demands for a civil list, a yearly appropriation covering the King's expenses, which would prevent him from spending as he chose; for the suppression of the Ferme générale; for the end of the venality of the seats in the Parlements; for a graduated and progressive income tax; even for the demolition of the Bastille. Finally, both the Tiers and the Nobility asked that Protestants be restored to their full civil rights; the Clergy, intolerant as usual, naturally opposed this.

There remained the great question of the vote within the Estates General; there the divisions appeared clearly. Almost without exception, the cahiers of the Third Estate asked for the one-man-one-vote rule, the *vote par tête;* with equal unanimity, those of the Clergy insisted on the vote by Orders; and the Nobility was split between the two positions, with, however, an almost general acknowledgment that, for questions of taxation, the vote par tête should prevail.

By early April most of this was known at Versailles. "It is as yet impossible to tell how far the effects of this madness will go," Mercy reported despairingly on the second, "but to judge by the sort of solitude in which the sovereign finds himself, by the weakness and fear in his ministry, by the audacity with which even the princes of the blood oppose the monarch, one must consider the entire subversion of the monarchy as entirely possible. . . . The Queen is greatly worried. . . . She tries to coax her august husband into being a little firmer."[37]

Amazingly, even though the situation could clearly be seen as dangerous, the government made no plans at all to deal with it. Already, Necker had firmly rebuffed all suggestions that he at least try to ensure the elections of Deputies friendly to himself and the King; now, he waited for the opening of the Estates and did nothing. As for Louis XVI, while it was always possible to force him to act in finite, precise occasions — the appointment or dismissal of a minister, for instance — there was no giving him the energy he did not have. Even the monarchy's supporters soon found that out.

One of these, Pierre-Victor Malouet, was a successful lawyer and a Deputy from Riom, in the Auvergne. Without any assistance from the government, he had fought hard to limit the demands of the local cahiers so as to preserve some of the King's power; this was noticed at Versailles. He reported in his memoirs:

> We were [on April 20] at M. de Montmorin's. "The King," M. Necker said to me, "has already read a great part of the cahiers and he saw in yours an article which pleased him, and which we would like to see in all. You give the Estates only the right to consent to the laws and taxes."
>
> "Indeed, yes," I said, "It is for you, for the King to propose. . . . If you take the initiative . . . you will keep it, for if we modify, we exaggerate [your proposals], you will always be able to say: I am the King, the keeper, the conservator of your oaths; and just as I neither can nor wish to go against the nation's wishes, you cannot either."[38]

Necker listened affably to this advice, and, as usual, failed to act.

That the King, aware of the contents of the cahiers, should have done nothing, said nothing, is scarcely believable: he was, clearly, about to lose his power, and, for all his passivity, he cared very deeply about its preservation. More astonishing is that Necker, who wanted limited reforms but certainly not a revolution, made not a single attempt to prepare for the opening of the Estates. No doubt he relied on his popularity; but popularity was no longer enough.

It is, of course, always easy to blame with the benefit of hindsight; but the contemporaries were just as struck by the government's immobility. Malouet, for one, complained bitterly. "It was no longer the King who spoke, it was the crown's consulting lawyer," he wrote, "asking everyone for advice and seeming to say to all and sundry: What should be done? What can I do? How far do you want to cut down my authority? What will be left to me?" and he adds: "They knew neither how to give nor how to hold back. . . . While the ministerial party, lacking consistency and a plan, hastened to its doom, the royalist courtiers, lacking equally in strength, wisdom and foresight, speeded up the cataclysm by declaring equally against the ministers and against the people."[39]

This kind of paralysis was widely discernible. Adrien Duquesnoy, another lawyer, but one who belonged to the extreme left, noted: "The extreme weakness of the government has been the reason why all power was broken, all the ties that bind men dissolved, and the King, constantly pushed from one system to the next, changing them, adopting them, rejecting them with the most astonishing lack of thought, showing strength, then giving in weakly; the King completely lost his authority."[40]

Duquesnoy was right. By recalling the Parlement in 1774 and giving in to the Queen's whims, Louis XVI had lost the power to change a blocked society; by backing, then rejecting, in turn Turgot, Necker, Calonne, and Brienne, he had shown that he was incapable of sustaining a resolution, that he could be pushed about by determined people. Now his total passivity invited the Estates General to take over. As April drew to its end, what the gathering Deputies witnessed was the spectacle of a King who would not lead and a government who would not govern.

CHAPTER NINE

From Estates to Assembly

. . .

THE Paris Season in the early spring of 1789 was among the most brilliant in memory. The nation was about to enter a Golden Age of justice and prosperity; the salons would find themselves more influential than ever as their members joined in the future, freer government; the people's burden would be lifted; and all this at virtually no cost. Even if the privilégiés found themselves paying a little more tax, this slight annoyance would be more than compensated by their newfound power in the forthcoming constitutional system. Never had conversation been so dazzling or so important: it was, after all, the future of the country that was being discussed in the great houses of Paris and Versailles. France, always at the forefront of civilization, was about to show the world yet again what progress was about.

That, at least, was the consensus in much of the elegant world, and, curiously, it was at one with the perspective of much of the country. In small provincial towns, among the lower middle classes of the great urban centers, everywhere except at court and in some rural areas, it was assumed that the Estates General would promptly bring about the necessary reforms, that the King would agree to them, gaining in popularity what he lost in power, and that, free at last, the French would prosper in a golden glow of national satisfaction.

Even the songs sung in the streets of Paris, which, until very recently had savagely attacked King, Queen, and government, were now praising them:

Louis comme le soleil brille
Par les rayons de sa bonté
Son peuple est toute sa famille
Voilà le moment désiré.
O Roi que j'aime et je révère . . .
Digne de régner sur la France
Par tes vertus, ton équité . . .
Le Clergé comme la Noblesse
Et le Tiers-Etat réunis
Tiendront à jamais la promesse
D'être tes enfants, tes amis . . .
Vive Louis! Vive Antoinette!
Vive leur ministre accompli . . .[1]

[Louis like the sun shines
With the rays of his goodness.
His people are his family.
Here comes the longed-for moment.
O King whom I love and revere . . .
Worthy of reigning in France
Through your virtues, your justice . . .
Clergy and Nobility
And the Third Estate as one
Will forever hold their promise
To be your children, your friends . . .
Long live Louis! Long live Antoinette!
Long live their accomplished minister!]

In this general atmosphere of goodwill and happy anticipation, with progress as the order of the day, it happened very naturally that women, those most civilized of beings, were more powerful than ever. "Women of a certain rank were involved in everything before the Revolution," Mme de Staël remembered. "Their husbands or their brothers always sent them to see the ministers; they could insist without lacking in propriety, even exaggerate without giving anyone the right to complain; and all the hints they knew how to give had a great effect on most of the men in office."[2] Now it was in the liberal salons that the future was being settled: Mme Necker, Mme de Staël, the comtesse de Tessé, and the duchesse d'Anville gathered the people who mattered and led discussions about the forthcoming constitution; as a result, it was clear that the dawning era would be one of liberty and refinement combined. That the ladies in their elaborate, fashionable dresses, that the elegant gentlemen who met thus happily might be in any danger of losing that *douceur de vivre,* that sweetness of life, which they prized so highly, seemed altogether out of the question.

Still, on April 28, when the riots ending in the sacking of the Réveillon factory took place,* the aristocrats might have wondered whether the change would happen as easily, as smoothly as they expected. But the Estates were about to open; the court was as splendid as ever; the very grandeur of the ceremonies that soon engaged everyone's attention buried the memory of that disagreeable moment.

First, on the day before the opening, the King, in his gala carriage, went to the church of Notre Dame in Versailles; the princes of the blood were there to greet him as he arrived. The Queen came soon after and was, in turn, received by the princesses. From there, a procession formed to go to the church of Saint Louis, where the mass was to be celebrated. First came the clergy of the two parishes in their full canonicals, then the Deputies. Of those, the Tiers came first (the place of least honor), dressed as prescribed in plain black and plumeless hats; then the nobles, wearing black silk coats lavishly embroidered in gold, gold vests, black breeches, white stockings, lace ties, and hats crowned with white plumes; finally, the Clergy, the cardinals in red, the bishops in purple. Like every other aspect of the ceremony, placement and costume answered to the unbreakable etiquette; but it required no great intelligence to understand the contrast between the unrelieved black of the Tiers and the gold and plumes of the nobles.

After the Deputies came the King, surrounded by the many splendidly dressed officers of his Household, followed by the princes of the blood royal and the dukes. The Queen, with her ladies, walked on the King's left; she wore the *grand habit,* a splendid embroidered dress spreading over vast side hoops, feathers in her hair, diamonds everywhere. It was a sumptuous show, but, in fact, the main actors did not enjoy it much.

---

* See Chapter One.

The shrewd American Gouverneur Morris noted: "The procession is very magnificent through a double row of tapestries [hanging from the windows]. Neither the King nor the Queen appear too well pleased. The former is repeatedly saluted as he passes with the Vive le Roi but the latter meets not a single acclamation."[3]

This is confirmed by the Spanish ambassador's report: "The acclamations and applause were unceasing," he wrote, "and the shared conviction of the sovereign's kindness and good intentions was expressed in enthusiastic ovations. But at the same time that these ovations filled even the most indifferent spectators with joy, one felt . . . ever more amazed at the deep and universal silence that accompanied the Queen . . . who has naturally suffered from the public's attitude."[4] In fact, upon returning to her apartments in the Palace, Marie Antoinette collapsed, sobbing heavily.

Before that, however, she sat through the mass at Saint Louis. There was a long sermon in which pointed allusions were made to the bad old times, now ended, and to the Polignac set. Duquesnoy, a Deputy, watching it all, remarked: "I noticed on the Queen's mouth an expression of anger [during the allusions to Mme de Polignac], otherwise the greatest coolness, the most intrepid assurance. . . . The King slept . . . some of the time. . . .

"As we came out of the church, complete silence greeted the Queen, the King received a little applause, the duc d'Orléans a great deal."[5]

All this, however, was only a preliminary. The first meeting of the Estates General opened, as scheduled, on the next day, May 5, 1789. That day at noon, the King, the Queen, the royal family, the princes of the blood royal, and all their suites left the Palace at noon for the short drive to the Hall of the Estates. This had been set up in one of the crown's buildings about a quarter of a mile down the avenue de Paris, the great thoroughfare that starts in front of the Palace and leads straight to the capital. The hall was thus not far from, but not within, the King's own residence. In fact, the building in question, the Hôtel des Menus Plaisirs, had been chosen because it had large interior spaces, previously used to store sets and decorations from the royal theater. The arrangement of the hall, which, as noted, contained smaller halls for the meetings of the first two Estates, was meant to underline the inferiority of the Tiers. The great hall, used on this day and always by the Tiers, was a vast, rectangular space lined with columns. It was occupied at one end by a platform set on three levels. On the top, carpeted in purple with gold fleurs-de-lis, stood the throne under a lavishly draped canopy. That, of course, was where the King sat when, at around 12:30, he came in, wearing an ermine-lined cloak and diamonds in his hat.

Just below, on the next step, was the Queen, sitting in an armchair, with her ladies behind her. Near her, on that second step, stood Monsieur, Madame, the comte d'Artois, Madame Elisabeth, the King's aunts Mesdames Adélaide and Victoire, and the comte d'Artois's two children, all with their attendants.

On the third step was a much larger group composed of the princes of the blood royal, the marshals of France, such peers as were not Deputies, the ministers, and the many officers of the royal Households, all splendidly dressed. It was immediately noticed that the duc d'Orléans was missing from his place; in what everyone construed as a deliberate insult to the King he had chosen to join the ranks of the Third Estate after having engineered his election as one of its Deputies.

All those on the platform faced the Assembly. Before them, on their right, was the Clergy; on their left, the Nobility; and in the center, a mass of men dressed in black, the Third Estate. At least, the Third Estate sat; research has disclosed that, before 1614, the Deputies of the Tiers had knelt while the King spoke; but finally it was decided that would be too antithetic to the spirit of the time.

The ambassadors sat between the columns, on the side, and behind them were more than two thousand spectators. "All the front benches were reserved for the ladies," Grimm noted, "and that courtesy greatly increased the pomp of the spectacle because of the elegance and richness of their dress."[6] All in all, it was a grand and majestic scene, the proper setting and the proper audience for the long-awaited regeneration of France.

Now it was up to Louis XVI. No one except those close to him knew what he was going to say, but it was generally expected that he would announce reforms, give orders about the voting method, define the topics to be discussed by the Assembly, propose a specific program: kings, after all, were supposed to govern. Had the Queen had her way, he would have done just that; it was time, she felt, to remind the French they owed the sovereign unquestioning obedience; and, of course, the three Orders would have been instructed to vote separately. "To the burden of the taxes and the debts of the state, there has been added a spirit of restlessness and innovation that will bring about the greatest disasters if it is not promptly checked," she wanted Louis XVI to say.* He was to continue: "I hope that this Assembly will show the obedience which [is] as necessary to the people's happiness as it is to the conservation of the monarchy. . . . I know that the power and authority of a just King are great,"[7] and after those menacing sentences, the end of tax exemptions was to be promised — provided, however, that the two privileged Orders agreed.

That position, in its uncompromising refusal to give an inch, along with the order to vote separately, might well have received the support of the Clergy and the Nobility; and at that stage the Tiers would almost certainly have obeyed. It would, however, have required the kind of firmness Louis XVI so conspicuously lacked; so, instead, he listened to Necker, without, however, showing himself as liberal as the minister would have liked. The result, as usual, was an uneasy compromise.

"The day my heart had been awaiting has finally come," the King said in a monotone,

> and I am amid the representatives of the nation I take pride in ruling. . . . The debt of the state, already immense when I came to the throne, has grown larger still under my reign; an expensive but honorable war is the cause; that forced the raising of the taxes and has made the unequal burden of them more evident.
>
> A general sense of disquiet, an excessive desire to innovate have taken hold and would finally completely mislead public opinion if it were not settled by wise and moderate measures.

Already, it was clear that the King was resisting real change: in saying that the deficit was due only to the war, he was ignoring the cost of the court and that of the pensions. He then went on to hope that the Clergy and Nobility would renounce their tax exemptions, and explained that retrenchment alone would not solve the financial problem: a whole new tax system, he said, was needed. He continued:

---

* The draft in Marie Antoinette's own hand has been preserved.

Agitation is everywhere, but an Assembly of the representatives of the nation will no doubt hear only the voices of wisdom and prudence. . . .

I know that the power and authority of a just King . . . are great; they have always given France its brilliance and its glory; I must, and always will, uphold them. But everything you may expect of the most loving interest in the public happiness, all that can be asked from a sovereign who is also his people's best friend, you may, you must expect from my feelings.

Gentlemen, may a felicitous concord reign in this Assembly, may this period become ever memorable for the prosperity and happiness of the realm! That is the wish of my heart . . . and what I expect as the reward of my good intentions and my love for my people.[8]

In its odd blend of authoritarianism, borrowed from Marie Antoinette's draft, and trust in the Deputies, of requests for reforms and warnings against excessive change, the speech had something to displease everyone. Still, Louis XVI spoke of his love for the people; he was generally believed to be well intentioned; and he had, after all, allowed the Estates to meet, so he was much applauded. As for the specifics of his program, that, the Deputies thought, would come next: after the King's, there were still two speeches to be delivered that day, one by Barentin, the keeper of the seals, and one by Necker.

Nobody expected much from Barentin, who, indeed, spoke so poorly that he was mostly inaudible; but it hardly seemed to matter. The savior of the country, the regenerator of France was next.

Necker was far and away the most popular man in the country. Not only did the Tiers believe in him, much of the Nobility did as well. It was understood the King was too grand for specifics; but here, at last, the Assembly knew it could expect details, concrete proposals, a blueprint for the rebirth of the nation. What it heard instead was one of the dullest speeches ever delivered to a parliamentary body, and one of such length, furthermore, that Necker, whose voice failed after a few minutes, had it read by Pierre Broussonet, one of his subordinates.

Blending high-flown platitudes with vague promises and technical details so complex that virtually no one could understand them, Necker proceeded thoroughly to disappoint the Assembly. (As for the King and Queen, who had already read it all, the boredom they must have felt is scarcely imaginable.) First, the minister gave a lengthy account of the budget, in the course of which he claimed, with his usual tendency to improve on the truth, that the deficit was only 56 million livres. "While France, while all Europe," he went on, "think that the Estates General were called because of the absolute need, the unavoidable necessity, to raise taxes, it can be seen, in the precise summary I have just given, that a King who feared for his authority would have found in the economies he was able to decree a solution adequate to the circumstances."[9] This, to say the least, was less than convincing: while Louis XVI was given full credit for not having tried to raise taxes by force, virtually no one believed that a few cuts here and there would have, of themselves, solved the financial problem. The King, himself, in fact, had just told the Deputies that taxes would have to rise.

Having thus lost a good deal of credibility, Necker went on to say that the financial problem must have absolute priority, but a new order was needed that would guarantee the nation healthier finances. And then, he added, that while reforms were needed, he was not about to define them. There should be, he explained, regularly held sessions of the Estates. "We have gathered, for this one time, the ruins of an old temple; it is up to you, Messieurs, to look them over and see how they can be better ordered."[10] Nothing, given the mood of the country, could have been more dangerous: unlike the Queen, who wanted nothing changed except the tax system, Necker admitted reforms were badly needed; but instead of telling the Assembly what he recommended, what the King was prepared to accept, he simply changed the subject to the role he hoped might be played by the provincial assemblies.

That, in turn, brought him back to the Estates General, whose competence, he said, was unrestricted. "The King, Messieurs, considers you as associated, from this moment, with his Council; he will listen with attention and interest to your suggestions and your proposals, and His Majesty will also communicate to you all the ideas he feels are worth being examined. It is through perfect closeness between the King and this august Assembly that the business of the King and the nation will be best handled and understood."[11] Considering the contents of the cahiers, this was obviously asking for trouble: the minister was quite aware that Louis XVI had no intention of granting most of their demands. It is, in fact, hard not to suspect that he hoped to force the King's hand by creating a situation where those demands would become irresistible; but then again, he was so optimistic, so sure of himself and his popularity that he may well have believed that once the transformation began, he would be able to stop it when he chose.

Before suggesting that the Orders remain separate, except for common meetings when needed, and that the Clergy and Nobility give up their exemptions, he did, however, include a note of warning: "His Majesty will weigh the character of your deliberations; and if it is such as he hopes, such as he is entitled to expect, such, finally, as the healthier part of the nation wishes and requests, the King will carry out your wishes . . . and will find glory in carrying them out."[12] Nothing could have been better calculated to annoy without frightening: after asking them to reform the government, Necker was telling the Deputies that, in effect, the Estates General was merely a consultative assembly, none of whose decisions could stand up itself; and yet there was no threat of repression, of dissolution if the King was dissatisfied.

The speech was followed by much applause, after which the King and court left the hall; but, in fact, the disappointment was universal. The reactionaries were furious because Necker had suggested giving up certain privileges, the liberals were disappointed because they felt that the minister had not gone far enough, besides which everyone agreed that the speech had been long, confusing, and dull.

Duquesnoy described it tersely: "Then came M. Necker. As he stood up to speak, he was applauded. He spoke for at least three hours. Virtually no one was pleased with what he said. . . . [He offered] no new ideas either in administration or finance. . . . [There was] no applause, most often only a frozen silence."[13] Even Mme de Staël, devoted as she was to her father, was unable to pretend it had been otherwise: "As they left the sitting, the people's party, that is, most of the Third Estate, a minority of the Nobility, and several members of the Clergy complained that M. Necker had behaved as if he were addressing a provincial assembly by speaking only of the measures to be taken to guarantee the debt of the state and to improve the tax system."[14] Worse, at the end of the day, the really urgent question, that of the mode of voting, had been left unresolved.

As things stood, the Tiers alone easily outnumbered the two other

Orders combined. The Clergy had 308 Deputies, 205 of whom were priests who, because they were themselves poor and underprivileged, were likely to sympathize with the Tiers. The Nobility's 285 Deputies appeared more homogeneous: 266 were nobles, nineteen were members of the Parlements, and therefore likely to be among the most reactionary of all; but even here, there was a significant minority of young, enlightened men who thought that the separation of the Orders was antiquated and wrong. Finally, there was the Tiers with its 621 Deputies.

Although the electorate of the Third Estate included a great mass of very small farmers, it was men of property or influence who had been chosen: a few nobles, of course, but mostly professionals who knew what they wanted — 214 lawyers, 158 judges of the lower courts, 178 merchants. They all could read a contract and understand legal language; they all were accustomed to power, each within his domain; and they felt their time had come.

Still, nothing could happen until the Deputies verified their election; and so paralysis promptly set in. The privileged Orders wanted to do so on a separate basis, since they intended to keep to the old formulas; the Tiers, intent on establishing the vote par tête, wanted the three Orders to proceed together and in the absence of the other two Orders refused to do anything. It was a grotesque and dangerous situation: the hopes raised simply by the meeting of the Assembly were so high that no one could tell what would happen if they were disappointed.

A government, if it wishes its orders to be respected, must govern; yet, in this, the first crisis of the Estates General, the King and Necker did absolutely nothing. "The public thinks that these events cause the King to feel nothing but indifference and boredom," Mercy noted on May 10. "The ministry is fearful, without vigor, inactive; [Necker] alone faces the storm, but he is isolated, without help, without support, and attacked by a cabal all the more dangerous in that the King's two brothers support it, thus giving more scope to the Clergy and Nobility, who, on their side, are conspiring against the government."[15] Thus the picture was clear: the privileged Orders, with the court behind them, were conspiring to continue an inquitous situation, and the Third Estate began to fear that, as the result of yet another intrigue, Necker would be dismissed and the Estates General dissolved. As for Louis XVI, while it was still assumed that his intentions were good, he was apparently incapable of doing anything for himself — again, not least perhaps because he was ruled by his wife.

"The Queen's position," Mercy went on, "has become impossible. All eyes are turned toward her because of the inertia generally believed to afflict her august husband. The result is that she is held responsible, all the more unfairly since whatever the Queen . . . proposes is rarely carried out."[16] As the days passed, in fact, it became ever clearer that no one at court, except perhaps Necker, really wanted reforms; that the King was only interested in food and the hunt; and that the Queen was determined to block any change. Little more was needed to make the Tiers fear it was being betrayed; yet the ministry did nothing. Necker, as ever, was an optimist who thought that when the crisis came he would solve it single-handedly; the other ministers were completely out of their depth.

Even Necker's firmest support in the Council, Montmorin, the foreign minister, was evidently overwhelmed. On May 25 he wrote his Spanish counterpart a letter that, in its whining puzzlement, must be nearly unmatched in this sort of correspondence. "Our interior affairs are in a very difficult position," he complained. "We are where we are because of the series of mistakes that have been made for the last twenty years, and the road out of our difficulties is full of obstacles. The least error can have the most dreadful consequences; we are forced to hesitate and yet hesitation itself may be a mistake. The entire nation is stirring. . . . What do we need? Better ordered minds and a firmer government."[17] Coming from the second most influential member of the government in question, that last statement is little short of startling.

In the presence of this paralysis from above, the Tiers tried to negotiate some sort of agreement with the other Orders, but to no avail. By the time ten days had passed, it was becoming clear that anger was replacing the desire for compromise. The Nobility created more ill will when, having verified the elections of its members, it declared itself able to function as a separate Order on May 14, and so notified the Tiers. "The proud and insolent manner in which the duc de Praslin spoke at the head of the deputation from the Nobility has upset even the most moderate members of the Third Estate," Duquesnoy noted;[18] the upset was general particularly since the nobles' move implied a rejection of the vote par tête. Duquesnoy added: "The King's silence is to despair."

By the next day, the reaction to the Nobility's action was well under way. Malouet suggested that a way to change the Nobility's position might be to guarantee its precedence and its estates; he was promptly booed. Then things began to move. On May 19 the Clergy announced, first, that it was not ready to function as a separate Order, but that, in any event, it gave up all its tax exemptions: this, of course, was the work of the priests as opposed to the bishops. By breaking the united front of the first two Orders, it comforted the position of the Tiers.

At that point, commissions were appointed by the three Orders and charged with negotiating a solution; they met on May 23 and 25, wholly without success. Then, on the twenty-sixth, the Tiers sent a deputation to the Clergy asking it, "in the name of the God of Peace and the interest of the nation," to join them in the great hall so as to devise an agreement.[19] This, however, the Clergy was as yet reluctant to do, and the paralysis continued.

It was widely felt, however, that the first Order was not really to blame: even before the Estates assembled, the aristocracy, by its greed and arrogance, had earned itself the singular hatred of much of the nation. "There exists in the Assembly an extremely violent party that is against the Nobility, [including] the Deputies from Brittany, the Franche-comté, Provence, part of the Languedoc," Duquesnoy noted. "The storm is nearing."[20]

At that point, finally, Louis XVI, spurred on by Necker, intervened, but in the least active way imaginable. On May 28 he wrote the three Orders and asked them to hold a conference of conciliation in the presence of his own envoys led by Barentin, the keeper of the seals. It quickly became obvious that this measure was a complete waste of time, partly because Barentin hoped the Assembly would just go away, partly because the Nobility reaffirmed its position in the most uncompromising terms: by 202 votes, it decided "firmly to maintain the custom of voting separately as being part of the nation's constitution."[21] As a result, a further conference on May 30 proved just as sterile, in spite of Necker's presence. And no one doubted that the Nobility's stand was being strongly supported by the court, the royal family, and, probably, the Queen herself.

The better to continue the fight, the Tiers elected a president, Sylvain Bailly, the distinguished astronomer, with strongly liberal views; the group was obviously moving to the left as a result of the stalemate. That, in turn, alarmed Necker; consequently he asked the King to intervene in person by ordering that the verification of the election be carried out by each Order separately, then communicated to the others. On June 5 the Nobility flatly refused to do so on the grounds that the Tiers was not entitled to any such communication; thus the situation remained unchanged. It is, however, worth noting that when it came to disobeying the King, it was the Nobility that set the precedent. So far, the Tiers had proved itself willing to cooperate; the Clergy clearly wished to do so; only the nobles disdainfully refused to compromise.

This naturally did not escape the Tiers; increasingly conscious of its dignity, it now began calling itself the Commons — a clear reference to the powerful British House of Commons. On June 6 a deputation came to the King and complained about the immovability of the second Order. The deputation then went on: "Sire, your faithful Commons will never forget what they owe their kings; they will never forget the natural alliance of throne and people against the several aristocracies whose power can prosper only on the ruins of the King's authority and the people's happiness. . . . Thus you can tell, Sire, whether it is not the Commons who are the most eager among your subjects in upholding the rights, the honor, and the dignity of the crown.''[22] It was a telling rebuff to the Queen's position; it was also a dazzling offer: Louis XVI, who had indeed suffered from the selfishness of the privilégiés, was offered the chance of punishing them while earning for himself enormous popularity. A clever, forward-looking monarch would have taken it; a truly reactionary one would either have sided with the Nobility or have dissolved the Assembly. Louis XVI, as usual, did nothing.

The King and Queen may, however, be partly excused for a degree of distraction in the midst of these grave events: on June 4 the little Dauphin finally died of his protracted and painful illness. It was a great blow to both parents, and within a few days they left Versailles for the relative seclusion of Marly, that gathering of pavilions set in a vast and lush water garden some two miles away from the Palace; the move helped to distance them from events.

While they mourned, the Commons acted. On June 10 they passed by a very wide margin a motion presented by the abbé Sieyès: "The Assembly,'' it said, "deems it can no longer wait idly for the privileged classes without being guilty to the nation,"[23] and it urged the other two Orders to join in. Nothing much came of it that day; but on the thirteenth the Deputies of the Clergy, slowly at first, began to drift in; by the fifteenth most of them had joined the Commons; and so Sieyès proposed a new motion. It went a good deal further than his earlier one: "This Assembly," it said, "is already composed of the Deputies sent directly by 96 percent of the nation. So great a mass of deputation cannot remain idle just because of the absence of a few classes of citizens. . . . It is this Assembly's right, and its exclusive right, to interpret and express the will of the nation."[24] After that, there was just one more step, and Sieyès took it the next day when he asked the Deputies to proclaim themselves the National Assembly. On June 17, by 480 votes to 89 — there were a good many abstentions — that revolutionary step was taken and greeted by shouts of "Long live the King! Long live the National Assembly!" At one blow, the Nobility and the Clergy had ceased to exist as separate Orders, and the King found himself alone before the nation's representatives: the Estates General were over.

The Assembly then took one step further: it declared all existing taxes illegal, but added that they would continue to be collected until the system had been reformed, providing the Assembly remained in session. Thus, quickly and easily, it took over the power of the purse, and with it the government, all without referring to the King or asking for his agreement: it was the end of the ancien régime. As if to underline that, Bailly, the president of the brand-new National Assembly, then called on Barentin to tell him that a deputation wanted to see the King, and he added: "The Assembly hopes that its deputation will be received with the dignity suitable to its new status."[25]

Just ten days earlier, the Commons had offered Louis XVI their alliance; now it was too late. Instead of an advisory body, called and dismissed by the sovereign at will, there was an indissoluble Parliament. This time both the King and Necker realized they had better act; so the minister came up with a proposal for two declarations to be made by the King to the Assembly in the course of a *séance royale*.

In the first of these, the King would announce that henceforth the Orders would deliberate together about all the business of government, including the constitution of the future Estates; that he would never allow a legislative body composed of a single chamber; and that all titles, honors, and precedence connected to a fief would require the separate consent of each of the three Orders prior to any modification.

In the second declaration, the King would make the Parlements subordinate to the Estates; confirm the need for taxes and loans to be voted by that Assembly; announce that all provinces would have their assemblies set up according to the vote par tête; support the end of the taille, the tax paid only by non-nobles, and other similar taxes, along with the reform of indirect taxes and the game preservation laws;* end all tax exemptions; guarantee the freedom from arbitrary arrest and the freedom of the press; and finally open all civilian and military positions to non-nobles.

Louis XVI was shown these proposals by Necker on the eighteenth, and he told the minister that he approved of them. In fact, they contained everything that the minister had wanted all along without daring to tell his master: here was the liberal state within a strong monarchy he thought best for France. It must be noted, in particular, that while the Estates were given control over taxation, they had none over nonfinancial laws.

Had these reforms been offered to the Estates on May 5, they would have stood a very fair chance of approval, but now it was already too late. The new National Assembly was not about to transform itself back into the Commons. Even so, Necker's proposals horrified almost everyone at Marly. On June 19 the minister, upon arriving there for the Council at which the King's speech was to be discussed, was told by the Queen and the King's two brothers that they were strongly opposed to his proposals.

That became clearer the next day, June 20. In a series of meetings, the second of which lasted until ten at night, before a silent King, Necker's plan was strongly attacked by opponents made all the bolder since that minister, whose sister-in-law was near death, was not present. He was much reproached, in particular, for suggesting that non-nobles could become army officers, Barentin pointing out that the armed forces were the King's alone and that the Estates had no claim on them. As for the composition and periodicity of the future Estates General, that, too, it was claimed, was beyond the Assembly's competence, and could be settled only by the separate Orders. And there was a new source of

---

* Game, which the peasants were forbidden to hunt, often spoiled their crops, as did the noble hunters who rode carelessly through their fields.

pressure on the King: by June the vast majority of the Clergy had joined the National Assembly, and sixty nobles had voted to do the same; it was already becoming clear that a new era had begun; suddenly the great aristocrats, who had begun the Revolution, realized that, far from gaining greater power, they were about to lose all their privileges, so they flocked to Marly and added to the royal family's arguments. As of June 20, it seemed not at all unlikely that the monarch would listen to them, though once again, nothing was decided. A new meeting was set for the next day at five, when the royal family would be back in Versailles. The séance royale, originally to be held on the twenty-second, was set for the twenty-third.

Meanwhile, a little before seven on the morning of June 20, Bailly had received a letter suspending the Assembly's session. The note in question was from the marquis de Dreux-Brézé, grand master of ceremonies, and it read: "The King having ordered me, Monsieur, to announce . . . His Majesty's intention of holding a séance royale on Monday the twenty-second of this month, and at the same time the suspension of the Assemblies required by the preparations to be made in the hall, I have the honor of notifying you of this."[26] In fact, this representation was perfectly accurate: the King was not about to dissolve the Assembly; the hall did have to be prepared.

Smelling a rat, however, Bailly promptly answered that he had not heard from the King and would therefore open the day's session at eight, as planned. Brézé reiterated that he was obeying a specific order, that the building would indeed be closed, and that the sessions were to be suspended until the twenty-second. That, in one respect at least, is what happened: when, at nine, Bailly and the Deputies began to arrive, they found the door to the building guarded by regular troops and were forced to wait outside in the pouring rain. Eventually, the officer in charge came out, and told Bailly that he and the Assembly's two secretaries were free to come in and fetch what papers they chose, but that no one else could enter. Indeed, as they entered the hall, they saw that the benches were already removed and that the necessary conversion work was being carried out.

By then, posters had gone up in the building's courtyard and on the outer walls stating that, because of the forthcoming séance royale, just two days thence, the building would be closed and the sessions suspended;

it was still raining. Had the Deputies trusted the King, they could have waited for the required forty-eight hours; but they knew about the attitude of the Queen and the court, they knew that Louis XVI was weak, and they expected the worst, so rather than disperse, they looked for shelter.

They found it, just a few doors down, in an indoor tennis court, a large, empty rectangular hall; and, having entered, they were not in a happy mood. Mirabeau described it in a widely published letter to his electors. "The Hall of the Estates General closed to the representatives of the people at the moment when they were beginning their activities; the unbelievable spectacle of the National Assembly forced to seek an asylum, to behave like a lawless crowd, to have only precarious sessions; everything, including the very pretext given to justify this incredible attempt against public liberty, everything seemed to announce the most sinister projects."[27]

This eloquent paragraph is typical of its author; but, for all of Mirabeau's unique ability to describe the affront, he had in the weeks preceding been alarmed by the impending clash between King and Assembly. While he wanted freedom and a constitutional monarchy, he also feared the complete collapse of the system. Improbably enough, he was on friendly terms with the staid Malouet. "It is now a question," he had told Malouet, "whether the monarchy and the monarch will survive the coming storm or whether past mistakes, and the mistakes that will undoubtedly still be made, will drown us all."[28]

Now, with the Assembly angrily gathered in the tennis court, Mirabeau began to show what he could do when he was on the attack; he was among the most eloquent on that day, June 20. The result, the Oath of the Tennis Court, has become one of the great symbolic moments in French history.

Until then, although the Assembly had already broken all precedent by creating itself as an institution and giving itself the power to tax, it had not claimed a power and permanence equal to that of the King, or indeed demanded control over anything more than finance; nor had it demanded this one control in direct opposition to the monarch. Now, for the first time, it willfully disobeyed a royal order — to suspend its sessions — and claimed to have as fundamental a role in the government as the King himself. Late that morning, by 638 to 1, some nobles and Clergy included, it voted the following decree:

The National Assembly, considering that its task is to settle the constitution of the kingdom, bring about the regeneration of public order, and maintain the true principles of the monarchy; that nothing can prevent it from continuing its deliberations no matter where it may be forced to gather, and that, finally, wherever its members meet, there is the National Assembly;

Resolves that all the members of this Assembly will this moment take a solemn oath never to separate and to meet wherever the circumstances may dictate, until the constitution of the kingdom is established on solid foundations. . . .[29]

The official journal entry adds that the oath taking was followed by shouts of "Long live the King."

Here, indeed, was a break with the past: by claiming the right to settle the constitution, the Assembly had given itself powers far exceeding those of the King, since it could now define his position. Moreover, it had at one blow changed the source of all legitimacy. Until then, the King ruled because he was chosen by God and all authority, therefore, derived from his person. Now the Assembly, as the representative of the nation, could delegate such powers as it chose to the monarch. Legitimacy had passed to the people, and the crown became only one of the parties in a social contract. No longer God's representative on earth, the King was suddenly reduced to being merely the chief civil servant of the nation. That day, modern France was born.

While Louis XVI could hardly be expected to recognize this, even he must have somehow felt the Assembly had gained new importance. On June 20 it had seemed sufficient to have Brézé warn Bailly that the Assembly would be closed; now the King wrote Bailly in his own hand, a little after midnight: "I warn you, Monsieur, that the session I had called for tomorrow Monday will only take place on Tuesday at 10, and that the hall will only be opened then."[30] Upon which, dauntless, the Assembly met the next day in the church of Saint Louis.

In one other way the oath had an immediate effect: to the Council held on the twenty-first, the King called, not only all the ministers but also his two brothers, who were known to be opposed to Necker's declarations; and indeed, although the minister argued in favor of his plan with all the energy he could muster, the majority, outraged by the Oath of the Tennis

Court, went against him — as the King no doubt expected. It was decided, that day, to maintain the separate Orders except for certain cases, defined by the King, when the vote par tête could prevail; to annul all the Assembly's decisions, starting with those of June 17; to forbid any common deliberations about a future constitution; and to close the Estates General to the public. Another meeting was then called for the next day to consider the rewritten speech.

That, naturally, turned out to be very far from what Necker wanted, but when Montmorin tried to defend his friend's policy, the King interrupted him, saying coldly that the only question was whether the speech reflected the previous day's decisions. Instead of resigning on the spot, Necker stayed in office, but refused to appear the next day at the séance royale, thus disassociating himself from whatever Louis XVI might say.

In fact, and although he did not quite realize it yet, the King's position was already untenable. On the twenty-first, Duquesnoy perceptively noted: "What can the King do? If he sides with the Nobility, the kingdom will drown in blood; if he sides with the Commons, he ceases being king, and no one yet knows to what extremity they [the Commons] will go. . . . The most exaggerated ideas, the most incendiary propositions no longer cause any surprise."[31] In the shorter term as well, by allowing Necker to stay away from the séance royale while yet remaining in office, Louis XVI doomed himself to fail. It could now be assumed that he had, yet again, given in to pressure from the Queen and court, but that countervailing pressure from the Assembly would force him to heed Necker instead. Thus, before he spoke a single word, it was clear that he would not be obeyed.

In spite of this, his speech is not without interest. Here, uniquely, is a clear summary of just what Louis XVI was prepared to concede of his own free will, a definition of his political position. Anything more would have to be forced out of him, anything more he therefore would consider invalid.

Speaking now like his ancestors — "I want, I order" — the King announced that the separate existence of the three Orders was maintained as being a fundamental law of the state, and that therefore, each would sit in its own chamber; that he annulled, as illegal and unconstitutional, all the actions of the Third Estate as of June 17; and that while he hoped that the three Orders would unite for the deliberation of common business, he did not order the Clergy and Nobility to do so. As for the future form of the Estates, and anything concerning feudal and ecclesiastical rights and privileges, that must be debated by the Orders separately. The end of the privilégiés' tax exemptions was now left to the "generosity of the two first Orders"; and while freedom from arrest and the freedom of the press were granted, there was no more question of making civilian and military offices open to all regardless of birth.

Then the threats came. "If, by a fatality which I am far from expecting, you abandoned me in so fair an undertaking," the King said, "I would, alone, look after my people's welfare, I would, alone, consider myself as their true representative. . . . Remember, Messieurs, that none of your proposals, none of your resolutions can become law without my specific approbation. . . . I now order you immediately . . . to go off each to your particular chamber."[32] Compared with the situation only two months earlier, the King's new position undoubtedly represented progress; compared with the claims made by the Assembly in the last six days, the retrogression was vast. As a result, the King, while applauded by the Nobility, was heard in freezing silence by the great mass of the Assembly.

Worse yet, from his point of view, was the fact that he was in no position to carry out his threats. In a memorandum written a few days earlier, Necker had pointed out one key element of the situation: "If," he told the King, "the fatal secret of the army's unreliability were known, how could we restrain the factions?"[33] Without the support of the army, there could be no question of dissolving the Assembly; and by June 23 Louis XVI knew from his ministers and his generals that most of the armed forces were not willing to serve against the people or its representatives. In the hope that the foreign troops, at least, might obey, a regiment of Swiss Guards was transferred on the twenty-second from Soissons to Paris.

Even then, the King was able to see clearly on the twenty-third how helpless he had become. Immediately after he left the Assembly, most of the Nobility and some of the Clergy followed; since the enlarged Commons remained in place, the master of ceremonies came in and told them they must go. There was a silence, then Mirabeau stood up. "Monsieur," he said, "we have heard the decisions which were suggested to the King." That remark, in itself, implied that, because

Louis XVI had been influenced by others, what he had just said that day did not represent his true intentions and could thus be disregarded. Then came the challenge: "You, who cannot represent him before the Estates General," Mirabeau continued, "you, who have here neither place nor vote, you are not qualified to remind us of his speech. However, in order to avoid all misapprehension and all delay, I tell you that if you have been asked to put us out of this hall, you will have to request an order that force be used, for only bayonets can make us leave our place." The issue was squarely joined, and the King knew it. When he was told that the Assembly would not go, he answered sullenly: "They want to stay, well, fuck, let them."[34] As for Mirabeau's words, slightly altered ("We are here by the will of the people and will leave only by the force of the bayonets"), they have been taught to every French child from that day to this.

For the first time also, the immensely popular Assembly had refused to obey the King's direct orders, given in person. Indeed, it immediately went further: that afternoon, it voted to confirm its earlier decisions and to make the persons of the Deputies inviolable; to arrest any one of them would be to flout the will of the nation. From that moment on, it became clear that power had passed to the Assembly, and that, at most, Louis XVI might delay but never prevent.

The fragility of his position was underlined the afternoon of that same June 23. At noon, Necker resigned. "Immediately, the news spread and the streets of Versailles were filled by people shouting his name. The King and Queen called for him . . . that evening and asked him to take back his office in order to save the state; the Queen added that the safety of the King's person depended on his remaining minister. . . . The Queen solemnly swore to be guided by his advice only. . . .

"M. Necker agreed to remain. . . . Leaving the King to go home, [he] was carried in triumph by the people."[35] In fact, the maddened people had been stopped by the Guard at the very door of the King's apartment: it was a good preview of what was likely to happen if Louis XVI tried again to resist the reforms. It was also the beginning of a brand-new way of behaving for the distraught monarch: if forced, he would seem to acquiesce, while doing the best he could to reverse the situation. In this case, the King's attempt at reversal meant immediately breaking a promise: Necker had implored the King not to call in any troops as it would then become clear to all that they were not prepared to obey him. At least, while people still thought the army might be sent in, the King retained some little bargaining power, and Louis XVI had agreed to follow this advice. Instead, on June 24 he ordered a concentration of troops around Paris involving some 30,000 men, and on the twenty-fifth he wrote to the old maréchal de Broglie, giving him the command of these forces.

These orders remained secret a little longer, but events did not wait. On June 24 the majority of the Clergy joined the Assembly; on June 25 forty-seven nobles, led by the duc d'Orléans, did the same; most of the rest of the Nobility followed on the twenty-sixth; and on the twenty-seventh the King, showing yet again what a little pressure would do, asked the remaining nobles to do the same. That was the end of the Estates General: from then on, the National Assembly was an accepted fact for all except the King, his family, and most elements at court.

Although we do not know exactly what Louis XVI thought at the very end of June, it is clear that he felt resentful and abused: an act of generosity, the calling of the Estates, had been turned against him. Besides, he was quite clear about one thing: his chief duty as a monarch was the transmission to his successor of the powers he had himself received; and those powers were being ripped from him by the Assembly. There can be no doubt, therefore, that he meant to use the troops he was gathering: there would be a change of ministry — Necker lost the King's confidence for good on June 23 — and the illegal body that had replaced the three Orders would be dissolved.

It would not have been the first time, or the last, that an authoritarian government used troops to put down the people; only it was perfectly evident to all sensible observers that royal commands were less and less likely to be obeyed. At the same time, rebellion spread. There were riots in many provincial towns; in the countryside, the peasants were beginning to attack the castles belonging to their lords; Paris itself was virtually out of control. The mob had already taken over the gardens of the Palais Royal, and the gardes françaises were fraternizing with them.

If the King could no longer rely on the gardes françaises, at least he still had the bodyguard regiments, composed entirely of noble officers, who would no doubt be ready to protect his person — or so he thought. But then, on June 28, the minister of Saxony reported, "a sergeant has come to tell the duc de Guiche, captain of the Guard, in the name of the [bodyguard] troop that it was their duty to keep and protect the King, but not to get on their horses and fight with the mob; and that consequently they would not go on patrol duty. . . . The fidelity of the foreign regiments is also becoming uncertain."[36] Indeed, on July 2 the minister added, speaking of the 30,000 men being gathered outside Paris: "It was the maréchal de Duras who suggested that the maréchal de Broglie be appointed commander as he is trusted by the men and may get them to do their duty."[37] The signs were not very encouraging for the King.

While all this was happening, the Assembly began organizing itself. It deplored on July 1 the disorders in Paris, and on the sixth it chose a committee to write the constitution, although there was as yet no agreement as to what that document should prescribe. Gouverneur Morris, who had been a member of the American Constitutional Convention in 1787 and understood, therefore, what it was all about, noted in early July: "They want an American constitution, with the exception of a king instead of a president, without reflecting that they have not American citizens to support that constitution. . . .

"The King . . . is an honest man and wishes really to do good, but he has not either genius or education to show the way toward that good he desires."[38] Morris was right: no one in France had any notion of how to write a workable constitution, and the American model, touted by La Fayette and his friends, hardly applied to an old, centralized country. There was also one further problem, perhaps the most insoluble of all: while it seemed obvious in early July 1789 that the monarchy must endure and that a republic was both inappropriate and impossible, the very notion of a constitutional, or limited, monarchy supposed the existence of a monarch willing to rule under such constraints as might be devised. Unfortunately, Louis XVI regarded all such ideas with abhorrence; perhaps he might be forced to accept them, but that hardly augured well for the future regime.

On July 8, however, as the troop movements became common knowledge, it seemed there might well not be a constitution, or indeed a National Assembly, if the King had his way. That day, Mirabeau proposed a motion asking "that a very humble address be made to the King to advise him of the strong alarm felt by the National Assembly because of the abuse of the name of a good King which has caused artillery and numerous troops both foreign and national to be gathered outside the capital and the town of Versailles.

"Let His Majesty be humbly begged to reassure his faithful subjects by giving orders . . . for the dismissal of these troops."[39]

A deputation of the Assembly did, in fact, carry the motion to Louis XVI; it was coldly received. While no one knew just what would happen next, it was plain that a crisis was brewing. The King was dissatisfied with the situation; the Queen had turned, once more, against Necker; the troops were still gathering. It seemed most likely that, in a moment of violence, Louis XVI would reach for the power he had lost; and that is just what he did when, by dismissing Necker, he provoked the storming of the Bastille. The two years that passed from that moment to the night of June 20, 1791, were packed with various, sometimes surprising events; but they were all finally the consequence of the fact that Louis XVI, while unable to govern, refused to be less than an absolute king. In July 1789 he was still cheered by his subjects; in June 1791 he could hear from his windows the crowd clamoring for his death; at neither time did he understand what caused their behavior. Obviously, flight was his only remaining hope.

PART THREE

CHAPTER TEN

Varennes and Back

:   :   :

ACTION, or what looks like it, can sometimes be a supreme expression of passivity. When, on the night of June 20, 1791, the royal family fled from Paris, its apparently bold move was only the latest expression of Louis XVI's inability to assert himself. He had failed to be an effective ruler on countless occasions in the seventeen-year course of his reign; he had shown, again and again, that he could neither impose his will nor concede gracefully. Now he simply withdrew.

Even then, there are all kinds of withdrawals: monarchs, on occasion, have fled after losing a hard fight, and, being clever and determined, have lived to return; others, like the incompetent Charles I, have known how to win even when they lost, turning their martyrdom into the seed of a future restoration. A bumbling, ill-planned flight, with no real plans about what must come next, obviously belongs in neither category; but that, typically, was what Louis XVI settled for.

Because, as everybody knows, the royal family was stopped at Varennes, it has been widely assumed that the enterprise was hopeless from the start, an assumption that has not prevented endless speculation as to what would have happened if . . . if, for instance, Drouet had not recognized the King's profile, if the troops had been where they should have been. In fact, it was not so difficult to escape: Monsieur, Louis XVI's brother, also left on the night of June 20; being smarter than his brother, he made it safely to, and beyond, the border, living eventually to become King Louis XVIII by the grace of God and the Tsar of Russia. Thus, Louis and Marie Antoinette's flight was less a voyage than the final, irretrievable demonstration of their incompetence, even when it came to organizing an escape.

It was also more than that. On a human level, the long, agonizing trip — away fast, back slowly — was a spirit-breaking ordeal, the start of the calvary that ended on the scaffold. On a political level, Varennes was the most convincing political argument ever conducted in the history of French politics. By the time it was over, the magic attaching to the person of the King, the mystic powers conferred on the sovereign by his coronation, were gone: Louis XVI was just a politician like any other, and a failed politician at that. In the few days of the journey, in fact, modern France was born in the hearts of the people.

At the same time, the story of Varennes has all the suspense of a good thriller: from first to last, uncertainty and anguish are the rule. We feel for the protagonists even as we see their doom approaching and deplore their inadequacies; and because so much is known about the episode, we can accompany the royal family, in its large, lumbering carriage, from the first step of the flight to the last humiliation of the return.

One reason for our knowledge is also one of the reasons why the escape failed: the presence with the royal family of Mme de Tourzel, the governess of the children of France. Mme de Tourzel, herself a devoted mother, had been appointed to this eminent position when, on July 15, 1789, the duchesse de Polignac had left in the first great wave of emigration. Unlike the Queen's former friend, Mme de Tourzel was neither greedy nor ambitious; all through the various shocks that subsequently shook the royal family, she remained true to her charges. Because the still sacrosanct etiquette prescribed that, in spite of their having a numerous staff, she must always be with the children, she had, in the growing isolation of the Tuileries, become very close to the Queen.

As a result, she was told about the planned escape; indeed, so were most of the Queen's favorite Women of the Bedchamber. Mme de Tourzel pointed out that her position gave her the *right* to go along with the royal family on the flight. This was the sort of right with which the King and Queen were thoroughly familiar: the right of duchesses to be seated (on a stool) before Their Majesties, the right of the First Gentleman of the Bedchamber to walk immediately behind the King; so they did not think of refusing her. It is from her that we know what happened inside the carriage: she lived, eventually, to write vivid, detailed, and accurate memoirs.

Although Mme de Tourzel's presence is a great retrospective convenience, it was a serious mistake at the time. Horse-drawn conveyances depended on small size for speed: the larger and heavier they were, the slower they went. Thus, a single person traveled fastest of all, two still fast, but six, with abundant luggage, very slowly indeed. Yet that was the way Louis XVI and Marie Antoinette had chosen; and because neither the Queen nor Mme de Tourzel wanted to leave their maids behind, they were followed by another coach in which these servants traveled, along with two of the royal bodyguards. That other coach also required horses at every post; and given the disturbed state of the country and the general flight of the aristocracy in the last two months, there was every chance that post horses would, in fact, turn out to be scarce. Monsieur understood all this: he left, alone with his wife, in a light carriage that traveled with all the speed possible.

Not only did the King and Queen take Mme de Tourzel along; they were also accompanied by Madame Elisabeth, the King's twenty-seven-year-old sister. All present took along the clothes they expected to need when holding court in Montmédy, thus adding large and heavy trunks to the weight of the already massive carriage, which now required six fresh horses at every post. Bouillé, who had helped to plan the trip, had begged the King to travel with his family in two light carriages, but he was firmly ignored.

At first, though, and in spite of some delays, it looked as if the flight might succeed. On the afternoon of June 20 Marie Antoinette took her children to the Tivoli Gardens in a successful effort to make everything look normal. She even gave instructions about the next day's outing when she returned to the Palace. The rest of the evening was spent as usual; at ten, the Queen announced that she was retiring for the night. In fact, she went to the Dauphin's bedroom, where she met Mme de Tourzel. The six-year-old boy was quickly awakened and disguised by being given a girl's dress; his thirteen-year-old sister joined him, and, together with their governess, they passed down to the ground floor of the Palace, using two supposedly walled doors that gave into the apartment of the First Gentleman of the Bedchamber, the duc de Villequier, who was absent that night.

It had been arranged that the royal family should meet on the rue Saint-Honoré, not very far from the Palace, and go on together to the city gate, where the traveling coach would be waiting for them. Madame Elisabeth, the King, and the Queen were to walk there separately; a coach was provided for the children, who were to be the first to go. Armed with a letter from the King stating that she was acting on his orders — this was in case she was caught — Mme de Tourzel waited for the coach to appear; the distance was too great for the little Dauphin to walk. Once it had come, the governess wrote, "the Queen herself went to look at the courtyard, and seeing that it was quiet, she embraced me and said: 'It is with entire confidence that the King and I are entrusting you with those dearest to us; all is ready, you must go.' . . . We came out through a seldom-used door and got into an antiquated carriage which looked like a hansom and was driven by Count Fersen."[1]

At a quarter to eleven, Fersen brought this carriage to the appointed spot on the rue Saint-Honoré; there he entered into conversation with other hansom-cab drivers while, in great anguish, Mme de Tourzel and the children waited. "I was on tenterhooks," she remembered, "although I appeared to be carefree, when Madame [Royale] said: 'Here is M. de Lafayette.' I hid M. le Dauphin in the folds of my skirt and assured them both there was no reason to be worried, although I was, terribly. M. Bailly followed just after [Lafayette]; they both passed without noticing anything, and soon afterward I had the consolation of seeing Madame Elisabeth arrive: it was a first hope."[2] The King himself came a little after midnight; Marie Antoinette, who got lost on the way, arrived last.

Both had been severely delayed. Lafayette and Bailly, who were attending the King's coucher, had begun to chat, and in order not to make them suspicious the monarch had joined the lengthy conversation; after which he had undressed, gone to bed, dressed again in a gray, liverylike suit, put on a wig, and left. As for Marie Antoinette, she had crossed Lafayette's path as he left the Tuileries, and only the darkness had concealed her from him. Thus, by the time the entire party, now ensconced in Fersen's hansom, left the rue Saint-Honoré for the barrière Saint-Martin, one of the city's gates, where the traveling carriage was supposed to be waiting, they were well behind schedule; and then they had difficulty finding the carriage. In fact, by the time they went off for good, it was two-thirty instead of midnight, and then they got lost again on their way to Laye, the first post, where Fersen left them, because he was unfamiliar with the streets in that part of Paris.

This mattered enormously: the troops that were to escort them once they reached Pont de Sommevel, just after Châlons, were led by the duc de Choiseul, a brave but untried and not very bright young man, who was prepared to retreat, so as to avoid exciting suspicion, if the King did not appear at the agreed-upon time. Just as dangerous was the fact that, firmly ignoring all advice to the contrary, the King had insisted on taking along the useless Mme de Tourzel instead of either the marquis d'Agoult, a highly resourceful officer, or Fersen himself. Thus, starting at Laye, the royal family was left to itself; no one was really in charge anymore.

Of course, they traveled in disguise. Fersen had obtained from Montmorin, the foreign minister, a passport for a Swedish lady, Mme de Korff, and her family. Mme de Tourzel was playing the role of Mme de Korff; the royal children were supposed to be her own, Louis XVI her majordomo, and Marie Antoinette and Mme Elisabeth a governess and a maid; all of which they found quite comical.

From the first, the atmosphere within the carriage was extremely cheerful. It began with embraces all around, Louis telling Marie Antoinette: "How happy I am to see you here at last!"[3] Then the King began to talk about his plans. He would, he said, either settle in Montmédy or move on to some more convenient town, leaving France only in order to reach this new residence faster, but never stopping on foreign land. "I am at long last out of this city of Paris where I have suffered so bitterly," he told his fellow travelers. "You can be sure that once I'm up in the saddle, I will be quite different from the way you have always known me."[4] He talked at length about the happiness of France once he was free and in charge, enjoying in advance his reunion with his brothers, planning to restore the Church and undo the effect of the Assembly's laws. Then, Mme de Tourzel goes on, "he looked at his watch, which showed it was eight [A.M.]. 'Lafayette', he said, 'is now having a hard time of it.' "[5]

That was putting it mildly: the scene in Paris, on the morning of the twenty-first, was one of horrified consternation. Lafayette, as the commander of the National Guard, was promptly denounced by the Jacobins for having allowed the King to flee and, indeed, for having been his accomplice — an accusation that was very likely to have immediate consequences; but, almost worse, the regime he had set up and to which he was absolutely committed had just collapsed in the space of one night. After two years spent in pretending that Louis XVI was the kind of monarch the as yet unfinished constitution demanded, Lafayette and his political friends now found themselves without a king, that is, without the keystone of their system. And, just in case anyone felt any confusion about the disappearance of the royal family, Louis XVI had left behind a declaration damning the Revolution and all its works.

"As long as the King could hope to see the realm ordered and happy through the means chosen by the National Assembly and through his residence near that Assembly in the capital, he accepted every personal sacrifice," it said.

> He would not even have pointed out that his absolute lack of freedom made all the measures taken since October 6, 1789, null and void if that hope had been fulfilled; but today the only reward for so many sacrifices is to see the destruction of the monarchy, all the [legitimate] powers disregarded, property violated, the safety of the person endangered everywhere, crime remaining unpunished and a complete anarchy taking over in spite of the law, while the phantom authority given the King by the new constitution is too weak to address a single one of the ills ruining the realm. The King, therefore, makes this solemn protest against all acts forced from him during his captivity, and thinks it his duty to offer to the eyes of the French, and to those of the universe, this account of his own behavior and of that of the government which has established itself in the kingdom.[6]

There followed complaints about the events of October 6, 1789, the dismissal of most of the Royal Guard, the insolence of members of the National Guard, the discomfort of the Tuileries Palace; but most of all, Louis XVI emphasized his own powerlessness when it came to the actual government of France. "The King," he repeated, "had become a prisoner in his own country. . . . He had no part in the making of the laws . . . and the administration is altogether in the hands of the départements, the districts, and the municipalities [whose civil servants were elected]. . . . He does not choose the judges but merely signs their commissions. . . . There is one last prerogative, the fairest of all, that of suspending or lessening criminal sentences; you took it away from the

King.* . . . The King is supposed to be the supreme head of the army, but all the work is done by the National Assembly's committees without my participation.'' Then, having thoroughly denounced the new system, Louis XVI went on to the peroration: ''Frenchmen . . . do you want the despotism of the clubs to replace the monarchy under which this realm has prospered for 1400 years?'' and, denouncing once again the mob that had prevented his move to Saint-Cloud in April, he ended: ''These motives, and the King's inability to prevent evil, have naturally determined him to seek his own safety.''[7]

It could not have been clearer: free at last to tell the truth, Louis XVI firmly rejected the Revolution and almost all its works. Worse, the declaration was immediately published: nothing, in the panic of that morning, could remain a secret. What, then, were Lafayette and the other supporters of a constitutional monarchy to do? It was clearly impossible to find a substitute king: Monsieur was also gone, and the only prince left in Paris, the duc d'Orléans, was so thoroughly discredited that no one thought for a moment of giving him the crown. Clearly, therefore, Louis XVI must be brought back; but if he was simply caught like any other fleeing criminal, he would obviously not be much good as a monarch anymore. It was crucial to save his and everyone else's face. So, on his own responsibility, Lafayette issued orders to seek and apprehend the King, at the same time coming up with a convenient fiction first publicized in a message that morning to the Deputies: ''The Assembly is aware,'' said the General, ''of the attempt made against the King and part of his family last night by the enemies of France's welfare, in the shameful hope of compromising our liberties.''[8]

Henceforth that was to be the official line: his declaration notwithstanding, the King had been kidnapped, and was to be ''freed'' and brought back with all possible speed. Messengers galloped off in all directions. The Assembly, after a moment of hesitation, decided to take all royal prerogatives unto itself during the King's absence, and it, too, issued a proclamation. After describing the declaration as a ''text forced from a seduced King,'' it went on to say: ''A criminal attempt has just taken place. The National Assembly was reaching the end of its long

---

* On June 5 the Assembly had decided to withdraw the power of reprieve or commutation from the King.

efforts; the constitution was complete; the storms of the Revolution were ending; and that is when the enemies of our welfare have tried, by committing this crime, to sacrifice every Frenchman to their vengeance. The King and the royal family have been kidnapped.'' After vowing that this would not alter the new system, the proclamation ended: ''Frenchmen! The King's absence will not halt the activities of the government.''[9]

This was all very well; unfortunately, it was also mostly untrue. To begin with, the constitution was nothing like complete; it eventually took another three months of efforts to reach that stage. The unrest in Paris, the riots in the provinces, far from abating, were daily growing in violence. Finally, of course, it was quite plain that Louis XVI had not been kidnapped. Never more than on that day did the main actors of the drama act on the mistaken belief that eloquent words can substitute for reality, that, as long as everyone pretended that the King had not left of his own free will, both his flight and his proclamation somehow did not count. Two months earlier, the Assembly had mendaciously told Louis XVI that his subjects loved him; now they mendaciously told the people that he had not wanted to leave.

The purpose of the lies, in both cases, was not only to save face, it was also to improve the situation by describing it as better than it was. Once again, the Deputies were behaving as if the Assembly was just a larger salon, where battles could be won with words. On June 21 there was also a third aspect to this: by pretending the King had not run away, the Fayettists and the triumvirs were saving their own skins. No one knew what would happen if the monarchy collapsed, but it was not likely to be pleasant for the Assembly's majority, so it leaped onto the slim plank of safety offered by Lafayette, and agreed to pretend the King had been kidnapped.

This kind of concerted illusion tends not to work very well even when everyone agrees it is necessary; in this case, there was a whole, important group that stigmatized the pretense as a pitiful — and guilty — lie: the Jacobins. On the first day after the King's flight, Robespierre spoke at the club, and he made it all perfectly clear: ''I am not the sort of man to whom the flight of the first civil servant will seem to be a disastrous event. This day could be the best of the Revolution, it may be still.'' What he was saying was that here, in fact, was the perfect occasion to do without a king. As for the kidnap theory, Robespierre poured scorn on the moderates: "Louis XVI . . . writes . . . that he is *taking flight* and the Assembly, in a cowardly . . . transparent . . . and treacherous lie . . . pretends to think the King's flight is a kidnapping!"[10]

After Robespierre came Marat, in a speech he printed the next day in *L'Ami du peuple*: here was passion instead of cool reasoning, but each was all the more effective for the other:

> All France remembers the disgusting speech that Louis XVI recited to the National Assembly on April 18 to complain, like a punished schoolboy, that the people of Paris had prevented him from going to Saint-Cloud, that is, to Brussels. Last night Louis XVI, wearing a cassock, fled with the Dauphin and the rest of the family. This perjured king, without honor, without shame, without remorse, this monarch unworthy of the throne was not stopped by the fear of being infamous. The thirst for absolute power that devours his soul will soon make him into a ferocious murderer; soon he will swim in the blood of his compatriots because they refuse to submit to his tyrannical sway. . . . Now is the time to behead the ministers . . . Motié [Lafayette] . . . Bailly."[11]

It could not be clearer; like Robespierre, Marat was telling the Jacobins that the King had provided them with an immense opportunity: not only was the throne vacant but also the majority in the Assembly was hoist on its own monarchist petard. Of course, both of them made the justifiable assumption that Louis XVI was gone for good; but even as they spoke, Lafayette and the Assembly were doing their best to recapture the errant but necessary King.

Whether they would succeed depended not just on the speed of the couriers that had been sent racing in several directions, but also on the attitude of the people in the towns the royal family would be crossing and, of course, on the military protection set up in advance to shield Louis XVI from his pursuers. As the heavy coach lumbered along the road to northeastern France, stopping to change horses every four hours or so, stopping yet again because part of the harness had broken, it was this protection that was eagerly awaited. "The further we came, the more hopeful we were," Mme de Tourzel remembered. " 'Once we are past Châlons, we will no longer have anything to fear,' the King would say;

'we will find the first body of troops at Pont de Sommevel, and then our trip will be a success.' We passed through Châlons without being recognized. We felt then perfectly secure.''[12]

That happy feeling did not last long. There were no troops at Pont de Sommevel or, indeed, anywhere near the next relay, a village called Orbeval; and, obviously, the travelers could hardly ask for them. Worse, as it grew later, the chance of the carriage's being discovered by the Assembly's couriers grew, and the atmosphere became more tense with every moment.

Soon the horses had to be changed yet again, so the carriage stopped at Sainte Menehould. There a captain in the duc de Choiseul's regiment sidled up to the carriage. "He whispered to me," Mme de Tourzel writes, " 'the measures are poorly organized; I will go now to avoid making them suspicious.' Those few words terrified us, but we went on because there was nothing else we could do.''[13] The captain was right: the duc de Choiseul had brought his men to Pont de Sommevel by telling them they were to escort a shipment of gold. When the royal family failed to arrive at the appointed time — it was more than six hours late — he waited a little, then decided that something had gone wrong and took his troops back toward Verdun. By a fatal stroke, he decided to use a back way instead of the main road, where the carriage might have caught up with him. So it was that neither at Pont de Sommevel, nor at Sainte Menehould, nor at Clermont, the next relay, were there troops ready to protect the King.

Because it is always tempting to wonder what might have happened if — if Cleopatra's nose had been longer, if the duc de Choiseul had not left so soon — it has been generally assumed that if indeed Choiseul's troops had met the carriage at one of the relays, the royal family would have been safe. As a result, the blame for the failed escape has been spread evenly: Choiseul should have waited; the flight should have been better organized; the carriage should have been lighter and faster. In fact, two key questions have been ignored: Would the soldiers who thought they were escorting a gold shipment have obeyed orders to protect the King instead? Would the towns through which the group was to pass have allowed it to continue unhampered? Given what Bouillé kept saying about the unreliability of his troops, the first is highly doubtful: there is every probability that the troops would have refused to obey orders. As for the second, the events in Clermont answer it fully.

There, according to Mme de Tourzel, the comte de Damas, who had not followed Choiseul's order to retreat, came up to the carriage; he told the King that the whole region was full of movement, and that he would try to leave the little town with his dragoons so as to provide the needed escort. When he did so, the townspeople refused to let them through, and the dragoons refused to obey; nor could Damas tell his troops they were to escort the King since that would have obviously led to the royal family's immediate arrest. It thus becomes clear that Fersen's plan was based on pure illusion: there was no longer any place in France where an escaped Louis XVI could be safe; there were no longer any troops willing to fight for him. We are therefore justified in providing a new answer to the old question: even if Choiseul had not panicked, even if the carriage had been on time, there is every reason to think that the King would have been arrested. Louis XVI himself understood this; when next he saw Lafayette, he told him: "I had thought you were surrounding me with a whirlwind of people of your opinion, but that the French did not agree with you. I have seen clearly, during this trip, that I was wrong, and that yours was the prevalent opinion."[14]

That, in the late afternoon of June 21, was still in the future; but even as the carriage, having left Clermont, rolled on toward Varennes, a man was riding as fast as he could along a shortcut connecting the two small towns. His name was Drouet, he was the postmaster of Sainte Mene-hould, and he had recognized Louis XVI, making sure that the familiar-looking profile of the traveler was indeed the King's by comparing it with the picture printed on the assignats. As it happened, Drouet, like most of his compatriots, approved of the Revolution; he, like almost everybody, had heard the rumors that the King was preparing to flee; and he saw it as his duty to prevent this. So he rode ahead, and by the time the carriage arrived at Varennes the population was ready.

Varennes itself was so small that it did not even have a post. A relay was supposed to have been arranged by Choiseul at one of the outlying houses, but as the travelers arrived, they saw no signs of it. Stopping, they knocked at a door and asked about it, but were told there was no such thing. They then asked the postilions to double the post, that is, to drive on to the next relay, and offered them a substantial tip, but the postilions answered that the horses were too tired, and that it could not be done. The travelers then decided to stop for dinner at an inn on the other side of town and to leave only once the horses were properly rested; but it was too late even for that. Drouet, who had reached Varennes earlier, had blocked the bridge the carriage needed to cross by upsetting a cartful of furniture on it; he had also warned the local authorities and roused the National Guard. Thus the carriage, together with that of the maids, which preceded it, was stopped as it was passing the house of the procurator of the commune. It was now eleven-thirty at night.

Still, the travelers hoped it was no more than a temporary halt; their passports were demanded, but they were in order; and Marie Antoinette, saying that they were tired and wanted to get to the inn, asked that they be let through. This the rapidly growing crowd refused. At that point, the two bodyguards who had been traveling with the maids asked the King whether he wanted them to try to get through by force; Louis XVI refused, in part, no doubt, because he was always reluctant to shed blood, but also because there was not much two men could do against an armed crowd. By then, the bells were tolling, and it was clear that the King had been recognized. The royal family was asked to leave the carriage for the procurator's house: there was no resisting, and one of the people who had stopped them confirmed that it was indeed the King; by then, Varennes was surrounded by 4,000 members of the National Guard. The escape plan had failed.

Even so, Louis XVI tried to go on. "He announced that he was indeed the King," Mme de Tourzel wrote, "that he was leaving Paris as the result of the daily insults he had had to bear, that he had no intention of leaving France, but simply wanted to go on to Montmédy. . . . Both King and Queen used all possible means to soften the hearts [of the crowd] and reawaken the old love of the French for their King."[15] That was when Louis XVI learned his great lesson: not even the population of a small town far away from Paris was willing to let him go. There remained a small hope: Choiseul and his men might still appear. In fact, as the King soon discovered, the troops were unwilling to obey. He was now well and truly a prisoner.

By then it was after two in the morning; the Dauphin and Madame Royale were in a room upstairs, fast asleep; Louis XVI, Marie Antoinette, Madame

Elisabeth, and Mme de Tourzel were still up, in the main room of the house, exhausted and begrimed by the dust of the long trip. At three their fate was finally sealed: Lafayette's envoys — Romeuf, his aide-de-camp, and Baillon, a battalion commander of the Paris National Guard — arrived in Varennes and were promptly led to the royal family. They carried with them the decree ordering that the King was to be protected from all attempts against him and speedily brought back to Paris.

"When the Queen saw the two men, who had always said they were devoted to the royal family," Mme de Tourzel noted, "she was unable to conceal her indignation, reproached them for the difference between their behavior and their daily protestations of fidelity, tore the decree from their hands without even wanting to hear it read out, and would have destroyed it if the King had not stopped her; she merely threw it down with contempt."[16]

It was a painful situation. The King was now surrounded by some twenty of Choiseul's officers, who had returned to Varennes but did not dare to try to free him for fear he would be massacred by the ever-growing crowd. Baillon kept urging an immediate departure for Paris, and indeed, the horses and carriage were waiting outside; Louis XVI, arguing that he did not want to wake up his exhausted children, kept postponing the departure in the hope that Bouillé and his troops might appear at any moment. Finally, at eight, he gave in. The children were awakened, and the family reentered the carriage.

Away in Paris, the climate was growing uglier by the moment: when he ran away, the King also forfeited what remained of his subjects' love. There were still many people, Lafayette first and foremost, who were prepared to argue that a constitutional monarchy was the only possible regime; but no one even tried to defend Louis XVI.

"The King's portrait, which each citizen liked to carry, has been thrown in the gutter," the *Chronique de Paris* thundered. "What regret could we feel for a prince who thus voluntarily abdicates, who, in order to restore the usurpations of the crown, does not fear to expose twenty-five million people to the horrors of war. . . . He takes our indignation and our contempt with him."[17] Admittedly, this was a left-wing paper, but that day it expressed a widely shared attitude: most people thought that a foreign invasion was bound to follow once the King was gone.

No matter what the Assembly might pretend to believe, in fact, it became clear that day that Louis XVI had been lying for two years; whatever credibility he had had was now gone; and some people began asking why it was so necessary to have a king after all. That, however, still sounded shocking to most. When the Cordeliers, agreeing with Robespierre, decided that France should become a republic and communicated that demand to the Jacobins, it was firmly repulsed: the constitution, nothing but the constitution, was to be the rule.

Any remaining uncertainty, however, about the King's flight did not last long. The King had fled on the night of the twentieth; his absence had been discovered on the morning of the twenty-first; and he was stopped that night. By the afternoon of the twenty-second, the news had reached Paris. On the morning of the twenty-third, the press reported: "The arrest took place without difficulty."[18] The key word here is *arrest*; there was no pretense about freeing the royal family from their kidnappers.

Even so, it was an immense relief for Lafayette and the Assembly. Already three commissioners had been chosen to bring back the royal family: Barnave, one of the triumvirs; Charles de Latour-Maubourg, a close friend of Lafayette's; and Jérôme Pétion, Robespierre's associate and a member of the Assembly's left. As soon as it heard the news, the Assembly sent the commissioners off; the fate of the royal family was decided. According to the decree passed that day, the King, Queen, and Dauphin were to be kept under close guard; all those who accompanied them were to be arrested; the monarchs themselves were to be "heard" — which is to say, interrogated — about the flight; the Assembly's decrees were to have force of law without the King's signature; and the ministers were to govern without reference to the sovereign. It was a monarchy without a king.[19]

Louis XVI himself, in fact, was now despised not just by the people, but by the very men who worked hardest to maintain the regime. "Two hours after my appointment," Pétion reported, "I went to M. de Maubourg's house where we were all to meet. . . . [Duport and Lafayette arrived.] . . . There was a long discussion as to what should be done with the King. Everybody said that 'the fat pig was really a nuisance.'

" 'Should he be jailed?' some would ask; 'should he reign?' others wondered." The conversation continued as the three commissioners made their way toward Varennes. "Maubourg said," Pétion reported,

The attempted demolition of the Vincennes fortress by the mob, February 28, 1791.
The National Guard, led by Lafayette, is about to intervene.

The arrest of the royal family at Varennes, June 21, 1791. Louis XVI, wearing his
hat, Marie Antoinette, and their children are sitting at a dinner table.

The arrival of the royal family in Paris after the flight to Varennes, June 25, 1791.

The mob invades the Tuileries Palace, June 20, 1792; a cannon is dragged toward the stairs.

The storming of the Tuileries, August 10, 1792. By this time—around nine A.M.—the royal family had already left the Palace and taken refuge in the National Assembly.

The transfer of the royal family to the Temple, August 13, 1792. The tower-prison is seen in the background.

The Massacre of September, September 2–5, 1792. A severed head is carried on a pike, while prisoners are bludgeoned in the foreground.

The execution of Louis XVI, January 21, 1793. The King is seen trying to address the people; his voice was covered by a drum roll.

J.P. MARAT.

l'Ami du Peuple,

Second Martir de la Liberté.

Né à Genève en 1743 Assassiné le 13 Juillet 1793.

Marat crowned with oak leaves, a symbol of civic virtue; the scroll on the right reads: "The Friend of the People and the warmest defender of our rights."

The cannon pointed at the Convention, June 2, 1793, which forced the arrest of the Girondins.

The assassination of Marat by Charlotte Corday, July 13, 1793. The journalist is in the bath that was supposed to relieve his skin disease.

Arch of triumph to celebrate the ratification of the new constitution, August 10, 1793. The constitution was immediately suspended until the end of the war, and annulled before it could go into effect.

" 'It is really difficult to know what to say; he's a stupid man who allowed himself to be influenced; now he is so wretched that, in truth, I pity him.' Barnave added that, in fact, he could be considered an imbecile.''[20] The word here has its eighteenth-century meaning of more than merely stupid, almost retarded: the royal prestige could hardly have fallen lower.

That was manifest as well to the royal family at Varennes. No sooner had they installed themselves back in the carriage, a little before nine o'clock, when Choiseul and his officers were arrested in spite of the King's pleas. The coach as it set off was surrounded by the population, members of the National Guard, and soldiers from the very regiment that deluded officers had planned to use as an escort to the fleeing King. All were shouting, "Long live the nation and the National Assembly!"

"The sufferings of the royal family during this wretched trip cannot be imagined,'' Mme de Tourzel remembered. "Moral sufferings, physical sufferings, they were spared nothing. In the places where we were forced to go slowly, the shouts of 'Long live the nation and the National Assembly!' deafened us and redoubled in the villages we were crossing. The mayors of the towns, as they presented the King with the keys, reproached him bitterly for leaving Paris, and the way in which they offered what should have been a mark of respect was a new insult.''[21] Worse, the royal family had reason to fear for their lives. Near Sainte Menehould, shots were heard: a nobleman who had tried to approach the carriage had just been killed.

"Those who surrounded the carriage talked to Their Majesties anytime it suited them* with the most insolent familiarity, and answered their questions in a disgustingly rude manner,'' Mme de Tourzel goes on. "The kindness with which the royal family treated them and the patience with which it bore the discomforts caused by the heat and the dust, which were extreme, and which it seemed to feel only because of the young prince and princess, should have touched less hardened hearts, but they had one feeling only: their enjoyment of their triumph and of the humiliation of the royal family.''[22] It is a vivid picture: the bumpy ride in the crowded carriage, the heat, the dust, the lack of sleep and, right

---

* People were not supposed to address the King; as is still the case in England, they were to wait until the monarch had spoken to them first.

outside, the angry escort: Louis XVI and Marie Antoinette must have wondered if they were about to be massacred in front of their children.

This continued at Sainte Menehould, where the royal family stopped for dinner. ''The King,'' Mme de Tourzel noted, ''was forced to listen to the reproaches of the president of that city's district who . . . went so far as to criticize him bitterly because, he said, the King, in leaving France, was leaving it open to foreign invasion.''[23] When they reached Châlons, where they were to spend the night, however, things improved. The town was still largely royalist, so the monarchs were greeted with respect and made comfortable. Still quite unsure that their lives would be protected, Louis XVI the next morning asked that he be allowed to await the Assembly's commissioners there; this, however, was not allowed, and at midday, they were off again, this time surrounded by revolutionaries from nearby Reims who demanded that the carriage move only at the slowest possible pace.

It was then that a telling incident took place. Some of the men who walked next to the coach complained of being hungry; the Queen took some cold meat from a hamper and offered it to them — at which point shouts rent the air: ''Don't touch it, it is poisoned!'' Angrily, all the occupants of the carriage ate pieces of the meat, and the escort, reassured, followed suit. That people could really believe that Louis XVI would deliberately poison them shows, obviously, to what absurd extremes the antiroyalist feeling could go; but also it made very clear that the King had been rejected by the nation and now survived on sufferance only.

At Epernay, where the royal family stopped to eat, the effervescence was such that the meal had to be interrupted as soon as it had begun, and the carriage sent on its way. Finally, a little way past Epernay, the commissioners reached the royal family. ''We arrived at the door of the carriage and it was opened immediately,'' Pétion reported:

> The Queen, Madame Elisabeth, seemed very upset, in tears. ''Messieurs,'' they said quickly, . . . ''let no misfortune occur, let the people who came with us not be victims, let them not be killed! The King did not mean to go outside of France!''
>
> ''No, Messieurs,'' said the King volubly, ''I was not going abroad, I said it, that is true.'' [After the commissioners had squeezed into the

carriage] we had hardly gone ten paces before they started to say again that the King had not meant to leave France. . . .

The first chatter over, I noticed an air of simplicity, of family affection, which pleased me. . . . It would not have been possible for the travelers to have been dressed more simply. The King's linen was quite dirty; the women were wearing the most ordinary little morning dresses. . . . The King's expression is always cold, without animation; . . . his difficulty in speaking makes him shy, as I saw clearly several times; those who did not know him might well mistake this shyness for stupidity, but that would be wrong. . . . I never heard him say anything stupid. . . .

The windows were always down; we were baked by the sun and choked by the dust . . . but it had to be done this way because people wanted to see the King. . . .

"Everyone blames the King," the Queen said, "but no one understands his position; he is constantly given contradictory information; he does not know what to do."[24]

This sympathetic account is all the more interesting because Pétion was a deeply committed revolutionary, who told the King that, although he wished for a republic, he did not think France was ripe for one yet, and that he did not even expect it would be in his own lifetime. Even he was almost converted when, for the first time, he saw the royal family, not as the emblem of a hated regime, but as real, and distressed, human beings.

That this should happen was no accident. Maubourg did not think highly of Louis XVI, but he was thoroughly convinced that France must remain a monarchy; so he deliberately gave up his tour of duty and traveled in the second coach in order to give the royal family a better chance to impress his colleagues. The maneuver worked, to a degree at least, as Pétion himself makes obvious. Barnave, the other commissioner, was even more ready to be converted. It was Barnave whom Madame Elisabeth and the Queen really addressed as they tried to convince the commissioners that life had been made impossible for the King; indeed, during those endless, intolerably hot and dusty hours in the carriage, the two women held something like a political science seminar. The result was to convince Barnave — less, perhaps, because he paid attention to the arguments than because, according to Mme de Tourzel's account, he fell flat out in love with Marie Antoinette. Here, again, was an example of that personal magnetism which she retained to the last: while she often appeared to crowds as arrogant, in private she seemed both seductive and caring, proud yet weak enough to require support.

Still, the slow trip went on. After the night at Châlons, there was one at Dormans and one at Meaux. The travelers, now sunburned and filthy, lacked even the most ordinary comforts. The heat, unusual for June in northern France, was fierce, and the dust raised by the troops and crowds surrounding the carriage was so thick as to resemble the densest fog: it was actually hard to breathe. Then, on the twenty-fifth, the carriage started on the last lap. As it neared Paris, the people became progressively angrier. " 'The whore, the trollop,' " Pétion remembers men shouting, " 'she can show us her child all she likes, we know he [Louis XVI] is not the father!' The King heard all this clearly. The young prince . . . began to shriek in terror; the Queen held him on her lap, tears were falling from her eyes."[25]

In Paris itself things were very different, though no better. The people had been told to wear their hats, a sign of disrespect since one normally took off one's hat to the King. An English visitor reported: "Profound silence was recommended to the people on the entrance of the royal family and it was in general observed. . . . An officer passed us about half an hour before the King's arrival and called out as he passed: 'Chapeau sur tête' [Hat on your head]. This order was punctually observed. . . . I have heard very little violence against the King, more against the Queen, but still more against those who assisted their escape. 'Le gros cochon' [the fat pig] is the most common appellation."[26] It was indeed an impressive scene. An immense crowd filled the Champs-Elysées and the Place Louis XV (now the Place de la Concorde), men and women together, some quite well dressed, others obviously small shopkeepers or artisans in their well-worn clothes, still others sans-culottes — all side by side, filling every open space, perched in every tree, looking down from every roof. The silence as the carriage entered Paris and slowly drove through its streets was complete: instead of the usual bustle, the noise of traffic, the cries of the street vendors, all now was quietly menacing. And every man had his hat on his head. Finally, after passing through these walls of staring, silent people, the royal family reached the Tuileries. There the King found Lafayette awaiting him while, vocal at last, the huge crowd shouted: "The law! The law!"[27]

At that point, finally, the royal family was allowed to go and clean up: there was hot water to wash with, clean clothes to wear; but the family was also, and clearly, in prison. Guards stood at every door, often within every room. It was only with the utmost difficulty that Marie Antoinette convinced her guardians not to spend the night in her room; so they stayed at the door and at frequent intervals barged in to make sure she was still really there. Nor was this limited to the adults: the six-year-old Dauphin, too, was under constant watch, as, indeed, was Mme de Tourzel; only Madame Elisabeth and Madame Royale were allowed to lead a relatively normal life.

It was during the trip to Varennes and back that Louis XVI and Marie Antoinette first fully realized the horror of their position. Until then, they had either hoped for a reaction against the Assembly or kept a flight in reserve as their most extreme decision; but, except on October 6, 1789, they never really thought they were in immediate danger. Now they knew better, and it showed. When Mme Campan, the queen's First Woman of the Bedchamber, saw her mistress again in July, she noted: "Her face was not very much changed; but, after the first few kind words she addressed to me, she took off her cap and told me to see the effect her sufferings had produced: in one night her hair had become as white as that of a seventy-year-old woman."[28] (Marie Antoinette was in fact thirty-five.) As for the Spanish ambassador, who saw her even earlier, he reported: "The Queen is so weak, so broken that those who see her can barely recognize her."[29]

The monarchs now knew they were trapped; for the Assembly, there remained the unsolved question of what to do with them. Louis XVI was officially "suspended" — he no longer functioned as a monarch — but that could hardly be a permanent solution. Before one could be devised, however, there were some important formalities: the Assembly sent commissioners over to the Tuileries to question all those who took part in the flight. Although they were not allowed to communicate with each other, both Louis XVI and Marie Antoinette said essentially the same thing, exonerating their companions (Mme de Tourzel, the maids, the bodyguards), and claiming that they had merely wanted to move to some city other than Paris. "The reasons for my departure," the King explained to the commissioners, "are the insults and menaces my family and myself had to bear on April 10. . . . I thought from that moment on that we could not safely, even decently, stay in Paris.

"I decided therefore to leave the city. Since I could not do it publicly, I decided to do it at night, and without an escort. Never did I mean to leave the kingdom. I reached no agreement about all this with foreign powers, my relatives, or any of the other French people abroad."[30] That, of course, was a lie: together, the King and Queen had arranged for the presence nearby of Austrian troops that were to enter France; and while it is true that the comte d'Artois had not been warned about his brother's flight, this was only because of his well-known indiscretion. The King's other brother, the comte de Provence, had been told about the plans; he had, as we have seen, left at the same moment; and he had now safely arrived in the Austrian Netherlands.

As it was, however, not only were the commissioners unable to prove the King was lying, they actually had no desire to do so. Marie Antoinette, who had secretly written Fersen on the twenty-sixth, "Take comfort, we are still alive," went on to add on June 29: "We are guarded day and night. Do not worry, nothing will happen to us, the Assembly means to treat us well."[31] And so it did: it really had no choice. If a constitutional monarchy was to be maintained, it would need a King, and the one now imprisoned in his Palace was the only one readily available.

That did not mean the life of the royal family was pleasant, however. "The King and Queen, who did not want to be seen as prisoners by the National Guard or to be exposed to the insults of a misled multitude, no longer left their apartments and refused even to go and breathe a little fresh air in the Dauphin's little garden,"* Mme de Tourzel wrote. "The uncertainty of their fate, the hostility of the public, the discomforts of a crushing heat, all made their situation even more difficult. . . . The royal family's only pleasure was the time it came together [for dinner] and when it watched the prince and princess at play."[32] As for the political prospects, they seemed even bleaker: Louis XVI still loathed the very idea of being King according to the constitution the Assembly was at last completing; he distrusted the Deputies and dreaded the people of Paris. Since, obviously,

---

* A section of the Tuileries gardens had been screened off for the Dauphin's exclusive use.

he was in no position to attempt a second escape, there was, as far as he could see, only one way out, and he tried to take it.

"No one in Europe is unaware of the King's love for his people, and the generosity he has shown them," he wrote Leopold II sometime early in July. "[He] has been paid back by countless insults to him and his family and by the captivity in which he has been kept for the last two years. . . . As he confides his sufferings to the Emperor, his brother-in-law, he feels sure he [Leopold] will be prompted by his generous heart and take all the measures necessary to rescue the King and France."[33]

At the same time, Louis brought his brothers into play. On July 7 he sent them a full delegation of power, carefully written in invisible ink: "I trust absolutely in my brothers' affection for me, in their love and attachment for their Fatherland, in the friendship of the sovereigns, my relatives and allies, and in the honor and generosity of the other sovereigns to agree together about the ways and means to be used in the negotiations whose object must be to reestablish order and tranquillity in the kingdom."[34] This was enclosed in a letter from Marie Antoinette to Fersen, now safely residing in Brussels, in which she gave him his instructions: "[The King] wants his captivity to be thoroughly acknowledged by the powers . . . [who will then convene] a sort of Congress which would open negotiations, with of course a large enough army to back it, but far enough away not to provoke crimes and massacres [of the royal family]."[35]

For the next few months, in fact, Marie Antoinette spent much of her time in writing and ciphering, or reading and deciphering, this secret correspondence that again and again urged all other European monarchs to help Louis XVI — but discreetly enough so as to avoid a new and final uprising in Paris.

On its side, the Assembly finally reached a solution to its virtually insoluble problem: the King, it determined, would remain suspended until the constitution was finished; then, if he formally accepted it and swore to observe it, he would be reinstated; in the meantime, so as to avoid the public trial urged by much of the left, it voted to make his person inviolable, like those of the Deputies themselves. Obviously, if he could not be punished, he could not be tried.

It was the most uneasy of compromises; but, as so often, Louis XVI had no one to blame but himself — for having allowed the political situation to deteriorate so drastically that flight was the only solution, for having organized the flight so badly, for having been caught. In many ways, in fact, the King's arrest in Varennes seemed emblematic of his entire reign: the half-measures adopted too late, the disasters that invariably followed, the invincible lethargy that precluded rapid, effective action, all played their part in this final failure.

Yet, Varennes was also something new. Until then, to varying degrees and in varying ways, the image of the King retained something of its old authority, something of its old magic: the monarch, no matter how attacked and diminished, was still the fetish of the tribe. When he fled, Louis XVI ended all that. It was not merely that he had been caught, and brought back a prisoner. Far worse, he was suddenly nothing more than a failed politician.

CHAPTER ELEVEN

At Last, the Constitution

:   :   :

NEVER, perhaps, more than in the measures they adopted after the capture of the royal family did the members of the National Assembly show themselves statesmanlike. Far from wanting revenge, or even yearning to punish Louis XVI for the very unpleasant surprise he had given them, their one thought was to set up a fair and free system, a constitutional monarchy in which the gains of the Revolution could be embodied. Of course, in doing all this, the Assembly was moved by several considerations. One, obviously, was that its majority consisted of men of property, who saw with terror the Revolution sliding too far toward the left. They did genuinely want a free government, but they had no intention of losing anything that belonged to them; and if Marat and his friends were allowed to depose the King, they might well call for sharing the wealth as their next objective. Thus it was essential to stop the Revolution and establish a stable regime.

Then, there was Leopold II's proclamation; dated July 6, it asked the other European sovereigns to join him in ensuring the respect of Louis XVI's freedom and honor. The Assembly therefore had to recognize the distinct possibility that any act ending the monarchy would, eventually, bring about an anti-French coalition; and men like Lafayette and the triumvirs had few illusions about the current condition of the army. Indeed, on July 25, the powers opened talks aimed at convening an antirevolutionary European congress — thus beginning to fulfill Marie Antoinette's wishes.

Finally, the Deputies who lived and worked in Paris were painfully aware that the mob's effervescence was extremely dangerous. Not only did they have to pass through it every day on the way to the Assembly, they could also see and hear it as it filled the tribunes. In the course of their normal lives — visiting friends, going to a café, attending the theater — they saw the mob everywhere. Worse, the mob was now being purposefully excited by its leaders — not the Jacobins, who insisted upon remaining strictly within the law, but the Cordeliers, where the most inflamed speeches were made — and of course by Marat, ever present in print. On June 25, *L'Ami du peuple* made his position clear: "Who can be so blind as not to see that the King, who not only fled but denounced the constitution . . . has thus forfeited all right to the crown. If the Assembly were not the accomplice of Louis XVI's treason, it would have deposed him. . . . The indignant nation . . . declares Louis XVI unfit to reign. . . . The wife of the ex-monarch, that ferocious mover of the court's crimes, must be shorn and jailed."[1] A slightly more moderate paper suggested simply replacing Louis XVI with his six-year-old son.

From then on, the attacks were relentless — against Lafayette, who was accused of being the King's accomplice; against Bailly, because he was too moderate; against the Assembly; and, of course, against Louis XVI, who from that moment on is referred to as Louis Capet. On June 27 Marat wrote: "He has been brought back within our walls, this crowned brigand, perjurer, traitor, and conspirator . . . as cowardly as he is stupid."[2] On the thirtieth his headline read: "Observation on the declarations made by Louis and Antoinette. Contradictions, falsehoods, lies, and gross imposture which they contain. . . . Urgent reasons for deposing and jailing the fat Capet."[3]

Although Marat's rage is not without its unpleasant aspects, it cannot be denied that he had a point. The King, who had sworn (several times) to observe the constitution, had denounced it as he was leaving; his behavior from July 1789 to June 1791 had been an extended lie. Marat was less convincing when he attacked the Assembly: at the beginning at least, it had defended the rights of the people. Now, however, it seemed to side with the monarch inasmuch as it could without provoking an instant uprising: not only had it firmly declined to depose him, or indict him for breaking his oath, it went on to order Bouillé's trial by the High Court for kidnapping the King, when everyone knew full well that Louis XVI had left of his own free will. In fact, this was a purely theoretical gesture since Bouillé had emigrated; but it was enough to madden the mob. As if that were not enough, 293 of the Deputies, all, of course, from the right, withdrew in protest against the suspension of the inviolable King and appealed for foreign help. So a new journée was planned, a mass demonstration at the Champ de Mars, that vast esplanade where the Fête of the Federation had taken place; and its announced purpose was to demand the end of the monarchy.

The nearly five thousand people who met there on July 17 were the most angry of groups, a blend of the mob proper and some small shopkeepers. They were alone, too: the bourgeoisie had broken with them; even the Jacobins refused to participate on the grounds that they were breaking the law in demanding the King's deposition. Martial law was proclaimed, and when the demonstrators refused to disperse, the National Guard, eager for once to obey Lafayette, opened fire, killing some fifteen people. That was the end of the demonstration, but, even so, the Assembly was not satisfied. It promptly passed laws closing the Cordeliers and forbidding the circulation of inflammatory publications, and these laws were effective enough to make Marat go underground.

There remained, however, one ineradicable fact. When he fled to Varennes and was ignominiously brought back, Louis XVI not only lost whatever shred of prestige, whatever sacred aura he had still possessed, he also revealed himself for all to see as a mere agent of the aristocratic plot. For quite a while, the left and the mob had thought that the Nobility was planning to recover what it had lost. As long as Louis XVI was seen to side with the people, as he appeared to do on a number of occasions, he was popular; the moment he was seen as a tool of the enemy, he became the most hated man in France. The fact that there really was no aristocratic plot did not matter; from June 1791 on, it was plain to all that Louis XVI was an enemy of the people.

This greatly complicated the task of the moderates who were desperately holding on to their hopes for a stabilizing constitutional monarchy. In response, they made a highly significant move: on July 16 more than half of the Jacobins' members split off to found a new club, the Feuillants. The idea was to provide the new moderates with a political tool similar to the ones enjoyed by the left. Further, in an attempt to rally some of the disaffected Catholics, the majority removed the Civil Constitution of the Clergy from the realm of constitutional law. This meant not only that the Civil Constitution could now be modified like any other ordinary enactment but also that the people who would be required to swear allegiance to the constitution could do so without ceasing to be devoted Catholics. For the first time since 1789, the Assembly had taken a major step backward.

Still, it could hardly forget the presence, in growing numbers, of the ever more angry mob, frustrated now because the King had not been deposed; so it also passed a number of measures that were meant to please the left. All officers who had emigrated were to be tried as deserters if they reentered France; all decorations, orders of knighthood, and other distinctive signs were abolished; priests were forbidden to wear ecclesiastical dress outside of their churches; and finally, on August 17, the émigrés were enjoined to come home within a month or be declared outlaws.

The debate on the constitution continued all through August, but it was clear that it would be over by the beginning of September, that it would then be presented to the King and the King would approve it; he hardly had any other choice. At this time the Assembly would dissolve itself and give way to the new legislative body stipulated in the constitution.

The elections, in fact, had already started, in June. There were to be two separate procedures. First, all the "active citizens," that is, those paying a minimum tax, gathered in a primary to elect the electors. There were, as noted, nearly 4 million active citizens, a very high figure in a country with a population of 20 million, considering that women did not vote; they came together starting on June 10. These primaries were then interrupted by the King's flight and resumed after his capture, with very obvious results as to the choices being made. Then, the electors chose the Deputies over a ten-day period from August 25 to September 5. This in itself was a great novelty: the elections to the Estates General had taken place in an entirely different fashion, so no one could even guess at what the results were likely to be, especially since none of the sitting Deputies was allowed to run again. At Robespierre's urging, the Assembly had voted on May 15 to make the members of the Assembly ineligible to sit in the first legislature to be elected under the new constitution.

Although the Assembly did not complete that document until September 3, its shape was already clear enough by August to be firmly rejected at both ends of the political spectrum. On the seventh, Marie Antoinette wrote to Mercy in Brussels: "You must have already read the Charter; it is full of impracticable absurdities."[4] On the twenty-sixth she added: "The King cannot possibly refuse to accept [the constitution] because of his position here. . . . Our only hope thus lies with the powers."[5] Marat, on the other hand, exclaimed in *L'Ami du peuple:* "So here it is at last, that much-praised French constitution, fresh from the impure labyrinth of our decree-makers, this work of madness, venality, dishonesty, and perfidy, except for a very few laws that only a salutary fear has wrenched from our representatives. It can now be seen plainly in the light of day, that shameful monument of oppression and slavery. . . . O turpitude! O treason!"[6]

It was not a happy omen. The King, who was supposed to guard and apply the constitution, thought it as hopeless as the people whom it was supposed to satisfy. Louis XVI felt it weakened the executive so radically as to make all government impossible; Marat and his friends at the soon to be reopened Cordeliers no longer wanted a monarchy at all. What, in fact, was this long-celebrated, long-awaited constitution like?[7]

To begin with, it set forth the rights enjoyed by all citizens; these were the Rights of Man as passed in 1789. It provided that all civil servants, all military men, all priests, and all members of the National Guard were to swear loyalty to the nation, the law, and the King. It made a major change in the everyday life of the French by stating that marriages could henceforth be considered valid only if they were performed by a representative of the state; religious marriages were allowed but not recognized in law.

Next, the separation of powers was clearly stated: to the National Assembly went the legislative power, to the King the executive, to judges elected for a term by the people the judicial.

The Assembly sat in permanence; its members were elected for two-year terms; it was composed of a single chamber; it could not be dissolved by the King. It was to comprise 745 Deputies, 247 elected by territorial districts, 249 representing the excess of population in certain of those districts, 249 representing those who paid more than a certain sum in taxes. These Deputies were to be chosen by electors who were to be nominated in primary assemblies composed of those "active citizens" who fulfilled the following conditions: each must pay a tax equivalent to the value of three days of work; be at least twenty-five years old; serve in the National Guard; not be a domestic servant; and have taken the oath of fidelity to the law, the nation, and the King. The electors, in turn, had to own estates providing an income equal to the value of 200 days of work or pay a rental equivalent to 150 days of work. All active citizens could be elected, but any employee of the executive had to choose between his job and being a Deputy; the Deputies could serve only for two consecutive legislatures; they were exempt from all legal pursuit.

On the whole, so far, this was a fair system. Almost every man was allowed to vote — in England, by comparison, there were fewer than 100,000 voters. Any voter could be elected even if he was not rich enough to be an elector. The reason why the two-tier electoral system was chosen was to avoid having temporary popular emotions influence the legislature; given the volatility of the electorate in 1791, it was perhaps no bad thing. Even then, one major ambiguity remained. It was well understood that the Deputies' powers accrued to them solely as representatives of the people, as the men in charge of expressing the will of the nation. What was not at all clear was who the nation was. Just the active citizens? All men over a certain age? The entire population, men and women alike? Was the mob in Paris actually the people, or a fraction of them? And, if so, could they impose their own will on the Assembly because they actually *were* the nation that the Deputies merely represented? To what degree, in other words, was the Assembly a sovereign body? The questions remained unanswered, for a while at least, but their resolution soon played a major role in the development of the Revolution.

The situation was even more confused when it came to the balance of powers, to the functioning of the government. In defining the executive, the Assembly had behaved as if the government were too powerful, as if the chief danger to the state came from the King. In fact, the government was virtually powerless, the administration at a halt; the King, even before 1789, far from being too powerful, had demonstrated time and again his inability to make his policies prevail.

As it now was, Louis XVI was given a new title: he was no longer King of France (that implied divine right) but King of the French, which meant they had chosen him. His person, like that of the Deputies, was inviolable, but he reigned only so long as he was faithful to the oath he swore to the law, the nation, and the constitution. He would, in particular, be deposed if he led an army against the nation or went out of the realm without authorization; in that case he could be tried and judged. He was given a civil list and a Guard of 1,200 foot and 600 horse. His family were to be called French princes, without title or other privilege. In other words, he was little more than a hereditary president.

Nor was the King allowed to govern. He appointed the ministers but could do nothing without them, and the ministers were responsible to the Assembly. He could not offer any bill to the Assembly, could merely point out a problem and ask the Assembly to solve it. He could not dissolve the Assembly or have anything to do with the budgetary process: that belonged entirely and exclusively to the Deputies and not even the King's suspensory veto applied to it. Only the Assembly could decide on the size and nature of the army; it could indict the ministers and have them tried by the High Court; it declared war, ratified treaties, controlled the armed forces within a twenty-mile radius of the place where it sat.

And this was not all. While the King was indeed given a veto, it could be overriden by the next legislature but one. He could address the Assembly but must leave immediately upon having spoken. No minister could be a Deputy, so there was no one to defend the government in the Assembly.

In principle, the King was the supreme head of the kingdom's administration, and he did appoint ambassadors and the general commanding the army; but he could choose only half the superior officers, one-third of the colonels, one-sixth of the lieutenants. He had no control over the civil servants: within each département, an elected administrator was in charge; the King could neither hire nor fire him.

It could not have been clearer. The King had no real control over the administration or the armed forces; he was excluded from all budgetary matters; he could not ask the Assembly to consider a bill; he had no way of providing for a defense of his administration during the Assembly debates; he could not appoint the judges. He was, in fact, a mere figurehead, presiding over an executive branch without power or real responsibility. Even his one important prerogative, that of choosing the ministers, was made virtually void by the Assembly's power to indict them. However, he remained subject to attack by people who thought, old habits being hard to shake, that he was still in charge. And in front of him, the all-powerful Assembly could do essentially what it pleased, except for the veto. It was hardly the recipe for an efficient or solid government.

The conditions in which the constitution was to be promulgated were also equivocal at the very least. It would officially come into being when the King accepted it, and at that moment he himself would be reinstated into his proper powers; but it may well be asked how a suspended monarch could at the same time validate these new fundamental laws; and in the unlikely case that he should choose to reject them, what was to happen? Either the constitution was granted by the King — but then he could not be suspended; or it was purely the will of the people — and then it required no royal approval at all. Robespierre as usual saw it clearly when he told the Assembly on September 1: "Only one condition need be fulfilled for the constitution to come into being, and that is its acceptance by the nation. . . . Its fate is therefore independent of Louis XVI's decision."[8]

Robespierre has been represented as a bloodthirsty monster for so long that it is difficult to recognize him for what he actually was: a man who saw through pretense and obfuscation, had ideals, and acted on them. That, more than his oratorical powers, is what gave him such power, such ability to convince; but in this case, he got nowhere at all. On the evening of September 3 the constitution was solemnly brought to the King, who for the next ten days played his part in the charade by pretending to examine it; on the thirteenth, he notified the Assembly that, upon careful consideration, he had decided to accept it.

He did not do so, however, without comment. In a long letter to the president of the Assembly, Louis XVI carefully rewrote history: "From the beginning of my reign, I have wanted to bring about reforms," he claimed.

When . . . you started to put in place the first elements of your work, I did not wait until the constitution was finished before assenting to it . . . and although the disorders that accompanied almost all the periods of the Revolution too often afflicted my heart, I hoped that the lawful authorities would regain their strength. . . .

When I left Paris . . . the power of the laws seemed to wane daily. . . . Only the most extreme ideas seemed successful; the licentiousness of the press was extreme; no power was respected . . .

but since then you have shown you wanted to reestablish order. . . .
You have transferred certain articles out of the constitution. . . .
Therefore I can no longer doubt that [it] represents the wish of the
people.[9]

Then Louis XVI went on to urge, first, a return to civil peace, and,
finally, a general amnesty covering all accusations and convictions linked
to the events of the Revolution.

If not fully convincing, the letter was at least good enough. The
reasons for which the King had fled no longer existed; he was willing to
work with the constitution; he hoped for a return to tranquillity.
Unfortunately, his statements were also untrue. Once again, many in the
Assembly relied on the magic of the word: if Louis XVI *said* things had
changed, then they really would change; if he *said* he freely accepted the
constitution, then the hoped-for regime did really exist. In fact, no one in
the know supposed for a moment that the wretched monarch actually
meant any of those things; they understood that he had no choice, and so
did the mob.

Still, he was, once again, cheered to the echo, both just before his
acceptance, since it was plain that it was forthcoming, and on September
14, when, with the Queen, he went to the Assembly and solemnly swore
to respect the constitution. "The royal family appeared [in the Tuileries
gardens] in the evening," Samuel Romilly reported, "and were well
received though perhaps with less enthusiasm than Lafayette. . . . Last
night [September 19] the royal family were at the Opera; the Boulevard
and the house as full as they could hold, and the most enthusiastic
applause without any alloy. One verse, 'Régnez sur un peuple fidèle'
[Reign over a faithful people], was encored, and amazingly clapped; and
the applause, as far as I could judge, was distributed to Their Majesties
very equally. They have been very popular ever since their
enlargement."[10] Indeed, upon leaving the Opera, the King and Queen
slowly rode down the Champs-Elysées amidst tremendous shouts of .
"Long live the King"; but, as Mme de Staël aptly observed: "These
were the same people who had insulted the same King when he came
back from Varennes."[11] What the acclaim reflected, in fact, was not
Louis XVI's popularity but the fact that he had done what the people
wanted. It was not unlike the praise given a performing animal that has

just done a difficult trick; and it was equally likely to be replaced by punishments if the monarch ever failed, in the future, to behave in such a way as to please the Parisians.

As for the King's own feelings, amid all the huzzahs, they were anything but pleasant. On his return from the Assembly on September 14, Mme Campan noted, the King came into the Queen's apartment through a private door. "He was pale; his face was extremely drawn. The Queen exclaimed in surprise on seeing him thus. I thought he was about to faint; but . . . then I heard that unfortunate monarch say, as he collapsed into an armchair and held his handkerchief over his eyes: 'All is lost! Ah, Madame, and you were the witness of my humiliation! What! You came to France in order to see. . . . ' The Queen said to me, 'Oh, go, go!' with a tone of voice which meant only: do not remain here to see your sovereign's despair!"[12]

Outside of Marie Antoinette and Mme Campan, however, no one positively knew how the King felt; as a result, he was attacked once more by the extreme right: earlier, they had deplored his weakness; now they found themselves outraged by his compliance. "A great number of *aristocrates* have lately quitted the kingdom," Romilly wrote home. "They all appear so mortified with the King's acceptation and subsequent conduct, that I have not the least doubt of his sincerity."[13]

By now, in fact, it was not only right-wing aristocrats who were leaving. The princesse de Chimay, the duchesse de Duras, and most of the Queen's ladies had gone, of course, and so had most of the King's Household, the marquis de Duras, the duc de Villequier, and the others, along with Cardinal de Montmorency, the Grand Almoner of France. That was to be expected. But they were also joined by people like La Marck, Mirabeau's great friend; the comtesse de Tessé, the liberal hostess; the vicomte de Noailles, who, on August 4, 1789, had proposed the end of feudal privileges; his friend Mathieu de Montmorency; and many others. Even then, some remained: Lafayette, who professed the utmost confidence in the future; Mme de Staël, who felt protected because her husband was ambassador from Sweden; the duc de La Rochefoucauld-Liancourt, who still felt a duty to the King. One person actually came back from emigration. Mme de Lamballe had fled Paris at the same time as the royal family and successfully made her way to London; now she returned, resuming her office as Superintendent of the Queen's Household, because, no matter how great the danger, she would not leave her friend alone.

Because, in the nineteenth century, historians were given to simplification, the Revolution is still often seen as a clear-cut battle: the King and the upper classes on one side, the bourgeoisie, peasants, and lower classes on the other. In fact, Louis XVI found himself under attack, not just from Marat or Robespierre but also from most of his former courtiers, who found his lack of resistance deplorable and looked instead to the émigré princes for leadership. This fact added greatly to his agony — and to Marie Antoinette's indignation. By late October she was writing Fersen: "Our family circle is unbearable; with the best intentions in the world there is nothing one can say. My sister [Madame Elisabeth] is so indiscreet, surrounded by intriguers and, above all, dominated by her brothers abroad, that we cannot converse without quarreling all day. I think that the ambition of the people around Monsieur will sink him altogether."[14]

Still, in mid-September it looked as if the King's acceptance of the constitution might give him new leverage. La Marck, who, after Mirabeau's death, continued to advise the Queen, wrote her from Brussels on September 16:

> The decision the King has just carried out, and the Queen's agreement, manifested by her presence [at the Assembly] have already produced a great effect on the revolutionaries and inclined the people to a more trusting attitude that it would be easy to encourage. This is an example of the power the Queen could exert if she could constrain herself sometimes to cajole this changing and frivolous people.
>
> I understand how it offends the Queen's dignity to have to flatter a misled multitude. But when the most imperious need makes it essential, when the antirevolutionary party offers no strength on which to count, when there is no solid hope of a foreign intervention . . . it is necessary to follow the policy the Queen has already endorsed.[15]

As it turned out, La Marck was preaching to the converted: Marie Antoinette had no compunction about pretending to like the constitution if it could save her and her husband; the only problem was that, as usual, she completely misunderstood the real situation.

"We have been in a new position since the King's acceptance," she wrote Fersen on September 26. "It would have been more noble to refuse but it was impossible given the circumstances. . . . The follies of the princes and the émigrés also forced us to this; it was essential to accept in such a way that people could not think it was not in good faith. I think the best way to disgust them with all this is to appear to believe in it; they will soon see that nothing works."[16] It was the same old policy that had already failed so spectacularly.

At least, on September 14, the Deputies voted the amnesty the King had requested: this primarily helped the former privilégiés, if they were willing to come forward; but, of course, most of them remained safely abroad. Moreover, on the thirtieth, the very last day of its existence, the Assembly passed a law punishing the excesses of the clubs. Now all depended on the new legislature, which met on October 1. Within the week, it became evident that the aftereffects of Varennes were far from over.

Because the elections had taken place just after the flight, they reflected the people's indignation; as a result, the Deputies were, on the whole, significantly more revolutionary than most of their constituents. They were also mostly naive and inexperienced: because the members of the first Assembly were automatically disqualified, the political experience gathered by the Deputies during two and a half turbulent years was essentially lost. Some of the departing members remained important, however: Robespierre, himself no longer a Deputy, was still the Jacobins' leading orator and therefore extremely influential. The departing moderates left no legacy at all.

Essentially, the new Legislative Assembly was divided into three main groups. On the right were the Feuillants, those moderates who had split off from the Jacobins; they were a largely inchoate mass of about 250 men, whose leaders were either gone — Lafayette soon retired to his estate in the Auvergne — or ineffective — Barnave was no longer a Deputy, and the Feuillants, as a club, was never really powerful. It should also be emphasized that, in the previous Assembly, this group had occupied the center left; now, as a result of the overall slide to the left, it sat on the right-wing benches.

The center, consisting of some 350 men, was leaderless and distinguished mostly by the mediocrity and inexperience of its members. It stood for the preservation of the monarchy, but with a further dose of reforms, and quite failed to realize that this must, in the end, bring about a radically different form of government.

Finally, on the left, some 150 Deputies ranged all the way from the Jacobins to the Cordeliers; all were hostile to the King, all demanded radical change, and most were ready to work together with the Paris mob, whom they often harangued and with whom they met at the clubs. It was within this group that the few Deputies of talent were to be found. They were as yet unknown, but ready all the same for radical change; and, just as important, they were hungry for power.

Under the circumstances, the new Assembly represented a clear and present danger to the system set up by the constitution. Because it was essentially manipulated from the outside, whether by leaders like Robespierre or by the actions of the mob, it could not reach compromise solutions, and its debates were essentially meaningless. This awkward fact was soon perceived by both sides. On October 31 Marie Antoinette wrote Fersen, "There is nothing to be done with this Assembly: it is a mass of villains, of madmen, and of idiots"[17]; while the mob discovered that occupying the tribunes was a highly effective means of pressure: the terrified Deputies being then likely to cave in while pretending they were acting according to their convictions. It needs little insight, however, to guess the effect of tribunes packed with hundreds of menacing, vociferating sans-culottes on the legislators — middle-aged men, most of them, who had until then led sedate lives.

Indeed, the mood was set on October 5, the first real workday of the new legislature. Georges Couthon, a member of the extreme left and a friend of Robespierre, demanded the suppression of the titles of "Sire" and "Majesty" (Louis XVI to be addressed only as King of the French), adding for good measure that the King, when he appeared before the Assembly, should be given a seat identical to that of the president, and that the Deputies, wearing their hats, should sit even when he stood bareheaded. In a burst of enthusiasm, his motion was passed; upon which, it occurred to a majority that they had virtually ended the monarchy; so the next day, the Deputies voted to reverse themselves.

It was a practical thing to do; but a pamphlet that appeared a month later showed clearly the way the wind was blowing. Its author, Charles Barbaroux, a radical lawyer from Marseille, was busy organizing the local Jacobins so that they soon became one of the most important

revolutionary forces in the country. Although, with a few local exceptions, the larger provincial cities were much more conservative than the
capital, many of them, especially the ports, had an equivalent of the Paris
mob, composed mostly of sailors and dockers who were unemployed as
a consequence of the virtual end of foreign trade. France no longer had
much to export, and was hardly in a position to pay for imports. These
men, poor, uneducated, and dissatisfied, were ready to listen to the local
Jacobins, whose clubs had been chartered by the Paris Jacobins, and who
were told at length, in correspondence and through the left-wing press,
just how to proceed. Because the middle-class inhabitants of these cities
were even more timid than their Paris brethren, it was possible for a small
group of activists to gain a disproportionate influence there. Paris, of
course, was where key events took place; but the extremists in Paris were
reinforced by the success of their affiliates in the provinces.

"The word 'Majesty' denotes the fullness of the sovereign power,"
Barbaroux wrote. "We refer to the majesty of God because He is the
source of all being. . . . People used to refer to the majesty of kings
because they were the source of all the evils that ravaged the world. . . .
The title now belongs only to the 25 million men who form the French
nation because it is in them that the sovereign power resides, because they
have made the constitution and the King."[18]

Barbaroux was a little ahead of the Assembly, and even of the majority
of the Paris Jacobins — but not much. Logic was on his side, and logic,
while it had a tendency to disappear when the people rose, played a key
role in bringing about these very uprisings. The English, who may fairly
be said to have invented the notion of constitutional monarchy, understood the value of a compromise and the merits of vagueness; the French
did not. A line of reasoning, once started, was likely to be pursued to its
ultimate end; and Barbaroux's argument was nothing more than one more
step in the clarification of the new polity. If the people were indeed
sovereign, if their will as expressed by the legislature was indeed the only
legitimate source of power, then there really was no room for a hereditary
monarch. When the mob made menacing noises in the tribunes of the
Assembly, it was, of course, expressing the pent-up rage of centuries
rather than support for a line of logic; but the line of logic, by justifying
radical change, made it far easier for the rage to be legitimately vented.

In spite of its occasional crises, the Revolution so far had progressed with a minimum of violence. Now that all changed. The tourists who had still flocked to Paris in the spring and summer of 1791 stopped coming; those who were there began to leave: there was no telling anymore when you might find yourself faced with a menacing, hostile mob, which might well insult you, might even assault you, and, in any event, would terrify you. As it surged in from the faubourgs, the mob seemed to become established in the center of the city; it was recognizable, not just by its appearance and smell but also by its utter lack of ordinary politeness.

By the late fall, in fact, the capital was becoming a dangerous place. Order was supposed to be kept by the National Guard, but now it gave up even the pretense of doing so. Some of its members, of course, sympathized with the mob, but most were just plain frightened. The election that took place on November 14 showed it plainly.

Bailly's term as Mayor of Paris expired on that date, and he had no thought of running again, largely because he had been one of the Cordeliers' targets and was therefore hated by the mob. That should have made no difference: the mob did not vote, as virtually none of its members paid enough tax to qualify as an active citizen; but the secret ballot had yet to be invented, and the voters had no intention of becoming the victims of the violence consequent on Bailly's possible reelection. As it worked out, the two candidates in the field, Pétion and Lafayette, were both perfect representatives of the two great movements within the Revolution.

The General, who resigned as commander of the National Guard in order to run, was the most visible incarnation of what might be called the liberal party. He stood for the new constitution and a moderate policy that would guarantee the conquests of the Revolution while preventing further radicalization; and, of course, he was immensely well known, both for his exploits in America and his role since 1789. Even more important, he still believed he was popular.

In contrast to so famous a figure, Pétion, a former Deputy and current Jacobin, looked almost insignificant, though among the radicals he was not. His most glorious moment had come as one of the commission sent to bring the royal family back from Varennes. He belonged to the fringe of the extreme left, being politically situated somewhere between Marat and Robespierre, and made no secret of his republican feelings. Born in 1756 and, until the Revolution, a resident of Chartres, Pétion had led an uneventful life there as a lawyer. Immediately upon his election as a Deputy to the Estates General, however, he began to be noticed. Tall, handsome, with the kind of stentorian voice eighteenth-century orators needed (there were no microphones), he also proved to be eloquent in just the right way: in this age when sentimentality was universal, he was well able to move his audience to tears. With that, and from the beginning, he always placed himself at the extreme left. As Robespierre's closest friend, he had a great deal of influence at the Jacobins, and together with him, was triumphantly acclaimed there when the National Assembly dissolved itself, upon which he was elected president of the Paris Criminal Court. All this hardly measured up to Lafayette's fame or accomplishments, obviously; Pétion, however, did have one essential qualification for the post of Mayor: he could be relied on not to keep order in Paris, but instead to help any future uprising. Given the limitations on voting, that last qualification hardly seemed likely to appeal to a majority of the 80,000 active citizens of the capital.

The campaign opened in mid-October, and it was immediately obvious that while large and angry crowds supported Pétion, Lafayette, whose mere presence once drew hundreds of admirers, was badly behind when it came to the people's favor. But then, neither the upper middle class nor most of the petty bourgeoisie really wanted disorder: if the King and Queen had been so warmly cheered in mid-September, it was because such Parisians assumed that, with the new constitution firmly in place, life would return to normal, and with normality would come prosperity. It was high time, really. Not only was unemployment spreading and business suffering, the assignats, which had been printed in huge quantities, were losing their value with worrying speed. In January 1790, 100 livres assignat were still worth 96 gold livres; by January 1791, after a dip, their value had risen again to 91; but in September it was only 82, and in December, 77. The assignats, in other words, had lost a quarter of their value, while gold and silver had become so rare as to be invisible. All transactions, therefore, were made in a rapidly depreciating currency: obviously, only civil peace and the return of prosperity could prevent a further, even more disastrous plunge.

Under those circumstances, Lafayette should have won by a landslide. Instead, he lost by two to one: he received 3,126 votes to Pétion's 6,728. That was startling enough, but the really significant figure was that of the abstentions: of the 80,000 potential voters, almost 70,000 failed to attend the election. It could hardly be clearer: seven-eighths of those who had something to lose were too frightened to vote. The middle class, who had made the Revolution, was now out of the circuit, out of power. The Assembly, watching the results, knew exactly what they meant: for many of the frightened Deputies, the only safety lay in moving closer to the radicals. Just as important, the Jacobins themselves were being pushed to the left: the Cordeliers had far more influence on the mob than they did, and the Jacobins could not afford to look like moderates. The result, therefore, was a visible speeding-up of the revolutionary process.

This movement was reinforced, as usual, by a great flood of pamphlets and other publications. There was *L'Ami du peuple,* of course, with its provocative headlines. After the retraction of the motion ending the titles of "Sire" and "Majesty," for instance, Marat proclaimed: "The New Assembly Undoes Today What It Did Yesterday — The People Can Feel Little Trust in the Enlightenment and Energy of Its Representatives — Ruin of the Fatherland Prepared by Its Enemies."[19] And he kept it up. On November 7 he announced: "Picture of the Calamities About to Desolate France"; on November 9: "Picture of Several Notorious Facts Proving the Tuileries' Plot to Sell France to Its Enemies"; on December 1: "Secret Means used by the Minister To Corrupt Almost All the Deputies in Very Little Time"; on December 11: "The Legislature, Rotten to the Bone, Displays Its Prostitution to the Cabinet. Pétion, the Model of Intrepid and Incorruptible Magistrates."[20]

That took care of daily political events; but there was also a great burgeoning of the anonymous attacks against the King and Queen, which had been current all along. Typical of this sort of invective was the pamphlet entitled *Death sentence pronounced by the monarch of Hell against the king and queen of the French and the National Assembly.* The point was simply to discredit the monarchs, make them look like criminals, and create an atmosphere in which their deposition would seem both logical and unavoidable; thus, specific issues are seldom mentioned; character assassination is the aim. It would be tiresome to quote at any length from this or other pamphlets: a few selections will suffice to give their flavor. "Brutal and ignorant prince, lascivious and perverted princess," the *Death sentence* proclaimed, you are despised and mocked by the men and women who so abundantly abused your weakness. . . . Yes, monarch more stupid than Midas, you would not [otherwise] have sacrificed the blood of your subjects to the vile embezzlers who, by their insatiable greed, have finally brought the hatred and contempt of a sensitive and generous nation on your head and that of your detestable wife. . . . And you, lubricious Antoinette . . . you will wander for centuries on the banks of the Styx with your criminal favorites and your cowardly lovers. . . . You will account for the treasures of France you lavished on your ambitious brother.[21]

It must be noted that in 1791 the attacks still remain centered on Marie Antoinette. Louis XVI is pictured as stupid, weak, undeserving, but not evil; his wrong policies are due not to his own wickedness, but to that of his wife; and the canard about the cartfuls of gold supposedly sent to Austria by the Queen is endlessly revived. The King might be *le gros cochon,* the fat pig; Marie Antoinette, after being Madame Deficit, was now Madame Veto. That, in fact, is her title in one of the most popular revolutionary songs, the "*Ça ira.*" By the end of 1791, it could be heard all over Paris, including just outside the royal windows.

Like other such songs, the "*Ça ira*" had a rapidly changing content so as to reflect current events, but the core remained the same: "*Ah, ça ira, ça ira, ça ira / les aristocrates à la lanterne / Ah, ça ira, ça ira, ça ira / les aristocrates on les pendra. / Le despotisme expirera / l'égalité triomphera*" (Oh, it will go [in the sense of: things will be as they should], it will go, it will go / the aristocrats to the lantern [the streetlights from which Berthier and Foulon had been hanged] / Oh, it will go, it will go, it will go / the aristocrats, we will hang them / despotism will die out / equality will triumph).[22] To this much was added; in early 1792, for instance, one verse began: "Madame Veto had promised / that she would burn Paris down."

These songs, all set to catchy tunes, culminated in the "Marseillaise," named after the battalion sent by the Marseille Jacobins to Paris in July-August 1792. That a revolutionary song should still be the national anthem two centuries later says something about the hold of these songs on the minds and hearts of the French; and, indeed, they are still taught to schoolchildren. In 1791, however, they were also an easy way of defining someone's politics; the separation lay between the people who sang and those who refused to sing. The songs could be used to humiliate and frighten the *aristos* who were sometimes forced to join the singers; they kept the street tensions high; and as they drifted in through the Tuileries windows, they reminded the royal couple and what remained of their court that their position was precarious in the extreme.

The "Ça ira," the "Marseillaise," and the other revolutionary songs, while often violent, were relatively clean; but at the same time a great flood of obscene pamphlets spread over Paris, and eventually, the rest of the country. Again, their chief purpose was to discredit the figures depicted in them by showing them to be immoral, uncontrolled, despicable. They were widely read and very often believed: many of the accusations against Marie Antoinette, for instance, were taken up again, quite seriously, at her trial.

Here, too, detail is hardly necessary: nothing is duller or more monotonous than this sort of writing, and a few, very brief samples will suffice to indicate tone and content. There was, for instance, a rhymed brochure entitled *Fureurs utérines de Marie Antoinette* (Uterine rages of Marie Antoinette), in which she says to herself: *"Louis est impuissant, mais Artois ne l'est pas / D'Artois est aussi beau que le fringant Narcisse / D'Hercule il a la force, il aura mes appâts"* (Louis is impotent, but Artois is not / D'Artois is as handsome as lively Narcissus / As strong as Hercules, I'll give myself to him). The writer then comments: *"L'amour a le dessus et le foutre ruisselle . . . / Le fort dix fois repris fut dix fois emporté"* (Love triumphs in rivers of fuck / The fortress, ten times assailed, is ten times conquered). Nor are the Queen's female friends left out: *"Elle donne à Polignac son coeur et ses attraits . . . / Chaque femme à la fois fut tribade et catin"* (She gives herself to Polignac, heart and body . . . / Each woman is both a dyke and a whore).[23]

This pamphlet, at least, has a specific political purpose; there were also similar pamphlets, written in the most obscene language possible, and in which the attacks included anyone at all famous, whether on the right or the left. A good example of this is the *Bordel patriotique institué par la reine des Français pour le plaisir des députés à la nouvelle législature* (Patriotic brothel set up by the Queen of the French for the enjoyment of the Deputies to the new legislature), which came out in November 1791. After setting out the cost to the subscribers to the brothel — twenty-four hundred livres for a prince or princess, two thousand livres for a cardinal, three livres for a soldier or an actress, forty-eight livres for the Deputies — it goes on to depict the activities therein in the most vivid fashion. Of course Marie Antoinette presides, and the various characters are represented as insatiable if female, and demanding to be sodomized if they are male: in this latter category, the reader finds, not only Lafayette, Bailly, and Barnave but also Marat and the rising hope of the extreme left, Danton. Because these brochures are usually very short — they range from six to forty pages — they were cheap to print, and so they flooded the streets. Even if much of the mob was illiterate, there were enough men and women who could read so as to ensure that this outpouring reached a very wide audience.

This great flood of mud is due in part, no doubt, to the overall breakdown of the old, polite society, and of the relationships that derived from it; it is unquestionably a reaction against the extreme refinement of the upper classes before 1789. But it is also something more: the direct expression of an unloosening of the popular soul. Respect, indeed deference, had been demanded of the lower classes for centuries. Now that equality prevailed, or was meant to, everything that had been repressed for so long came out with tremendous force. We are, after all, never more like one another than when we are having sex — peasants and kings behave in much the same way under those particular circumstances — and that, in part at least, is what the pamphlets tell us. Then, too, in a country where "sodomized one" (in a less polite form) is a standard form of insult, the representation of the likes of Lafayette and Marat — who had many rivals on the left — as begging to be sodomized made a real contribution to the breakdown of their popularity.

Short of another escape attempt, nothing could have been more dangerous for the monarchy than these pamphlets; it had relied for centuries on an inchoate belief that the King was different from all other men. Once that aura was gone, it was up to the individual monarch to impress by his prowess — the very last thing of which Louis XVI was capable. His awkwardness, his slowness all worked against him, as did his utter inability really to understand what was happening. He knew that he, and the monarchy, were in desperate danger, but the Revolution seemed to him a natural catastrophe on the order of a hurricane or an earthquake: there just was not very much he could do about it. This resigned passivity was noticed by friends and enemies alike: the testimony of Antoine Bertrand de Molleville, whom the King made minister of the navy in late September 1791, is particularly telling.

Bertrand, who had been a high-level civil servant, was one of those pillars of the ancien régime who saw the progress of the Revolution with consternation. As early as late May 1789, he had advised the King to dissolve the Estates General; he was a devoted monarchist; and yet, in his own account of his appointment, the King looks as weak, as deluded, as usual.

The appointment process had, indeed, begun badly. Bertrand, on being told Louis XVI was about to give him the navy ministry, let it be known he would refuse to serve on the grounds that it was impossible to govern in the circumstances. The choices open to the King were so few, however, that he went on pursuing Bertrand. On September 27 he wrote the reluctant appointee: "In a word, I am confident that your services would be useful to me and the state. I know your attachment to me and expect, in the present emergency, that you will give me this proof of your zeal and obedience." Even that, however, failed to sway Bertrand, who sent back a letter declining the appointment. Bertrand goes on: "The King, after having read my letter, said to M. de Montmorin, who had delivered it: 'But ask M. Bertrand, then, how I am to find ministers and what is to become of me if persons such as he, who profess themselves attached to me, refuse their services and abandon me?' "[24]

That pathetic plea convinced Bertrand it was his duty to serve, so off he went to the Tuileries. He tells us what happened next:

As it was the first time that I had ever had the honor of speaking to His Majesty, on finding myself tête-à-tête with him, I was so overwhelmed with timidity that, if it had been my part to speak first, I should not have been able to pronounce a sentence. But I acquired courage on observing that the King was more embarrassed than myself. He stammered out a few words without connection, but at last recovered himself. . . .

"I am far" [he said] "from regarding this constitution as a chef d'œuvre, I believe there are great faults in it and that if I had been allowed to state any observations upon it, some advantageous alterations might have been adopted. But of this there is no question at present. I have sworn to maintain it, such as it is, and I am determined, as I ought, to be strictly faithful to my oath; for it is my opinion that an exact execution of the constitution is the best means of making it thoroughly known to the nation, who will then perceive the changes proper to be made."[25]

It is all there: Louis XVI's extraordinary and frantic shyness, which often made him appear half-witted; his calling upon a man devoted to himself and an opponent of the constitution, only to discourage him by telling him he meant the constitution to be strictly observed; the fact that this was a lie, and he really hoped the system would soon collapse before the onslaught of foreign armies; and, finally, the fact that Louis XVI utterly failed to comprehend that Bertrand was quite incapable of serving usefully under the circumstances. Indeed, the new minister, disobeyed by his civil servants and unable to conciliate the Assembly, was forced to resign within six months.

This kind of mistaken choice, of halfway measure, was typical of the King. Malouet, who had led the monarchists in the Estates General and the Assembly in the summer and fall of 1789, was still in touch with the royal couple; he saw, with sadness, that it was incapable of saving itself: "The Queen [when speaking privately to those she trusted] . . . would have nothing to do with anyone who believed in the constitution. . . . Alone, the King would have been disposed to adopt a more reasonable stance. His mind was perceptive enough to show him the needs of his position, but the weakness of his character prevented him from taking any strong, decisive measures."[26]

Another friend, La Marck, having watched Mirabeau's efforts and seeing the uselessness of his own, wrote much the same thing in a burst of despair; unfortunately, his assessment was perfectly accurate. "Louis XVI is unable to reign — through the apathy of his character, that rare resignation, which he mistakes for courage and which makes him almost unaware of the dangers of his position, and finally through his invincible repugnance for the work of thinking, which makes him change the subject whenever there is a discussion about the dangerous situation in which his kindness has placed his kingdom and himself," he noted in a letter to Mercy, the former Austrian ambassador:

The Queen, who is more intelligent and very brave, still misses all the occasions of taking over the reins of government and of surrounding the

King with people who are faithful to her, want to serve her and save the state with her and through her.

When one tries to discover the causes of the lack of decision, of the slackness which pervade the Tuileries, one discovers that, through laziness of mind and character, and also perhaps through the exhaustion which often follows on prolonged reverses, the King and Queen hope only in whatever chances the future may bring and in the results of a foreign intervention . . . and they think that, in the meantime, a few private efforts* will ensure their personal safety.[27]

It would be hard to imagine a better recipe for disaster. As the Revolution accelerated, as the disorders became more dangerous, the center grew weaker every day. Instead of trying by any available means to recover a measure of control, the bemused King and Queen just sat back and waited for the next crisis. Unpredictable though the future might be in a number of ways, the one certain thing was that there would indeed be a next crisis.

All through the last months of 1791 and the beginning of 1792, the situation was allowed to drift. The executive branch of the government had virtually stopped governing; the Assembly moved steadily to the left; and the royal couple secretly tried to arrange a foreign invasion, partly through Breteuil, Louis XVI's secret envoy, partly through Mercy and Fersen, with whom Marie Antoinette kept up an abundant correspondence. That a war was the only solution she made clear again and again. On November 25, for instance, she explained: "Our ostensible policy is forced on us by our position; we must win the confidence of the majority no matter what the cost, but we neither want nor can approve of a constitution which has caused our sufferings and is ruining the kingdom; [instead] we wish to arrive at an order of things that is desirable but cannot be established by the French. . . . The powers must therefore come to our help."[28] Even so, the Queen realized that if Prussia, Austria, Spain, and Sardinia declared war on France, the mob was likely to assume this was all — as in fact it was — a royal plot, and end it by expeditious means. Thus the new plan was to arrange for France to start the war, with the King's approval, so that he would seem merely to be

---

* The "private efforts" are the bribes the King was distributing on a fairly large scale among supposedly influential men on the left.

obeying the people's will; an Austrian victory would then save the monarchy. That possibly the French might not be beaten occurred to absolutely no one involved in this plot.

By adopting that position the King, blind as ever, missed a splendid chance of splitting the left and moving the Revolution back toward the center. Because of Leopold II's declaration at Pillnitz in August, which was aimed at protecting the royal couple, and because virtually every foreign government clearly loathed the principles of the Revolution, it had occurred to some of the Jacobins that it might be best to start the war rather than wait to be attacked. This was the position Pierre Vergniaud, one of the extremist Deputies, took in a speech as early as October 24. To all appearances, therefore, the royal plan was well on its way to being a success.

At the same time, however, another important section of the extreme left, the one being led by Marat, opposed the war, which it saw, accurately, as a trap set by Louis XVI and his fellow monarchs: "Ministerial Plots to Bring the Nation into a Disastrous War while Blaming the Legislature for it," *L'Ami du peuple* headlined on December 1.[29] For Marat, it was more important to consolidate and extend the civil conquests of the Revolution than to impose its principles on the rest of Europe: a war might be lost, he pointed out; and even if it were not, he dreaded the new power the King would acquire as constitutional head of the armies. Robespierre, now no longer a Deputy, entirely agreed with this analysis. All through this period, he spoke often and vigorously at the Jacobins' meetings against any warlike policy, basing his reasoning on the idea that the key triumph of the Revolution was the constitution; that it must be obeyed, and preserved, absolutely; and that a war might well endanger it by transferring power to the army. That, however, was an unpopular stand because the mob thought Europe would crumble just as the monarchy had done, and the great influence the orator had won for himself waned rapidly; by March 1792 he looked very much like a spent force, a legalist at a time when the law no longer mattered.

This split was obviously Louis's chance: if, instead of waiting passively, he had tried further to divide the pro-war and antiwar factions, he might well have found himself more in control of the situation than he had been since May 1789; but, once again, that would have required just the kind of intelligence and energy he so conspicuously lacked. Instead,

Louis XVI refused to deal with his countrymen, knowing, however, that the situation grew more alarming with every passing day.

"Our position right now is appalling," Marie Antoinette wrote Fersen on November 25. "The factions are always busy; the people are ready to rise at any moment and to commit horrors; and the republicans are doing their best. I still think that, by being quiet, we will, through the very excesses of it all, be able to do something sooner than one thinks, but great prudence is needed. Without foreign help, we will do nothing."[30] On December 7 she went on: "How happy I will be if only I can become powerful enough, one day, to show all these blackguards I was not their dupe! . . . As for me, I feel better than I should considering the prodigious fatigue of mind I bear while hardly ever going out: I have hardly a moment to myself because of the people I must see, my letters and the time I spend with my children. This last occupation . . . gives me my only happiness and when I am too sad, I take my little boy in my arms, kiss him with all my heart and that consoles me for the moment."[31]

The "blackguards" in question knew very well how the Queen — and the King — felt; and they acted in consequence, both by passing new laws and by pressuring the ministers. On October 31 Montmorin, who had been foreign minister for more than four years, was forced to resign as being insufficiently progressive, although, in 1789, he had shared Necker's popularity as one of the most forward-looking ministers. He was replaced by the interior minister, Valdec de Lessart, a mediocrity whom Louis XVI appointed to ministry after ministry and who did equally badly in all of them, while another nonentity, Cahier de Gerville, became interior minister. These changes, while faithfully reflecting the King's weakness, had disastrous consequences in that Lessart caved in to the pressures in favor of war, while Louis XVI, who was unwilling to do without Montmorin's advice, set up a secret committee composed of the latter, Malouet, and Bertrand de Molleville.

He could hardly have made a worse move. The committee was supposed to be secret; but of course it was not. Its existence thus became yet another proof that Louis XVI and Marie Antoinette were secretly conspiring against the regime; soon dubbed the Austrian Committee, it was assumed to be plotting the defeat of France in the forthcoming war, and was used by the leaders of the mob as proof that the monarchy must be ended. All this would have been a heavy price to pay even for the best of advice; but, in fact, while Louis XVI listened to the three men, he never carried out their recommendations, thus typically having the worst of both worlds.

At the same time the Assembly moved to protect the new regime. Until now the émigrés had done nothing illegal; it was their right to reside abroad if they so chose. Now that freedom was abrogated. On October 31 a decree was passed enjoining Monsieur to come back to France or lose all rights to the throne; on November 9 another that would punish all the émigrés who failed to return with the loss of their estates and the death penalty in absentia. Both decrees were vetoed by the King, but the trend was clear, and because he realized that his veto was likely to cause a riot, Louis XVI at the same time wrote his brothers an open letter asking them to come home. To no one's surprise, both Provence and Artois refused to obey on the grounds that the King was neither physically nor morally free.

In theory, once Louis XVI had vetoed the decrees, the matter was closed; but everyone remembered that there was a simple way to make him change his mind; the causes for a new, large-scale uprising began to accumulate. Yet another was added when, on November 29, the Assembly voted to require all non-juring priests to take an oath of obedience to the constitution or be arrested as suspected of rebellion. Once again, the King killed the bill; once again, the move was highly unpopular; but this time, his effort was unnecessary. That Louis XVI should refuse to force his brothers to come back is understandable. That he should also feel compelled to protect the émigrés from so extreme a punishment is also defensible, although many of them were engaged in treasonable activities. An émigré army was being formed; its specific purpose was to invade France and force a return to the ancien régime: it was perhaps a little much to expect that they should enjoy their incomes unhampered. If, however, there is a rather slender case to be made for that veto, there is no defending the King's killing of the non-juring priests bill.

The Assembly had every reason to look at the non-jurors with extreme suspicion: the French Church, always intolerant and reactionary, was rapidly identifying itself with the counterrevolution. Now that the Civil Constitution of the Clergy was just an ordinary law, there was no religious reason for the priests not to take the oath to the constitution proper, since it did not imply allegiance to the schismatic Church. Theirs, therefore, was a purely political stand, a refusal to obey the laws of their country even though the laws in question did not limit their ability to preach and practice as they chose; the sympathy they have since received from a number of conservative historians is thus wholly undeserved, if perhaps not very surprising; and the support Louis XVI gave them unquestionably hurt his cause.

For the first time in the course of the Revolution, in fact, the Catholic Church chose to take the clear and permanent political stand opposing progress and liberty that it maintained throughout the nineteenth century and most of the twentieth: freedom of speech, freedom of the press, freedom of religion, constitutions, elections, and parliamentary governments, all were anathema. That religion was not really the issue behind the non-juring priests' attitude is made particularly clear by the behavior of the Protestant ministers and Jewish rabbis: so long as they were allowed to practice their creeds, they were perfectly content to obey the law. Thus, what has sometimes been seen as religious persecution should be reassessed in light of the Church's politics: although there were a few liberal clerics, most priests were bigots; they were also rabid reactionaries who, as has so often been the case since then, were not afraid to use their office to resist any deviation from their own narrow views.

Much of the blame for the spreading so-called religious disturbances, in late 1791 and early 1792, must therefore be placed where it belongs: when the non-juring priests excited the faithful to riot, they did so mostly in the hope of reversing the reforms. This was the case in the Vendée and Avignon in October, in the Mayenne in November, and in countless villages thereafter. These riots took the form of attacks on the juring clergy, where it existed, and on the civic authorities. Just as the mob in Paris believed what it wanted to believe, even if it was patently untrue, so these religious mobs listened to priests who told them that they would all be killed because they were Catholic, that their children would be taken away from them, and other similar nonsense. All this worked best in the country and in very small towns. Except for Avignon, which had until 1790 been a papal possession, the population of the larger centers was less credulous — at least of suggestions from the Church. That eventually the Assembly should have felt the need to retaliate is hardly surprising.

In December 1791, however, what seemed to matter far more than the factious disobedience of a few priests was the rapidly approaching war. Both secretly and publicly, Louis XVI did his best to fan the flames. On December 3, for instance, he sent off a secret letter to the King of Prussia; routed via Brussels, it arrived in Berlin on January 12. "I have heard," he told Frederick William II,

> of the interest Your Majesty has shown not just toward me personally but also in the good of my kingdom. Your Majesty's willingness to prove it in all cases where it could be useful to the welfare of my people touches me deeply. I ask for it at this moment when, in spite of my acceptation of the new constitution, the factions clearly show their intention of destroying entirely the remains of the monarchy. I have just written the Emperor [Leopold II], the Empress of Russia, the Kings of Spain and Sweden to suggest the idea of a congress of the main European powers relying on an armed force as the best way of stopping the factions here, giving me the means of reestablishing a more desirable order of things and preventing our disease from contaminating the other European states. I hope that Your Majesty will approve of my ideas and keep this as the most absolute secret; you will easily understand that the circumstances in which I find myself demand the greatest circumspection.[32]

There is nothing like a good circumlocution to avoid embarrassment: in his twining, twisting sentences, Louis XVI was simply asking the King of Prussia and the other European monarchs kindly to massacre his subjects so as to restore him to the plenitude of his powers, and using a hint of blackmail — the "disease" was about to spread — to strengthen his argument. This alone is enough to end the myth according to which poor Louis was bumbling and ineffective, but well-meaning. It is perfectly true that, providing he remained an absolute ruler, the King wanted to make his subjects happy — not enough, however, to resist his wife's demands or his courtiers' begging; but, for all that, he had a very clear notion of what came first: the restoration of the monarchy as it was before 1788. Unfortunately, calling in the enemy to accomplish one's own political purposes does have a name, treason, for which the penalty, in France and elsewhere, was death.

Given the fact that, except for a few friends, she had never really liked the French, it is not surprising that Marie Antoinette yearned for a good, destructive war even more ardently than her husband: he would have been content with a return to the past; she could not wait for what would be spectacular revenge. "I think that we are about to declare war," she wrote Fersen on December 9, "not against a power that might be dangerous, we are too cowardly for that, but . . . to a few German princes in the hope that they will be unable to defend themselves. The imbeciles do not see that if they do this, they will actually serve me because, after all, once we start, the powers will be forced to come in. . . . But they must be thoroughly convinced that the best way to serve us is to attack us mightily."[33]

In early December, Duportail, the minister of war, resigned. A friend of Lafayette's and a competent general, he had been a weak minister who found himself under attack from the right for tolerating indiscipline in the army, and from the left for insufficiently preparing for the war; he resigned, in fact, as the result of an attack from Couthon, the Deputy who had proposed abolishing the titles of "Sire" and "Majesty." His departure left the army thoroughly disorganized, but his successor, for once, was chosen with the utmost care.

The comte de Narbonne, a handsome, vain, and not particularly intelligent young man — he was thirty-six in 1791 — was widely believed to be an illegitimate son of Louis XV. Be that as it may, he harbored great ambitions that were warmly encouraged by his mistress of the moment, Mme de Staël. It was partly thanks to her influence that he was appointed minister. Many of her friends still played an important role in politics and the government, so when, as in this case, she exerted herself, she was able to make a real difference. Not only did the other ministers suggest Narbonne to the King, not only did the moderate press sing his praises, many Deputies also indicated that his appointment would meet with their approval. What Mme de Staël did not know, however, was that the royal couple was eager to be influenced. Because they found Narbonne both silly and hopelessly inefficient, they thought he would make an ideal war minister; his job, after all, would be to lose the war, without his realizing that this was the case; and so he joined the government.

There followed a scene of high comedy. "Prompted by his natural vanity and the counsels of Mme de Staël," Bertrand de Molleville noted,

M. de Narbonne demanded an audience of the Queen, with whom he flattered himself he possessed more influence than he had with the King, who never appeared to have any confidence in him. . . . After expatiating on the difficulty of reestablishing the King's authority and saving the state, he proposed, as the only remedy, to place at the head of government, in the quality of first minister, a man who . . . had acquired a reputation for abilities, wisdom, activity, etc., and who possessed such a degree of popularity as to overawe the Assembly; one who, in addition to these advantages, possessed an unshaken fidelity, an unbounded attachment to the King. . . . The present emergency required that the King and Queen should place an entire and exclusive confidence in him, but without allowing it to appear; and that Their Majesties should devolve on him the power of forming a new administration, and of naming to all the different employments all the persons he judged most capable.

"All this is very fine," said the Queen . . . , "but unfortunately impracticable; for where can we find such an admirable and unparalleled person for a minister? And even if it were possible . . . , the King could not give him all the powers you mention because, by the constitution, His Majesty has not the power of appointing a *prime* minister. He is obliged to name six, each one of which must have the full direction in his own department."

This objection did not disconcert M. de Narbonne. He was very certain, he said, that the King might very easily prevail on the Assembly to depart from the strict letter of the constitution, for the sake of getting such a man at the head of affairs.

"Well," said Her Majesty, "suppose the Assembly to have this complaisance, still I ask, where is this wonderful man to be found?"

To this, M. de Narbonne, with apparent confusion and with the voice of modesty, answered, that many people supposed that he himself, whether from nature, or education, or good fortune, or all three, nearly united all the qualities he had enumerated. The Queen, breaking into laughter, merely said: "*Etes-vous fou* [Are you mad], M. de Narbonne?"[34]

More than just a comment on Narbonne's vanity, this little scene tells a good deal about the caliber of the most important minister as war loomed, and about the way the royal couple thought of their government. Having obviously given up any attempt at showing the country he was still capable of governing, Louis XVI was merely waiting for a general collapse. It remained to be seen whether he would not be trapped under the wreckage.

That left the question of the proposed conflict. On December 10 the Emperor, acting on a resolution of the Imperial Diet, made it public that he would defend the German princes whose possessions in Alsace had been confiscated by the National Assembly. To Louis XVI, of course, this seemed a God-given opportunity. On December 14 he demanded that the Archbishop of Trier, a small state near Alsace, expel the French émigré army. On the twenty-first the Emperor retorted with a note advising the French government that he would defend Trier against any attack.

On December 14 Narbonne, appearing before the Assembly, strongly argued for a declaration of war. On the twenty-seventh, the King appointed Generals Rochambeau and Luckner, both elderly, both veterans of the American campaigns, to head the armies of the North and the Rhine, and, for good measure, created them marshals of France. Lafayette, eager to be in on the coming conflict, returned from the Auvergne and made it plain that he, too, supported the war. The next day, the Assembly decreed the creation of battalions of volunteers, and two days later provided 20 million livres for the first costs of the war, while on the thirtieth, Isnard, an extreme radical from Marseille, spoke in favor of a war without which, he said, the Revolution would never be complete. What no one, except for Marat and Robespierre, seems to have asked is whether France was ready to fight the rest of Europe.

If fighting there had to be, however, it might have made sense to foster the greatest possible degree of national unity; but on December 31 the Assembly, in a blatant insult to the King, decided not to send him its wishes for the new year. That same day, one of Marie Antoinette's ladies, the princesse de Tarente, remembered, "finding myself next to the Queen, I offered her my wishes. 'The end of last year,' she told me, 'was very different: then I had great hopes; this year, I foresee only unhappiness, and no means of avoiding it.' "[35] Many people in Paris might have said the same. Even though she wanted the war, Marie Antoinette knew that it might also create a situation in which she and the King would become victims. Much was likely to happen within the next twelve months, but no one knew whether 1792 would end with the triumph of the Revolution, the triumph of the powers and the King, or simply widespread calamities.

CHAPTER TWELVE

War, Glorious War?

. : . : . :

GAIN or loss: that was the question for France and Europe at the beginning of 1792. What no one expected, or wanted, was that things would remain the same. For the émigrés, vengeance accompanied by the reinstatement of all their feudal rights was the goal. For the powers, it was becoming urgent to prevent what they saw as the contagion of revolutionary ideas. For Louis XVI and Marie Antoinette, whose position was indeed well-nigh unbearable, a good war would lead to the restoration of the ancien régime. For Narbonne, Lafayette, and their friends, the war was to be a means of stabilizing the Revolution (victorious troops, they thought, would help them to restore order in Paris and the provinces). For Robespierre, Marat, and their followers, finally, it seemed all too likely that 1792 would be the year of the foreign invasion and their own defeat.

With a King yearning for enemy invasion, an Assembly eager for war, and the rapid radicalization of politics, a crisis was obviously at hand. It was brought on, however, less by all these obvious causes than by the grave economic problems that affected the whole country, and Paris most of all, in the first months of 1792. The cause this time was not, as usual, a bad crop: it was the rapid drop in the value of the assignats. As noted, in December 1791 the bank notes were down to 77 percent of their nominal value. In January they sank to 72 percent, in February to 61, in March to 59. Under those conditions, anyone exchanging his merchandise for paper money was obviously making a fool's bargain; and the metallic currency had virtually disappeared, so much so that even the King received only 300,000 livres a year in specie. The balance of the civil list, 24.7 million livres, was paid to him in paper.

The results of this rapid depreciation of the assignats were immediate. The peasants stopped bringing their crops to the market and stocked them, instead; that, in turn, provoked severe shortages and a rapid rise in the price of bread. In January riots occurred in Paris and several other cities, motivated not by politics, but by need. From that, it was a very short step to a belief that these shortages were, once more, artificially induced by the court and the rich to punish the people; the consequence was further rapid radicalization of the lower bourgeoisie and the artisans. Back in September, the signing of the constitution had seemed to promise an era of prosperity. Now the times were harder than ever and the people were all the angrier since their hopes had been so high.

The crisis was compounded by the fact that some, at least, among the extreme left realized that the French army was in no state to wage a successful fight, and that the King and Queen were busy passing any useful information to the prospective enemy. With treachery at the center and inefficiency on the battlefield, the result seemed a foregone conclusion. Of course, at the Tuileries, the royal family was busy pretending to be patriotic, the idea being to fool people long enough to avoid the risk of another burst of Revolution; but even that policy was carried through with characteristic incompetence.

Because so many courtiers had emigrated, by January 1792 the King's and Queen's Households no longer had their full complements of attendants. How to replace them was a question that, though it may seem unimportant in the context of the crisis, gravely worried Louis XVI, and Bertrand de Molleville recorded a typical discussion about this. " 'I feel,' said [the King], 'that the Queen cannot without inconvenience retain the wives of the emigrants about her, and I have already spoken to her upon the subject: but it cannot be expected that she is to form her society of Mme Pétion, Mme Condorcet, and women of that stamp. With respect to myself, those whose services were most agreeable to me have deserted me; and among those who remain here, there are some who are the torment of my life: for instance, there is Chauvelin, who is a spy in my family, always commenting upon what is said and giving a false account of all that passes.' "[1] It obviously never occurred either to Louis XVI or to Marie Antoinette that they might gain themselves sympathies by receiving the upper middle class at their court; or that if they had had nothing to hide, they would not have felt so worried about the possible lack of-discretion of some of the people who served them.

They did, however, have a great deal to hide, so much so that, with the help of a single working man, Louis hollowed out a cache in one of the walls of the Tuileries and closed it with a metal door he had hammered himself: lock-making had always been his favorite hobby. But not all the treasonable correspondence went into this hiding-place. There was the letter that Breteuil sent to Frederick William II on January 4, for instance, in which he said: "I believe I can assure Your Majesty that the influence of the seditious factions will end as soon as it becomes apparent that there is enough force to defeat them," adding, however, "my zeal forces me also to mention how important for the King's safety it is to keep all this a secret."[2] Ten days later, Frederick William decided the time had come to write Louis XVI directly. "I am very much inclined to share in Your Majesty's views as regards the setting up of an armed congress," he announced. "In consequence, I will immediately ascertain the feelings of His Majesty the Emperor [Leopold II], with whom I have so far maintained a secret accord regarding the affairs of France." That cheerful announcement was followed by a demand for a financial indemnity: if Louis XVI expected to be restored to his former powers by Prussian troops, he would have to pay for them.[3]

Of course, the King felt the price was well worth paying. He made a sharp distinction between the bloodshed resulting from a foreign invasion and that caused by a civil war: the first was fine, the other to be avoided. "He blamed Charles I for having taken up arms against his subjects," Malouet noted, "and refused to imitate him. He was resigned to suffering in order to avoid being considered as the cause of a civil war." These sufferings, however, were expected to remain bearable. "The Jacobins," Malouet continues, "were considered by [the royal family] with even more contempt than fear; they could not believe that party might be really strong or that the revolutionaries would not be restrained by the measures announced by the powers. . . . They thought [the Jacobins] more corrupt than fanatical, hence that fateful trust in the efficacy of the money they spent."[4] What Malouet is referring to here is the policy mentioned earlier that the King and Queen followed all through the first seven months of 1792: they thought that by bribing various Jacobins they would ensure their safety. Thus whatever these men might say seemed unimportant to the royal couple; worse, they never considered the possibility that they were being tricked, that the revolutionaries might take the money, use it for antimonarchist propaganda, and, at the right time, behave exactly as if they had received nothing.

Although, in retrospect, this attitude seems extraordinarily foolish, it is easier to understand in the context of the time: the King and Queen, after all, had lived all their life in the middle of a greedy and corrupt court; they were accustomed to buying support, and thought it could still be done with a new set of recipients. Then, too, they felt nothing but disdain for the lower class of the people: obviously, money properly distributed would contain them. That there were idealists who really hated the monarchy and yearned for a republic under which all men would be equal simply never occurred to them.

Still, they *did* worry about the mob. In a conversation with one of her favorite ladies, the princesse de Tarente, Marie Antoinette mentioned one day how upset she was because of the anonymous letters that she received daily. "The details in these letters, together with a shot she heard close to her window — she lived on the ground floor overlooking the terrace," the princesse reported, "filled me . . . with a deep worry. 'Don't cry,' she told me, 'your King will survive; I alone am in danger.' "[5] No doubt, the Queen was seeing herself in her favorite role, that of a brave and selfless heroine.

When it came to business, however, and she was no longer striking poses, she expressed herself very differently. "Let the Emperor . . . show himself at the head of the other powers with . . . an imposing force and I assure you that all here will tremble," she wrote Mercy in early February. "There is no need to worry about our safety now; it is this country which is provoking a war, it is the Assembly that wants it to happen. The constitutional behavior of the King protects him, and his existence and that of his son are so necessary to all the blackguards who surround us that we are in no danger. . . . We can no longer hope for help from inside France."[6] This realization, accurate as it was, hardly shocked the Queen, who had distrusted the French ever since the summer of 1789. That Louis XVI should now understand it as well marked a new step in his hatred of the Revolution; as long as he could think that outside Paris great masses of faithful subjects yearned to obey his commands, he had not lost heart. Varennes had begun to disprove this fantasy; the political complexion of the new Assembly completed the process. As a result, he now made it a practice, not only to distrust his ministers but also to give in automatically to virtually every change, pursuing this old policy for a new reason: none of it mattered since it would all be canceled when, at long last, Leopold II restored him to his rights.

We know exactly how he felt, in fact, because Fersen, who had made a brief and secret trip to Paris, had a long conversation with him on February 14 and promptly recorded it:

> He wants the congress to be concerned only with his requests, and if [the Assembly] agreed to them, the powers should insist that he leave Paris for an agreed-upon place where the ratification would be carried out. If [the Assembly] refuses, he feels the powers must act and he will then bear any danger in consequence of this. He does not believe he is running any risks because the rebels [the revolutionaries] need him to represent France at its capitulation to the powers. . . . He can see that force is the only way out but he is so weak that he thinks it impossible to resume his full authority. . . . Then he told me: "Well now, we are alone and we can speak freely. I know I am reproached for my weakness and my indecisiveness, but no one else has ever been in my position. I know I missed the moment, it was on July 14 [,1789]. I should have left and wanted to, but what could I do when Monsieur himself was asking me to stay, and when the maréchal de Broglie, who commanded the troops, told me: 'Yes, we can go Metz, but what will we do when we are there?' I missed the moment then and have not been able to find another one since. Everybody has abandoned me."[7]

Louis XVI was not alone in feeling alarm: the Jacobins, too, were appalled, but by opposite aspects of the situation, of course. What worried them was the weakness and disorganization of the country. When Barbaroux, the committed revolutionary lawyer from Marseille, decided to move to the capital, he found that traveling was no longer either quick or easy: "We have arrived in Paris after seven and a half days on the road," he wrote home on February 11, 1792, "and they were not without danger due to the inconceivable degradation of the highways, or without worry because of the endless difficulties with our postilions, who refused to be paid with assignats of five livres."[8] When the people providing goods and services refuse to accept the only available currency, the results quickly become intolerable, both in terms of human survival — how are the poor to eat? — and in terms of the country's economic survival, especially in a preindustrial society. By the early spring of 1792, there could be no doubt: the French economy was slowly disintegrating.

That, in turn, caused a great split in the ranks of the former Third Estate. Although the Feuillants, who governed, and the Jacobins, who attacked them, obviously had their differences as to the chosen means of preserving the conquests of the Revolution, and the need for extending them, they were at one on a key issue, that of the necessity of liberty and the defense of the constitution. Now, faced with a new list of popular demands, they began to disagree about that as well. For the Feuillants, and a section of the Jacobins that at first included the ever-legalistic Robespierre, absolute economic liberalism was an untouchable principle: the ancien régime had tried to control the economy through a variety of devices — price controls, production controls, occasional forced distribution — and in doing so had been tyrannical. The great new principle was that of Liberty, and it must apply also to economic exchanges: there could be no question, therefore, of setting food prices, forcing the peasants to sell their withheld stocks, or allowing working men to combine so as to pressure their employers into paying them a decent minimum wage.

As is so often the case, however, these lofty precepts served to disguise a very different reality: the men who had made the Revolution as members of the first National Assembly, and their successors in the current legislature, belonged, most of them, to the propertied middle classes; they had much to gain by insisting on economic liberty, much to lose as soon as the sacrosanct principle of the inviolability of property was breached. Thus, with self-interest bolstering their position, they were not about to be moved by a little noise in the streets.

For the first time, however, another section of the left, composed in part of the remaining Jacobins and of almost all the Cordeliers, took a diametrically opposed attitude. The newly impoverished artisans and shopkeepers who were rampaging in the streets of Paris — and, of course, the mob — demanded a return to a controlled economy: maximum prices (price controls) were to be set, the peasants forced to disgorge, the "monopolists" punished. This was a potent battle cry, one with a long history. All through the ancien régime, famine had loomed as a menacing possibility whenever the crop was less than good; speculators had been prompt to take advantage of the fact. By buying grains at the beginning of the season, and holding them until the prices had risen to a peak, they made great fortunes on the backs of the hungry people, and were loathed for it. That practice was stopped by the royal government in the 1760s; but the people then assumed that any trouble was the result of the King's speculating for his own account. In 1792, obviously, the King was no longer in a position to do this, but, with the newly established economic freedoms, any rich man could trade on the shortages. So, along with demanding price control and forced distribution, the angry people readily demanded laws making speculation impossible and insisted upon the prosecution and punishment of the speculators.

It was this infringement of their economic privileges that a large part of the Deputies now prepared to resist; the split thus caused was deep and permanent: the great opposition between the cautious Robespierre and the irrepressibly radical Danton was born of it, and conditioned all the further development of the Revolution. But this split could not be fully revealed as long as both factions had a common enemy. Survival, after all, required tactical compromises that all the leaders were fully prepared to accept; and the enemy, in the spring of 1792, was highly visible, inside and out, in the persons of the King and his secret allies, the monarchs and armies of the powers.

In many ways, Georges Jacques Danton was the very image of a revolutionary. A lawyer before 1789, he had immediately found his way to the most radical groups; he was among the founders of the Cordeliers, and Marat's close friend and defender — so much so, in fact, that in 1790 he escaped arrest only through his election to the Commune. From that moment, he had defended the most extreme positions: he extolled the mutinous soldiers in Nancy, attacked Lafayette and the moderates in terms that had not yet been heard in political discourse, and utterly refused to observe the rules of (relative) politeness that still largely obtained. For Danton, only the oppressed people mattered; they were right by definition no matter what they did, and their long sufferings called for the most exemplary vengeance. It was thus logical for him to be one of the organizers of the antimonarchy petition and the uprising that followed in July 1791.

Of all the riots since 1789, however, this alone was successfully repressed, and Danton was forced to flee the country in order to avoid arrest, but he was back in October when an amnesty was proclaimed in honor of the new constitution. Since then, with Marat and Antoine Santerre, a rich brewer who had been a radical from the start, he had continued his attacks, not just on the King, but also on all who he thought too moderate, including even Robespierre; in the process, he earned himself the latter's hatred.

In December 1791 Danton took a very large further step: until then he had been simply an agitator, albeit a very successful one; now he was elected administrator of the Département of Paris, a position that gave him wide powers, and second assistant to the Paris district attorney. That, and his friendship with the Mayor, Pétion, and the district attorney, Louis-Pierre Manuel, meant he could now use the very institutions he so decried in order to speed up the Revolution. It also, for a while, looked as if he might replace Robespierre as the leader of the extreme left. From April to August 1792 Robespierre had no official position whatsoever; he was not a member of the Assembly; he depended completely on his influence at the Jacobins, even as the club began to be overshadowed by the Cordeliers, whose star was of course Danton.

As if that were not enough, Danton had all the characteristics most likely to make him seem equally repulsive to the moderates and to Robespierre. A massively built, spectacularly virile man with a voice of brass and just the kind of eloquence that could rouse the people, he was often dirty, sloppily dressed, and obviously careless of appearances.

Antoine Thibaudeau, one of those prudent men who managed to pass unscathed through the Revolution, knew the fiery tribune well. "Danton was always easygoing, and sometimes kind," he noted. "His appearance, which was ferocious when he addressed [the convention], was otherwise calm and sometimes even inviting. His principles were incendiary, his speeches violent and furious; but in private, he was easy, had the loosest morals and was utterly cynical. He loved women and despised life. He had a soul; his eloquence was volcanic; he was built altogether to be the spokesman of the people."[9]

That, too, made him both hated and irresistible. His debauchery, his gambling, his scatological expressions, which horrified Robespierre, held great appeal for the people: the mob followed Danton, and Danton spurred them on.

Meanwhile, daily life in most major cities was becoming increasingly violent and dangerous. While the Feuillants were fully prepared to resist any attempt at controlling the economy, they were very willing to trade political extremism for economic reforms. The people could be, if not quite appeased, at least made less dangerous, by the passing of radical political measures; and that is just what, to Louis XVI's increasing horror, the majority of the Assembly proceeded to do.

Thus the Revolution entered on a completely new phase. In its first incarnation, it had been intent on the widest possible liberty, on dismantling the old structures that restricted it, and on lessening the role and importance of government. In its second period, it reversed itself completely. Liberty became secondary to the needs of the people as expressed by an ever more centralized state; opposition was to be suppressed; perceived enemies were to be prosecuted, then executed. All freedoms — of the press, of speech, of religion — were to be abridged or ended in order to pursue the revolutionary struggle. It is customary in histories of this period to make a break at the fall of the monarchy; but even that major event was only a consequence of the new attitude that emerged in February and March of 1792.

For a while, however, many of the main revolutionary figures failed to perceive this. It was at first simply a question of appeasing the angry people until the war could be won (or lost); then, victory (or defeat) would so change the situation as to rob the "passive," nonvoting citizens of the power they owed to repeated insurrection. Still, on February 1 the Assembly passed, and the King signed, a new law pregnant with possibilities for oppression: henceforth, a passport was required in order to travel within France itself. On the ninth the Deputies' intentions with this law became quite clear, as they passed an additional decree confiscating the estates of all French citizens who resided abroad.* One way or the other, the remaining aristocrats and the increasingly apprehensive members of the upper bourgeoisie were to be prevented from

---

* Most of them were about to bear arms against their country.

leaving the kingdom, or even getting closer to the borders. And while there was, as yet, no thought of tyranny, it may be observed that the requirement of a passport for internal travel has been a trusted tool of both the tsarist state and the Communist government in Russia.

These new decrees quite failed to pacify the people, however: empty stomachs have no ears, a French proverb says. In fact, the food riots continued: on February 13 the silos at Monthléry, outside Paris, were pillaged; on the fourteenth the people of Dunkerque seized the provisions kept there by the navy; on the eighteenth a regiment in Bethune mutinied out of sympathy with the starving artisans; on the twenty-third crowds stopped a shipment of grain from Beauvais; on the twenty-sixth dissatisfied peasants, led by non-juring priests, occupied the southern town of Mende; on March 3 the mayor of Etampes was murdered by a mob; on the eighth an uprising in Conches was — suprisingly — put down by the army. From one end of the country to the other, order was breaking down as misery spread, but the reaction long expected by the royalists never materialized. The starving people, far from yearning for the good old days, tried to take over themselves. Of the revolutionary trilogy, Liberty, Equality, Fraternity, the first and third concepts had ruled at the beginning; now the day of Equality was dawning, and it was not likely to prove pleasant for the propertied classes.

Outside France, too, events were speeding up: on February 7 a military alliance was concluded between Prussia and Austria, formerly the bitterest of enemies. While its main object was a further — and definitive — partition of Poland, the French question was also raised: any declaration of war against the Emperor, therefore, must now include Prussia as well, and the latter was widely recognized as having a virtually unbeatable army. Then, on March 7, the Duke of Brunswick was made commander-in-chief of the two armies: it was now a united Austro-Prussian force the French would have to face.

All this, of course, could only please the Tuileries; no one was more conscious than Louis XVI of the army's deficiencies. And just as the Emperor seemed to take a more moderate stance, the Assembly voted to send him what amounted to an ultimatum — which he eventually rejected: he was to declare that under no circumstances would he oppose himself to any French movement into the Rhenish states. That was the work of Edmond Gensonné, a Deputy who belonged to a new, clearly recognizable political group, the Brissotins, which took its name from Jacques-Pierre Brissot, a hitherto unsuccessful journalist. The appellation, however, was misleading: Brissot was quite incapable of leading anyone. Intelligent but weak and unprincipled, he had been involved in a variety of dubious projects and interesting publications before the Revolution; his description of the United States, in particular, remains intriguing today. Now because he spoke and wrote eloquently, he briefly gave his name to a group also called the Girondins because many of its members in the Assembly came from the département of the Gironde.*

The Brissotins belonged mostly to the middle middle class; many were lawyers, some owned small estates, a few were journalists; they stood for a deep, romantic commitment to the Revolution. Brissot himself — who was then not yet a Deputy — had demanded the deposition of Louis XVI after Varennes; he was openly republican; he thought that the declaration of war would be followed by a general European rising so that the conquering French armies would bring liberty to the entire continent, thus, not incidentally, precluding any reaction in France itself. That, of course, supposed that the armies in question would be allowed to win, so the group kept up a steady barrage against the ministry. Only if they were in charge, by holding the ministerial positions themselves, could they be confident that all necessary measures would be taken, since it was perfectly obvious that the King longed for a defeat.

The constitution, however, gave the power of appointing ministers to the monarch, and Louis XVI naturally detested the Brissotins; so in January and February their accession to power seemed unlikely in the extreme, in spite of the fact that the government was virtually paralyzed. The lack of contact with reality at the Tuileries is manifest in another scene described by Bertrand de Molleville, who, as minister of the navy, was naturally present at all Council meetings.

M. Cahier de Gerville [the minister of the interior] read aloud the draft of a proclamation relative to . . . the acts of violence, at that time very frequent. . . . [In it] was the following sentence: "These disorders interrupt the happiness we at present enjoy." He had no sooner pronounced it than the King said: "That sentence must be altered." M.

---

* The area around Bordeaux.

de Gerville . . . replied: "I perceive nothing that needs to be altered, Sire."

"Do not make me speak of my happiness," resumed His Majesty with emotion. "I cannot authorize such a falsehood. How can I be happy, M. de Gerville, at a time when no one is happy in France? No, sir, the French are not happy; I see it but too well; they will be so, I hope; and I wish it very ardently. When that time arrives, I also shall be happy, and shall then be able, with truth, to declare it." These words which the King uttered with a faltering voice . . . [were] followed by a general silence.[10]

This is a revealing exchange, notable in particular for the pretense, expressed by the minister's disputed sentence, that the current disturbances were a mere interruption of the general felicity. Far from being a personal aberration, this extraordinary denial of reality represented the official view: day after day, as the economic and political situation deteriorated, the French were told that the Revolution had ushered in a Golden Age, that the country basked in freedom and happiness. Obviously, this kind of pretense went a long way toward discrediting the men who kept it up, the Feuillants. Since this was essentially their regime, the one they had set up after Varennes, and their constitution, they felt unable to admit that anything was seriously wrong; and as a result they lost their popularity along with their ability to resist the mob. Nor, obviously, was the King a help. "The King was endowed with a very just judgment, but unhappily was of so timid a disposition, and so distrustful of himself, that he was apt to prefer the opinions of weaker people to his own, and always adopted that of the majority of his Council," Bertrand de Molleville pointed out.[11] Given the markedly low caliber of the ministers, this would have been a recipe for disaster in the best of times; in the middle of a Revolution, it was bound to be catastrophic.

On March 1 the Emperor Leopold II died, and was succeeded by Francis II, his twenty-four-year-old son. Although Leopold was Marie Antoinette's brother, the two had scarcely known each other and shared no particular mutual fondness. While Francis was only the Queen's nephew, instead of her brother, he was known to be far less hesitant, far more inclined to war than his father; thus his accession to the throne promised to speed the armed congress. This apparently favorable event was followed by a setback on March 29: with the assassination of Gustavus III of Sweden, the royal couple lost their most ardent defender, but his weight in the European coalition then forming had always been rather slight.

Still, even under the best of conditions — that of a successful congress or invasion — the King and Queen now realized that ruling France would not be easy. "It is impossible suddenly to reestablish the old order as it was," Marie Antoinette wrote Mercy on March 2, "but at the same time no part of the current one can be allowed to endure. . . . The multiplicity of powers, the holding of elections, the strength given the people finally, all prolongs the anarchy and consequently must bring about the complete ruin of the monarchy."[12] For once, the Queen was right. The monarchy was indeed doomed; even if the powers restored the King's authority, the ancien régime could not be revived. It was finally and perfectly clear to her that the French would not stand for it, and that they could not be held down indefinitely. Yet, at the same time, the only people who extolled the old absolute system, the émigrés, were forming their own army, and they were resolved to accept nothing less than a full return to the ancien régime. They were, after all, its chief beneficiaries. Centered around the princes, as they were known — Monsieur, the comte d'Artois, the prince de Condé — they ranged from former ministers like Calonne to great aristocrats like the duc de Luynes, the prince de Rohan, or the duc de Montmorency, and equally aristocratic clerics. As for the mass of their little army, it consisted mostly of emigrated officers and members of the lower nobility who had lost their incomes with their feudal rights. By 1792 money was becoming scarce even for the leaders, so they felt there was no time to be lost. They wanted to invade France and wipe out the very memory of the Revolution; unlike Louis XVI, they had no scruples at all about shedding blood.

The situation in France suddenly became much more acute on March 10. As long as the Feuillant ministry endured, things might go on more or less as they had; there was no immediate crisis. The Brissotins, however, took advantage of a new development to push the Assembly further to the left. On March 9 Louis XVI, who had always distrusted the comte de Narbonne, finally decided to dismiss him. This could easily be presented as an attempt to cripple the country's defense: the minister had been at one with the Brissotins in wanting the war, while the other ministers were seen as no more than lukewarm; they were often accused of being in league with the King, the Queen, and their imaginary "Austrian Committee." Thus Narbonne's ouster was a godsend, since it seemed to confirm that the Tuileries was preparing for defeat, especially since Narbonne was replaced by the colonel-marquis de Grave, an honest nonentity distinguished only by links to the duc d'Orléans.

In the Assembly, the reaction was both strong and immediate. First, on the ninth, it voted that the departing minister took the nation's regrets with him; then, on the tenth it proceeded to impeach Lessart, the foreign minister, who was thought to be responsible for his colleague's dismissal; worse, Lessart was promptly arrested and sent off to be judged by the High Court. The rest of the government understood the hint: except for de Grave, the remaining ministers resigned. "The King," Bertrand noted, "was reduced to the fatal necessity of forming a ministry at a time when he had not the power of appointing a single individual in whom he could place confidence. Sensible of the dangers which surrounded him, he now showed evident anxiety about his situation. Instead of the contempt and indifference with which he had supported the outrages which he had hitherto been exposed to, sorrow and consternation were strongly marked on his countenance during the sad Council of the ninth of March."[13]

It was, in fact, the first time since the return from Varennes when both the King and Queen realized that they were in danger no matter what happened. Not only was the ministry obviously at an end, the means adopted — the referral of Lessart to the court in Orléans — hinted at punishments much more appalling than the mere loss of office.

The scene in the Assembly was described by Barbaroux, who had just arrived from Marseille and was burning with revolutionary zeal. "The Assembly's recent attitude," he wrote on March 13,

has saved the state. The minister de Lessart has been indicted. We were in the tribunes with a few young Jacobins. . . . When we saw a considerable number of patriots moving from the right side to the left, so as to frighten the supporters of the ministry, we felt sure that the minister's fate would be decided then and there, and as we saw some of M. de Lessart's friends leaving, we felt sure they were going to urge him to flee, so several among us went to warn M. Pétion of this, while others, reinforced by several private citizens, went to block the exits of his house. These measures were effective; the minister did not dare flee, the decree of accusation was brought to him, and that same night he was taken to Orléans.[*] . . . On Sunday, the [former] minister Duport was denounced.[14]

Obviously, there could be no question of replacing the departing ministry with another batch of Feuillants. The Brissotins had control of the Assembly; they would have to form the next government. That, in itself, does not sound so dreadful: in a constitutional monarchy, the parliamentary majority normally provides the government; only here the majority consisted of men who openly advocated the establishment of a republic, men who had been denouncing the Queen as a traitor and the King as her accomplice. Asking Louis XVI to appoint a Brissotin ministry was not unlike asking the Shah of Iran to make the Ayatollah Khomeini his prime minister. It is no wonder, therefore, that fear and consternation reigned at the Tuileries.

As it turned out, de Grave remained as war minister. Antoine Duranthon, a friend of Gensonné, was made minister of justice. An attorney by profession, he behaved in much more moderate ways than might have been expected: he tried to protect the King, banned *L'Ami du peuple,* and pursued a policy of appeasement. Elie Lacoste, a nonentity, was given the navy. The finance ministry went to Etienne Clavière, a Swiss speculator who had served Mirabeau and was a friend of Brissot, who saw to his appointment. A man neither honest nor competent, he was also a violent and open antimonarchist, and proceeded to be as unpleasant as possible to the King.

All these were essentially second- or third-rate men: the leaders in the ministry were Jean-Marie Roland at the interior, and Charles du Périer Dumouriez at foreign affairs. Both were entering on a phase of their lives during which they would play a major role in the Revolution.

Roland, who was fifty-eight, had had a successful, if undistinguished, career under the ancien régime as an inspector of manufactures, his area of specialty being the Lyons silk industry. In 1780 he had married a bright and charming young woman, Manon Phlipon, who was twenty years younger than he. That proved to be his making. Mme Roland was

---

[*] Lessart was massacred as he was being brought back to Paris on November 9, 1792.

amazingly well read; she knew all about ancient Greece and Rome, resented the inequalities to which the French were subjected, and liked to pose as an austere reformer. For her, the Revolution was a godsend. When her husband moved to Paris in 1789 and became the friend of Brissot, Pétion, Buzot, and other extreme revolutionaries, she encouraged him to bring them home. Soon she was running a salon where the Brissotins gathered: indeed, it was to her nurture, as much as to Brissot's ideas, that the party owed its existence. Much more intelligent and incomparably more energetic than her rather stodgy husband, she pushed him relentlessly until he became one of the leaders of the party. As for herself, her ambition was simple: her husband was to run the Republic, and she would run her husband. With all that, she loved liberty and resented privilege; she wanted power, of course, but also the happiness of the people. She despised Louis XVI and Marie Antoinette.

Roland was thus an extremely uncomfortable interior minister for the King to have about. Dumouriez proved far more amenable. A cautiously ambitious man, aged fifty-three, he had pursued an adventurous and on the whole unsuccessful career, first in the army, then in the course of often rather shady diplomatic missions. An enthusiastic convert to the Revolution because he thought it would win him fame and fortune, he was a close friend of Brissot and among the most enthusiastic members of the war party; but he had also been careful to have himself recommended to the King by the administrator of the civil list. Thus, having offered a secret allegiance to Louis XVI, he entered the ministry with the favor of both the Brissotins and the King himself; and, indeed, as a known anti-Austrian, he provided the royal couple with a form of insurance, in that the war ministry could no longer be said to be disorganized by the "Austrian Committee." It was also in his interest to spare Louis XVI, at least for the moment: if France won the war, he expected to be created a marshal of France and become the most important man in the government — and that would require the King's support. If France began to lose the war, he was prepared to blame his predecessors and co-opt popular support to become a military dictator in charge of organizing a successful resistance to the enemy.

Thus, all in all, Louis XVI could have been even worse off than he was; but that, understandably, was a meager consolation. With the advent of the Brissotin ministry, it became apparent to the royal couple that they were rapidly becoming the main figures in a tragedy: they were doomed no matter what they did — except, of course, in the event of a rapid, successful invasion by the Austro-Prussian forces, a development that the King at least had about given up on.

"It was impossible to see a sadder position than that of the royal family at this time," Mme de Tourzel noted;

> The ministry included its most deadly enemies, who surrounded it with spies, even in its private apartments, so that the King and Queen several times had recourse to my own footman to introduce into their studies people to whom they wished to speak in secret. All their letters were opened; and to remedy this, they were forced to use a cipher which it took a long time to write or read, but which could not be broken. . . . The Queen spent her mornings writing, the King read and made notes on the events. . . . He felt sure he would end up as a victim of the factions; but since he also thought that whatever was done to help him would only hasten the last moment and endanger his family as well, he was resigned to his fate and courageously waited for whatever fate held in store.[15]

As for the Queen, who was not so passive, she complained bitterly that neither Mercy nor Breteuil was exerting himself sufficiently; however, she turned down a proposal that she, alone, escape from Paris.

Unlike Louis XVI, in fact, she still hoped that a foreign invasion might save them, and she tried to make very sure it succeeded by passing on the French military plans to the enemy. On March 30, for instance, she wrote Fersen: "The plan is to attack through Savoy, and in the direction of Liège. . . . I warned Turin* three weeks ago. . . . It is essential to be ready in the Liège area. Our position is still dreadful, but not as dangerous as long as it is we who attack."[16]

While Marie Antoinette did her best to ensure the defeat of France, the ministers tried hard to prepare for war, and, at the same time, they made very sure to receive proper credit: they claimed (truthfully) all responsibility for the popular measures they took, while, equally truthfully,

---

* The King of Sardinia, whose capital was Turin, was also Duke of Savoy.

they blamed Louis XVI for the rest. As a result, far from being credited with at least compliance to the people's wishes in appointing the Brissotin ministry, Louis XVI found himself more hated than ever.

Dumouriez's plan of operations was simple: the French armies were to take defensive positions wherever there were natural boundaries (mountains, large rivers) while attacking elsewhere. Instead of invading Savoy, as Marie Antoinette had reported, he tried to seduce the King of Sardinia into an alliance by promising him Milan once Austria was defeated; but the main offensive was indeed to be into the Austrian Netherlands. Equally, he was intent on attacking first: coalitions were notoriously unwieldy, the Prussians and the Austrians had been enemies until very recently, thus a triumph in the area of Liège and Brussels might well be enough to convince Frederick William II to forget about the war.

As a result, an ultimatum was sent off to Vienna on March 27; France would take any continuation of Austria's arming as a declaration of war. On April 19 Marie Antoinette warned Fersen: "The ministers and the Jacobins will force the King to declare war on the House of Austria tomorrow. . . . The ministers hope this will frighten [Francis II] and that negotiations will open within three weeks. May God prevent this so that at last we may be revenged for all the outrages inflicted upon us in this country."[17]

As predicted, on April 20 in the Assembly all but seven Deputies voted in favor of the war; and the decision was immensely popular; but Marie Antoinette was wrong to rejoice. It was already clear that the King, the Queen, and her imaginary "Austrian Committee" would be held accountable for any French losses. That l'Autrichienne hoped for her nephew's victory was a universally known fact. Although Louis XVI wrote the King of Prussia in early May, asking him to issue a proclamation holding the French responsible for the royal family's safety, the popular reaction, in case of an early defeat, was likely to be violent and uncontrollable — and the French army, as it hesitantly went on the offensive, was anything but ready. Indeed, it lacked nearly everything.

In the first place, there were almost no leaders; of the 9,000 officers in place before 1789, only 3,000 were left. As for the men, they, too, were in short numbers, although patriotic volunteers were beginning to join. Worse, the foreign regiments who, together, amounted to almost a fifth of the troops, were extremely unlikely to fight at all.[*] Then, too, supplies of all kinds were either very scarce or altogether missing. From gunpowder to shoes, all seemed lacking, so much so that Lafayette complained on May 6, in a letter to the minister of war, about the foolhardiness of declaring a war under these conditions. Finally, the commanding generals themselves were less than enthusiastic. Rochambeau, when he understood the situation, resigned. Lafayette made it plain that even putting up a defensive action would severely tax his resources. Luckner, who was seventy, lapsed into inaction. As for Arthur Dillon — a former friend of the Queen who had gone over to the Revolution — he did try to march toward Tournai, but retreated immediately upon meeting with an Austrian corps, and was massacred by his infuriated troops. That left the duc de Biron, who first advanced toward Mons and then, not trusting his men, also began a retreat.

These dubious maneuvers should have been the preliminaries to a disaster. In fact, they were not; neither Prussia nor Austria was anxious to fight. With the final demise of Poland at hand, they realized that Catherine II of Russia was likely to take advantage of their being engaged in France to help herself to the remains of that wretched country, so nothing much happened on France's northern border. In Paris, where the army's retreat looked very like a royalist conspiracy, things were quite different. At one with the Assembly, the Brissotin ministry reacted by taking radical measures. It ordered the printing of another 300 million's worth of assignats and the raising of a further thirty-one battalions, along with the dissolution of the Royal Guard accorded the King by the constitution; docilely, Louis XVI signed all this into law. Things changed, however, when he found himself faced with a decree exiling all non-juring priests — who were no doubt praying for the triumph of Austria — to Guiana; and another calling together 20,000 men of the National Guard, who were to gather in a huge camp at the gates of Paris. These, greatly to his ministers' anger, he vetoed.

That created an impossible situation for the Brissotins, now generally called the Girondins. Since the war had begun so badly, Robespierre and the pacifist left, while endorsing the greatest possible efforts to reverse

---

[*] The ancien régime army had included some Swiss and German regiments from areas traditionally allied with France. These regiments were, of course, paid by the French treasury.

the situation, at the same time heaped scorn on those who had been so foolhardy as to declare war when the country was unprepared. "When the orators excited us to war," Robespierre wrote in his *Défenseur de la Constitution,* "since they described to us how the Austrian armies, deserting the banners of despotism, would fly to the tricolor, and how the whole of Brabant would rise to come under our laws, we could have expected a more successful beginning and believed that the measures needed to realize these splendid predictions had been taken!"[18] With this kind of opposition on their left, Roland and his colleagues could hardly allow the King's vetoes, and so they told him, in a letter outlining the likely consequences of angering the people. At that, on June 12, with the genius for mistiming that characterized him, Louis XVI dismissed Roland, Clavière, and Joseph Servan, who had replaced de Grave at the war ministry only a month earlier, while Dumouriez, still attempting to bridge the unbridgeable, went from the foreign ministry to the war ministry.

Immediately, the Assembly reacted. On the thirteenth it affirmed its confidence in the dismissed ministers while beginning the process that would have resulted in Dumouriez's indictment, upon which the latter prudently resigned. It took the King only another two days to appoint new ministers; but they were such nonentities that it was obvious, first, that he was scraping the bottom of the barrel, and, second, that the government would be less than ever able to govern. In fact, in the two-month period between June 10 and August 10, there were three foreign ministers, one of whom lasted only four days; three war ministers; two finance ministers; and three ministers of the interior. As if that were not enough, the Assembly on June 17 appointed a committee of twelve Deputies to supervise the ministers, thus taking openly unto itself the executive power. To all intents and purposes, after only eight months, the constitution had become a dead letter, and the one man in France who was most directly responsible for its existence, Lafayette, saw it clearly.

On June 16, therefore, he sent the Assembly a letter:

The state is in peril, and the fate of France depends mainly upon its representatives. The nation expects its salvation from them; but when it gave itself a constitution, it also prescribed for them the only way in which they could save it. . . .

Can you refuse to see that . . . the Jacobine faction has caused all the disorders? . . . Organized like an empire throughout the country, blindly led by a few ambitious men, this sect forms a separate body amid the French people whose powers it usurps by subjugating its representatives. . . .

Let the royal power remain intact, for it is guaranteed by the constitution; let it be independent, for that independence is one of the mainstays of our liberty; let the King be revered, for he is imbued with the nation's majesty; let him choose a ministry free from the bonds of faction.[19]

It was a bold move on the General's part, especially since it showed how much further the Revolution had progressed since the days of his popularity. Amazingly, except for the Jacobins, the Assembly took it well: there were many Deputies who, bereft of the courage of their centrist convictions, yearned for someone else to put down the radicals. Had Lafayette appeared at the gates of Paris with his army, they would no doubt have greeted him ecstatically, but the troops were no more ready to back a counterrevolution in 1792 than they had been willing to fight for absolutism in 1789.

Thus Lafayette's letter, although in many ways justified, turned out to be counterproductive. It helped to establish further the myth of the aristocratic conspiracy. The court and those who had, in the past, seemed to back the Revolution were coming together in a fearful plot: that is what Marat, Danton, Santerre, and the other leaders were telling the mob, and they were believed. As the French army retreated, as it seemed possible that the Austrians might reach Paris, fury and resentment were blended with fear to produce a highly explosive mixture. It needed only a match, and this the Girondins happily provided.

They knew they ran almost no risk at all: with Pétion as Mayor of Paris, and Danton as assistant attorney general of the city, it was clear that the municipal authorities would not only ignore but positively encourage a new uprising. Roland had as good as warned the King of this on June 10: "If the law against the priests does not take effect, the départements will be forced . . . to adopt violent measures in its stead. . . . The situation in Paris, its proximity to the borders have created the need for a camp [of armed men] in its environs. . . . A little more delay, and the saddened people will become the friend and the helper of those who conspire [against you]."[20]

The King knew what to expect; so did the Assembly; starting on the tenth, there was a constant parade through its hall of armed "volunteers." Their message was clear: should the people rise, force would be on their side, and the Deputies could not rely on being protected. If they wanted to survive, therefore, they would have to side with the rising. Indeed, on the sixteenth they were told, officially, that the citizens of the Faubourgs Saint-Antoine and Saint-Marcel, *fully armed,* would bring the Assembly and the King petitions relative to the recent events. What would happen next was so obvious that on the nineteenth the Directory — or local government — of the Département of Paris warned the National Guard to be at the ready; but the Guard, after all, was composed of men who were not at all eager to fight an infuriated and well-armed mob; it required no great intelligence to see that if the faubourgs rose, the Guard would stay at home or join the rioters.

Naturally, Marat did his best to see that the mob would rise. The headline of *L'Ami du peuple* on June 15 read: "Death blow against liberty and public safety dealt by the National Assembly in cahoots with the court,"[21] and he, Danton, and Santerre were busy in the faubourgs. Their task was easy; not only was the mob infuriated by what it saw (accurately) as the King's treason, the economic distress had raised its anger even higher, and since the government and the Assembly were not prepared to help them, they were quite ready to punish them for it.

Now the Girondins were ready to join the Cordeliers: the King must be punished for dismissing them, the vetoed decrees must be signed, and, most important of all, the party must regain its credentials as the leading edge of the left: all was ready for the assault on the Tuileries. Seen from the distance of two centuries, this deliberate provocation to riot may seem like an inexcusable form of subversion; it was, certainly, unconstitutional: the legally elected Deputies and the legitimate monarch were to be forced to do the will of the mob. And yet, it must also be remembered that these were exceptional circumstances; that Europe had a long history of revolts followed by bloody repression; and that the enemy was on the march.

We know just what the mob and their friends were thinking in June 1792, through the notes kept by Pierre Gaspard Chaumette and completed by him late in 1792. Born in 1763, Chaumette had drifted until he went to Paris in 1790 as a medical student. Immediately joining the extreme revolutionaries, he had found employment writing for the *Révolutions de Paris* and quickly understood that the mob could easily be manipulated because of its extreme poverty, complete lack of education, and credulity. A leading member of the Cordeliers, he had demanded the abolition of the monarchy after Varennes, and was now given the task of master-minding the insurrection.

It is important to know what Chaumette wrote. With very few exceptions, the revolutionary leaders, even when they were using the mob for their own ends, actually believed what they were saying, dreaded the perils they were predicting. Unlike Lenin, who wanted his party to lead what he saw as the dumb and amorphous masses, men like Danton, Marat, and Chaumette were part of the people and felt, with good reason, that they were expressing its will.

In reading Chaumette, however, it must be remembered that while he believed what he said, it was not necessarily the truth. Because a plot against the Revolution seemed so likely to exist, people believed that it was a reality; because the court was known to be reactionary, it seemed evident that it must be organizing a massacre. Here precedent seemed more important than fact, especially since it is in the nature of plots to be secret. At the same time, Chaumette is not infrequently right: his first sentence, for instance, is dead on target.

"The fanatical non-juring priests," he wrote in early June,

were starting a civil war. . . . The émigrés made frequent trips into France and left again loaded down with the court's gold; they were arming themselves . . . were putting together great quantities of foodstuffs and ammunition under the protection of the foreign powers, who, on their side, were in league as they brought their armies closer to France. Our borders were unprotected, open, betrayed. General Lafayette had perverted a great part of the army. . . . The city of Paris was rife with those debauched, shameless men who make it their job to betray their Fatherland, and these men were given office by the court. . . .

The court had called to the government two or three men [namely,

Roland, Servan, Clavière] who . . . had acquired a sort of reputation for patriotism. These men were persecuted by the royalists . . . and the people felt insulted in the persons of those who then enjoyed its trust.[22]

In fact, the émigrés knew better than to reenter France; Lafayette had tried to indoctrinate his army so that he could then use it against the Jacobins — but to no avail; as for the "debauched, shameless men," they are purely imaginary.

Later, Chaumette went on:

Ministers held in contempt by the public replaced those in whom the people had placed its trust. . . . The National Assembly [was] without strength or consideration, divided against itself . . . , humiliated by an arrogant court. . . . That awoke the courage of the friends of liberty [and] provoked them into making a brilliant demonstration [on June 20], which then served the court as a pretext for further treasons, treasons so atrocious and so openly plotted that they caused the fall of a throne whose only guard was crime, whose only defense was crime, whose only support was crime again.[23]

Apart from this last rhetorical flourish, Chaumette's point is very simple, but only an extreme revolutionary could have thought the Assembly was humiliated by the court when the reverse was true: what looked like cravenness to him was simply moderation.

Given the situation as the radicals saw it, there was only one thing to do, especially since "that abominable court was ready to . . . provoke disorders in Paris, assemble its cohorts, and lead them to massacre [the people]. . . . After that expedition, the National Assembly was to be dissolved . . . , the generals would have opened the borders to the enemy. . . . Then the ancien régime would have come back to life."[24] With the encouragement of the Girondins, therefore, Chaumette, Santerre, and a few others marshaled the mob and on June 20 led it to the Tuileries. Just how successful they were, we have seen. The doors of the Palace were smashed, the cannon was dragged up the stairs, the King was threatened and forced to wear the Phrygian cap, the Queen was chased from room to room. Finally, there was the interminable parade past the royal family barricaded behind a table. For the first time, revolutionary

Paris had not only broken into the Palace but proved that there was no force left either able or willing to stop it.

Even though the royal family survived, it had become clear to all that the Tuileries were indefensible, that the National Guard would not protect the King, and that the Assembly could easily be cowed. "The events of the twentieth of June . . . dissipated the prestige of the inviolability of the Palace, of the King's person, and of the monarchy. The throne still stood, but the people had sat on it and had taken its measure."[25]

It was reasonably obvious to all, on the evening of the twentieth, that the events of the day would be repeated; the mob, having found its way into the Palace once, was not likely to hesitate if it wanted to return; next time it was probable that the royal family would not come out of the invasion unscathed. At the same time, while the revolutionaries rejoiced, and the Girondins gloated about the lesson they had just taught the King, many people felt upset and uneasy. The prestige of the throne had certainly shrunk, but perhaps it was not actually all gone.

On the twenty-first the *Journal de Paris,* reflecting much of public opinion, wrote: "Yesterday's events have left a deep and painful impression."[26] In the next few days, a petition deploring the invasion of the Tuileries and asking that the rioters be punished received 20,000 signatures. Louis XVI did his best. Naturally, he sent a message to the Assembly in which he tried to encourage the reaction: "Paris is no doubt appalled; France will learn [about the events] with an amazement blended with sorrow," he wrote. "I leave it to the Assembly's prudence to seek the causes of this event . . . and to take the measures needed to maintain the constitution and ensure the inviolability and the personal safety of the hereditary representative of the nation."[27] This was, at least, cleverer than usual: by letting the Assembly determine the causes of the rising and the means of preventing its recurrence, he was shifting the onus of the repression away from himself. It would not be a monarch returning to his old, tyrannical ways that the people would see but their representatives ensuring that the constitution was obeyed. Unfortunately, this supposed that the Deputies were willing and able to put down the mob: in reality, they were not only scared but impotent. No one in Paris could count on the number of obedient soldiers this policy would have required.

At the same time, in an attempt to appeal to the moderates in and out of the capital, Louis XVI issued a carefully worded proclamation:

> The French will not have learned without sorrow that an armed multitude led into error by a few factious men broke into the King's residence, pulled cannon as far as the Guard Hall, broke down the doors of his apartment with axes, and there, abusively claiming to be the nation, tried to obtain by force the consent that His Majesty constitutionally refused to two decrees.
>
> The King met the menaces and the insults of these factious men with no force other than his conscience and his love of the public welfare. . . .
>
> If those who want to end the monarchy need yet another crime, they may commit it. In its current state of crisis, the King will give to the last moment . . . an example of the courage and firmness that alone can save France.[28]

In its blend of resistance and dignity, this was by far the best public statement Louis XVI had ever made, and it met with widespread approval; but words could not disarm the mob.

At least, for the first time in a while, the King had help: the first great hero of the Revolution, Lafayette, was now determined to save the monarchy. On June 27, having left his army, he arrived in Paris and the next day was heard by the Assembly. There he explained that, having provided for his army's safety, he had come to protest the invasion of the Tuileries; he then made a plea for a return to a strict application of the constitution. A violent debate followed, with the left demanding the General's head, but many of the Deputies still warmly remembered the Fête of the Federation, and, in the end, a majority approved the General's actions. Still, it was easy to see that, given a new effort by the Jacobins, that majority would not hold; so Lafayette came up with a new plan.

Now that he was back in the capital, he would join the King, who was to review a general parade of the National Guard; he would then harangue the gathered men, lead them against the Faubourgs Saint-Antoine and Saint-Marcel, restore the rule of law, and return to his army as the benefactor of the nation. There were only two problems with this: first, Lafayette felt sure that his popularity with the Guard was as great as ever, a most doubtful assumption; and second, he required the King's cooperation. It seems certain that the latter was refused. Marie Antoinette distrusted Lafayette's politics and clearly understood that he was no politician. In any event, and characteristically, the plan was leaked, Pétion forbade the parade, and there was nothing left for the disappointed General to do except go back to his army.

By now, at the Tuileries, something very like despair prevailed. Bertrand de Molleville, who still saw Louis XVI secretly and often, described the King's mood.

> All that now remained for him was to fly from the capital; but the consequences of the journey to Varennes, and the many mortifications that attended that event, connected every enterprise of that kind with reflections so bitter, that nothing could have induced him to listen to any plan of escape but the most positive assurances that the lives of his family were in danger, and that flight alone could secure them from the poniards of assassins. . . .
>
> He frequently read the history of Charles I of England: his chief attention was to . . . avoid whatever might serve as a pretext for bringing him to a legal trial. . . . He wished to die by the hand of an assassin, that his murder might be considered as the crime of a few individuals, and not a national act. . . .
>
> [Upon my urging him to flee, he said]: "There may be a possibility of my escaping; but still there are many chances against it; and I am not lucky. I might risk another attempt if I were alone. Oh! if my wife and children were not with me, it would soon appear that I am not so weak as is imagined."[29]

It was a convenient excuse; when it came to avoiding a trial, Louis XVI was not quite as cautious as he told Bertrand. His correspondence with foreign monarchs continued, and so did Marie Antoinette's. On June 5 she had written Fersen: "There are orders for Luckner's army to attack; he is against it, but the ministry wants it. The troops lack everything and are in the greatest disorder."[30] On June 23, she added: "Dumouriez is joining Luckner's army tomorrow; he has promised to create an insurrection in Brabant."[31] If the enemy was not thoroughly aware of what the French were doing, it would certainly not be the Queen's fault.

At the opposite end of the political spectrum, too, there was activity. Barbaroux's report to the municipality of Marseille was typical of the

Jacobin line, which was being defended by the club throughout the country.

> The King, who had put on the cap of Liberty and who himself had told several deputations from the National Assembly that he felt safe amid the people of Paris has just ordered that legal procedures against the people be started. . . . Because the people, who were eager to present their petition, have forced two locks, arrest orders will no doubt be given. . . . The King, further, has written the Assembly a letter in which he complains of so-called excesses against his person. . . . [T]his has all been combined by the new ministers, the Austrian committee and the members of the right. . . .
>
> The peril now comes from the constitution itself: it gave the King a veto to be used for the people's safety and that veto is killing the people. We must give the executive a good scare or submit to being murdered by him in the name of the constitution and according to its rules.[32]

There is a certain humor in the description of the two broken locks; but one thing is plain: for the Jacobins, the King felt threatened only because he was resisting the will of the people, because he felt guilty; compared to that overwhelming fact, a little insurrection hardly mattered.

In Paris, power had completely slipped away from the legal authorities. The Assembly could always forbid armed men to gather within its precincts, as it did on June 21; it might seem disposed to punish the leaders of the uprising: none of that made a difference anymore since it no longer had the power to enforce its decisions. Any doubts as to that should have been dissipated by a letter Chaumette wrote on behalf of the inhabitants of the Faubourg Saint-Antoine on June 25. "There are threats to prosecute the leaders of the gathering [*sic*] which took place on Wednesday. We come to oppose them. . . . It is we . . . , fathers, citizens, soldiers, victors of the Bastille; it is we who, tired of seeing so many plots, so many insults to the nation and the legislature, tired also of the division created by perfidious men between the two powers[*] . . . , outraged at the dismissal of patriotic ministers . . . have decided to offer the King the spectacle of twenty thousand armed men. . . . Yes,

---

[*] The executive and the legislative.

legislators, let us die rather than lose our honor!''[33] Against that, the review by the King and the royal family of one of the very few loyal battalions of the National Guard would hardly have counted; even if the "twenty thousand men" were, in fact, probably no more than five to six thousand, it was still quite enough.

Certainly after Lafayette's plan failed, the Assembly understood its own impotence in the face of the mob perfectly; that, together with the progress of the enemy, whose armies had now breached the borders, created a new mood within the legislature. Not only was the country in danger, the Deputies themselves had quite a precise notion as to their likely fate if the ancien régime were to be restored, and so they turned entirely against the King. On July 1 they decreed that all administrative bodies must hold their sessions in public, thus, in effect, giving them the choice between obeying the mob or being massacred on the spot. This ensured that, henceforth, none of the King's legitimate orders would be obeyed. Then, on the second, they called for a meeting of all National Guards in Paris on July 14, the pretext being a celebration of Bastille Day: the camp of armed men just outside the capital would now take place despite the King's veto.

At that, Louis XVI decided to strike back, and he chose the Mayor of Paris as his target. On June 20 Pétion had sided with the mob. Three days later, when it looked as if another assault against the Tuileries was being planned, he softened his stance and issued a proclamation that apparently was intended to help the King: "Protect the King and constitution with your arms," it said, "surround his person with respect; let his residence be sacred. . . . Do not gather in arms, the law forbids it."[34] Still, when he presented himself before the monarch, his attitude seemed hardly loyal.

Mme de Tourzel noted:

Pétion arrived [at the Tuileries] around seven P.M. . . . He went up to the King and had himself announced as Mayor of Paris. . . . "Sire," he said, "we are told that you have been warned of a gathering that was marching on your abode; we are here to inform you that this gathering is composed only of unarmed citizens who are coming to plant a tree of Liberty. I know, Sire, that the municipality has been slandered, but Your Majesty knows how it has behaved."

"France," the King answered, "knows how it has behaved. I accuse no one, I saw everything."

"Without the precautionary measures taken by the municipality, far more untoward events might well have occurred, not against your person (and here he stared at the Queen who was standing next to the King); you must know, Sire, that your person will always be spared."

The King looked at him indignantly and said: "Am I being spared when armed crowds break down the doors and force their way in? What happened here, Monsieur, has scandalized everyone; you are answerable for order in Paris."

"I know the nature of my duty and will fulfill it," Pétion answered, looking insolently at the Queen.

"This is too much," the King said in a menacing voice, "keep quiet and leave."[35]

Following this encounter, it seemed quite logical for Louis XVI to choose the Mayor as a tool for a reassertion of royal authority. He asked for Pétion's suspension.

It was already too late, however. On July 3 Vergniaud, in the Assembly, had denounced the King as a traitor, thus aligning the Girondins with the Cordeliers in the republican camp. The suspension, at the monarch's behest, of Pétion as Mayor merely angered them further; it was all the more dangerous since Pétion was now the most popular man in Paris. The Deputies knew it, of course; on the thirteenth, quite unconstitutionally, they annulled the suspension; the King, realistically, signed the bill. Indeed, the fermentation in Paris was such that any other course would have been suicidal; whether the royal family would survive the summer now seemed very doubtful.

"All is lost," Marie Antoinette wrote Mercy on July 4, "if the factions are not stopped by the fear of a punishment in the near future. They will do anything to install a republic and, in order to have their way, they will assassinate the King. It is necessary that a manifesto should make Paris responsible for his life and that of his family."[36] That plea was duly transmitted. In the meantime, Lafayette tried once again: he let the King know that he was prepared to join him in Compiègne with an army that would then crush the Jacobins; but the project was, as usual, completely unrealistic — the army was not about to let itself be used in this way — and Louis XVI distrusted the General; so, as the temperature mounted, paralysis continued at the Tuileries.

It was at this point that a most peculiar episode took place. On July 7 the constitutional, juring bishop of Lyon, Lamourette, who was a Deputy, made a highly emotional speech in the Assembly. Arguing that with the borders already breached by the enemy, any internal division might be fatal, he urged all parties to be reconciled in a new spirit of patriotism; and amid frantic applause and cheers, the Deputies agreed, shaking hands, hugging, even kissing in a great orgy of newfound brotherhood. It was all so astonishing, in fact, that the King, upon being told of it, insisted on addressing the Assembly. "My heart is most deeply touched," he told the Deputies, "by this spectacle in which all unite to save the Fatherland. I have long hoped for this salutary movement; my wish has come to pass; the nation and its King are one. . . . Their union will save France. The constitution must be the standard of every Frenchman."[37] This, too, was followed by frantic applause. But hardly had Louis XVI regained the Tuileries than it was all over: as if the last few hours had been nothing more than a momentary aberration, the Assembly divided once more into angry factions, and the dream of union, apparently realized in the mid-afternoon, had become nothing more than a bad joke by the evening. Within two days, the attacks on the King and the monarchy resumed.

Indeed, on the eleventh, the Assembly took a new step away from the constitution: it declared the Fatherland in danger, which in turn justified any exceptional measure it felt like taking. It was a slap in Louis XVI's face; the Deputies, not trusting him to direct the war, had just taken on that task themselves. After that, there really was no reason why the monarchy should survive: all power was concentrated in the legislature; the constitution was, to all intents and purposes, a dead letter; and the royal family was hated as it had never been before. "There is no day on which I do not tremble for the lives of the King and Queen," Montmorin wrote on July 13. "They are as well guarded to stop them from getting away as they are poorly defended against those who want to force their way in."[38] He was right. Nor could there be any doubt that the Tuileries would indeed be invaded again sometime soon. On the fourteenth the King and Queen took part in a new Fête of the Federation. Once again, they drove from the Palace to the Champ de Mars; once again, Louis XVI swore to observe the constitution. Two years earlier, he had been greeted with universal applause. Now he was met with jeers, insults, and menacing gestures.

Mme de Staël, that stalwart liberal, that friend of the constitution, was there. "I will never forget the expression on the Queen's face," she wrote.

> Her eyes were swollen with crying; the splendor of her dress, the dignity of her stance contrasted with the cortege that surrounded her. Only a few National Guards separated her from the populace. The armed men gathered in the Champ de Mars looked as if they had come there for a rising rather than a festivity. The King walked from his pavilion to the altar set up at the end of the Champ de Mars; that was where he was to swear allegiance to the constitution for the second time. . . .
>
> It required Louis XVI's character, his acceptance of martyrdom, for him to bear his position. . . . I saw from afar his powdered head among all the heads with black hair; his suit, still embroidered according to the old fashion, clashed with the clothes of the mob that hemmed him in. When he walked up the steps of the altar, he looked like a holy victim going willingly to the sacrifice. [39]

That last touch is perhaps a little fanciful, but, otherwise, Mme de Staël does not exaggerate: many witnesses attest to the constant cries of "Long live Pétion!" "Down with the veto!" "Hang the aristocrats!"

Indeed, the only question now remaining was just when the monarchy would end. On July 20 Marat wrote: "It is only once you make the royal family your hostage that you will be able to reform the monstrous vices of the constitution." [40] It was an idea that had a future. Another plan was for a Jacobin government to take the royal family with it to the south of France, where the government would be safe from the Austro-Prussian invasion, and the monarchs could be used as a bargaining chip. That did not happen, but no one thought the royal family would remain much longer at the Tuileries. On her side, Marie Antoinette sent off ever more frantic letters asking for a manifesto that might still save the royal family by frightening the Parisians. In the meantime, with the weather hot and sunny, the court was penned in the Palace: every attempt at taking the air in the gardens was met with loud, hostile demonstrations.

It was then that the "Marseillaise" was heard for the first time. Written in late April by Rouget de Lisle as "The Song of the Rhine Fighters," a purely patriotic song, it was appropriated by the Marseille volunteers who had come to Paris for the July 14 celebration, and it was from them that it took its permanent name and its revolutionary connotation. The latter was so strong, in fact, that a century later, the "Marseillaise" was still loathed and dreaded by reactionaries of every stripe. The text bears out that interpretation, especially if it is remembered that people suspected Louis XVI of yearning for an enemy victory. Set to a lastingly catchy tune, this most enduring of revolutionary anthems does not mince words.

> *Allons, enfants de la Patrie,*
> *Le jour de gloire est arrivé!*
> *Contre nous de la tyrannie*
> *L'étendard sanglant est levé!*
> *L'étendard sanglant est levé.*
> *Entendez-vous dans les campagnes*
> *Mugir ces féroces soldats?*
> *Ils viennent jusque dans nos bras*
> *Egorger nos fils et nos compagnes:*
> *Aux armes, citoyens!*
> *Formez vos bataillons!*
> *Marchons! Marchons!*
> *Qu'un sang impur abreuve nos sillons!*

[Come, children of the Fatherland
Our day of glory has come!
Against us the bloody flag of tyranny is raised!
The bloody flag is raised.
Can you hear in the country
The shrieks of those ferocious soldiers?
They come to our very arms
To slaughter our sons and our wives:
To arms, citizens!
Form your battalions!
March forth! March forth!
Let their impure blood water our fields!]

Seldom has the soul of a people been so rousingly expressed. What to the King and Marie Antoinette seemed yet another insult was in fact the proof that the France of 1792 had broken, once and for all, with its past: Liberty, love of the Fatherland, those were the powerful emotions which had replaced the old devotion to the monarchy; and as the people became aware of them, a new world was born.

Louis XVI knew it, too. On July 14 he had been asked to wear a bulletproof vest.* "I will consent to this nuisance to satisfy the Queen," he told Mme Campan, "but they will not murder me, that is no longer their plan, they will kill me some other way."[41] As for Marie Antoinette, she no longer even had hope: she knew that her husband was too passive to try to modify the situation. He did not lack courage and was able calmly to look death in the face, but he lacked the energy to rise against his fate. And every day the situation worsened.

On July 15 the Assembly passed a decree sending all regular troops away from Paris, thus leaving it completely undefended against the mob. That same day, speaking at the Jacobins, Jacques Nicolas Billaud-Varenne, a failed lawyer who had become the club's vice president, demanded that the King be deported to some distant French possession, and the Cordeliers passed a motion calling for the election of a constitutional convention, while, north of Paris, the Austrians took Orchies. The next day they took Bavai, and, away in the southwest, the city administration of Angers asked for the King's dethronement. On July 25 the Assembly authorized the Parisian sections, where the most revolutionary elements prevailed, to sit in permanence; upon which the latter created a central office so that they could act together and fast. On the thirtieth the Deputies voted to allow "passive" citizens into the National Guard, thus satisfying one of their grievances and making it exceedingly probable that the distinction between voting "active," and nonvoting "passive" citizens would soon be eradicated, while, at the Champs-Elysées, in the course of a banquet given by the city to the Marseillais, a number of National Guards who were known to be faithful to Lafayette were severely beaten. In those circumstances, it required only one incident to set off a new rising; this the Duke of Brunswick, in a misguided effort to save the royal family, provided.

---

* It was lined with thickly wadded cotton.

It must be said that in issuing his famous Manifesto on July 25,[*] he was just taking a step urged repeatedly by Marie Antoinette and her envoys abroad. Not surprisingly, he used the tone of a feudal overlord warning his vassals. Nothing, obviously, could have been more maddening to the already excited Parisians.

"After having arbitrarily appropriated the rights and possessions of the German princes in Alsace and Lorraine," the Manifesto said,

after having perturbed and then ended order and the legitimate government, and carried out against the sacred person of the King, and against his august Family, attempts and violences which are renewed every day, those who have usurped the reins of the administration have finally filled the cup by injustly declaring war on the Emperor. . . .

To [the defense of the Empire] another equally important goal is added . . . ; it is to end the anarchy within France, to stop the attacks against Throne and Altar, to restore the legal power, to give the King again the freedom and safety of which he has been deprived and to so place him that he can exert the legitimate authority which is his alone.

Convinced as I am that the healthy part of the French nation abhors the excesses of a faction which has subjugated it . . . and is impatiently awaiting the coming of help to declare openly against the odious enterprise of their oppressors . . . I declare . . . that the two allied courts . . . wish only to free the King, the Queen, and the royal family from their prison. . . . The city of Paris and all its inhabitants will be made to submit immediately to the King. . . . Their Imperial and Royal Majesties[**] hold all the members of the National Assembly, of the districts, of the municipality, and of the National Guard of Paris personally responsible for all events; they stand to be punished militarily and with no hope of pardon. . . . If the Palace of the Tuileries is assaulted or invaded, if the least violence, the least insult is directed at Their Majesties the King and Queen, or at the royal family, if their safety . . . and their freedom are not immediately provided for, an exemplary and ever-memorable vengeance will follow and the city of Paris will undergo a military execution.[42]

---

[*] It reached Paris three days later.

[**] Francis II of Austria and Frederick William II of Prussia.

It required no more, finally, to identify the monarchy utterly and entirely with the enemy. Late in July the Girondins, hungry for power, had tried to reach an accord with Louis XVI so as to be recalled to the ministry; but their new, moderate stance was widely denounced. On the twenty-ninth Robespierre, at the Jacobins, demanded — as the Cordeliers had days earlier — that a constitutional convention be called: the last bulwark of the constitution on the left had just given way. Now the entire Assembly could unite against the King. Once again, Marie Antoinette's calculations had proved wrong: the Manifesto designed to save the royal family was the deadliest blow yet struck against it.

Indeed, the King had no choice but to disavow his champion: on August 3 he sent the Assembly a patriotic letter in which he endorsed the regime and the war, but no one any longer believed him. That he was habitually lying in order to deceive the people had long been a universally accepted assumption. A pamphlet published that summer put it succinctly: "Either he is governing stupidly, or he is governing wickedly. Is he stupid? Then he is not capable of reigning. Is he wicked? Then, as a traitor, he is not entitled to any respect."[43] Now no one was willing to disagree with this. Paris was divided into forty-eight sections: on August 3 forty-seven of them demanded the King's dethronement in a petition presented by Pétion to the Assembly; the next day, the section of the Quinze-vingt called for the people to rise on the tenth if the Assembly had not yet deposed Louis XVI. At the same time the Swiss Guard, whose barracks were just outside the city, began camping in the courtyard of the Tuileries. A new assault was obviously imminent.

The Assembly's fate, if it failed to comply, was hardly likely to be any better. As it received a flood of addresses demanding the King's deposition, it gave up, under pressure, all control of the tribunes, which were constantly filled with menacing revolutionaries: they were now to be policed by their occupants, a measure that showed perfectly how powerless — and frightened — the Deputies had become.

Worse was yet to come. Lafayette, whom the Jacobins had indicted of treason, was acquitted by the Assembly on August 8. In this case, as in so many others, the Assembly, taking on the judicial power, acted as prosecutor, judge, and jury. Its decisions were without appeal. The very next day several of the Deputies who had voted to quash the indictment were beaten up by the mob, which was permanently swirling around the

Assembly's building on the edge of the Tuileries gardens. Any pretense that the legislature could function freely was thus ended.

"If they [the foreign armies] do not arrive, only Providence can save the King and his family," Marie Antoinette wrote Fersen on August 1.[44] She was right: Paris was about to rise again and make the earlier episodes of the Revolution look like child's play, and everyone knew it. Whatever happened would happen on August 10; everyone knew that, too; Pétion and Santerre had made sure of it.

As it turned out, the revolutionaries started a little ahead of schedule. On August 9, at 8:45 P.M., under the pressure of a vast, armed, and angry mob, the regularly elected and constitutional Commune of Paris was replaced by an insurrectional body. Paris, its forces, and its administration were now fully controlled by the extreme left. Then, Mme de Staël reported, "before midnight . . . , the bells of the forty-eight sections of Paris began to toll, and, all night, that quick, monotonous, lugubrious sound continued without cease. . . . We were told that the faubourgs, led by Santerre, were on the march. . . . No one could tell what would happen the next day, no one expected to live through it. . . . Suddenly, at seven in the morning, the dreadful sound of the faubourgs' cannon was heard."[45] It had been a very warm night, it was a hot, sultry morning. Paris had risen again, and, again, it was about to change the world.

CHAPTER THIRTEEN

The Monarchy Stormed

: : :

IT had taken only three years. The King who was so popular, so widely praised in the early summer of 1789, had become the enemy of the people: fiercely though they loathed the Queen, it was now unquestionably Louis XVI who was the primary target of the revolutionaries. The constitution, so widely revered throughout the Revolution, seemed no longer even marginally useful as an impediment to the royal prerogative. Those moderate Deputies, in the summer of 1791, had not gone far enough: now the people of Paris were ready to end the monarchy in a great wave of anger and disgust. As for the Assembly, it mattered almost as little as the monarch himself.

"I would not be surprised to see a constitutional convention set up in the very near future," the duc d'Orléans wrote his sons on July 26, 1792. "I think you must try to be elected to it."[1] If he could not be king, he hoped, according to his friends, at least to become president of a new republic; what he still failed to realize was that, although spared his cousin's unpopularity, he had become irrelevant. By August 10 all the old power structures were crumbling, and those who wanted to see a quick end to the monarchy could count on Louis XVI not to resist.

"The King," Marie Antoinette told Mme Campan at this time, "is not a coward, he has a great deal of passive courage, but he is crushed by the wrong sort of timidity, by a distrust of himself which comes from his upbringing as much as from his character. He is afraid to give orders and fears more than anything having to speak to large groups."[2] It is, in fact, the extraordinary truth that this man who was brought up to rule as an absolute king, who had always lived in the most splendid, most formal court in Europe, had the very qualities most appropriate to a martyr: he was prepared to suffer greatly for his beliefs, though he could not rouse himself to fight effectively for them. Thus, when the awaited assault on the Tuileries began, unable to sway the crowds, incapable even of rousing his few defenders, he would be a ready-made victim.

There were, early on that stifling morning of August 10, 4,000 men garrisoning the Palace. Not all were reliable, perhaps, but it is easier to defend than to attack; with spirit, and adequate planning, the assault might have been defeated, especially since the assailants, although numbering some 25,000 men, were completely inexperienced. Some 5,000 of them were the men of the Marseille Federation who had come for the Fête on July 14 — enthusiastic, no doubt, but not professional soldiers. As for the mob, which made up the rest of the gathering force, it was likely to be ferocious but unstable.

Unlike the dispirited defenders, though, it knew just what it wanted. Marat's latest pamphlet, *L'Ami du peuple aux français patriotes* (The Friend of the people to the French patriots), was passing from hand to hand, and it was heady stuff. First, the mob was reminded, it had been betrayed: "He [Marat] predicted that your armies would be led to the slaughter by their perfidious generals, and three shameful defeats have marked the opening of the campaign. . . . He predicted that the corrupt majority of the National Assembly would always betray the Fatherland: and its last two perfidious decrees, by arousing the public's indignation, will bring about the cruel but very necessary events of this day. . . . The glorious day of the tenth of August may be decisive for the triumph of liberty if you know how to use your strength. . . . Fear to listen to a mistaken pity."

Having thus urged the mob forth, Marat reminded it — as he had done so often before — that it was in danger itself; and, with the Austro-Prussians marching toward Paris, with the Duke of Brunswick's Manifesto still fresh in their minds, they were in a mood to believe him: "Fear the reaction," he wrote, "your enemies will not spare you. . . . You are lost forever if you do not lop off the rotten branches at the Municipality and the Département, along with the antipatriotic judges and the most gangrened members of the National Assembly. . . . The Assembly is your most dangerous enemy; as long as it keeps meeting, it will try to fight you.'' This last was a clever touch: with the Assembly scared, or dissolved, there was nothing to prevent the formation of an ad hoc revolutionary government. As to what needed to be done, Marat was equally clear:

> I therefore propose that you kill one in every ten of the counterrevolutionary members of the municipality, the courts, the département, and the Assembly. . . .
>
> Hold the king, his wife, and his son as hostages until they can be tried, let him be shown four times every day to the people. . . . Warn him that if, within two weeks, the Austrians and the Prussians are closer than twenty leagues [about fifty miles] to our borders . . . , he will lose his head. . . .
>
> Let all patriots bear arms. . . . Demand the calling of a national convention to judge the King and rewrite the constitution.[3]

Short of the one in ten killings Marat was advising, his advice prevailed: these became the demands of the revolutionary mob. Indeed, well before dawn on August 10, it had become clear that his plan was under way. The Tuileries gardens filled with an angry crowd. The cannon that had been posted at the Pont-Neuf was removed at District Attorney Manuel's order. There was nothing now to stop the insurrection from reaching the Palace.

Inside the Tuileries, the royal family knew what to expect. "The factions were bolder than ever since the arrival [on July 30] of the Marseillais,'' Mme de Tourzel noted.

> They even insulted the Queen through the windows of her private apartment which opened onto the courtyard. I no longer dared to receive Mgr the Dauphin in my own apartment, which opened onto that same courtyard and was on the ground floor.
>
> The Queen was so poorly protected, and it was so easy to force one's way into her apartment that I begged her to come and sleep in the Dauphin's bedroom. She was loath to do so as she did not want people to think she was afraid; but, as I pointed out that she could come down the young Prince's inner staircase, and that therefore nobody would know about this, she finally agreed to do so, but only on the days when there would be rioting in Paris.[4]

On the night of August 9–10, though, no one at the Palace was sleeping. No dispositions to defend the Palace were taken, either. Pétion came by, and gave the commander of the National Guard a written order to defend the Tuileries, so the men stayed on watch, without, however, receiving any further orders. A few noblemen, who wanted to be there to defend their King, trickled in; and everyone waited.

Late that night they were joined by Pierre Louis Roederer, the attorney general for the Département of Paris. A liberal who had belonged to the Parlement of Metz, Roederer had been a member of the first National Assembly, where he sat on the moderate left. By August 1792 this effective civil servant, this honorable man, no longer knew what to do: not daring to oppose the mob, he still wished to protect the King and the royal family. And as the man in charge of the administration of justice in the Département (as opposed to the Commune) of Paris, his place was at the Palace. A little after 4:00 A.M. on August 10, "dawn began to appear," Roederer noted. "Madame Elisabeth went to the window; she looked at the sky, which was a deep red, and said to the Queen, who had remained in the back of the room: 'Sister, come and see the rising of the sun,' and the Queen joined her. At about the same time, the King, who had withdrawn to his bedroom, came back to his study. He must have slept, for he had lost all the powder from his head and his curls were flattened on one side." At that point, Marie Antoinette called Roederer over and asked him what should be done. "I answered," Roederer goes on, "that I thought it necessary for the King and Queen to go to the National Assembly . . . but that I was only suggesting this as the least dangerous thing to do. The Queen then answered in a very firm tone of voice: 'Monsieur, we have men here; it is time to find out at last who will be the stronger, the King and the constitution, or the factions,' and when the officer commanding the National Guard complained about the crowd in the apartments, the Queen spoke up again, saying: 'I will answer for all the men who are here. They will march in the front, in the rear, in the ranks as you please; they are ready to do whatever is needed; they can be counted on.' "[5]

In Paris the renewed Revolution had already begun. Danton, urging on the mob to the Hôtel de Ville, had the city government surrounded. Antoine de Mandat, the commander of the Paris National Guard, was called in, told he was replaced by Santerre, and, when he protested, killed on the spot. The Guards at the Tuileries were now without a leader, even as the gardens filled up with an angry mob. As for the Assembly, it had resolved to sit uninterruptedly; but, terrified by the crowds, it proved incapable of adopting any resolution. The only determined people left in Paris were the leaders of the insurrection.

Just as, at a little after four, Madame Elisabeth and the Queen were looking at the blood-colored sky, Louis XVI, as placid as usual, tried to go for a walk in the gardens, but within minutes was forced to come back by the crowd's violent hostility. Soon, at the Queen's urging, he went down again, this time to review the troops defending the Palace. "I can still see him," a witness recorded, "walking along our line with his awkward, waddling gait, mute, worried, as if he were telling us: 'All is lost.' "[6] In fact, he eventually tried to address the troops, but spoke low, and, failing to receive any response, he went back into the Palace. By then, it was already six. From the Hôtel de Ville, two municipal officers came with the news of the Commune's takeover by the insurrection, adding that all Paris was in arms.

Over in the National Assembly, the terrified Deputies kept leaving the hall, thus making sure there was no quorum: no initiative could come from the legislature, no resistance from the government, while all through the center of Paris a great wave of sound, a distant roar, came ever closer.

At the Palace, some of the newly arrived battalions were urging the National Guards to defect. "One heard them shout: 'Long live Pétion! Long live the nation! Down with the traitors and the veto!' " Mme de Tourzel wrote.

Entire regiments of the National Guard went over to the rebels so that the King could count only on the Swiss Guards, six hundred men of the National Guard, and about three hundred more persons, noblemen, [former] officers of the Royal Guard, and servants, all armed only with swords and pistols. . . .

Some twenty grenadiers of the National Guard were posted in the Council Room, to whom the Queen said: "Messieurs, all you hold dearest, your wives, your children, depend on our existence; we have a common interest"; and showing the little group of noblemen: "You can trust these brave people who will share your dangers and defend you to their last breath.'' Moved to tears, they swore to die, if need be, to defend Their Majesties.[7]

That was all very well, but there was not much a handful of men, now lacking leadership and shrunk in number by defections, could do. No doubt the Queen, who spent much of these early morning hours going from group to group, urging on the men, thought that heroics might still win the day; but it was much too late for that. Outside, the gunmen who were supposed to defend the royal family took the ammunition out of the cannons, which were ranged in the courtyard, and deserted to the mob; when the King asked the Assembly, in a message, to send a deputation to harangue the mob, he was told that the lack of a quorum prevented any such endeavor.

The situation was now absolutely clear. The King had no defenders left; the constitution, which proclaimed his inviolability, was forgotten; there was no significant body of troops left to impose order — a few hours more and it seemed likely that the corpses of the royal family and their defenders would lie abandoned in the devastated Tuileries. It was at this point that Roederer, the legally elected representative of the Département of Paris, intervened again; his own report of the advice he gave Louis XVI is confirmed by other witnesses.

This is the scene, at a little before seven, as he describes it:

"Sire," I said in the most urgent tone, "Your Majesty does not have a minute to waste. Your only safety lies in going to the National Assembly. The Département [of Paris]'s opinion is that you must go there immediately. You do not have in the courtyards a large enough number of men to defend the Palace; they are also not well disposed toward you. The gunners, who were simply given the order to shoot defensively, have taken the ammunition out of their cannons.''

"But," the King said, "I did not see much of a crowd in the Carrousel.''

"Sire, there are twelve cannons and a huge crowd is coming in from the faubourgs.''

"But, Monsieur," the Queen said, "we have defenders.''

"Madame, all Paris is marching.''[8]

Then, according to Mme de Tourzel, who was present, Marie Antoinette pointed out that it was impossible to abandon the volunteers who had come to defend their sovereign. The governess goes on:

" 'If you oppose my advice,' Roederer said to her severely, 'you will answer, Madame, for the King's life and those of your children.' That unfortunate princess said no more, but the shock was such that her face and neck immediately turned a mottled red.'"[9] Immediately turning to Louis XVI, Roederer added, he tells us:

"Sire, time is passing; it is no longer a plea we are making; it is no longer a piece of advice we take the liberty of giving you; there is only one thing to be done, we request your permission to take you away." The King raised his eyes, looked at me fixedly for a moment, then, turning to the Queen, he said, "Let us go," and stood up. Madame Elisabeth, passing behind the King . . . said to me: "M. Roederer, you will answer for the King's life?"

"Yes, Madame, on my own, I will walk directly before him." The King looked at me trustingly. [I said]: "Sire, I ask that your Majesty not take along any of your courtiers." . . . The Queen asked: "And Madame de Tourzel, M. Roederer, my son's governess?"

"She can come, Madame."[10]

And so a little group came together, composed of the King and Queen, she holding her two children by the hand, Madame Elisabeth, Mme de Tourzel, Mme de Lamballe, who as a relative* was given permission to come along, and the remaining ministers, with Roederer in the lead and a few National Guardsmen as escorts. Just before leaving, the King turned to the noblemen around him and said, in a faltering voice: "Messieurs, I ask you to leave and end a useless defense; there is nothing more to be done here, either for you or for me."[11]

"We were walking," Roederer continues, "on leaves that had fallen during the night. 'So many leaves,' the King said, 'they are falling early this year.' "[12]

It was during that short walk across the Tuileries gardens to the Assembly that the monarchy finally ended, after nearly a thousand years of existence. Subjected to hoots and insults from all sides, the little group

---

* The princesse de Lamballe was the widow of a member of a distant branch of the royal family.

was finally met by a deputation from the Assembly; " 'Sire,' its leader said, 'the Assembly, eager to ensure your safety, offers you and your family asylum among itself' ";[13] but for a while, it looked as if the crowds would actually massacre them before they reached the Deputies. "One National Guardsman said to the King . . . 'Sire, don't be afraid, we are good people, but we won't be betrayed anymore. Be a good citizen, Sire.' "[14]

Finally, the bedraggled group made it into the hall. Although it was barely seven, the heat was already intense. The disheveled King, the red-eyed Queen, the terrified women and children looked like what they already were, refugees. Still, Louis XVI went up the steps to the president's chair and said: "I have come here to avoid a fearful crime and believe that I cannot be safer than in your midst, Messieurs," while the Queen and the women sat down on the ministers' bench opposite him. Vergniaud, the president, answered: "You can count, Sire, on the firmness of the National Assembly. Its members have sworn to die for the rights of the people and the defense of the constitutional authorities."[15]

That was hardly reassuring: the Assembly had been demonstrating its cravenness for the past two days. Throughout the King's and the president's speeches, the mob in the tribunes shouted threats, and then, as if nothing unusual were happening, one of the Deputies pointed out that the constitution prohibited the Assembly from deliberating in the King's presence. Still, he could hardly be thrown out to the crowds, so he was moved, along with his family, into a tiny room that opened into the hall just behind the president's chair and that was normally used by the men who took down the debates in shorthand. They remained in this tiny, airless space for the rest of the day. Food and drink were occasionally passed in through the opening by some of the King's surviving servants (those who had escaped the Palace), but discreetly, because the tribunes remained filled with an angry mob.

It was now barely seven-thirty. In the Assembly cannon and rifles could be heard firing in the distance: the Swiss Guards, who knew what to expect if they were taken prisoner, were trying to defend themselves. Some hundred assailants were wounded or killed and the attack was falling back when, under pressure from the Assembly, the King sent the Swiss Guards the order to cease resisting. In a last show of fidelity, they obeyed, and were massacred by the mob, as were most of the men still inside the Palace. Although no exact count was ever made, it seems probable that there were at least eight hundred dead.

Within the hall of the Assembly itself, the disorder was scarcely less. The tribunes were full of armed men who alternated between shouting antiroyalist slogans and demanding the King's deposition; by ten, both the Deputies and their president were ready to cave in. Interrupting the debate in which Danton had demanded the King's dethronement, and firmly ignoring the constitution, Vergniaud proposed suspending the King and moving the royal family to the Palace of the Luxembourg. That, however, was considered too grand, so instead the Assembly decided that the Chancellery, on the Place Vendôme, would suffice. In the meantime, Louis XVI and his family were to remain within the precincts of the Assembly: no one was in any doubt as to what would happen if the mob got hold of them.

That was still not enough. Marat had done his work thoroughly; the Assembly was distrusted by the Parisian revolutionaries, so it did all it could to please. It passed the following decree:

> The National Assembly . . . , considering that the ills [of the Father-land] derive principally from the mistrust inspired by the behavior of the head of the executive branch and that this mistrust has given rise, in various parts of the country, to a wish tending to the revocation of the authority delegated to Louis XVI . . . decrees:
>
> Article 1. The French people are invited to elect a National Convention.
>
> Article 2. The head of the executive branch is provisionally suspended until the National Convention has made clear the measures it means to take to ensure the sovereignty of the people and the rule of liberty and equality.[16]

Of course, it was the second time the King had been suspended; but this time it was clear to all, including the former monarch, that there would be no reinstatement. The very conditions in which the royal family were kept made it plain: after a long, hot day spent in the tiny room behind the president's chair, they were taken to the former convent of the Feuillants across the street; there, without water to wash or clean clothes into which to change, they were left to spend the night. Everything they owned had remained in the Tuileries, and it was now lost. Louis XVI, as usual, slept well, as did the terrified but exhausted children; Marie Antoinette was heard sobbing until the morning. The next day, August 11, they were brought back to the same little room off the Assembly's hall, only to return to their convent cells at night.

As they saw and heard, more than the King's suspension had been accomplished. The civil list had also been suspended and its ledgers sent for, a development fatal for the monarch since it would now become known that Louis XVI had engaged in large-scale bribery. As for the rest, the delighted Barbaroux, the lawyer from Marseille, wrote his friends at home: "the king and his family remain as hostages, the ministry is dissolved . . . and [the Assembly] has itself appointed the new ministers. They are: Roland at the interior, Servan for war, Clavière at the public contributions [This in itself was a significant name change: since the Assembly intended to control the finances itself, the new minister was charged only with overseeing the tax administration], . . . Danton at justice, [Henri] Lebrun for foreign affairs."[17] It could hardly have been clearer. Roland and the Girondins had warned Louis XVI that they would have their revenge; now the suspended King was a hostage and they were the government. Even the appointment of Lebrun at the foreign ministry was an indication of Roland's power: a clerk who had prospered in the leader's entourage, he had neither knowledge nor talent. Obviously the interior minister would be foreign minister as well.

Still, there was one discordant appointment, that of Danton at the ministry of justice. That he owed his place to his role in the uprising everybody knew. With Santerre, he had been the main agent of the assault on the Tuileries, and his fiery eloquence had had a powerful effect throughout. It was Danton who had brought about the takeover of the Commune by an insurrectionary committee, it was he who was responsible for the dismissal (and death) of Mandat. Within a ministry of the moderate, not-quite-Republican left, he represented not just the Montagne — the Mountain, so called because the extreme leftist Deputies sat in the top benches of the semicircular hall — but, within it, the most radical of its tendencies. He stood, in fact, well to the left of Robespierre.

The violence of Danton's views terrified the Girondins, who could see that they were about to be outflanked from the left, and angered Robespierre, who thought them irresponsible. Worse, it looked as if he might become the most powerful man in France: the Paris mob — who never cared much for Robespierre, his fussy, old-fashioned appearance, or the often dry and legalistic tone of his speeches — was always ready to hear Danton.

It is clear, therefore, that his inclusion in the new ministry was forced on the Girondins; again, as the man most directly responsible for the events of the day, he could not be left out; and it was thought that, as minister of justice, he would not really be in a position to do much. That was a serious mistake: promptly hiring Camille Desmoulins and Fabre d'Eglantine, a gifted minor poet and violent revolutionary, surrounding himself with a judiciary commission composed of other men of the Montagne (Danton asked Robespierre to serve on the commission, an act of condescension that infuriated his rival, who refused the appointment), Danton made his ministry the center of the Revolution. It was soon noticed that, at the councils, the force of his personality overawed his weaker colleagues, Servan first and foremost. How could an incompetent minister of war resist the man whose battle cry was: *"De l'audace! Encore de l'audace! Toujours de l'audace!"* (Audacity! More audacity! Always audacity!)

France needed to be defended: obviously, the Revolution was doomed if the Austro-Prussians reached Paris. For Danton, though, it was not merely a question of personal survival. The triumph of his political ideals mattered as well, and so did the greatness of his country: a restored Louis XVI, deep in debt to his fellow monarchs, was not likely to do much for the pride, or even the independence, of the nation. "All belongs to the Fatherland when the Fatherland is in danger," he told the Assembly on August 28, adding, five days later: "All are moved, all are in arms, all burn to fight. . . . The bells that are about to toll will not give the alarm, they will launch the attack on the enemies of the Fatherland."[18] Danton, therefore, spent a good deal of his time overseeing Servan's activities, urging him on, and providing for the armies.

That was all outside his own department; but, as minister of justice, he could also further the cause of the Revolution by seeing to it that the "guilty" were punished. Here, for the first time, we encounter the modern version of class justice. In the Middle Ages and, indeed, until the end of the ancien régime, what was a crime for one category of people —

peasants, for instance — was not for another. Commoners and nobles were tried by different courts, under different laws; they were subject to different penalties. Now, with Danton, "revolutionary justice" was born. Here, too, different people were judged by different criteria: what mattered was defending the Revolution; anyone who got in the way was, or should be, removed. The criterion was not individual, proven guilt, but the overall welfare of the people. And that signaled a drastic radicalization of the revolutionary process: until then, change had come about as the result of laws passed by the Assembly and promulgated by the King. Now, the very minister whose job it was to ensure obedience to the law asked for the execution of legally innocent men.

On August 23 Arnaud de Laporte, the administrator of the civil list, was tried before a specially set-up criminal court. He was accused not only of having released funds to finance anti-Jacobin posters but also of having arranged for the quarters of the Swiss Guards at the Tuileries on August 9. He was speedily found guilty and executed, before a cheering crowd, the very next day, while a journalist, Durosoy, was being tried. Because the latter was a royalist, he was deemed to have been part of a conspiracy against the people and executed on August 25. Then it was Montmorin's turn: the former foreign minister — he had left office in mid-November 1791 — was, in fact, acquitted of treason, but the public protested so strongly that he was taken back to jail.

All the while, nobles and priests were arrested as such: it was assumed that they, too, must have been part of the "conspiracy" that was invented as a sufficient reason for the assault on the Tuileries. Again, that fateful modern invention, revolutionary justice, differs from ordinary justice in that it requires no proof of guilt, but condemns men and women for what they have been rather than what they did. Indeed, Danton found the judicial process altogether too slow. Rather than a few seriatim executions, what he wanted to see — and he said so often — was a general uprising that would massacre those who were as yet merely imprisoned.

As it became clear that the 30,000 prisoners kept in the Paris jails were actually in danger of being massacred, Danton's attitude was unequivocal: "I don't give a fuck about the prisoners," he told a colleague, "whatever happens to them, happens," adding the same day: "The people want to carry out justice on all those imprisoned blackguards."[19] This utter disregard for the value of human life, this travesty of justice, must weigh in the balance against the popular image of Danton as the brave revolutionary, the inspired and freedom-loving orator.

Priests and nobles were all very well: better dead than alive, better jailed than free, but even so they were not the chief culprits — that distinction belonged, Danton and his friends agreed, to the suspended King. Something would obviously have to be done about Louis XVI.

Once again, in fact, the Assembly was ignored. It had decided to move the royal family to the Chancellery; but when, after two days (August 10 and 11) spent in the shorthand writers' room, it was finally thought safe for them to leave the Assembly precincts, the insurrectionary Commune had other notions. The Assembly had not voted to imprison Louis XVI, Marie Antoinette, their children, or Madame Elisabeth. The insurrectionary Commune — the new Council, composed of 288 representatives of the sections, led by Pétion and Danton — refused to accept this. Faced with a deputation demanding that the royal family be imprisoned, the Assembly caved in yet again. New orders were given, a carriage was brought forth, and the hostages were sent on their way.

At first, when they left the Assembly, their carriage traveling through violently hostile crowds insulting the fat pig and the whore, the royal family were told they were being taken to the Temple, and, Mme de Tourzel tells us, they breathed a sigh of relief. Named after the old fortress of the medieval Knights Templars, the Temple consisted of two fourteenth-century towers, long disused, and a large and sumptuous house built in the middle of a park by the prince de Conti, one of Louis XV's distant cousins. On his death, the estate was given to the comte d'Artois, who made it one of the prettiest residences in Paris. Under the circumstances, therefore, although it was not a royal palace, it seemed like a highly acceptable place.

It was indeed to this house the royal family were taken; but then they were told that by that evening they would be moved to the fortress, which was hurriedly being outfitted with the necessary furniture. "The royal family first lived in the smaller of the two towers," Mme de Tourzel noted.

The princesse de Lamballe stayed with them, and the Queen occupied the second room opposite that of Mgr the Dauphin. The King was on the floor above the Queen and guards were stationed in the room next to his. Madame Elisabeth was placed in an appallingly dirty [former] kitchen which opened into the guardroom. . . .

Since the Queen's room was the largest, the days were spent there. . . . Their Majesties did not even have the consolation of being alone with their families; a representative of the Commune, who was changed every hour, always stayed in the room with them. The royal family spoke to them all with such kindness that it was able to soften several. At mealtime, they went down to a room below that of the Queen's and, around five, Their Majesties went for a walk in the garden.[20]

Eventually, the prisoners were moved to the larger tower, where their quarters were a little more spacious. On August 18 Mme de Tourzel, Mme de Lamballe, and the servants were taken away and jailed separately.

As it was, a new routine was soon established. The royal family's usual tradespeople quickly brought over new clothes (the bills had not yet been paid when Napoleon became Consul in 1799). Every day, Louis XVI gave his children lessons; Marie Antoinette and Madame Elisabeth watched him. All looked forward to their daily walk in the garden, but by the end of August this was forbidden because the crowds on the other side of the wall were getting increasingly violent, and it was feared that, if they broke in, secret royalists might help the family to escape. So they stayed in their sad little rooms and waited, Louis XVI without much hope, Marie Antoinette firm in the belief that they would soon be freed by the victorious Austrian troops.

If, for a while, nothing more happened to the royal family, it was for a series of very good, but temporary reasons: not only were they useful as hostages, but also there was very considerable disagreement among the victors as to what should be done with them. For Danton and the extreme left, which, in this case included Robespierre and his friends, both Louis and Marie Antoinette were traitors who should be tried and executed; to this Marat naturally agreed. The Girondins, however, were much less sure that this was desirable.

For them, August 10 had been a triumph; the insurrection had swept them into power, and they were all the freer to govern since the unpopular, discredited Assembly had only a month left to live. The Convention, named after the American Constitutional Convention of 1787, was to meet on September 21, and the Girondins firmly (and rightly) expected to be the largest, most influential group in this new Assembly. Even better, they were no longer hampered by the Constitution of 1791: with the suspension of the King, with the unofficial but real end of most civil liberties, it had become clear that a new charter was needed; in the meantime the Girondins seemed free to do whatever they wanted.

This, however, was only an illusion. First, of course, there was the war: on August 19 Brunswick crossed the border and the next day set siege to Longwy; on the twenty-third Longwy capitulated. On the thirtieth the Austro-Prussians set siege to Verdun; on September 2 it capitulated; by the fourteenth, ponderously moving forward, they crossed the Argonne river. The émigrés who fought with them spoke confidently of being in Paris within two weeks. The Paris revolutionaries, therefore, had good reason to worry.

Then, there was the pressure of what might be called the professional, full-time sans-culottes. Some five thousand strong, aided and sometimes led by Danton, Pétion, Marat, and Santerre, they had become an irresistible force. Filling the tribunes of the Assembly as well as the center of Paris, they could impose their will from day to day. The National Guard was a mere phantom; there was no police, no army, no one at all, in fact, to stop them. So it was that the Assembly, in its last days, voted a whole series of measures that went far beyond the wishes not only of most Deputies, but even of the Girondins, who were supposedly in power.

On August 14 a new oath sworn to Liberty and Equality was required of all ecclesiastics and the property of the émigrés was confiscated, even as Lafayette, who had tried and failed to march on Paris with the army he commanded, was forced to flee abroad. On August 15 the Assembly did refuse to create a "People's Court," but two days later, under pressure from the sans-culottes, it set up the Criminal Court, which condemned Laporte and the others. On August 18 the last legal religious orders were suppressed. On the twenty-first Collenot d'Angremont, a royalist whose opinions were his only crime, became the first victim of the newly installed guillotine. On August 22 the Commune demanded replacement of the appellation of "Monsieur" with that of "Citizen." On the twenty-sixth all priests who had not taken the new oath were expelled from France. On August 30, finally, more than three thousand suspects were arrested and jailed by the new, often volunteer, police of the Criminal Court; it needed only a spark to start the general massacre that Danton favored.

This was all much more than the Girondins had wanted. Although, to Louis XVI and Marie Antoinette, they had looked like bloodthirsty monsters, they were, in fact, surprisingly moderate. They favored, it is true, a more democratic system than the one set up by the constitution; they thought the King was still too free to interfere; but they were no longer entirely convinced republicans. Belonging, by and large, to the small and middle bourgeoisie, they felt no qualms about dispossessing the Nobility and the Church, but they also believed that property was sacred, that order must prevail. Nor were they without social ambitions: a monarchy where the King would have been a mere cipher, as the Queen of England is today, a reformed court in which Mme Roland might have shone, were not unappealing notions for them.

Roland, almost completely controlled by his wife, had few political views, and those few he did have were muddled; Mme Roland, to compensate, knew very well what she wanted: to become the most important person in Paris. "Mme Roland was not a real beauty, but she was very attractive," an observer noted. "She had lovely fair hair and wide-open blue eyes; her figure was graceful, her hand elegant. Her glance was expressive and her expression was noble and appealing even when she was relaxing. She had no need to talk for one to become aware of her intelligence; but no woman talked with more clarity, more grace, more elegance. . . . The harmony of her voice was heightened by gestures that were full of truth and nobility, by the expression of her eyes, which became animated as she spoke. . . . To such rare natural gifts she also added much natural wit, extensive knowledge of literature and of political economy."[21]

With all that, Mme Roland had principles. The partly self-educated daughter of a shopkeeper, she had read widely as a young girl, shared the prevalent craze for Jean-Jacques Rousseau, and thoroughly believed in his political ideas. She had also read much Latin literature, histories especially, and soon began contrasting the corrupt and unequal society of France in the 1780s with what she saw as a Roman Republic of free and equal citizens. It was a misreading: Rome before the Empire was an aristocratic society ruled by a few great families; but for Mme Roland, it became a burning ideal; and to this ideal she converted her rather slow, rather passive husband and his friends the Girondins, who, until then, had been just a small part of the Assembly's left. From the beginning of 1792, in fact, it was in her salon that the Gironde met, and her role as queen of the up-and-coming party, a queen with whom many men were in love, tickled her vanity even as it confirmed to her mind her superiority over other women.

In one respect, therefore, the Girondins were just what Louis XVI and Marie Antoinette imagined them to be: democrats who wished to bring about an open, privilege-free society. But they were also very much more conservative than Marat and the Dantonists, or even than Robespierre; while they believed in political equality, they also preferred the state to have as small a role as possible. Where the Cordeliers demanded greater centralization and a dictatorship of the people, the Girondins were essentially federalists who thought that each locality should be self-governing, and that the property of the middle class should be protected. The extreme left felt the state had an economic role to play as it discharged its responsibility for the poorer class of citizens; the Girondins were ardent believers in an absolutely free market (although they did not call it that) and felt that taking from the prosperous to help the poor was simple robbery.

Unfortunately for them, however, in their effort to recover power, the Girondins had become the prisoners of the mob: the very assault on the Tuileries that gave them the government also put Paris at the mercy of the sans-culottes; so Roland, Brissot, and their friends were constantly forced to be untrue to themselves. Both Brissot and Roland had opposed the King's deposition and by September were becoming one of Robespierre's favorite targets. In order to survive, they had to appear far more revolutionary than they actually were, and, even then, they never quite dispelled the mob's suspicion. "Men, during revolutions, often have more to fear from their successes than from their reverses," Mme de Staël wrote,[22] and it was undoubtedly true of the Girondins: their very triumph condemned them to be other than they were. This was true in all respects except one: the war, which the Girondins were just as anxious to win as anyone.

Indeed, the left's victory over the monarchy, far from appeasing it, had made it hungrier than ever. On August 13 Marat was denouncing "The cowardly Louis [who] is seeking an asylum amid his accomplices while announcing that he fled in order to spare the people, whom he was going to massacre, the great crime of punishing him [Louis] for his misdeeds."[23] On the nineteenth he warned: "The infamous senators at the [Assembly] are betraying the people."[24] And in September he went on to denounce "the odious maneuvers used successfully in the provinces to elect to the Convention the traitors who have always been the people's most cruel enemies."[25] By this last he obviously meant the Girondins, who were at that moment winning the elections.

Marat was not alone in his sentiment. Inspired by a heady mix of triumph and fear — of the invasion — Paris throughout August and September was seething. It was then that new revolutionary songs appeared, first and foremost the "*Carmagnole.*" Set to a vibrant, catchy tune that even today has lost none of its power to rouse, the "Carmagnole" was also meant to be danced by revolutionary groups, whom the music, the rhythm, and the steps would bring to a new pitch of fervor. As for the words, they were plain enough:

> *Dansons la Carmagnole,*
> *Vive le son, vive le son,*
> *Dansons la Carmagnole,*
> *Vive le son du canon.*
> *Veto femelle avait promis*
> *De faire égorger tout Paris.*
> *Ses projets ont manqué*
> *Grâce à nos canonniers . . .*
> *Veto le mâle avait promis*
> *D'être fidèle à son pays.*
> *Mais il y a manqué*
> *Le fourbe est encagé.*[26]

> [Let us dance the Carmagnole,
> Long live the sound, long live the sound,
> Let us dance the Carmagnole,
> Long live the cannon's sound.
> Veto female had sworn

She would massacre all Paris.
Her plans failed
Thanks to our gunners . . .
Veto the male had sworn
He'd be faithful to his country.
But he had lied to us
The traitor is in a cage.]

From there to direct retaliation, it was a short step. The Girondins dared not oppose it; Danton wanted it; so did Robespierre. On August 17, in an appeal to the future Convention, he told the insurrectionary Commune, of which he had become a member: "The guiltiest of the plotters did not show themselves on August 10. . . . Should Lafayette, who was perhaps not in Paris then, but who could have been there, thus [escape] the nation's vengeance? . . . We beg you to rid us of all duly constituted authorities."[27] Obviously, wide-scale punishment was the order of the day, and for that the new Criminal Court, whose members were elected directly by the sections, and who judged without appeal, was already deemed to be too slow; but there was a way around it.

On September 1 Manuel, the Paris district attorney, and Billaud-Varenne, his assistant, saw to it that many of the people who had been, or were just being, arrested were removed from their several places of confinement to two prisons, the Abbaye and La Force, where they were concentrated. These transfers were widely publicized; now if the people — who could, by definition, do no wrong, as Danton constantly pointed out — wanted to wreak their vengeance, they would know where to find their enemies. The hint could hardly have been clearer.

The next day, however, it was made clearer still. Throughout Paris, a "patriotic fête" was organized; its avowed purpose was to stimulate the people's warlike spirit, a necessity, it was explained, when the enemies' march on the city seemed unimpeded. Given the general mood, it was not hard to jump from recruiting volunteers to making sure that those remaining behind would not be stabbed in the back. One of the sections demanded that all the prisoners be put to death before the new battalions left the city; within a very few hours, most of the other sections added their agreement.

Now all that was needed was an incident, and Manuel considerately provided it. Early in the afternoon, he sent a convoy of twenty imprisoned priests from the City Hall, where they had been kept up till then, to the Abbaye. This was enough; upon seeing them, the maddened crowd tore them off the carts and massacred them. Having thus begun, it moved to the prisons themselves, where it demanded that thirty detained Swiss Guards be brought out. The prison authorities, who throughout the next three days proved eager to cooperate with the most bloodthirsty elements of the mob, promptly brought them out and watched as they were massacred. At that point, though, a deputation from the Hôtel de Ville begged the mob to stop, and proved so convincing that they were given an hour in which to produce a plan whereby the "royalist conspirators" could be immediately punished.

This was all Billaud-Varenne needed. He was a somber, uncommunicative and bloodthirsty lawyer whose recent title of assistant district attorney gave him just the power base he sought. At the meeting of the Commune following the return of the deputation, therefore, he was listened to carefully when he suggested that all prisoners implicated in the August 10 "plot" be turned over to the people for summary judgment; it was still thought not quite right to execute the prisoners without a semblance of a trial. Given the state of the capital, this was an irresistible suggestion, and indeed he was promptly set off to the Abbaye, where he was to carry it out.

It must be stressed at this point that the pretext repeatedly invoked — the royalist conspiracy — was nothing more than a fantasy. Marat and his friends claimed that they had taken the Tuileries and ended the monarchy on August 10 because, otherwise, the "conspirators" would have carried out an antirevolutionary massacre on Louis XVI's orders. This is an absolute untruth. There was no such plan; there never had been. Louis XVI's only, feeble effort had been so to garrison the Palace as to ensure its defense; and even then, he had finally given his defenders the order not to fight. Thus the rationale for the developing massacre of early September was simply a pretext invented by men eager to kill those who disagreed with them.

As quickly became evident, the Commune's plan worked perfectly. When he arrived at the Abbaye, Billaud-Varenne met a dubious character named Stanislas Maillard. A small-time crook, the half-mad Maillard, who was already suffering from advanced tuberculosis, now suggested to the crowd that a twelve-man people's court be created, that it sit right in the prison, and that it judge the inmates, its decisions to be carried out on the spot. The delighted Billaud-Varenne hastened to concur, the court was indeed set up, and some twenty men volunteered to act as executioners.

That might have seemed expeditious enough; apparently it was not. Several prisoners were murdered as they crossed the prison's courtyard on their way to the court, Montmorin, the former foreign minister, among them. That, of course, in no way prevented the court from going to work on its own. Naturally enough, knowledge of these events spread rapidly, reaching the Assembly by the late afternoon. What, then, was the legislature to do? Since the King's suspension, it represented the only legal authority in France. Alone it could, if it chose, modify the court system. Now, in its very city, illegal tribunals were being set up to carry out widespread massacres. Obviously, this not only made a mockery of the Assembly, it also violated a number of the provisions contained in the Declaration of the Rights of Man. Clearly, something had to be done, and it was: the Assembly sent a deputation over to the Abbaye. There, the Deputies were refused entrance and told that if they valued their own lives, they had better make themselves scarce; so they returned to the Assembly, which, in the late evening, washed its hands of the situation by decreeing that it "no longer has any means of causing the law to be obeyed."[28]

By then, the massacres were spreading. At the prison of the Carmes, set up in a former convent, the mob started the evening by tearing the Archbishop of Arles limb from limb, and went on to murder some hundred and fifty priests. At another prison, La Force, a people's court, set up a little after midnight, immediately began ordering executions. Early on the morning of September 3, Mme de Lamballe, the Queen's great friend, was "tried," found guilty, and massacred on her way to her execution. Immediately, her head and private parts were cut off, stuck at the end of a pike, and promenaded through Paris. At the Temple, the grisly remains were held outside Marie Antoinette's window. Called by the shouts of the mob, the Queen looked out, recognized the head of her friend, and fell in a dead faint. In the streets outside the prisons, where the pavement literally ran with blood, the revolutionary crowds showed no such reaction: all through the day, the massacres continued.

Indeed, by noon on September 3, virtually all the city's prisons were involved. At the Conciergerie, where a people's court was dispatching prisoners with exemplary speed, it was supplemented by men wielding iron bars, as was also the case at the Châtelet. At the Salpêtrière, a women's prison, the inmates also fell to the mob; it is one of the distinguishing characteristics of the September massacres that, for the first time in the history of popular violence, women were no more spared than men.

Very rarely, a few of the accused survived. Early on the third Maillard saved 238 Swiss Guards who had been imprisoned at the Palais Bourbon — for no discernible reason. Sometimes, it was the local people's court that let itself be touched, either by a pathetic plea or by a spirited self-defense: that was the case for Mme de Tourzel. And gradually, lassitude began to set in. On the morning of the fifth Pétion wrote, "only a very small guard stood before the gates [of La Force]; I went in . . . and saw two officers wearing their scarves of office. . . . Three men were quietly sitting at a table, the prison registers open before them. They called the prisoners, other men questioned them, others still acted as jurors and judges; a dozen executioners, their arms naked and covered with blood, held dripping cudgels, sabers, and knives and carried out the judgments in the instant."[29] Still, by then, there were fewer capital sentences, and on the sixth, its fury finally exhausted, the mob went home. Although exact numbers are hard to determine — the people's courts were not good record-keepers — it seems virtually certain that some thirteen hundred were killed in the course of the massacres: few by the standards of our century when victims are often counted in the millions, a shocking and inexcusable number by any civilized reckoning.

All through these five days, Danton, the minister of justice, sat quietly at the Chancellery, carefully refraining from any interference and letting it be known that, in his view, the massacre was necessary and, in fact, overdue. If the people, the sole legitimate source of power, chose to mete out vengeance, then, as Danton had always said, it was right by definition. Worse, Roland and the Girondins, who, unlike Danton, held no such theory, did absolutely nothing. They knew that the massacres were an indelible blot on the Revolution, but they also knew that any opposition to them would cost them their power — such as it was; and so they remained passive.

It is easy enough to understand *how* the massacres happened; a more meaningful question is *why* they should have occurred, what prompted the famously polite and civilized French to turn on mostly innocent victims in an orgy of murder and savagery. The answer can only be that the long-repressed anger of an exploited people had finally burst forth. All through the ancien régime, whatever the respective positions of the nobility and the upper middle class, it was, in the end, the people who paid the bills, literally and figuratively. Centuries of bearing the tax burden, of forced obedience, of exaggerated deference, needed compensation, and the early Revolution provided virtually none. As long as Lafayette and the moderates were in charge, it was the well-to-do who were given political and economic power; the main difference, as far as the people were concerned, was that the press was free, and could tell them daily that they had been, and still were, exploited. With the assault on the Tuileries, actual street power passed to these same resentful masses. Now they took their vengeance; and the fact that they needed to do so, that they were in a position to do so, is a searing indictment of the Girondin government and of the Assembly.

It also meant that, as long as Paris remained the capital, the legislature and whatever executive it created would be in thrall to the sans-culottes, with a double result: first, national policies would be very much more extreme than those desired by a majority of the French; and second, in reaction to this, towns and provinces would rise against the Paris government. This began to happen as early as August 17, when Carcassonne and its region rebelled, continued on the twenty-second, when the Vendée followed, and was thenceforth manifested sporadically throughout the country.

By September the old Assembly was thoroughly discredited; just before dissolving itself, however, it earned the gratitude of posterity by decreeing, on September 19, the creation of the Louvre Museum, thereby preserving the huge and glorious royal collections and ensuring that they would eventually be open to the public. On the morning of the twentieth, it gave further proof of its enlightenment by decreeing the creation of birth and death certificates — until then the Church had kept often inaccurate registers — and by making divorce legal. Then, at the end of the morning, it separated. Within the hour, its successor, the *Convention nationale,* met behind closed doors and elected its officers. A new era had begun.

What the new Deputies gathering in Paris did not yet know was that they had just received the best present imaginable: on that same September 20, at Valmy, the Austro-Prussian troops under Brunswick, faced with unexpectedly enthusiastic resistance on the part of two French armies, one under Dumouriez, the other under Kellerman, turned tail after a minor battle and began their retreat. It was the end of many illusions, and the proof that, in spite of all its disorganization, revolutionary France remained a potent adversary. On September 22 a French corps conquered Savoy, going on to Nice on the twenty-ninth. Away on the Rhine, Speier was taken on the thirtieth, Basle on October 3, Worms on the fifth, Mainz on the twenty-first, Frankfort on the twenty-fifth. On the twenty-seventh Dumouriez broke into Belgium; by November 14 he was in Brussels.

Politically, this had enormous importance. First, it provided apparent proof for the suspicion that earlier defeats had been due solely to the King and Queen's treachery. Also, it made the Convention feel that it was now free from external attack. That, in turn, meant that Louis XVI lost all use as a hostage, and could safely be disposed of; indeed, the discussion concerning his fate began on November 23.

Moreover, these victories indicated that the Revolution, which could not be stopped by force, was capable of spreading to the rest of Europe. On November 16 Chaumette, in a speech before the Commune, predicted that the rest of the continent would soon join France in proclaiming the Republic: the Revolution now had a universal and messianic mission.

At the same time, the war continued, and that meant there was a need to reorganize the country so as to wage it more efficiently. Liberty was curtailed, or even dispensed with, in the interest of national salvation. As previously noted, it was replaced by equality as a principal motivation — a handy way of decimating whatever remained of the elites.

Thus, as the Convention first came together, a different France was emerging. Goethe, when he heard about the battle of Valmy, said that a new world had just been born. Even that genius did not imagine how very right he was.

CHAPTER FOURTEEN

Revolution by Trial

: : :

WHEN, on September 21, 1792, the Convention nationale met for the first time in open session, it was, or seemed to be, omnipotent. Charged with writing a new constitution, it was free to do just what it chose. The past was dead and had left no surviving limits, no surviving institutions. Furthermore, the Convention, unlike its American predecessor, was also the government. Whatever executive it selected to set up would be its creature, to be dismissed and replaced at will. It could appoint ministers, generals, and prosecutors. It could set up new courts and close older ones, create new prisons, decree the arrest, indeed the execution, of anyone it wished. It could seize property, set prices, censor the press: subject only to the disorganization of the country, it ruled France far more absolutely than any of its kings had ever dreamed possible.

There was, in fact, only one limit on its freedom to act; but that, in the end, proved insuperable: the will of the Paris sans-culottes as led by Marat and Danton on the one hand, that of the middle and lower bourgeoisie represented by Robespierre and his friends on the other. And so it was that an Assembly where the Gironde predominated went on to implement the policies of the Montagne — a repeat of the same process as that which had transformed the previous Assembly.

Even so, the Convention was most probably more revolutionary than the country as a whole. There can be very little doubt that the general atmosphere of antimonarchical violence prevented not only right-wing voters but also many moderates from going to the polls. The secret ballot not having yet been invented, electors voted by proclaiming their choices out loud; and with the local Jacobins watching and listening — there was an affiliated club in every city and most of the towns — many men simply ignored the election. Although universal male suffrage was now the rule, it seems very probable that only some 10 percent of the electorate actually went to the polls.

As a result of its left-wing bias, the very first item of business the Convention took up, on September 21, was the nature of the regime, and its decision was both unanimous and enthusiastic: the monarchy, it decreed, was abolished. France was now officially a Republic, and all public acts were dated from Year I of the new regime.

The 749 members of this omnipotent legislature were, first of all, young: 75 percent were between thirty-one and fifty. They were, most of them, part of the solid middle class: 47 percent were lawyers, 10 percent former civil servants. Among them were about a dozen former priests or bishops, and about the same number of army officers. Celebrities were present as well: Marat had been easily elected, and also Jacques-Louis David, the painter (an ardent revolutionary); Boursault, a well-known actor; Antoine Fourcroy, a brilliant chemist; Condorcet, the great mathematician and philosopher; and even a foreigner — but what a foreigner — Thomas Paine himself. Finally, and perhaps more surprising, seven former marquises who had long ago renounced their titles and embraced the Revolution sat in the Convention, as well as the former duc d'Orléans, who had just decided to change his name and announced that he was henceforth to be called Philippe Egalité (Philippe Equality).

Just as important were the political divisions. It very soon became clear that the Girondins numbered about 200, of whom some sixty belonged to the inner circle around Brissot and Roland. The Jacobins, a group stretching from Danton to Robespierre, numbered about 110. The rest of the Convention, close to 440 men, were unaffiliated and undecided; they were quickly dubbed *le Marais* (the marsh) because they were as shifting as a marsh, or *la Plaine* (the plain), in contrast to the Montagne (the extreme left).

Obviously, the balance of power rested in the hands of the Marais, but Paris being what it was, these men could be intimidated by the crowds filling the Convention's tribunes and swirling around its doors. Before it happened, therefore, the Girondins decided to set the tone. Anxious to make up for their passivity during the September massacres, they began by attacking the power of the Parisians. Lasource, a provincial Deputy, asked that Paris, being only one of eighty-three départements, be reduced to an influence of one eighty-third, and he was followed by Rebecqui, who denounced Robespierre as a potential dictator, upon which the discussion shifted to Marat; the latter, brandishing a pistol, announced that he would shoot himself if the Convention decided his arrest.

At that point, Danton, well aware that most of the Convention considered Marat to be directly responsible for the massacres, tried to change the subject by appealing to his colleagues' patriotism, and demanding unity before the enemy, but he was not heard. It was finally Couthon, soon to become one of Robespierre's associates, who ended the debate when he asked the Convention to vote on his motion that the Republic was one and indivisible. It was both an affirmation of the new regime and a blow to the federalist Girondins, and it passed easily.

Soon, however, the latter regained the advantage. Danton was replaced at the ministry of justice by Garat, now a politically neutral Deputy. Like all departing ministers, Danton was supposed to account for the public funds entrusted to him at the moment when he passed on his powers; but he was quite unable to do so, and although he was not prosecuted — the Convention would not have dared — he lost much of his credibility. This was a major step forward for the Girondins, who especially dreaded Danton because of his influence on the mob. Next, they turned to Robespierre, attacking him because, they said, he had terrorized the administration of the Département of Paris and aspired to become dictator. Of course, Robespierre defended himself vigorously: he pointed out that revolutions were, by definition, illegal and that therefore his actions, though illegal, were legitimate. This answer is so good that it has been used repeatedly from that day to ours, but the very fact that he had been attacked somehow seemed to diminish him in the eyes of his colleagues. There could be no doubt about it: the Gironde, relying on its numbers, had won an important victory.

Never has a victory been so short-lived. What mattered was not so much what the Deputies thought as what the Parisians could pressure them into doing. Of course, Brissot and Roland were aware of that, so they proposed that the Convention have its own 5,000-man guard recruited from the rest of France. The Commune protested violently at first, then greeted the arriving guards in such a way as to co-opt them. Eventually, the guards disappeared among the greater number of Parisians, and the Convention was again left defenseless.

By December, therefore, it was clear to the Marais that, if they defied Paris, they were quite likely to lose their lives and, further, that they could not rely on the leaders of the Gironde. Just as in September, Roland and Brissot had proved both powerless and craven, so it became clearer every day that they were political incompetents compared with their rivals. Brissot, wrote a successful fellow politician, "was as naive as a child, always easily duped and incapable of duping others. . . . [He] had much wit and no ability to foresee the future, he knew history very well and men hardly at all, he had a wide circle of political friends and saw no further than the tip of his nose. Eager to prove that he was right, he did not know how to be actually right. In a word, he had all the qualities required to reach the leadership of a party and lead it to its death."[1] Given that, and Roland's utter lack of common sense or firm resolution, the Girondins' positions as ministers did not make much difference: from the very beginning, the Convention decided to govern directly, through permanent committees in charge of the various important questions of the day. As for the new constitution, it was to be the work of a committee as well: composed of eight Girondins and Danton, it set to work on September 29, but soon spaced its sessions, and did not come up with a draft until April 1793.

That left the Convention to deal with a singularly embarrassing problem: the fate of the former king. The papers that had been seized at the Tuileries by the Commune were now transferred to the legislature, and it soon became obvious that they contained enough evidence of Louis XVI's counterrevolutionary efforts to form the base of an indictment.

This was enough to condemn the ex-King; but whether it was desirable to do so remained a very large question for the Girondins and the Marais. Marat and Robespierre, who wanted the ex-King tried, represented just the segments of the extreme left they most feared, the ones who were even now attacking Brissot and Roland: trying the ex-King was all too likely to strengthen them.

As it was, the Brissotins, as they were now called, already found themselves under constant attack. On September 28 Marat, in his new paper, the *Journal de la République française,* had denounced the "plot formed by the Brissot faction to libel the Paris Deputies,[*] crush the most energetic among them, and cause the friend of the people to perish under the sword of tyranny."[2] He was joined in early October by the enormously influential Camille Desmoulins, who claimed that "Robespierre [was] the least ambitious of men except in his desire to best serve the cause of liberty,"[3] adding, in his next issue: "There is . . . a monstrous system which claims that the best friends of the people are agitators because they say out loud . . . at the podium of the Jacobin Club that they will call for an insurrection against the Convention itself if . . . it tries to restore tyranny. . . . The people know their rights, and will not hesitate to claim them."[4] Then, as if that were not clear enough, Desmoulins added a week later: "There is a party who wants to partition France, who wants to create federated republics and is the main source . . . of the criticism against Paris."[5]

Obviously, the Brissotins were not about to allow their enemies to triumph without a fight; so, on October 29 Jean-Baptiste Louvet, a member of Brissot and Roland's inner circle, accused Robespierre of wanting to become a dictator but also of having engineered the September massacres in the hope that the Girondins would perish as well. When two parties accuse each other of murderous intentions, the split is irreconcilable: obviously, the Convention would soon have to take sides. Under those circumstances, the fate of the ex-King provided a highly complex challenge.

It could, on the one hand, unify the revolutionaries: if they agreed that the former "tyrant" was to be punished, then they might also come together on other issues; but it could, on the other, divide them according to how they saw the future of France: if a moderate — that is, Girondin — regime were about to prevail, then there was no sense in shedding more blood and deepening the divisions between lukewarm royalists and moderate republicans. Adding yet further confusion was the fact that the Revolution was only forty months old and that many remembered the time when Louis XVI had enjoyed the people's loyalty: depending on their current feelings, they wanted either to punish his treachery, or to spare him for old times' sake. In both cases, they tended to be highly emotional about their point of view.

---

[*] Marat and his friends, that is.

Still, there was no avoiding the question. On October 1 a committee of twenty-four Deputies, with a Girondin, Charles Valazé, as chairman, was set up: this move at least postponed any resolution. On October 4 the committee came up with a preliminary report. There were, it said, mountains of documents that seemed to bear proof of a royal conspiracy; more work was needed, however, so teams of Deputies were set up to go through all those papers, and a full report was promised for a later date. That came on November 6, the very day the Austrian army was badly beaten at Jemmapes, and it was just as vague as the first report. Clearly, the Convention (as a whole) would have to make up its own mind.

For the Montagne, the elimination of Louis XVI was highly desirable, both as a way to prevent any possibility of a restoration and as a way to speed up the Revolution. For the Girondins, who were anxious to preserve the status quo, and perhaps eventually even willing to put a figurehead on the throne — the little Dauphin was the best candidate — as a means of ensuring stability, it was obviously not a good idea to kill the ex-King. Worse, it might lead to a renewal of the September Terror in which they would be the victims. That left the Marais to decide between these opposite points of view; but it could not do so in a vacuum. The Convention had just proclaimed the Republic; the revolutionary fervor was heady and widespread: it was tempting to fling a gauntlet in the face of monarchical Europe by trying and beheading Louis XVI.

For the extreme left, the very debate denoted a lack of revolutionary fervor. "You are republicans in name only," Marc Antoine Jullien, a Montagnard, told the Convention in mid-November. "If you were real republicans, you would not give so much importance to the fate of a dethroned tyrant. . . . You say you want to teach the nations how to judge their kings? No, citizens, teach them how to destroy these scourges in the most prompt and efficacious way."[6] And, of course, the Jacobin press continued its pressure. On November 10, Marat argued: "The nation that has just brought down the monarchy means to have Louis Capet tried. He cannot be without revealing the names of his accomplices."[7] Here was a new argument: the only way of getting at the royalist "conspiracy" was by forcing the ex-King to admit all in open court, that is, before the Convention sitting as a tribunal.

Before arguments like these there was no possible resistance. Once again, the Girondins held an untenable position: it was more than their lives were worth to defend Louis XVI in November1792. There was only one possible solution. The Constitution of 1791 had declared that the King's person was "inviolable and sacred," and that he was himself not accountable, that is, all constitutional responsibility for the government's actions was to be borne by the ministers. Strictly speaking, his actions could be judged only according to the rules of the constitution in effect at the time. Under those circumstances, how could he be tried? How could he be punished?

This was the question — one of constitutional law — which Jean Mailhe, one of the members of the committee on legislation, addressed in his November 7 report to the Convention. "Never did [the constituents] mean to say that this inviolability . . . could be opposed to an Assembly holding all the powers of the nation," he wrote. "They could not even have allowed themselves such an assertion without putting themselves at odds with the decisions of the constituent body which ordered the King's arrest at Varennes, which suspended him, which ordered him to give in writing the reasons for his flight, and which would not have had the right to do all this if it had not deemed that the King's inviolability must give way to this sovereign tribunal." This, on the face of it, is a specious argument: the Constitution of 1791 came into being only *after* the events in question, and it did not provide for the possibility of suspending the King's inviolability.

"Citizens," Mailhe went on,

> is not your duty made plain by all that has happened? . . . Can you not hear in your hearts the voices of the citizens who died [on August 10] before the Palace of the Tuileries? Can you not hear the entire Republic reminding you that this is one of the primary reasons for your presence here? Can you not see all the nations of the world, all the generations present and future . . . waiting . . . until you show them . . . whether the inviolable King has the right to murder citizens and groups without punishment; whether a monarch is a god whose strokes must be blessed or a man whose crimes must be punished.
>
> Louis XVI can be judged. He must be judged for the crimes he committed when he was on the throne.[8]

That, at last, was clear enough: revolutionary logic had replaced constitutional law. The dead of August 10 — who had died as members of an insurrection against the constitutionally established monarchy — preempted all else. There was still another question to be decided, however, and Mailhe went on to tackle it.

"[Louis's] inviolability disappears only when confronted with the nation; only the nation can call Louis XVI to account. . . . [I]n consequence, the Convention [as the nation's representative] must itself decide on his crimes, or ask the whole nation to be the judge, [but] the Convention represents the nation entirely and perfectly."[9] Besides, Mailhe pointed out, penalties can be ordered only by the judges present at the trial. Therefore only the Convention could decide on the ex-King's punishment.

With Mailhe's report went a draft decree: "1. Louis can be tried. 2. He will be tried by the Convention. 3. Three commissioners taken from within the Assembly will gather the documents and proofs relative to the crimes of which Louis XVI is accused [points of procedure follow]. 9. The Convention will vote on the sentence by nominal roll call."[10] That last point was the most controversial: given that the Convention's tribunes would be packed with sans-culottes, many of its Deputies would fear to vote openly against the death penalty. While, therefore, most of the decree was in fact passed, that last provision gave rise to violent discussions.

The debate on the report began on November 13, and an obscure Deputy, Asselin, expressed what many of his colleagues thought: "When a nation gives itself a king," he said, "it is so that he will govern it wisely. . . . If, putting aside this sacred duty, he declares himself its enemy through perverse maneuvers, through treacheries of every kind . . . then the nation has the right, not merely to dethrone him, but also to call him to account for his misdeeds and to punish him for them."[11] This made eminent sense: by 1792 Jean-Jacques Rousseau's notions about the social contract that should bind government and governed were widespread. That the King had a duty to the nation was therefore self-evident; and it was equally clear to most of the Deputies that Louis XVI, never having accepted the Revolution, had lied to the French and connived with foreign powers to restore the old order — a belief that is very close to the historical truth. If the moral law were to prevail over the constitution, and a recent, discredited constitution at that, then, clearly, Louis XVI deserved to be tried and punished.

What seems logical to us in the twentieth century was amazingly new at the end of the eighteenth, however. Just a very few years earlier, it had been widely accepted that Louis XVI was King by the grace of God, and that meant that he had been chosen by the Deity to rule over the French; his semidivine character had been confirmed at his coronation when he was anointed with the sacred oil brought down (it was asserted and believed) from heaven by an archangel in the eighth century. Such a King was untouchable, superior in essence to his subjects, and certainly not such as to be either deposed (no King of France had ever been) or judged by his subjects. While Asselin had obviously forgotten about the old legends, Louis himself had not: at the Temple as at Versailles, he always remembered that he was the chosen of God: to do so was part of his intense Catholicism.

In a little over three years, the old beliefs had been shattered, and, of course, the flight to Varennes had been one of the major reasons for the change of attitude. There was also the fact that Louis XVI was both so unimpressive in person and so ineffective as a ruler. Even so, that Asselin should have expressed what turned out to be a widespread and common-sensical opinion shows vividly how far the Revolution had gone in burying the old world and creating a new one.

Compared with this display of cool reason, Marat's speech seemed unimpressive: he was always at his best in writing, and did not have anything new to say; but it was important, all the same, because of its effect on the sans-culottes in and out of the tribunes. "Louis XVI's crimes are unfortunately only too real," he told the Convention. "They are well established, they are notorious. . . . He hid behind the mask of hypocrisy to plot against [the nation] more securely."[12] Marat ended by demanding first the ex-King's trial, then his execution.

One interesting linkage is perhaps worth noting here. It is customary, in Anglo-Saxon law, to assume innocence until guilt is proven; but in France and most of the Continent, guilt was assumed, and the purpose of detention and trial was to prove it, to make the criminal tell all, so that the effect of the trial would be a sort of catharsis, rather than an adversary proceeding, which, if properly conducted, would establish the truth. Thus, until Louis XVI decreed its end in 1787, torture was regularly used as part of the pre-trial procedure, to make sure the criminal would indeed tell all. In the case of the ex-King himself, with so overwhelming a presumption of guilt, it never occurred to anyone that he might be tried and found innocent; that made the real question not so much the outcome of the trial, but the nature of the punishment. Naturally, Marat was all for a capital sentence; the more moderate Asselin eventually voted for a suspended death sentence.

Although Marat himself seemed less than compelling, the Montagne did not lack for orators. Robespierre naturally demanded a swift trial with a subsequent execution, but it was Saint Just whose fiery eloquence was found the most moving by his colleagues.

Young — he was only twenty-five — handsome and passionate, Saint Just, who had trained as a lawyer, was a troubled figure who had written an erotic novel, *L'Organt,* full of rape and violence. He fancied himself a theoretician, and became the author of a singularly turgid tome entitled *Les Institutions républicaines,* in which he recommended, among other things, that children be fed a vegetarian diet and that unmarried girls be allowed out only if accompanied by their parents. What really mattered, though, was his burning faith in the most extreme revolution possible, and his ability to communicate his beliefs. His utter lack of personal ambition coupled with his fierce denunciations of the Gironde and all those he conceived to be lukewarm endeared him to Robespierre, whose close friend and ally he became. When he spoke on November 13, his was the voice of the new Republic.

"The Committee's only object was to convince you that the King must be judged like any other citizen," he began, "but I say that the King must be judged as an enemy, that it behooves us less to judge him than to fight him. . . . Posterity will be surprised if it sees that, in the eighteenth century, we were less advanced than in Caesar's time; that tyrant was sacrificed in the Senate with no formality other than twenty-two knives plunged in his breast, with no laws other than the liberty of Rome. And today, we would respectfully try an assassin taken in the act, his hands red with blood! . . .

"Louis is a foreigner among us. He was not a citizen before his crime; he could not vote, he could not bear arms; he is even less a citizen since he committed his crime." And in what is probably the best existent definition of antimonarchism, Saint Just ended: "It is impossible to reign and be innocent: all kings are rebels and usurpers. . . . French people! If ever the King should be declared innocent, remember we will no longer deserve thy trust.''[13]

Saint Just had spoken for the new revolutionary faith; Thomas Paine, like the Englishman he was, added a practical note, which, however, led him to the same conclusion: "There exists, between the crowned brigands of Europe, a conspiracy against, not just the liberty of France but that of all the other nations as well. . . . Louis XVI, taken as an individual, does not deserve the attention of the Republic, but, taken as a member of that band of plotters . . . he must be tried.''[14]

After that, it was of no use for some of the more legal-minded Deputies to point out that the only penalty contained in the 1791 Constitution was the King's dethronement, and that, since it had already been carried out, the ex-monarch should now be a free man: the Convention wanted a trial.

Then, on November 20, more of the ex-King's papers were discovered in that hollowed-out spot in the stones of the Tuileries walls. The locksmith who had helped him make the door and the lock now revealed the cache's location. Although normally passive, the King was also secretive, and he liked manual labor: hollowing out the cache, making the door and lock were thus perfectly in character. Naturally, the documents in question were the most sensitive: they provided abundant proof that the King had been paying Mirabeau, that he had bribed many other revolutionaries, that he had corresponded secretly with his fellow monarchs and urged them to give him assistance against his people.

After that, it became obvious that a trial *must* take place. On December 5 the Assembly ordered that all the seized documents be printed and made public. Among the ones that most exasperated the sans-culottes was a letter from Louis XVI to the Bishop of Evreux: "You know the sad position I find myself in because of my sad acceptance of the decrees concerning the Clergy [that is, the Civil Constitution],'' the King had written early in 1791. "I always considered that this acceptance had been forced on me and am firmly resolved, if I recover my power, to reestablish the Catholic Church.''[15] It needed no more to convince everyone that there had indeed been a royalist-clerical plot against the Revolution.

Not that the Convention needed what it considered to be merely added proof. On December 4 it voted the death penalty against all who advocated the restoration of the monarchy. Now, with the Girondins thoroughly swamped by the leftward trend in the Convention, the very premise of the debate over the King's fate shifted.

On November 30 a Breton Deputy, trying to save the ex-King's life, had argued that clemency was a more effective way of strengthening the Republic: "Charles I has had successors," he pointed out, "the Tarquins[*] did not."[16]

The answer to this came from Manuel, one of the leaders of the mob on August 10 and now one of the Deputies from Paris. "The monarchy," he thundered, "was a conspiracy against the public weal. . . . Who still dares to ask whether the King can be judged when the entire people asks for his uncrowned head? . . . Legislators, hurry to pronounce the sentence which will climax the Revolution. . . . A dead king does not mean there is one man the less."[17] It was clear enough: kings were not even human.

It was left to Robespierre to put it squarely to the Convention. First, on December 3, clear and cold as usual, he ironically defined the situation: "The Constitution," he said, "forbids all you have done. . . . You did not have the right to imprison [the King]. He is entitled to demand that you free him and pay him damages. The Constitution condemns you: go then, and beg, at Louis's feet, for clemency. . . . " And having thus made fun of his colleagues' scruples, he went on: "The tyrant's trial is the [recent] insurrection; his judgment is his loss of power; his punishment is that demanded by the liberty of the people."[18] Here, clearly and finally, is a perfect definition of revolutionary legality: when the people rises, it creates a new law that supersedes the old. By deposing Louis XVI, the French had, in effect, judged him; beheading the ex-King would simply complete the process.

Robespierre's speech was immediately printed and released, as indeed were the speeches of all the other Deputies concerning the trial of the ex-King; but he did not think this was enough, and he went on to make his position clearer still in a letter to his electors: "[Louis] should have been judged as a tyrant condemned by the people's insurrection. He is about to be tried like a citizen whose guilt has not yet been established.

---

[*] The last kings of ancient Rome, who were deposed but allowed to live and were succeeded by centuries of republic.

The Revolution should have been consolidated by his death, and the capital penalty is now being discussed. He should have been judged according to the principles of the people's rights, and not . . . by an equivocal and monstrous blend of older laws and natural law."[19]

This is a crucial step, not just for the French Revolution, but for all those that followed. If the people is sovereign, if it is the sole source of legitimacy, then, when it rises and destroys a government, it also destroys the laws according to which that government functioned. *Salus populi, suprema lex* (the people's welfare is the supreme law) ran a popular Latin tag: on August 10, when it rose, the people had condemned Louis XVI; on September 21, when it formally ended the monarchy, the Convention had simply confirmed the people's judgment. After that, the massacre of September had shown what the people felt should be done with their enemies — always providing that the Paris mob was in fact the people. It followed, then, that Louis XVI, too, must be executed.

As usual, Robespierre not only was being logical, he was carrying his logic as far as it would go: this set an important precedent, for the development of the Revolution then under way, and for the future as well. Henceforth, revolutionary leaders were to base their claims to power and punishment on the principles so succinctly defined by Robespierre: dethroned kings and emperors would be guilty by definition, revolutions would be bloody by right. Once again, the new world Goethe had perceived was being created.

There now only remained to put all this in the form of a decree, and this is what Augustin Robespierre, Maximilien's younger brother, proceeded to do. Had the Convention followed him, it would have decided that "Louis will be brought before the Convention so that he may name his accomplices, hear his capital sentence, and be taken forthwith to the scaffold."[20] The Convention was not ready to go so fast, however; the draft decree was never passed. Instead, on December 6, the Convention first debated a motion presented by Marat demanding that sentence be passed on the ex-King by nominal roll call as opposed to secret ballot, a process that would allow every latitude for the sans-culottes to exert pressure from the tribunes, where some two thousand of them would be sitting and watching the Deputies. Because they were already there, because these pressures were already being exerted, the Convention passed Marat's proposal, thereby almost certainly condemning Louis

XVI to die. Then, the Convention set up a special committee, composed of twenty-one members charged with "presenting on Monday morning [December 10] the act listing the crimes of which Louis Capet stands accused. . . . The next day, Louis Capet will be brought to the Convention to have this act read out to him. . . . A copy will be given him and the president will give him two days to answer. The day after this . . . , the Convention will decide Louis Capet's fate by nominal roll call."[21]

In many ways, Louis XVI had become an abstraction, the living symbol of "tyranny," a representative of all European monarchs, and he was, therefore, easier to condemn: it was no longer a man with a wife and children who was going to be executed, but an archetypal monarch. That helps to explain why the Girondins, anxious as they were to avoid the trial, were systematically outmaneuvered by the Montagne. Only the great issues at stake mattered. Concerning these, passions were so aroused as to defeat reason and, certainly, compassion; nothing the Girondins said could make any difference.

Still, away at the Temple, there was a man suffering an increasingly harsh fate. More and more, he was kept away from his family; the conditions of his imprisonment became increasingly strict, until he was allowed to see his wife, sister, and children only for a brief moment every day and forbidden the reading material he wanted. As to what it all portended, Louis himself had no doubt; for a long time now he had expected to be made a martyr; it was not for nothing he had kept the history of Charles I of England by his bed at the Tuileries. Before August 10, he had thought he would just be murdered; now, as he heard from his guards that the Convention was debating his trial, he felt quite sure that he would indeed be tried, condemned, executed. He was, of course, a fervent Catholic; he felt quite free of guilt since all his actions had been intended simply to recover his God-given power. What to the Convention looked like treason — the correspondence with the enemy, the open acceptance and secret plotting against most of the post-1789 changes — what, indeed, still seems like treason to us, struck him as an entirely legitimate way to behave. Further, according to Cléry, the valet who was allowed to attend him, he appears to have harbored a belief in the efficacy of his martyrdom; he thought his death would open the way to a restoration of the throne, to a revulsion against the Revolution from which his son would profit. He knew he had not been an effective king;

by giving his life to the cause of monarchy, he would make up for all his shortcomings; so it was that during all these days, and those that followed, he displayed the most perfect serenity, the most unruffled courage.

With that, unfortunately, went a certain lack of empathy for his family. To be sure, Cléry tells us, he loved his wife more, perhaps, than he ever had, and also his children, his sister; but his very acceptance of death removed him emotionally as he was being increasingly removed physically. As for Marie Antoinette, aged and unrecognizable although she was only thirty-seven, she sank into increasingly deeper depression. She looked after her children and went on feverishly doing her embroidery — she could not bear her hands to be idle — but also alternated between rage at her fate and despair at what the present and future had in store.

Pent up in her small room, with its rough furniture, unable ever to get a breath of fresh air, forced, for the first time, to dress and undress without help, the ex-Queen was also subjected to the insults of the guards: not only did they call her *Femme Capet* instead of Your Majesty, they denied her even the small courtesies accorded women everywhere. Sitting when she stood, blowing the smoke of their pipes in her face, they accused her of disgusting crimes and jeered at her supposed foibles.

On December 10, right on schedule, the committee presented its act of accusation to the Convention, but the ex-King himself was not brought before the Convention until the twenty-first. He was then told of the accusation and asked to choose his defenders. At that point Louis XVI could have followed Charles I's example (with which he was familiar) and simply denied that the Convention was competent to judge him; instead, he chose to defend himself. He appointed two lawyers, Denis Tronchet, a highly successful attorney who had sat on the right side in the first National Assembly; and Chrétien de Malesherbes, an eminent judge who had twice been a minister, first in 1775 under Turgot, then again in 1787–88. Both courageously agreed to serve. They chose a well-known lawyer, Romain de Sèze, to do the actual pleading for the defense and help them prepare for the trial.*

Unfortunately, these talented and brave men were altogether out of

---

* Malesherbes was arrested the following year and executed; de Sèze was jailed, but survived the Terror and was released.

their depth. Raised and trained in the complicated legal system of the ancien régime, they understood neither how to plead before a highly politicized legislature, nor how to defend Louis XVI on other than legal grounds. When, on December 26, they came to plead before the Convention, their attempt to exonerate the ex-King consisted of two parts: in the first, Louis denied that he had been plotting with any foreign power against the Revolution; this, of course, was a lie; but less was known then — his letters to foreign monarchs, for instance, were still secret — and some of the Deputies believed him. In the second, de Sèze argued that the Constitution of 1791 had made the King inviolable; and that if, in spite of that, he was to be judged, then it must be according to the prescribed legal forms, that is, through a grand jury indictment and a trial by jury. The Convention, he said, could not be the accuser, the judge, and the jury all in one. He then went on to defend Louis XVI's good intentions and pointed to the reforms of the mid-seventies. Although technically irreproachable, this was an extremely weak plea: the Convention had dismissed these arguments in its earlier debates and was obviously not about to change its mind.

Still, the debate over the decision to be made lasted from December 27 to January 7, and it included one last, desperate — but very roundabout — attempt by the Girondins to postpone the issue. They could not, of course, vote to exonerate the King without being immediately characterized as antirevolutionaries, but they tried at least to delay any resolution at all by arguing that the people had made the King inviolable in 1791, and that now only the people could decide on his fate. They asked, therefore, that the entire electorate become the judge of last resort; to make this palatable, they accompanied it with the most extreme anti-Louis XVI language. On January 1, for instance, Brissot put both aspects of the Girondin position succinctly. "That Louis is guilty of high treason, that he has deserved to die, those are points on which no man who has scrupulously examined the former king's actions can entertain any doubt. . . . But we must first consider the general interest." And he then went on to argue that the only unarguable decision would be that of the electorate itself. "How that mass of people commands respect," he continued. "How august a character it gives everything it does! . . . Then there can be no accusation of injustice, of partiality, of pusillanimity made against the Convention even among the members of the British

Parliament or among the friends of liberty. . . . Whenever we can, within one day, bring so many million men to make a decision . . . there can be no anarchy."[22]

Pétion, the Mayor of Paris, who had been moving toward the center, repeated the argument the next day with even greater vigor: "Louis has come off the throne; his entire life accuses him. . . . Louis, I will not look at whether you are guilty, that is a problem which no longer needs to be resolved; facts crowd around you and overwhelm you. . . . Your whole life is one long outrage against liberty: always a liar, always a plotter, cowardice and perfidy have accompanied your every act," he said, and having thus raged against the ex-King to match the best of the Montagne, Pétion went on: "I ask that Louis be condemned to die, and that this decree be sent out to be ratified by the voters."[23] This was yet another degree of obfuscation: Brissot had asked that the electorate, not the Convention, decide on the penalty; Pétion wanted to give the Convention a chance to vote for Louis's death, thus making itself look good to the sans-culottes, while the proposed ratification, which would almost certainly not be forthcoming, precluded any actual execution.

At first glance, the Girondins' dodge looks an ideal solution, one which would allow the Convention happily to have it both ways. In fact, as Robespierre was quick to point out, the most likely result would be a civil war. While substantial elements of the population undoubtedly sided with the Montagne, other, perhaps larger groups were very much opposed to the ex-King's execution: sending the decision down to the voters' level was therefore extremely likely to end in widespread local violence. It also invalidated the theory on which the legitimacy of the Convention rested, that of representative (as opposed to direct) government; and neither the Marais nor the group around Robespierre wanted this to happen, since it would support Marat's claim according to which it was always up to the people itself to decide any issue, thus, in effect, giving all power to the Paris sans-culottes, and to Marat himself.

It was Robespierre who led the assault against the plebiscite in an unusually passionate speech: "The sensitivity which sacrifices innocence to crime is a cruel one," he said.

When clemency is shown to tyranny, it is barbaric.
Citizens, it is of the supreme importance of the public weal I must

remind you. Why must we be concerned with Louis? It is not a desire for vengeance, which would be unworthy of the nation, it is the need to consolidate liberty and the public tranquillity by punishing the tyrant. . . . The voice of the alarmed Fatherland urges you to take the only decision in which it can find reassurance. . . .

I have proved that the proposal to submit Louis Capet's fate to the voters would bring about a civil war. If I cannot save my country, I wish it known at least . . . that I have tried to preserve it from the calamities which threaten it. I ask that the Convention declare Louis guilty and worthy of death.[24]

It was clear enough; but the feeling of the Montagne may have been better expressed by Anacharsis Cloots. Widely and rightly considered to be a clown, Cloots was a rich German established in Paris who in 1789 embraced the cause of the Revolution and, although a figure of fun, managed to get himself elected to the Convention. Having started out as a Brissotin, he joined the most extreme section of the Montagne out of rage at not being invited to Mme Roland's salon. Despite all that, something in his speech touched many of the Deputies.

"Let us hurry . . . and judge a monster whose head, as it falls, will bring all the crowns of Europe down into the dust," he said. "Some want to scare us with their big words about the aristocrats' Europe . . . as if, by taking measures which will speed up the world revolution, we did not have on our side the Europe of the sans-culottes, the sans-culottes [of] posterity, and our own sans-culottes' conscience."[25] Not eloquence of a high degree, but a powerful argument. The Republic, which had just conquered and annexed Savoy and Belgium, meant to be universal. It seemed evident that the peoples of the Continent, once they heard about the fall and death of one king, would rise against their own. The way to safety for France lay in the spread of revolution, and this could best be speeded up by the execution of Louis XVI.

The debate ended on January 7, 1793. On January 14 the vote began. Three questions were to be answered: first, whether the ex-King was guilty; second, whether to send the decision on sentencing to the voters; third, what the sentence was to be. By the fifteenth, the first question had been answered affirmatively by a virtually unanimous Convention: 693 out of 749 Deputies had, out loud, voted yes; there can be no doubt that this expressed their genuinely felt belief. The next vote, about whether to consult the electorate, was decisively against, although by a smaller majority: 424 to 287. The Girondins had been defeated by the Montagne and the Marais. That left the key question: was Louis XVI to be executed?

The vote on this began at eight on the evening of January 16; it closed exactly twenty-four hours later, many of the Deputies having not only pronounced for or against the death sentence, for or against its being suspended, but also giving the reasons for their decision; and throughout, the crowd filling the tribunes howled, screamed menaces, demanded the death penalty, and threatened those who opposed it. The outcome, under those circumstances, might seem utterly predictable. It was not: although the Convention did vote for the King's execution, it was by a plurality of only five votes, 366 out of 721. Moreover, an error in addition having been detected, it soon turned out that four of these votes were for a suspended sentence, so that it was in fact by a single vote that the death of Louis XVI was decided. It should be mentioned at this point that his cousin, the former duc d'Orléans, had voted for the death sentence.

This result was so very close that, the next day, an additional vote was taken about whether or not the sentence should be suspended. This time, the numbers for an immediate death rose and the suspension was rejected by 383 to 310. Now it was time to notify the condemned man.

On January 20, around two in the afternoon, a deputation arrived at the Temple and told Louis XVI that he was to die. Calmly, the ex-King asked to be given three days, to be allowed to see his family alone, and to be sent a non-juring priest. He was refused the first request but granted the other two, and at six the deputation returned with Madame Elisabeth's confessor, the abbé Edgeworth de Firmont. After a long private talk with the abbé, Louis XVI rejoined his family, who had been told of the sentence, though the little Dauphin was too young really to understand. Great efforts were apparently made by all to avoid a display of emotion; and in order to spare himself and his wife the pain of saying good-bye, Louis promised Marie Antoinette he would see her again briefly in the morning. He then returned to his room, ate his supper — two chicken breasts and cookies accompanied by Malaga wine — went to bed, and was awakened at five in the morning. After listening to a mass celebrated by the abbé Edgeworth, he decided not to see the Queen after all; asked to be allowed to cut off his hair himself, but was refused; and at eight-thirty was fetched by Santerre. Together the two men got into a carriage.

The weather on this twenty-first of January was rainy and foggy. It took the carriage an hour and a half to drive from the Temple to the Place de la Révolution (today Place de la Concorde), where the guillotine was set up. Some eighty thousand men armed with guns and pikes were lined up along the way; twenty thousand more, Parisians come to see the execution, waited silently around the scaffold. Shortly after ten, the carriage stopped at the foot of the scaffold. Louis came out, took off his coat and waistcoat; he had asked not to have his hands tied, but was refused, so the executioner now tied them. Then, with the abbé Edgeworth helping him, he went up the steps of the scaffold as the drums began beating. Once on the platform, he tried to speak but could not be heard over the drums; he is thought to have said: "I am innocent. I forgive the authors of my death and pray that France will not have to expiate my blood." Almost immediately, however, he was seen to kneel down and place his head on the guillotine. At ten-twenty, the blade fell. The executioner held up the still bleeding head, and the crowd shouted: "Long live the nation! Long live the Republic! Long live Liberty and Equality!" Away at the Temple, Marie Antoinette, her face awash with tears, knelt down before her eight-year-old son and saluted him as the new King of France.

The monarchy in France had already been dead for more than five months when Louis XVI ascended the scaffold, but as long as the King lived, albeit in prison, something of the royal mystique remained in the popular psyche. Unlikely though it seemed in January 1793, some felt there might one day be a restoration, and then Louis would have proved that he was God-chosen after all. When the blade of the guillotine came down, it not only ended a man's life, it killed the very concept of kingship. The French were eventually to have two emperors and three more kings before fully settling for the Republic, but none of them partook of the inevitability that alone can secure thrones; all except one[*] were deposed.

---

[*] Louis XVIII died on the throne in 1824; he had reigned for nine years.

Even more important, the execution of Louis XVI had a meaning far greater than that of Charles I because it seemed a logical step in the progress of human politics. The King of England had been condemned by his rebellious subjects, but the concept of monarchy was not really at stake. Whether or not Cromwell actually meant to become King Oliver I, his death was swiftly followed by a restoration. When Louis XVI died, all divine-right rulers lost their sanctity. From then on, they lived in fear of their subjects; and, except in England, a republic came to seem the natural regime for a free people. Saint Just's pitiless definition, "All kings are rebels and usurpers," became not a shocking attack, but an accurate description. It was admittedly, again, quite a while before France itself settled on a lasting republic: in 1804, Napoleon became Emperor, thus apparently ending the great experiment. Then, the Republic of 1848 lasted less than four years. It was not until 1871 that the French Republic became firmly ensconced. But the idea had been let loose in 1793; the modern world, however slowly, was ready to be born.

Oddly enough, and in spite of their speeches, most of the Deputies felt little or no personal animus against Louis XVI. Robespierre himself is said to have felt rather sorry for him. But they all knew that if the new regime was to last, if it was to spread to the rest of Europe, a great demonstration must be made. In that sense, Louis XVI was punished, less for his behavior (culpable as that was) than for his very existence.

What the Girondins at least did not realize, however, was that all those speeches denouncing "Louis Capet," insincere though they often were, had an enormous impact; predictably, the net effect of the King's trial was not to consolidate the Revolution but to speed it up. While the September massacres had been unreasoning, a spasm of violence, the death of Louis XVI began what might be called a process of rational terror, a cool, calculating use of murder. That, too, is a technique that has been well learned ever since; here again, the seeds of the modern world have been sown.

Beside the chief victim himself, those who suffered most from the trial and its outcome were the Girondins: they were now faced with radicalized public opinion and an Assembly leaning toward the Montagne; and, of course, the extreme left, having defeated them on this crucial issue, rushed to the attack with all the more vigor. On January 21 the Committee of General Safety was reconstituted, and, to everyone's surprise, since, after all, the makeup of the Convention had not changed, its new majority was composed of Montagnards. It was a clear indication that the Marais now supported the extreme left, and all the more important that the Committee was in charge of the police and the courts: the way was open again to the creation of special revolutionary courts.

In the press as well, the attacks against the Girondins continued fast and furiously, with Marat naturally in the lead. In December he printed his "Observations on the new perfidy of the Roland faction. The Penelope Roland is Regent of the realm."[26] Here, Marat means that, Penelope-like, Mme Roland was undoing secretly the work done overtly by the Revolution. In January, he offered his highly colored (and thoroughly libelous) description of "The life and mores of the woman Roland,"[27] going on to outline the "Dreadful plot of the leaders of the Roland faction as denounced by the friend of the people to the Convention."[28] The emphasis on Mme Roland was clever: she was already highly unpopular. "She loved all those who shared her opinions and hated those who did not," a friendly observer noted. "She saw talent, probity, virtue, enlightenment only in Roland and in her admirers; elsewhere she saw only baseness, ignorance, or treachery. She had inspired this extreme partisanship to all [the Girondins] and that had contributed not a little to alienate people and create hatred."[29] Add to that the obvious parallel with Marie Antoinette — a strong, domineering woman with a weak husband — and it is easy to see just how the attacks against her were so effective. Why end the monarchy if it was to be replaced by a new royal couple?

At the same time all the policies with which the Gironde was identified were unraveling. One of the consequences of Louis XVI's execution was a European coalition against France. On February 1, jumping before it was pushed, the Convention declared war on Great Britain and Holland, and, faced with so many powerful enemies, it also decreed the enrollment of 300,000 men. At that, Brittany and the Vendée, which had been smoldering quietly, burst into flame. It was no longer a question of local riots: the peasants, who were deeply attached to the Church and were horrified by the King's execution, were not about to fight for the Republic. On March 4, 1793, Cholet rose rather than provide the army with its quota of "volunteers." At that point, the rebels sought leaders and found them among the local aristocracy and gentry. Troops were formed, then small armies, and the civil war began. Not only did the two provinces refuse to obey the government, they actually set out to replace it by force. Within the first few weeks, major towns fell to the rebels, who advanced toward Angers. It seemed not unlikely that other parts of the country, encouraged by the example of the Vendée, might also rise against the Convention.

Concurrently, the army under Dumouriez underwent its first defeat at Neerwinden, in the Netherlands. Of course, that was still deep in conquered territory. But the rapidly increasing persecution of those ancien régime officers who were still serving and the dismay felt by some of the troops because of the recent political developments both helped to disorganize the fighting forces further. Then, on March 19, the troops sent to reestablish order in the Vendée were defeated at Pont-Charrault.

In Paris itself, life was rapidly becoming even more difficult than it had been. As the printing of the assignats speeded up — 800 million livres' worth were printed on February 1 alone — their value fell, from 72[*] in December to 51 in January and 43 in April. Because of the spreading civil war, the price of bread went up even faster. So far, the Revolution, instead of bringing about a new Golden Age, was making it increasingly hard to survive for the poor and the lower middle class, among whom unemployment was now widespread.

The result was, very naturally, that the frustrated and angry Parisians, many of whom already thought the Convention far too moderate because it had not ordered mass executions, food rationing, and a price freeze, now turned completely against it. By March, Thibaudeau, the moderate left-wing Deputy, noted:

> The Commune of Paris and the Jacobin Club were in open rivalry with the Convention and threatened the Girondins. The armies' defeats . . . and the failure of Robespierre's [earlier] motion to expel the Bourbons[**] gave rise to accusations of treason. People asked that suspicious groups [any, that is, not fervently endorsing the Revolution] be disarmed, that a new extraordinary tribunal be created. The section of the Tuileries decided to send to the other forty-eight sections a petition in which the

---

[*] 100 livres assignat were worth 72 gold livres, that is.

[**] Robespierre meant thus to get rid of Philippe Egalité, whom he greatly disliked; but his motion did not pass.

Convention was asked whether it thought itself fit to save the Fatherland. . . . The fermentation was extreme.

The Committee of General Defense [on March 27] sent for the ministers, the municipality, and the département to agree on the measures capable of preventing the impending riots. Before this began, Marat said these remarkable words: "It is not true that the sovereignty of the people is indivisible. Each commune of the Republic is sovereign on its territory when there is a crisis, and the people may take whatever measures their welfare requires."*

The Convention decided to tell the petitioners that it would save the Fatherland, but that it held the Paris Commune responsible for its own safety. This responsibility hardly worried those who controlled the Commune.[30]

A month earlier, at the end of February, in fact, the Commune had allowed riots to rage for two days; a new, solid currency and price controls were then among the rioters' demands. Eventually the National Guard, which still had an essentially middle-class membership, restored a measure of order. But Paris was obviously ready to erupt again, and the Convention's attitude toward the Commune showed clearly that it dared not oppose a new insurrection.

Again and again, through March and April, Paris rose against the government. These constant riots, together with the defeats abroad and the spread of the rebellion in the western parts of the country, transformed the Convention. Once again, the Revolution was developing its own, unexpected logic.

Originally, the Montagne was almost as strongly opposed as the Gironde to the installation of a controlled economy; but now, under pressure, it moved rapidly toward support of a centrally controlled plan, and the Marais followed. At the same time, what looked like an impending collapse — defeats, civil war, a nonfunctioning economy — transformed the moderates: they realized that the Revolution could be saved only by extreme measures, and so they joined the Montagne in a series of key votes.

This trend was already visible when, on March 9, the Convention made

---

* Marat was thus claiming that the Commune, not the Convention, was sovereign in Paris; it was within the Commune, of course, that his supporters were to be found.

two key decisions. First, it decided to send its own members, in teams of two, throughout the provinces to speed the call-up of the 300,000 men, and it gave these "representatives on mission" unlimited powers. These the representatives used in full: they ruled their areas just as they chose, created courts, had their decisions carried out, arrested people, seized property, even ordered capital executions. This move was necessary because France still functioned according to the decentralizing Constitution of 1791, which had set up the provincial administration so that it was locally controlled and virtually unresponsive to orders from Paris. Faced with the current crisis, national policies obviously had to be implemented fast and thoroughly.

As its second action that day, the Convention, at Danton's urging, went on to set up a new, Revolutionary Tribunal whose decisions were without appeal, whose sentences would be carried out immediately. This Tribunal would be composed of judges, jurors, and district attorneys appointed directly by the Assembly. It was to judge all counterrevolutionary activities, all attempts against the unity and indivisibility of the Republic and against the safety of the state, and all attempts to restore the monarchy. The Deputies then passed the laws that would make its work easier. On March 18 they voted the death penalty for anyone said to be an émigré and all non-juring priests. On March 19 they decided further that anyone wearing a white cockade, or exhibiting any other sign of "rebellion," would be deemed an émigré. On the twenty-eighth they decided that all the above laws applied also to minors, although girls under fourteen would merely be exiled. On March 29 it became compulsory to list on a panel outside each house the names of those residing inside, while to advocate the dissolution of the Convention became punishable by death; but then, to restore order, the Convention also voted the death penalty for those whose writings defended murder and looting. And to make sure no time would be wasted, the Deputies, when they learned that only ten of the twenty-four proposed jurors of the Revolutionary Tribunal had agreed to serve, decided that ten would be enough.

Now death became the standard punishment. On March 18 the Convention had also decreed capital punishment for anyone advocating theories subversive of property. This, in fact, was supposed to stop the *Enragés,* the "maddened ones." A group of Parisians, mostly of lower-middle class origin, led by Jacques Roux, a former priest, and Jacques Hébert, a journalist whose paper specialized in the use of scatological language, the Enragés, in spite of their name, were serious and rather dull; but the reforms they demanded were quite enough to terrify the Convention. Their program, in fact, is a preview of communism some seventy-five years before it was invented by Karl Marx: price controls on all foodstuffs, government seizure of all grain, a special very high tax on the rich, automatic death sentences for all hoarders and speculators, government control of the economy, and the provision of work and a minimum income to all. All these points were just what the bourgeoisie did not want. Of course, the Convention never considered implementing any of the Enragés' proposals; but the fact that they had been made showed that the margin in which the government could still function was extremely narrow, and that normal standards of humanity could no longer apply. Indeed, it was Marat, that tireless denouncer of tyranny, who proclaimed on April 6: "The moment has come to organize a temporary despotism of liberty to crush the despotism of kings."[31]

That very day, the government was reorganized. By delegating most of its executive power to the newly reorganized nine-man Committee of Public Safety, the Convention lost much of its power. From then on, the committee worked directly with the ministers, who became little more than secretaries: all the decisions as to policy and implementation were made by the committee. It was the committee who made appointments, ordered arrests, and raised men and provisions for the armies; and when legislation was required, the cowed Convention did what it was told. That, in turn, led to yet another escalation of the Revolution: for the first time, a highly concentrated, highly effective executive had been set up, and Danton's membership in the committee made sure that it would adopt extreme positions. Indeed, there was little dissent even within the Convention: the situation was so desperate that anything seemed permissible if it was a question of saving the Republic.

Even the Revolutionary Tribunal was no more than an arm of the Convention — and therefore of the committee. It began its functions on April 2. Revolutionary committees for every section — that is, the entire country — had been instituted on March 21 to identify and denounce all counterrevolutionaries. That the provender of suspicious persons would be abundant was ensured by a law which offered 100 livres for every denunciation.

It was in this overheated atmosphere that Paris heard about the treachery of the Republic's most successful general. Dumouriez had great ambitions that he felt were not properly recognized in Paris. He had also watched his army, eroded by lack of funds and discipline, wither away; he concluded that the way to his ambition was through an alliance with the countries he had been fighting. First, on March 27, he issued a proclamation denouncing the anarchy brought about by the Revolution; the Convention immediately sent the war minister and four representatives on mission to arrest him. Instead, Dumouriez arrested them and ordered his troops to march on Paris. Like Lafayette eight months earlier, he was ignored by his troops; and so on April 4 he went over to the enemy, accompanied by several of his subordinates, including Louis Philippe d'Orléans, Philippe Egalité's son.

To Dumouriez's first proclamation there was an immediate result: on April 2 an insurrectional committee of the Paris sections was formed, which demanded more extreme measures; also on that day Philippe Egalité was himself arrested. When the news that the French armies on the Rhine had been defeated as well reached the capital, the atmosphere grew still more volcanic, especially since the civil war was at the same time growing in intensity. The republican armies in the west — Brittany and the Vendée — found themselves fighting the kind of guerrilla warfare in which small groups of rebels would suddenly appear at the edge of a forest, kill the van of a regiment, and vanish; in which the people in towns supposedly controlled by the Republic were in fact helping the enemies. Then, too, there were pitched battles, after several of which the republican troops retreated in great disorder, regrouping late and sometimes not at all.

Nor was that the extent of it. In major cities like Lyons, an internecine warfare opposed revolutionaries and counterrevolutionaries. Heated battles between antagonistic groups of citizens took place in the streets; as a consequence, economic life virtually stopped. Even in smaller villages, large bodies of troops often had to be called by the representatives to quell the riots that erupted when men refused to be conscripted into the army; on occasion, the representatives themselves were forced to beat a hasty retreat.

As for the army itself, it seemed hardly to hold together. "The indiscipline of the troops had reached a climax," wrote Thibaudeau, one of the representatives on mission. "Entire battalions mutinied, sometimes because they had not been paid, sometimes because they wanted a raise. . . . In Niort, I myself arrested, in front of several assembled battalions, an officer who was preaching disobedience. . . . Every day, the sans-culotte generals denounced their more moderate colleagues; insubordination was general even among the soldiers who, out of ignorance or cowardice, kept shouting they were betrayed."[32]

All this affected Paris, the fount of the Revolution; there, events continued to speed up. On April 5 Marat was elected president of the Jacobin Club, a sharp blow to Robespierre and a presage of more uprisings to come; three days later the section of the Bon Conseil denounced twenty-two Girondin Deputies as counterrevolutionaries. This was no mere rhetoric: counterrevolutionaries were being sent to the guillotine in increasing numbers. That month in Paris alone nine men died solely for their opinions.

On April 11 the Convention, in an effort to pacify the Parisians, decreed that the assignat's value would be fixed by law, thus making depreciation theoretically impossible (although, as usual in these circumstances, the law proved useless). At the same time, on the twelfth, the Convention moved boldly to defend itself. Marat had been championing the primacy of the people, and their Commune, over the representatives in the Convention. This, if accepted, meant the end of the Convention, so, in an effort at reasserting itself, it voted Marat's arrest and his trial before the Revolutionary Tribunal. Robespierre followed this up on the twenty-fourth with a speech in which he denounced the Enragés and Marat and defended the rights of property, while trying to propitiate the more reasonable of the extreme revolutionaries. "Every citizen," he said, "has the right to enjoy and to dispose of that portion of goods recognized him by the law. The right of property is limited, like all the others, by the obligation to respect the rights of others. It can endanger neither the safety nor the liberty nor the existence nor the property of other citizens. All possession, all traffic which violates this principle, is immoral."[33]

It did not do much good. Marat, who had gone into hiding, had already reappeared on April 23; he was tried on the same day that Robespierre gave his speech, the twenty-fourth, and was promptly acquitted by the Revolutionary Tribunal, which faithfully reflected the atmosphere in the capital. On May 1 the Faubourg Saint-Antoine sent a delegation to the Convention: that birthplace of the Revolution demanded a forced tax on the rich and price controls, and there was nothing to do except give in. The Montagne, now converted to supporting a controlled economy, got the Convention to decree a sliding-scale type of price control for all grain; but the next day, in a move sure to speed up the already rapid rate of inflation, it also ordered the printing of 1.2 billion livres' worth of assignats. With taxes virtually uncollectible, the war somehow had to be paid for; printing money was the easiest way to do it.

It was clear, however, that dangers remained on both the right (that is, the civil war) *and* the left. The decree of accusation against Marat was an attempt to frighten the sans-culottes: even before that, to comfort them and solidify his growing power, Robespierre on April 10 had escalated his attacks against the Girondins. "In the sitting of the Convention on the tenth [of April]," a reporter noted:

Maximilien Robespierre denounced several traitors by name. After having gone over the constant efforts through which the leaders of the National Assembly had opposed the revolution of August 10 . . . he showed how they had soon seized power, handing offices out to their creatures, bringing their friends Servan, Clavière, and Roland into the ministry and entrusted that same Roland with numerous millions that he used to finance pamphlets against the Revolution. . . .

He denounced them further as having planned to flee with the royal family in September [1792].[34]

Obviously, these accusations were all nonsense, but in the climate of April 1793 they were thoroughly believable. By then, it was becoming an established fact among the Parisian sans-culottes that the Girondins were all crypto-royalists working in secret to betray the Revolution.

By the end of May the Jacobin line had become even harder: it was no longer enough to denounce the Girondins, they must be disposed of. On the twenty-seventh a newspaper, the *Sans-Culottes,* warned: "You are sleeping, Republicans, and your enemies are at work. They fill France with lies and hypocrisies and you satisfy yourselves with merely denouncing them before [the Convention]. . . . As soon as you have purged the government of those ambitious men who seek to return you to your ancient slavery, then all men will back you.''[35] By then, the lines had already been drawn. On May 22 Brissot, in an open letter to his electors, had demanded the dissolution of the Paris Commune and of the Jacobin clubs everywhere; four days later, in a most unusual show of agreement, Robespierre and Marat called for an insurrection of the people against the Gironde.

The stakes were clear: either the Gironde managed to cobble together a majority within the Convention and a reliable armed force outside it, or they would share the fate of the King they had brought down. In fact, it was no contest: the Marais, appalled by the catastrophes everywhere, thoroughly convinced of the need for extreme measures, was very familiar with the Girondins' incompetence; and no army near Paris was ready to back them. Thus, when Robespierre took the risk of calling for an uprising — the Girondins would have had his head if it had failed — he knew very well that he could not lose. Typically, however, what he called for was a sort of moral insurrection, which would bring such pressure to bear on the Convention that it would, of itself, eliminate the Girondins, as opposed to a direct attack on the Convention. He knew from experience, after all, that popular revolts often have unexpected and unwelcome effects.

Much the same attitude prevailed within the Commune and the Département of Paris; but already an insurrectionary committee had formed at the former archbishop's palace. On the morning of May 31 the bells tolled to signal the beginning of the rising. Several of the sections refused to be involved, and there were delays, but at 5:00 P.M. the Convention, now sitting at the Tuileries, was encircled by a few thousand fanatics. The deputation they sent the Convention carried a petition: it asked for the arrest of two ministers, of the twenty-two Deputies who had called for submitting Louis XVI's sentence to the people, and of the twelve members, all Girondins, of the committee recently set up to investigate the Commune. It also wanted the creation of an army of sans-culottes to pursue and punish all suspected persons, the institution of a tax on the rich, and the disenfranchisement of all non–sans-culottes electors. Bravely, the Convention resisted all these demands because it felt that its members should be inviolable, and it merely dismissed the committee of twelve. It was a major defeat for the Montagne and their Parisian supporters.

All that changed on the next day, however. By then, the revolutionary forces were largely in control of the city, and they proceeded to make arbitrary arrests, that of Mme Roland among others (her husband had already fled). The day after that, Sunday, June 2, was decisive. The revolutionary leaders had had time to organize their forces; they had also been joined by many workers whose day off this was. By the early afternoon, the Convention was surrounded by 80,000 men; 150 cannons were pointed at its section of the Palace: the great confrontation between Paris and the Convention was under way.

Around five, a few Deputies tried to leave the Palace; they were refused passage. At that, the entire Convention — less Robespierre and the Montagne, who stayed in their seats — presented itself at the door to the courtyard. Henriot, the commander of the Parisians, asked the Convention's president whether he was ready to turn over the twenty-two Girondins to the crowd; when the president refused to answer, Henriot gave his artillery the order to prepare for shooting. At that, the Deputies went back inside and tried to go out the other way, through the gardens; there, too, the Palace was guarded; so, returning to their hall, they voted the arrest of the Girondins.

There was perhaps not much else to be done; but the effect was great and immediate. "It was supposedly to protect the Girondins from the fury of the crowd that they were imprisoned," Thibaudeau, himself then a Deputy, lamented. "It would have been a hundred times better if the people had slaughtered them in their seats: at least the Convention would have preserved its independence and its honor . . . but when it mutilated itself, it gave all power to a faction and threw itself into the most shameful slavery."[36] Thibaudeau, of course, is right: from June 2 on, the terrified Marais followed the impulse — not to say the orders — of the Montagne: the price of resisting it was first imprisonment, then death, with the Revolutionary Tribunal making short work of the accused. There was, however, another side to this, and Napoleon saw it perfectly.

"The events of May 31," he said, "deprived France of greatly talented men who were also warmly attached to liberty and to the principles of the Revolution. That catastrophe was bound to cause sorrow among far-seeing men, but it should not have surprised them. It was impossible for a Convention that had to save France from so critical a situation to function when it harbored two parties that were passionate and unreconcilable.''[37] Given the attacks of the Montagne against the Gironde, given the desperate state of the country, one of the two parties was bound to perish. The Gironde, under whose leadership the current catastrophes had happened, obviously could not win. While it is easy to sympathize with the men and women who late that summer lost their lives on the scaffold, it is also fair to point out that they had largely brought about their own fall. When Mme Roland said — as she is believed to have done — just before her execution, "Liberty! What crimes are committed in your name!" she left a ringing cry to posterity; but she understood no more at the end than she did at the height of her power.

CHAPTER FIFTEEN

The Paroxysm

. : . : . :

ON June 4, 1793, Marat praised the Convention, which had, he said, at last "woken up from its lethargy."[1] Indeed, the work done by that body within the next thirteen months was prodigious. Lazare Carnot, a former artillery captain, took charge as a member of the Committee of Public Safety, of all military matters. Under his impetus the armies were reorganized and began, once again, to win battles. The economy, put in a straitjacket, served the Revolution. The last traces of the ancien régime were forever eradicated. In that year France entered the age in which it has lived ever since, even if many of the achievements of the Revolution remained to be codified by Napoleon.

Marat himself was murdered by Charlotte Corday on July 13. This young woman — she was just twenty-five — who came from an intensely Catholic and royalist family, loathed the Revolution; her two brothers had emigrated and were serving in the princes' army. She decided now that it was her turn to help the cause. Although unquestionably courageous, she was obviously not very bright: to her, all evil was incarnate in Marat; it was his incendiary words that had deluded the rest of the French. Once he was gone, she thought, the people would come to their senses and all would be well. So she bought herself a knife, left Rouen, where she lived, and came to Paris. There she ascertained Marat's address, made her way inside, claiming she had knowledge of a plot against the Republic, and found him in his bath, working on the next day's article. Without a moment's hesitation, as she talked to distract him, she took out her knife and plunged it into his breast. It was perhaps a not unfitting end for a man who had so often demanded that his opponents be killed; but what the naive young woman did not realize was that she had merely made Robespierre's life easier by removing his great rival.

After the arrest of the Girondins, a new constitutional committee was named. It finished its work within three weeks, and the document it produced officially gave the government to an all-powerful Assembly. It specified that the state must help the poor and the unemployed; it guaranteed religious liberty; it stated that the people had the right to revolt whenever it felt oppressed by the government. Finally, the constitution was to be accepted or refused by the electorate.

All through July, therefore, the people were asked to vote. They did so in very small numbers: 1,801,918 were in favor; 11,610 opposed; most of the voters prudently abstained. In any event, it hardly mattered: the constitution was supposed to come into effect whenever the war ended, but in fact it was never applied at all. Instead, even juring priests were forbidden to say mass, all other religious practices were banned, all liberties suspended. The Reign of Terror had begun.

It went slowly at first. Throughout that summer and fall, in Paris, the Revolutionary Tribunal passed an average of fifteen death sentences a month. In November, it condemned sixty-seven people; in February, the number was up to a hundred sixteen, by March, to a hundred fifty-five, and in July nearly eight hundred people were guillotined. When, on July 28, 1794, the Terror ended with the fall[*] of Robespierre — who had been governing France through his control of the Committee of Public Safety — the Tribunal had been responsible for 2,585 deaths, a number that shocked contemporaries, although, again, by twentieth-century standards, it seems amazingly moderate. Hitler, Stalin, and their many imitators had far greater numbers of people killed in a single day.

What mattered more than numbers, however, was the atmosphere — an atmosphere in which no one felt safe — and the results. France, which seemed about to fall to its enemies, domestic and foreign, in May 1793, had been saved a year later, even if it was at a tremendous cost. Those who lived through those fourteen months never forgot them. "In France, under the Terror," Thibaudeau wrote,

---

[*] Some hundred and six Robespierre followers were guillotined in the days following his fall.

no one was safe; it flew above all heads and chopped them off haphazardly, as arbitrarily and rapidly as the scythe of Death. The Convention and the people also paid the price. Danton, Camille Desmoulins, and the Paris municipality perished on that same scaffold where they had sent the Gironde, and the people applauded the end of the executioners and that of the victims equally. . . . It seemed as if the only way to avoid prison or the scaffold was to send others there. . . .

Just as, in ordinary times, one tried to rise, so, in this time of calamity, one tried to lower oneself so as not to be remembered. . . . One hid not just one's birth and one's wealth but also the advantages . . . received from nature or a good education. . . . One gave up costume, elegance, manners, cleanliness, ease of life, politeness, and proper behavior so as not to excite the envy of those who lacked all that.

The Convention itself became . . . a passive instrument of the Terror. On the ruins of its independence there arose that monstrous dictatorship so famous under the name of Committee of Public Safety. . . . The high benches of the Montagne . . . were crowded, the right side [of the hall] was deserted. . . . Those who were most afraid took no specific place but kept moving about . . . while the most prudent [of the Deputies] never sat down at all.[2]

Indeed, no one at that time could boast a charmed life, except, perhaps, the members of the committee; priests, aristocrats, the rich, the Deputies, all became fodder for the guillotine and were condemned, as we have seen, not for what they had done, but for what they were. Still, one category of men stood in particular danger: anyone who had played a major role in the Revolution, but was not part of the newly powerful elite, was doomed. This applied to scientists like Condorcet and to political leaders like Danton or Desmoulins; Bailly, the first Mayor of Paris, the man who greeted Louis XVI at the city gates on July 17, 1789, was taken like all the others. The more illustrious these men were, the worse they were treated.

"The time when [Bailly] was to be taken from his cell to the tribunal was a quarter of an hour's recreation for the jailers," a prisoner reported. "He was called in a mocking way and when he hurried to obey so as to end those shouts, the jailers pushed him the other way, shoved him back and forth, shouting: 'So there's Bailly! Bailly to you! Take Bailly!' and they howled with laughter at the sober mien presented by the wretched man in the midst of this dance of cannibals.''[3] The point was, indeed, not merely to kill, but to demean as well, something the crowds around the guillotine kept firmly in mind.

Bailly was arrested in October and beheaded in November; but earlier still, in the summer, it had occurred to the Committee of Public Safety that it held an even better-known, an even more exemplary person: Marie Antoinette herself. On July 1 her son was taken away from her in the midst of scenes of mutual despair; she never saw him again. Indeed, the Dauphin never saw any member of his family after that day. Raised by a semi-illiterate cobbler named Simon, kept much of the time in a damp, lightless room, he soon became ill, most probably of tuberculosis, and died, in deep secrecy, in June 1795.*

The former Queen, at least, had her daughter and her sister-in-law with whom to share her pain; but not for long. On August 1 the Convention decreed that she was to be judged by the Revolutionary Tribunal, and to be moved immediately to a cell in the Conciergerie, the medieval fortress-prison on the Ile de la Cité.** Madame Royale, the Queen's fifteen-year-old daughter, described what happened then:

> On August 2, at two in the morning, they came to wake us so as to read my mother the decree of the Convention . . . ordering her to be taken to the Conciergerie so that she could be tried. She heard this decree being read without emotion and without saying a word to them. My aunt [Madame Elisabeth] and I immediately asked to go with my mother, but we were not granted this favor. While she packed her clothes, the municipal guards kept watch over her; she was even forced to dress in front of them. . . .
>
> After having kissed me tenderly and told me to be courageous, to take good care of my aunt and to obey her as a second mother, my

---

* The Dauphin's grandfather, grandmother, and an uncle on his father's side, several close relatives on his mother's side, and his elder brother had all died of tuberculosis. In spite of subsequent legends to the contrary, there can be no real doubt that the Dauphin did, in fact, die on June 8, 1795, in the Temple. His death was kept a secret, however, so as not to create a stir at a time when a royalist party was reappearing.

** Her cell, which still exists, can be visited. Much of her furniture from the Temple apartments can be seen at the Musée Carnavalet.

mother . . . took my aunt in her arms and recommended her children to her. I could answer nothing because I was so frightened, knowing I was seeing her for the last time. . . . As she went out, she struck her head on the lintel, having forgotten to stoop; they asked her if she had hurt herself. "Oh, no," she said, "nothing can hurt me now."[4]

Nothing more happened for a month. In her small cell at the Conciergerie, the ravaged and sick woman waited for her life to end. Hardly able to eat, she also suffered from frequent menstrual hemorrhages, which weakened her further; but she still retained something of her old magic. The jailer's dazzled wife took great risks to improve the quality of her food and to find her better sheets and less rough chemises. On September 3 a commission from the Tribunal came to question her: they wanted to prove that she had betrayed France — which, indeed, she had — but, unaware of the facts, the specific crimes of which they accused her, such as having sent millions to her brother, the Emperor, were purely imaginary; she defended herself with firmness and dignity.

The outcome, however, was never in doubt: Marie Antoinette was too exemplary to be found innocent. Indeed, she was included in the new Law of Suspected Persons that the Convention passed on September 3: it referred to the Revolutionary Tribunal (now grown to four parts, so that four trials could be held concurrently) not only all suspected persons, a vague category if ever there was one, but also the husbands, wives, fathers, mothers, sons, daughters, brothers, and sisters of the émigrés, a category that obviously included the former Queen. Still, she was better known than most, her trial was to serve as a great public demonstration of the Republic's power, and even the most unjust show trials require an appearance of guilt.

On October 3 the Committee of Public Safety decided that Marie Antoinette would be tried within the week; but then, on the fifth, objections came from an unexpected source. Antoine Fouquier-Tinville, the district attorney who was known as the "Provider of the Guillotine," complained that he had no written proofs of guilt at all, and added that, under these circumstances, he was most unwilling to start the trial. On the tenth he asked to be given all the documents used in the trial of Louis XVI, in the hope that they would implicate the former Queen as well.

In the meantime, on October 6, a separate attempt to vilify the Queen was made, based largely on the beliefs resulting from the obscene pamphlets that had circulated so widely between 1789 and 1792. To people like Fouquier-Tinville, Marie Antoinette was a nymphomaniac and lesbian whose lusts were insatiable; it was that well-established legend he now decided to use. There was not much sense in looking for the Queen's supposed sex partners, who were either dead, like Mme de Lamballe, or safely abroad; but there was the Dauphin, who was only eight years old, had been separated from his family, and was now in the sole care of Simon and his wife: it would obviously be easy to get him to say almost anything at all.

This is what he is supposed to have admitted under questioning, as set down in an official declaration: " . . . Says further that, having several times been surprised in his bed by Simon and his wife while committing indecencies harmful to his health [masturbating], he admitted that he had been taught these pernicious habits by his mother and his aunt, that several times they had enjoyed watching him perform and that it often happened when he spent the night as all three shared the same bed." In an attached (but unsigned) note, the questioners go on: "that, according to the way the child explains it, his mother once called him to her, that they copulated, and that as a result he had swollen testicles, which the Citizeness Simon noted and for which he still wears a bandage;[*] that his mother asked him never to mention this; that this act has been repeated several times since."[5] The next day a committee that included David, the painter, interrogated Madame Elisabeth and Madame Royale about this; both denied indignantly that there was any truth to the accusation.

Obviously, it is quite easy to get a young, forlorn child to say anything; he had, no doubt, been well coached by the Simons; and, indeed, the accusation is so absurd that it fails of itself; but it was to be used at the trial. Oddly enough, however, this was coming to seem almost irrelevant. On October 10 the Convention proclaimed a revolutionary government giving all power to the Committee of Public Safety; arrests were multiplied; losing generals were tried, convicted, beheaded; another hundred Deputies were removed from the Convention and jailed. Under those circumstances, the ex-Queen hardly seemed to matter very much and indeed, as a person, she did not; but she was the last symbolic

---

[*] Swollen testicles can be a symptom of certain varieties of tuberculosis.

remnant of the monarchy. Louis XVI had been tried and condemned for his treachery to the people; Marie Antoinette was now to embody all the corruption, all the selfishness of the old system. Her trial would be not just that of a Queen but also that of the former upper classes, of the ancien régime as a whole, as opposed to the new Republican purity. Hence the importance of the Dauphin's declaration.

On October 10, the same day he had requested them, Fouquier-Tinville received all the documents belonging to the trial of Louis XVI; on the eleventh the former Queen was brought to the Tribunal, read the Act of Accusation, and questioned about it. It is worth noting here that the Convention itself had not thought her worthy of its attention: it had tried the King but it sent the Queen to the Revolutionary Tribunal as a common criminal.

Part of the Act of Accusation seemed simply feeble: it accused the Queen of having indulged in political intrigues, of having been a spendthrift, of having influenced Louis XVI, and these things were hardly crimes. Other parts were more serious: she was held to have inspired the antirevolutionary feelings at the banquet of the bodyguard on October 2, 1789, to have organized the flight to Varennes, to have forced the King into using his veto, to have brought the war about; and then there was the Dauphin's declaration. Throughout that day, Marie Antoinette, weakened, hemorrhaging as she was, stood up to her accusers.

She denied, of course, that she had given her brother millions, and that was true; but she also denied having corresponded with her family and other foreigners after 1789, which was an absolute lie. Then, according to the transcript, came the following question: " 'Wasn't it you who taught Louis Capet that art of deep dishonesty with which he fooled the good French people?'

"Answer: 'Yes, the people have been fooled, they have been cruelly fooled, but it was not by my husband or myself.' "[6] For a woman who was so weak she could barely stand, it was not a bad retort.

Then came many questions about the flight to Varennes, for which the Tribunal sought to make her wholly responsible; but here too she knew how to defend herself. She soon proved it again.

"Question: 'You never stopped for a moment wanting to destroy liberty; you wanted to reign at any price and reerect your throne on the corpses of the patriots.'

"Answer: 'We did not need to reerect the throne, it existed already; the only thing we ever wished for was the happiness of France. . . . '

"Question: 'Do you think kings are necessary for the happiness of the people?'

"Answer: 'A single person cannot decide this.' "[7] It was a clever evasion: obviously, Marie Antoinette believed that kings were indeed needed. But what is more striking than the evasions or the outright lies is the intelligence with which she answered difficult questions under difficult circumstances — so much so that, much to the prosecution's horror, the hostility that had greeted her when she entered the courtroom turned into something very like popularity. Her answers were often greeted with applause by the public, which filled the courtroom.

The trial itself — this was just a preliminary hearing — began on October 14; while this time Marie Antoinette had two lawyers to assist her, they had been appointed just the day before and handed a mass of documents which would have required two weeks to read. Nor would she, as the lawyers asked, request the Convention to postpone the trial: she knew very well what the verdict would be and would not lower herself by pleading for time.

In any event, it hardly made a difference. The prosecution knew her case no better than the defense; some of the accusations were simply farcical. Thus, because her full name was Marie Antoinette de Lorraine d'Autriche,* she was asked whether she had not planned to give Lorraine to Austria. Of course, she answered, she had not, upon which the district attorney gave her name as his sole reason for putting this to her; it was child's play then to answer that royal families bore the name of their country. So far, in fact, she was the clear winner.

It was then that the Dauphin's declaration was introduced as evidence. Looking disgusted, at first, she said nothing. Thinking he had at last scored, the prosecutor pointed out she had not answered him; at this, rising with indignation, she exclaimed: "If I did not answer, it is because Nature will not answer such an accusation made to a mother. I call upon all those who sit in this courtroom."[8] She was rewarded by thunderous applause. Robespierre, who was present, commented that evening to one

---

* Marie Antoinette's father was Francis of Lorraine, her mother Maria Theresa of Habsburg, of the House of Austria.

of the jurors: "That idiot Hébert! It is not enough that she should really be a Messalina, he has to make her into an Agrippina and give her a public triumph at her last moment."[9] Messalina, the wife of the Emperor Claudius, was famous for the number of her lovers; Agrippina, Nero's mother, is believed to have slept with her son in an attempt to keep her influence on him.

The public triumph, of course, changed nothing, nor did the failure of the prosecution to prove anything during the rest of the trial. At the end, however, Marie Antoinette was able to remark: "Yesterday, I did not know the witnesses, I did not know what they would say. Well! No one has accused me of any positive act. I end by pointing out that I was the wife of Louis XVI and that I was bound, therefore, to do what he wanted."[10] Rather like Mary, Queen of Scots, the selfish, vain, and frivolous Marie Antoinette had her finest moment as she was about to lose her life.

The expected verdict came on October 16 at four in the morning. When she was told that she was to die, one of her lawyers noted, "she gave not the least sign of fear, indignation or weakness. . . . She came down the steps without a word or a gesture, crossed the courtroom as if she saw and heard nothing: and when she arrived before the barrier holding the people back, she raised her head majestically."[11] Now there was not much more to be borne; she wrote her will and refused to see a juring priest; unlike Louis XVI she was not allowed a non-juror.

What happened next was described by a nonroyalist witness. "At eleven . . . fifteen, [Marie Antoinette] came out of the prison of the Conciergerie and climbed into the same tumbril as the other convicts who were being taken to the scaffold. She was wearing a simple white morning dress and a very plain bonnet, her hair had been cut off and her hands were tied behind her back. Her face was pale . . . because of a loss of blood she had just had in her cell, rather than because of the just punishment she was about to suffer, for, although her heart seemed oppressed as she climbed into the tumbril, she retained her grace, her pride, her majestic air." That, indeed, is how a sketch made by David shows her.

The witness continues: "From the [Conciergerie] to the scaffold, she looked quietly at the huge crowds shouting 'Long live the Republic!' When she arrived on the Place de la Révolution, she stared with some emotion at the Palace of the Tuileries. . . . The tumbril stopped before the scaffold; she stepped down quickly and easily without needing help although her hands were tied."[12] It was at this point that, by mistake, she walked on the executioner's foot. " 'Monsieur,' she said, 'I beg your pardon, I did not do it on purpose.'[13]

"She went up the steps of the scaffold with a brave air," our witness continues, "looking even calmer and more peaceful than when she came out of the prison. Without saying a word either to the people or to the executioners, she let herself be prepared, having herself shrugged off her bonnet. Her execution, together with its dreadful preliminary, lasted some four minutes. At twelve-fifteen exactly, her head fell under the blade of the law's vengeance, and the executioner showed it to the people who shouted repeatedly: 'Long live the Republic! Long live Liberty!' "[14]

AFTERWORD

ON November 6, 1793, the former duc d'Orléans, Marie Antoinette's great enemy, followed her to the guillotine, and so, thereafter, did many of her former courtiers. The Terror continued on its wild course until, at the end of July 1794, the rump of the Convention, in an act of desperate courage, outlawed Robespierre himself. After that, a new constitution was written, and a bourgeois Republic installed; it lasted until Napoleon put an end to it in December 1799. But with the death of the Queen the Revolution had essentially run its course. Although the following years offer a fascinating tale of fear, intrigue, corruption, and, eventually, wild enjoyment, what really mattered was that the monarchy and the society that supported it had been so thoroughly destroyed.

By 1794 nothing remained of the ancien régime: its constitutional structure, its laws, its class system, its judiciary, its tax system, its religious policies, its distribution of land tenure were all gone, never to be resurrected. The country that emerged from the great revolutionary storm shared little with the old France except geographical location. Much of its population, which had been landless, now owned enough acreage to prosper, thanks to the nationalization of all Church lands and many aristocratic holdings, which were then sold for devalued assignats, thus creating a new, rural, middle class. The hold of the Catholic Church on both the government and the daily life of the French was broken forever.

All that might have been expected to happen, slowly and eventually. What is astonishing, however, is that, from the day the Estates General first met to that when Louis XVI walked up the steps to the guillotine, less than four years had passed. Although the excesses of the Terror, and the figure of Robespierre himself, have fascinated from their day to ours, the real work of the Revolution had been done by the time Marie Antoinette, that vivid symbol of the ancien régime, was beheaded.

The Revolution brought into being another world, a world in which we still live, with its many positives — equality before the law, freedom of the press, of assembly, of religion — and its many negatives — the dictatorship of the state in case of crisis with the abrogation of all liberties, the notion that people deserve to die for what they are rather than for what they have done. For better or for worse, however, the twentieth century, in many ways, began between 1789 and 1793; and what astonished, thrilled, and horrified the contemporaries has become part of the very fabric of our lives.

NOTES

All quotations from the French have been translated by the author.

PROLOGUE

1. *L'Ami du peuple*, June 3, 1792.
2. Ibid., June 9, 1792.
3. Tourzel, II, 115.
4. Ibid., 138.
5. Ibid., 139.
6. Ibid.
7. Ibid., 140.
8. Ibid.
9. Klinckowstrom, II, 304.
10. Tourzel, II, 142.
11. Klinckowstrom, II, 304.

CHAPTER ONE

1. Ferrières, I, 8.
2. Malouet, I, 263.
3. Staël, 160.
4. Flammermont, *Correspondances*, 233.
5. Mousset, 46.
6. Archives Nationales, C185 (123.1).
7. Flammermont, *Correspondances*, 237.
8. Flammermont, ed., *Relations*, 16ff.
9. Bailly, I, 331.
10. Mousset, 51.

11. Flammermont, *Correspondances*, 238–239.
12. Flammermont, ed., *Relations*, 16ff.
13. Ibid., 21.
14. Mousset, 59.
15. La Rochefoucauld-Liancourt, 224.
16. *Nouvelle législation*, I, 264.
17. Arneth and Flammermont, II, 80.
18. Flammermont, *Correspondances*, 219.
19. Arneth, ed., *Briefwechsel*, 112.
20. Arneth and Flammermont, II, 223.
21. Ibid., 224.
22. Soderjhelm, 242.
23. Ibid.
24. Augeard, 193.
25. *Journal de Paris*, July 15, 1789.
26. Flammermont, ed., *Relations*, 22ff.
27. Campan, II, 58.
28. Ibid.
29. Flammermont, ed., *Relations*, 25ff.
30. Flammermont, *Correspondances*, 240–241.
31. *Nouvelle législation*, I, 265.
32. *Journal de Paris*, July 18, 1789.
33. *Révolutions de Paris*, No. 2.

34. Archives nationales, C185 (123.1).
35. Flammermont, ed., *Relations*, 30ff.

CHAPTER TWO

1. Egret, 314.
2. Staël, 179.
3. Ibid., 180.
4. *Nouvelle législation*, I, 1ff.
5. Mousset, 62.
6. Malouet, I, 277.
7. Ibid., I, 282.
8. *Journal de Paris*, Aug. 6, 1789.
9. Ibid.
10. *Nouvelle législation*, I, 83.
11. Ibid., IX, 85.
12. Mathiez, LXVII, 253.
13. Flammermont, ed., *Relations*, 367.
14. Arneth and Flammermont, II, 256.
15. *Le Publiciste parisien*, No. 1 (Sept. 12, 1789).
16. Anon., *Antoinette d'Autriche . . .* , 3–12ff.
17. *Le Publiciste parisien ou l'Ami du peuple*, No. 9.
18. Ibid.
19. *L'Ami du peuple*, No. 1.
20. La Marck, I, 112.

CHAPTER THREE

1. *Révolutions de Paris*, No. 12.
2. Ibid., No. 13.
3. *Discours de la lanterne*, 1.
4. Mousset, 85.
5. *Révolutions de Paris*, No. 13.
6. Egret, 365.
7. *L'Ami du peuple*, No. 25.
8. *Journal de Paris*, Oct. 8, 1789.
9. Flammermont, ed., *Relations*, 264.
10. Tourzel, I, 7–8.
11. Flammermont, ed., *Relations*, 264.
12. Ibid., 265.
13. Staël, 211.
14. Flammermont, ed., *Relations*, 266ff.
15. Ibid.
16. Campan, II, 78.

17. Flammermont, ed., *Relations*, 267ff.
18. Campan, II, 81.
19. Tourzel, I, 18ff.
20. Campan, II, 82.
21. Flammermont, ed., *Relations*, 269.
22. Flammermont, *Correspondances*, II, 272.
23. Campan, I, 86.
24. Flammermont, ed., *Relations*, 271–272.
25. Archivio Historico Nacional, Madrid, Papeles de Estado, 3942, 2.
26. La Marck, I, 120.
27. Ibid., 107.
28. Flammermont, *Correspondances*, II, 268.
29. Grimm, XV, 523.
30. *Nouvelle législation*, III, 1–4.
31. Staël, 197–198.
32. Romilly, I, 279.
33. Mathiez, LXIX, 57.
34. La Marck, I, 385.
35. Ibid., 390.
36. Ibid., 406.
37. Ibid., 413.
38. Ibid., 416.
39. Ibid., 417.
40. Romilly, I, 291.
41. *Révolutions de France et de Brabant*, No. 2.
42. Ibid., No. 1.
43. Ibid., No. 3.
44. *L'Ami du peuple*, Nos. 78, 79, 81, 82.
45. *Révolutions de Paris*, No. 22.
46. Mousset, 101.
47. *Nouvelle législation*, V, 1, 99.
48. La Marck, I, 436.
49. Orléans, 85.

CHAPTER FOUR

1. *Révolutions de Paris*, No. 27.
2. Ibid., No. 39.
3. *Nouvelle législation*, IV, 1, 300.
4. Mousset, 32.

5. *Révolutions de France et de Brabant,*
   No. 8.
6. La Marck, I, 460.
7. Morris, I, 277.
8. Klinckowstrom, I, lv.
9. Louis XVI, *Discours,* 1.
10. Ibid., 2–3.
11. Ibid., 3–4.
12. Ibid., 5.
13. Ibid., 5–6.
14. Ibid., 6.
15. Ibid., 8.
16. *Révolutions de France et de Brabant,*
    No. 12.
17. La Marck, I, 464.
18. Tourzel, I, 111.
19. Ibid., 110.
20. Staël, 228.
21. *La Chronique de Paris,* Jan. 19,
    1790.
22. *Le Junius français,* No. XI.
23. *Nouvelle législation,* VII, 89.
24. Ibid., 141.
25. *Révolutions de France et de Brabant,*
    No. 15.
26. Arneth, ed., *Briefwechsel,* 122.
27. La Marck, I, 139.
28. *Révolutions de France et de Brabant,*
    No. 19.
29. Orléans, 155.
30. Mousset, 231.
31. *Révolutions de France et de Brabant,*
    No. 21.
32. *L'Ami du peuple,* No. 107.
33. Ibid., No. 149.
34. Arneth and Flammermont, *Corre-
    spondance,* II, 301.
35. La Marck, II, 3.
36. Ibid., 11ff.
37. Ibid., 20ff.
38. Lafayette, II, 367.
39. La Marck, II, 25ff.

CHAPTER FIVE

1. *Le Junius français,* No. 28.

2. Ibid., No. 29.
3. Tourzel, I, 111.
4. La Marck, II, 34.
5. Ibid., 38.
6. Arneth, ed., *Briefwechsel,* 129ff.
7. La Marck, I, 191.
8. *L'Ami du peuple,* Nos. 148, 149.
9. Staël, 226.
10. Klinckowstrom, I, lvi.
11. Grimm, XVI, 40ff.
12. Staël, 227.
13. [Rivarol], *Dictionnaire,* 50.
14. Ibid., 85.
15. Anon., *Nouveau Dictionnaire,* 18ff.
16. *L'Ami du Roi,* Sept. 1, 1790.
17. La Marck, II, 162.
18. Arneth and Flammermont, *Corre-
    spondance,* II, 313.
19. *L'Ami du peuple,* Nos. 249, 250.
20. Anon., *Soirées amoureuses,* 11.
21. Ibid., 14–15.
22. La Marck, I, 230.

CHAPTER SIX

1. Klinckowstrom, I, lvii.
2. Grimm, XVI, 115.
3. *L'Ami des patriotes,* No. 3.
4. Ibid., No. 4.
5. *Journal de Paris,* Jan. 2, 1791.
6. Campan, II, 179.
7. Mousset, 239.
8. Ibid., 240.
9. Ibid., 242.
10. Klinckowstrom, I, lx.
11. Malouet, II, 107.
12. La Marck, I, 241.
13. Arneth, ed., *Briefwechsel,* 147.
14. Ibid., 151.
15. Mousset, 245.
16. Campan, II, 139ff.
17. Klinckowstrom, I, 83–84.
18. Ibid., 86ff.
19. *L'Ami du peuple,* No. 390.
20. *L'Ami des patriotes,* No. 17.
21. La Marck, I, 251.

22. Arneth, ed., *Briefwechsel*, 153ff.
23. Klinckowstrom, I, 88.
24. Ibid., 94ff.
25. Ibid., 103ff., for this narrative by Fersen.
26. *Journal de Paris*, April 20, 1791.
27. Ibid., Apr. 21, 1791.
28. *Nouvelle législation*, I, 311.
29. *Journal de Paris*, Apr. 20, 1791.
30. Tourzel, I, 243.
31. Mousset, 129.
32. Arneth, ed., *Briefwechsel*, 155.
33. La Marck, III, 143.
34. *L'Ami des patriotes*, No. 22.
35. *L'Ami du peuple*, No. 44.
36. Klinckowstrom, I, 111.
37. Ibid., 121.
38. Arneth, ed., *Briefwechsel*, 166.
39. Klinckowstrom, I, 132.
40. Ibid., 138.

CHAPTER SEVEN

1. Las Cases, I, 561.
2. Bernier, *Secrets*, 122.
3. Campan, II, 59.
4. Bernier, *Secrets*, 141.
5. Campan, II, 70.
6. Ibid., 73.
7. Vigée-Lebrun, 254.
8. Bernier, *Secrets*, 175.
9. Ibid.
10. Ibid., 183.
11. Egret, 124.
12. Mollien, I, 68.
13. Ibid., 196.
14. Arneth and Flammermont, *Correspondance*, II, 9.
15. Staël, 90.
16. Las Cases, II, 85.
17. Bertrand de Molleville, I, 29.
18. La Marck, I, 196.
19. Arneth and Flammermont, *Correspondance*, II, 77.
20. Ibid., 90.
21. Ibid., 92.

22. Ibid., 94.
23. Staël, 113.
24. Flammermont, *Correspondances*, 223ff.
25. Bernier, *Lafayette*, 174.
26. Arneth and Flammermont, *Correspondance*, II, 105–106.
27. Ibid., 112.
28. Ibid., 123.
29. Flammermont, *Correspondances*, 123.
30. Ibid., 125.
31. Arneth and Flammermont, *Correspondance*, II, 138.
32. Ibid.
33. Arneth, ed., *Briefwechsel*, 115.
34. Arneth and Flammermont, *Correspondance*, II, 182.
35. Flammermont, *Correspondances*, 40.

CHAPTER EIGHT

1. Arneth and Flammermont, *Correspondance*, II, 189–190.
2. Ibid., 197–198.
3. Ibid., 208–209.
4. Ibid., 194.
5. Ibid., 213.
6. Egret, 222.
7. Staël, 129
8. Grimm, XV, 312.
9. Romilly, I, 72.
10. Staël, I, 214.
11. Malouet, I, 293.
12. Egret, 234.
13. Grimm, XV, 344.
14. Ibid., 348.
15. *Procés-verbal de l'Assemblée des Notables*, 53ff.
16. Mousset, 41.
17. Grimm, XV, 369.
18. Sieyès, *Essai*, 1.
19. Ibid., 2.
20. Ibid., 16.
21. Egret, 241.
22. *Résultat . . . 27 décembre 1788*, 26.

23. Staël, 136.
24. Barentin, 65.
25. Ibid., 72.
26. Ibid., 73.
27. *Proces-verbaux* . . . *Dauphiné,*
    173–175.
28. Mousset, 41.
29. *Journal de Paris,* Jan. 11, 1789.
30. Arneth and Flammermont, *Corre-*
    spondance, II, 218.
31. Flammermont, *Correspondances,*
    228–229.
32. Sieyès, *Essai,* 27.
33. Ibid., 30–32.
34. Ibid., 57.
35. Ibid., 61.
36. Anon., *La Révolution* . . . *oculaires,*
    III, 65.
37. Arneth and Flammermont, *Corre-*
    spondance, II, 230.
38. Malouet, I, 257.
39. Ibid., 249–251.
40. Duquesnoy, I, 29.

CHAPTER NINE

1. Walter, *Révolution,* 521.
2. Staël, 101.
3. Morris, I, 72.
4. Mousset, 44.
5. Duquesnoy, I, 5–6.
6. Grimm, XV, 450.
7. Lefebvre, I, l, 243ff.
8. Ibid., 249ff.
9. Ibid., 320.
10. Ibid., 343.
11. Ibid., 324.
12. Ibid., 344.
13. Duquesnoy, I, 7.
14. Staël, 190.
15. Arneth and Flammermont, *Corre-*
    spondance, II, 239.
16. Ibid.
17. Mousset, 21.
18. Duquesnoy, I, 19.
19. *Journal de Paris,* May 27, 1789.

20. Duquesnoy, I, 13.
21. *Journal de Paris,* May 30, 1789.
22. Ibid., June 9, 1789.
23. *Nouvelle législation,* I, vii.
24. *Journal de Paris,* June 17, 1789.
25. Barentin, 169.
26. Lefebvre, I, 2, 174.
27. Chaussinand-Nogaret, 144.
28. Malouet, I, 277.
29. Brette, unnumbered page.
30. Ibid.
31. Duquesnoy, I, 113.
32. Lefebvre, I, 2, 284.
33. Staël, 151.
34. Chaussinand-Nogaret, 148.
35. Staël, 156–157.
36. Flammermont, *Correspondances,*
    226.
37. Ibid., 232.
38. Morris, I, 113.
39. *Nouvelle législation,* I, xxvi.

CHAPTER TEN

1. Tourzel, I, 305–306.
2. Ibid., 306.
3. Ibid., 307.
4. Ibid., 312.
5. Ibid.
6. *Nouvelle législation,* I, 351ff.
7. Ibid.
8. Buchez and Roux, X, 261.
9. *Nouvelle législation,* I, 379ff.
10. Buchez and Roux, X, 292ff.
11. *L'Ami du peuple,* No. 497.
12. Tourzel, I, 313.
13. Ibid., 316.
14. Bernier, *Lafayette,* 230.
15. Tourzel, I, 321.
16. Ibid., 324.
17. *La Chronique de Paris,* June 22,
    1791.
18. *Journal de Paris,* June 23, 1791.
19. *Nouvelle législation,* I, 401.
20. Mortimer-Ternaux, I, 353ff.
21. Tourzel, I, 327.

22. Ibid., 328.
23. Ibid.
24. Mortimer-Ternaux, I, 353ff.
25. Ibid.
26. Romilly, I, 327–328.
27. *Journal de Paris*, June 26, 1791.
28. Campan, II, 150.
29. Mousset, 283.
30. *Nouvelle législation*, I, 406.
31. Arneth, ed., *Briefwechsel*, 180.
32. Tourzel, I, 359–360.
33. Arneth, ed., *Briefwechsel*, 184.
34. Klinckowstrom, I, 145.
35. Ibid., 148.

CHAPTER ELEVEN

1. *L'Ami du peuple*, No. 501.
2. Ibid., No. 503.
3. Ibid., No. 506.
4. Arneth, ed., *Briefwechsel*, 196.
5. Ibid., 205.
6. *L'Ami du peuple*, No. 528.
7. See *Nouvelle législation*, I, 6–64, for the provisions of the constitution described in the next several paragraphs.
8. *Journal de Paris*, Sept. 2, 1791.
9. *Nouvelle législation*, I, 65ff.
10. Romilly, I, 334.
11. Staël, 250.
12. Campan, II, 169n.
13. Romilly, I, 338.
14. Klinckowstrom, I, 206.
15. La Marck, III, 227ff.
16. Klinckowstrom, I, 192.
17. Ibid., 207.
18. Barbaroux, 3ff.
19. *L'Ami du peuple*, No. 570.
20. Ibid., Nos. 590, 592, 594, 614.
21. Anon., *Arrêt de mort*, 2ff.
22. Walter, *Révolution*, 493.
23. Anon., *Fureurs Utérines*, no page numbers.
24. Bertrand de Molleville, I, 213.
25. Ibid., 215–216.

26. Malouet, II, 198.
27. La Marck, III, 248–249.
28. Arneth, ed., *Briefwechsel*, 231ff.
29. *L'Ami du peuple*, No. 614.
30. Klinckowstrom, I, 230.
31. Ibid., 270.
32. Flammermont, *Négociations*, 9ff.
33. Klinckowstrom, I, 271.
34. Bertrand de Molleville, I, 247.
35. Tarente, 41.

CHAPTER TWELVE

1. Bertrand de Molleville, I, 286.
2. Flammermont, *Négociations*, 11.
3. Ibid., 13.
4. Malouet, II, 229.
5. Tarente, 42.
6. Arneth, ed., *Briefwechsel*, 245.
7. Klinckowstrom, II, 6–7.
8. Barbaroux, 56.
9. Thibaudeau, I, 59.
10. Bertrand de Molleville, II, 16–17.
11. Ibid., 27.
12. Arneth, ed., *Briefwechsel*, 254.
13. Bertrand de Molleville, II, 99.
14. Barbaroux, 75.
15. Tourzel, II, 76.
16. Klinckowstrom, II, 220.
17. Ibid., 234.
18. *Le Défenseur de la Constitution*, May 17, 1792.
19. Bernier, *Lafayette*, 238.
20. Roederer, 9.
21. *L'Ami du peuple*, No. 666.
22. Chaumette, 3–4.
23. Ibid., 6–7.
24. Ibid., 26.
25. Roederer, 64.
26. *Journal de Paris*, June 21, 1792.
27. *Le Moniteur universel*, XII, 722.
28. Roederer, 79ff.
29. Bertrand de Molleville, II, 296ff.
30. Klinckowstrom, II, 289.
31. Ibid., 308.
32. Barbaroux, 182ff.

33. Chaumette, 21–24.
34. Roederer, 81.
35. Tourzel, II, 153–154.
36. Arneth, ed., *Briefwechsel,* 265.
37. Roederer, 169ff.
38. La Marck, III, 325.
39. Staël, 276.
40. *L'Ami du peuple,* No. 675.
41. Campan, II, 217.
42. *Le Moniteur universel,* XIII, 305.
43. Anon., *Têtes à prix,* no page numbers.
44. Klinckowstrom, II, 340.
45. Staël, 279.

CHAPTER THIRTEEN

 1. Orléans, 201.
 2. Campan, II, 231.
 3. Marat, *L'Ami du peuple aux français patriotes,* no page numbers.
 4. Tourzel, II, 194.
 5. Roederer, 352ff.
 6. Frénilly, 167.
 7. Tourzel, II, 211.
 8. Roederer, 354.
 9. Tourzel, II, 214.
10. Roederer, 355.
11. Tourzel, II, 215.
12. Roederer, 355.
13. Roederer, 356.
14. Ibid.
15. Ibid.
16. *Le Moniteur universel,* XIII, 380.
17. Barbaroux, 224.
18. Furet and Richet, 172.
19. Tulard, Fayard, and Fierro, 744.
20. Tourzel, II, 254.
21. Beugnot, 138.
22. Staël, 266.
23. *L'Ami du peuple,* No. 678.
24. Ibid., No. 680.
25. Ibid., No. 682.
26. Walter, *Massacres,* 513.
27. Wallon, *Histoire,* I, 5.
28. Walter, *Massacres,* 74.
29. Ibid., 152.

CHAPTER FOURTEEN

 1. Beugnot, 130.
 2. *Journal de la République française,* No. 4.
 3. *Révolutions de France et de Brabant,* II, 6.
 4. Ibid., 7.
 5. Ibid., 10.
 6. Convention nationale, Opinion de Marc Antoine Jullien.
 7. *Journal de la République française,* No. 42.
 8. Convention nationale, Rapport . . . présenté . . . par Jean Mailhe.
 9. Ibid.
10. Ibid.
11. Ibid., Opinion d'Asselin.
12. Ibid., Opinion de Marat.
13. Ibid., Opinion de Saint Just.
14. Ibid., Opinion de Thomas Payne [*sic*].
15. Louis XVI, in *Troisième recueil.*
16. Convention nationale, Opinion de Guy Kersaint.
17. Ibid., Opinion de Manuel.
18. Ibid., Opinion de Maximilien Robespierre.
19. Robespierre, V, 135.
20. Convention nationale, Opinion d'Augustin Robespierre.
21. *Le Moniteur universel,* XIV, 672.
22. Convention nationale, Opinion de J. P. Brissot le 1er janvier 1793.
23. Ibid., Opinion de Pétion le 2 janvier 1793.
24. Ibid., Deuxième Discours de Maximilien Robespierre.
25. Ibid., Opinion d'Anacharsis Cloots.
26. *Journal de la République française,* No. 72.
27. Ibid., No. 90.
28. Ibid., No. 91.
29. Beugnot, 139.

30. Thibaudeau, I, 23–24.
31. Wallon, *Les Représentants*, I, 82.
32. Thibaudeau, I, 25–27.
33. Mathiez, 508.
34. *L'Ami des sans-culottes*, April 14, 1793.
35. *Le Sans-culottes*, May 27, 1793.
36. Thibaudeau, I, 42–43.
37. Walter, *Actes*, 163.

CHAPTER FIFTEEN

1. *Journal de la République française*, No. 209.

2. Thibaudeau, I, 46–49.
3. Beugnot, 131.
4. Angoulême, 223ff.
5. Campardon, 112, n.l.
6. Wallon, *Histoire*, I, 319.
7. Ibid., 320ff.
8. Ibid., 331.
9. Ibid.
10. Ibid., 338.
11. Ibid., 342.
12. Walter, *Actes*, 134ff.
13. Wallon, *Histoire*, I, 351.
14. Walter, *Actes*, 137.

BIBLIOGRAPHY

The bibliography of the French Revolution is immense; some twenty years ago, its titles, in small print, already filled a sizable volume. The author has therefore listed only the material directly quoted, or immediately used, in this book.

PERIODICALS

L'Ami des patriotes
L'Ami du peuple
L'Ami des sans-culottes
L'Ami du Roi
La Chronique de Paris
Le Défenseur de la Constitution
Journal de Paris

Journal de la République française
Le Junius français
Le Moniteur universel
Le Père Duchesne
Le Publiciste parisien
Révolutions de Paris
Le Sans-culottes

BOOKS

Angoulême, Marie-Thérèse-Charlotte, duchesse d'. "Récit des événements arrivés au Temple," in *Collection des Mémoires relatifs à la Révolution Française*, vol. XIX. Paris, 1825.

Anon. *Les Adieux de Lafayette.* Paris, n.d. [1792].

———. *Antoinette d'Autriche, ou dialogue entre Catherine de Médicis et Frédégonde, reines de France.* Paris, n.d. [1789].

———. *Arrêt de mort rendu par le monarque des Enfers contre le roi et la reine des Française et l'Assemblée nationale.* Paris, n.d. [1791].

———. *Bordel patriotique institué par la reine des Français pour les plaisirs des députés à la nouvelle législature.* Paris, 1791.

———. *Fureurs utérines de Marie Antoinette.* Paris, 1791.

———. *Nouveau Dictionnaire Français.* Paris, 1790.

———. *La Révolution française racontée par des témoins oculaires.* Paris, 1960.

———. *Soirées amoureuses du général Mottier et de la belle Antoinette par le petit épagneul de l'Autrichienne.* Paris, 1790.

————. *Têtes à prix, suivi de la liste de toutes les personnes avec lesquelles la reine a eu des liaisons de débauche.* Paris, 1792.

Arneth, Alfred von, ed. *Marie Antoinette, Joseph II und Leopold II: Ihr Briefwechsel.* Leipzig, 1866.

Arneth, Alfred von, and Flammermont, Jules. *Correspondance secrète du comte de Mercy-Argenteau avec l'Empereur Joseph II et le prince de Kaunitz.* Paris, 1891.

Augeard, Jean Marie. *Mémoires secrets.* Paris, 1866.

Autié, Léonard. *Souvenirs de Léonard.* Paris, 1905.

Bailly, Sylvain. *Mémoires.* Paris, 1821–1822.

Barbaroux, Charles. *Discours sur les titres de Sire et de Majesté conservés au roi.* Marseille, 1791.

————. *Correspondance et mémoires.* Paris, 1923.

Barentin, M. de. *Mémoire autographe sur les derniers conseils du roi Louis XVI.* Paris, 1844.

Bernier, Olivier. *Lafayette: Hero of Two Worlds.* New York, 1983.

————. *Secrets of Marie Antoinette.* New York, 1985.

Bertrand de Molleville, Antoine François. *Private Memoirs relative to the last ten years of the reign of Lewis the Sixteenth.* London, 1797.

Beugnot, Jacques-Claude, comte. *Mémoires.* Paris, 1975.

Brette, Armand. *Le Serment du Jeu de Paume, fac-similé du texte.* Paris, 1893.

Buchez, B. J. B., and P. C. Roux. *Histoire parlementaire de la Révolution française.* Paris, 1834–38.

Campan, Madame. *Mémoires sur la vie privée de Marie Antoinette.* Paris, 1826.

Campardon, Emile. *Le tribunal révolutionnaire de Paris.* Geneva, 1973.

Carnot, Lazare. *Mémoires historiques et militaires.* Paris, 1824.

Chaumette, Pierre Gaspard (pseud. Anaxagoras). *Mémoires sur la révolution du 10 août 1792.* F. A. Aulard, ed. Paris, 1893.

Chaussinand-Nogaret, Guy. *Mirabeau.* Paris, 1982.

Cléry, Jean-Baptiste. *Journal de . . . la captivité de Louis XVI.* London, 1798.

Convention nationale. Printed Reports and Opinions, 1792–1793:

    Opinion de Marc Antoine Jullien.

    Rapport . . . présenté . . . par Jean Mailhe.

    Opinion de Saint Just concernant le procès de Louis XVI.

    Opinion de Thomas Payne [*sic*] concernant le procès de Louis XVI.

    Opinion d'Asselin concernant le procès de Louis XVI.

    Opinion de Marat concernant le procès de Louis XVI.

    Opinion d'Augustin Robespierre concernant le procès de Louis XVI.

    Opinion de Maximilien Robespierre concernant le procès de Louis XVI.

    Opinion de Manuel concernant le procès de Louis XVI.

    Opinion de Guy Kersaint concernant le procès de Louis XVI.

    Opinion d'Anacharsis Cloots concernant le procès de Louis XVI.

    Opinion de J. P. Brissot concernant le procès de Louis XVI, le 1er janvier 1793.

    Opinion de Pétion concernant le procès de Louis XVI, le 2 janvier 1793.

    Deuxième Discours de Maximilien Robespierre concernant le procès de Louis XVI.

[Desmoulins, Camille.] *Discours de la lanterne aux Parisiens.* Paris, 1789.

Duquesnoy, Adrien. *Journal.* Paris, 1894.

Egret, Jean. *Necker, ministre de Louis XVI.* Paris, 1975.

Ferrières, marquis de. *Mémoires.* Paris, 1821.

Flammermont, Jules. *Les Correspondances des agents diplomatiques en France avant la Révolution.* Paris, 1896.

———. *Négociations secrétes de Louis XVI.* Berlin, 1885.

Flammermont, Jules, ed. *Relations inédites de la prise de la Bastille par le duc de Dorset . . . et le comte de Mercy-Argenteau.* Paris, 1885.

Frénilly, baron de. *Souvenirs.* Paris, 1908.

Furet, François. *Penser la Révolution Française.* Paris, 1981.

Furet, François, and Denis Richet. *La Révolution Française.* Paris, 1973.

Godechot, Jacques. *Les constitutions de la France depuis 1789.* Paris, 1970.

———. *La Prise de la Bastille.* Paris, 1965.

Grille, F. *Introduction aux mémoires sur la Révolution française.* Paris, 1825.

Grimm, Friedrich. *Correspondance littéraire.* Paris, 1881.

Klinckowstrom, R. M. de. *Le comte de Fersen à la cour de France.* Paris, 1877.

Kuscinski, A. *Les députés à l'assemblées législatives de 1791.* Paris, 1900.

Lafayette, Gilbert, marquis de. *Mémoires du Général Lafayette.* Brussels, 1837.

La Marck, comte de. *Correspondance entre le comte de Mirabeau et le comte de La Marck.* Paris, 1851.

La Rochefoucauld-Liancourt, comte de. *Vie du duc de La Rochefoucauld-Liancourt.* Paris, 1827.

Las Cases, comte de. *Le Mémorial de Sainte-Hélène.* Paris, 1893.

Lefebvre, Georges, ed. *Recueil de documents relatifs aux séances des Etats Généraux, mai-juin 1789.* Paris, 1962.

Louis XVI, King of France. *Discours prononcé par le roi à l'Assemblée nationale le 4 février 1790.* Nîmes, 1790.

———. In *Troisième recueil, pièces imprimées d'après le décret de la Convention nationale du 5 décembre 1792.* Paris, n.d.

Malouet, Pierre-Victor. *Mémoires.* Paris, 1874.

Marat, Jean-Paul. *L'Ami du peuple aux français patriotes.* Paris, 1792.

———. *C'en est fait de nous.* Paris, 1790.

———. *Dénonciation contre Necker.* Paris, 1790.

———. *Infernal projet des ennemis de la Révolution.* Paris, 1790.

———. *Opinion de Marat sur le jugement de Louis XVI.* Paris, 1793.

Marion, Marcel. *Histoire financière de la France depuis 1715.* Paris, 1914.

Mathiez, Albert. "Les Journées des 5 et 6 octobre 1789," in *Revue historique,* vols. LXVII–LXIX (1898–99).

Molé, Louis Mathieu, comte. *Le comte Molé, sa vie, ses mémoires.* Paris, 1922.

Mollien, Nicolas, comte. *Mémoires d'un ministre du trésor publique.* Paris, 1845.

Mortimer-Ternaux, M. *Histoire de la Terreur.* Paris, 1863.

Mousset, Albert. *Un témoin ignoré de la Révolution, le comte de Fernan Nuñez.* Paris, 1923.

Nouvelle législation, ou collection de tous les décrets rendus par l'Assemblée Nationale constituante, aux années 1789, 1790 et 1791. Paris, 1792.

Orléans, L.-P., duc d'. *Correspondance de Louis-Philippe-Joseph d'Orléans avec Louis XVI, la reine, Montmorin . . . etc.* Paris, 1800.

Pasquier, Etienne Denis, duc. *Histoire de mon temps.* Paris, 1893.

Procés-verbal de l'Assemblée des Notables tenue à Versailles en l'année 1788. Paris, 1789.

Procés-verbaux des Assemblées générales des Trois Ordres et des Etats provinciaux du Dauphiné tenus à Romans. Paris, 1888.

Résultat du conseil d'état du Roi, tenu à Versailles le 27 decembre 1788. Paris, 1788.

[Rivarol, Antoine comte de.] *Dictionnaire national et anecdotique.* Paris, 1790.

Robespierre, Maximilien. *Oeuvres complètes.* G. Laurent, ed. Paris, 1910–1967.

Roederer, Pierre Louis. *Histoire de cinquante jours.* Paris, 1832.

Romilly, Sir Samuel. *The Life of Sir Samuel Romilly Written by Himself.* London, 1842.

Sédillot, René. *Le coût de la Révolution française.* Paris, 1987.

Sieyès, Emmanuel. *Essai sur les privilèges* (includes *Qu'est-ce que le Tiers-Etat?*). Paris, 1888.

Soderjhelm, Alma. *Fersen et Marie Antoinette.* Paris, 1930.

Staël, Germaine, baronne de. *Considérations sur la Révolution française.* Paris, 1893.

Tarente, princesse de. *Souvenirs.* Paris, 1897.

Target, G. J. B. *Les Etats Généraux convoqués par Louis XVI.* Paris, 1788.

Thibaudeau, A. C. *Mémoires sur la Convention et le Directoire.* Paris, 1824.

Thyl, Yves, ed. *Les cahiers de doléances de Haute-Alsace.* Colmar, 1974.

Tourzel, duchesse de. *Mémoires de Mme la duchesse de Tourzel.* Paris, 1883.

Tulard, Jean, Jean-François Fayard, and Alfred Fierro. *Histoire de la Révolution française.* Paris, 1987.

Vigée-Lebrun, Marie Louise Elisabeth. *Souvenirs.* Paris, 1869.

Wallon, Henri. *Histoire du Tribunal révolutionnaire de Paris.* Paris, 1880.

———. *Les Représentants du Peuple en Mission et la Justice révolutionnaire dans les départementes en l'An II (1793–1794).* Paris, 1889.

Walter, Gérard. *Actes du tribunal Révolutionnaire.* Paris, 1968.

———. *Les Massacres de septembre.* Paris, 1932.

———. *La Révolution française.* Paris, 1967.

INDEX

TO THE READER

The author wishes to express his gratitude to the New York Public Library, whose holdings, personnel, and facilities have, yet again, made research a pleasure.

This book, containing the essence of Mr. Bernier's understanding of the French Revolution, was the basis for his lecture series at the Pierpont Morgan Library, the eleventh series of Franklin Jasper Walls Lectures given there.

ABOUT THE AUTHOR

Olivier Bernier is a leading authority on French history and the author of, among other books, *Louis XIV: A Royal Life; Secrets of Marie Antoinette;* and *Louis the Beloved: The Life of Louis XV.* Born in the United States of French parents, he was educated in Paris, at Harvard University, and at the Institute of Fine Arts at New York University. In addition to writing, he has taught art history and is widely acclaimed for his lectures at the Metropolitan Museum of Art.